P9-CCI-297

Arguing about Art

CONTEMPORARY PHILOSOPHICAL DEBATES

Arguing about Art

CONTEMPORARY PHILOSOPHICAL DEBATES

Alex Neill
Trinity University

Aaron Ridley
University of Southampton

McGRAW-HILL, INC.

New York St. Louis San Francisco Auckland Bogotá Caracas Lisbon
London Madrid Mexico City Milan Montreal New Delhi
San Juan Singapore Sydney Tokyo Toronto

ARGUING ABOUT ART
Contemporary Philosophical Debates

Copyright ©1995 by McGraw-Hill, Inc. All rights reserved. Printed in the
United States of America. Except as permitted under the United States
Copyright Act of 1976, no part of this publication may be reproduced or
distributed in any form or by any means, or stored in a data base or retrieval
system, without the prior written permission of the publisher.

Acknowledgments appear on pages xiii–xv, and on this page by reference.

This book is printed on acid-free paper.

2 3 4 5 6 7 8 9 0 DOC DOC 9 0 9 8 7 6 5

ISBN 0-07-046191-0

This book was set in Aster by Ruttle, Shaw & Wetherill, Inc.
The editors were Cynthia Ward and David Dunham;
the production supervisor was Leroy A. Young.
The cover was designed by Jo Jones.
R. R. Donnelley & Sons Company was printer and binder.

Cover art: Courtesy of The Busch-Reisinger Harvard University Art Museums.

Library of Congress Cataloging-in-Publication Data

Arguing about art: contemporary philosophical debates /
  [compiled by] Alex Neill and Aaron Ridley.
    p.   cm.
  ISBN 0-07-046191-0
  1. Aesthetics, Modern—20th century.   I. Neill, Alex.
  II. Ridley, Aaron.
BH201.A74   1995
111'.85—dc20   94-14036

CONTENTS

3 The "Authentic" Performance of Music   58

What is it to give an "authentic" performance of a piece of music? Is it possible to reproduce the way a piece of music would have been performed when it was composed? Would an "authentic" performance have any aesthetic advantages?

4 Photography and Representation   85

Are we interested in photographs for their own sake, or are we interested in photographs only for the sake of what they are photographs of ? Is photography a representational art form? How does aesthetic appreciation of photographs differ from aesthetic appreciation of paintings?

5 Appreciation, Understanding, and Nature   122

Are there correct and incorrect ways of appreciating nature and appreciating works of art? How does our aesthetic appreciation of nature differ from our aesthetic appreciation of works of art?

6 Feelings and Fiction   161

Fictional characters aren't real. So why should we care about what happens to them? Is it rational to be moved by what we know it not real? What sorts of state are we moved to when we are moved by fiction?

11 The Idea of the Museum   319

Do museums distort the significance of art by detaching it from ordinary human experience? Or do museums rather make art available to many who would not otherwise be able to experience it? What should a good museum be like?

PREFACE

In producing this book, our aim has been to provide a collection of readings that is representative of ongoing debates in contemporary philosophical aesthetics, a collection which will enable students using it to engage with and join in those debates. Like many teachers of philosophy, we believe that the best, if not the only, way for students to learn philosophy, including philosophical aesthetics, is by *doing* philosophy, by engaging with and in philosophical dialogue and discussion. However, because most of the available anthologies designed for undergraduate courses in aesthetics are overwhelmingly historical in content, such an engagement can be hard to achieve. Many of the classic texts of aesthetics are extremely difficult, written in language that students new to the subject often find forbidding, and concerned with concepts which often appear to students—especially students specializing in subjects other than philosophy—far too abstract and embedded in difficult theoretical machinery to have any points of contact with everyday experience in the twentieth century. The historical nature of most anthologies can also make things difficult for the instructor who wishes to give a sense not only of the *history* of the philosophy of art, but also of the range of topics and issues that *contemporary* philosophers of art address and attempt to illuminate.

Our collection is not designed to substitute for collections of the classic texts of aesthetics, but rather to supplement them, so as to help an instructor overcome the difficulties described above. It contains eleven sections, each presenting a topic in contemporary aesthetics. As a glance at the Contents will show, it contains a very diverse selection of readings and topics, reflecting a wide variety of perspectives on philosophy and on art. Three factors have influenced our selection of topics. First, we have tried to produce a collection which is representative of ongoing discussion among contemporary aestheticians. As anyone familiar with the discipline knows, contemporary aesthetics exhibits no common agenda; there is no agreed-on set of questions or concerns which define the discipline.

We have attempted to reflect the diversity of interests and concerns pursued by aestheticians today in the topics we have selected. In doing so, we have included readings which focus on a variety of art forms: painting, film, photography, music, literature, and drama, as well as the natural environment. We believe that this variety will make the book usable and useful for a diverse audience, of the sort often found in courses on aesthetics: for students of literature and music, for example, as well as students of art, art history, and philosophy.

Clearly, some of the topics included are more venerable than others, and we do not suggest that they are all of equal importance. However, and this is the second factor which influenced our selection, we have found that these are topics which students take up and become involved with actively and readily. All of the readings here represent good examples of serious philosophical writing about the arts, which, we have found, work well in the classroom. They generate lively discussion and a feeling of genuine engagement with and in philosophical reflection about the arts. It is of course not easy to pick readings which will be accessible to every undergraduate reader and are also of philosophical and pedagogical value. However, we believe that this collection gets the balance about right.

Third, we have tried to include topics which make concrete many of the concerns raised in more abstract form by the classic texts of aesthetics, so that this collection can serve as an effective supplement to the latter. We begin with three topics that bear on originality and authenticity in the arts: Fakes and Forgeries (which in our experience works very well as the opening topic of a course), Colorizing Movies, and The "Authentic" Performance of Music. Next come two topics which raise issues central in the history of aesthetics: representation (here in the context of photography) and the nature of aesthetic appreciation (here in the context of the natural environment). We then move on to a cluster of four topics which focus on our emotional and intellectual engagement with art: Feelings and Fiction, The Pleasures of Tragedy, Sentimentality, and Musical Profundity. Finally, we turn to a pair of topics which bear on the institutions and the politics of aesthetics and the artworld: Feminism and Aesthetics and The Idea of the Museum. (We don't mean to suggest that the order in which the topics have been presented here is necessarily the best one. There are 39,916,799 other possible ways of ordering the topics, and we are sure that at least some of these will make as much sense as the one which we have chosen.)

The topics selected make it simple for an instructor to incorporate study of artworks into a course. For example, while reading and discussing the material on Colorizing Movies, a class might watch parts of both the original and the colorized version of Capra's *It's a Wonderful Life*. A visit to a museum or gallery may be useful when considering the material on The Idea of the Museum. Indeed, all the topics make it easy for the teacher to include material which should ensure that the course does not become wholly detached from the sorts of objects of experience which the readings are about.

Acknowledgments

As we have thought about and worked on this anthology, we have been greatly helped in many ways by a number of people. We would particularly like to thank Jay Bachrach, Curtis Brown, Allen Carlson, Sylvia Crisantes, David Dunham, Denis Dutton, Rick Flieger, Stan Godlovitch, Kathleen Higgins, Larry Kimmel, Flo Leibowitz, Jerrold Levinson, Doug McKenty, Marianne Neill, Ira Newman, Pat Powers, Jim Rather, Patty Rodney, Willis Salomon, Daniel Smith, Ann Spencer, Jay Thomson, Lee Thweatt, Dan Tures, Sue Weinberg, and our editor at McGraw-Hill, Cynthia Ward.

Finally, we would very much appreciate feedback about the book. Please let us know which parts of it have worked well for you, and pass on to us any suggestions for improvements. We would be particularly grateful for ideas about topics and readings which might be added in the future. Thanks!

Alex Neill

Aaron Ridley

ACKNOWLEDGMENTS

SECTION 1

Robertson Davies. From *What's Bred in the Bone*, by Robertson Davies. Copyright ©1985 by Robertson Davies. Reprinted by permission of the author and Viking Penguin, a division of Penguin Books USA Inc.

Alfred Lessing. "What Is Wrong with a Forgery?" From the *Journal of Aesthetics and Art Criticism* 23 (1965). Reprinted by permission of The American Society for Aesthetics.

Denis Dutton. "Artistic Crimes: The Problem of Forgery in the Arts." From the *British Journal of Aesthetics*, Vol. 19 No. 4 (1979), pp. 304-314. Reprinted by permission of Oxford University Press.

SECTION 2

Woody Allen. From "True Colors." First published in the *New York Review of Books*, Vol. 34 No. 13, August 13, 1987.

James O. Young. "In Defense of Colorization." From the *British Journal of Aesthetics*, Vol. 28 No. 4 (1988), pp. 368-372. Reprinted by permission of Oxford University Press.

Jerrold Levinson. "Colorization Ill-Defended." From the *British Journal of Aesthetics*, Vol. 30 No. 1 (1990), pp. 62-67. Reprinted by permission of Oxford University Press.

Flo Leibowitz. "Movie Colorization and the Expression of Mood." From the *Journal of Aesthetics and Art Criticism*, 49 (1991). Reprinted by permission of The American Society for Aesthetics.

James O. Young. "Still More in Defense of Colorization." From the *Journal of Aesthetics and Art Criticism*, 50 (1992). Reprinted by permission of The American Society for Aesthetics.

SECTION 3

Stephen Davies. "Authenticity in Musical Performance." From the *British Journal of Aesthetics*, Vol. 27 No. 1 (1987), pp. 39-50. Reprinted by permission of Oxford University Press.

James O. Young. "The Concept of Authentic Performance." From the *British Journal of Aesthetics*, Vol. 28 No. 3 (1988), pp. 228-238. Reprinted by permission of Oxford University Press.

SECTION 4

Roger Scruton. "Photography and Representation." From *The Aesthetic Understanding*, by Roger Scruton. Copyright © Roger Scruton 1983. Reprinted with the permission of the author and Methuen & Co.

William King. "Scruton and Reasons for Looking at Photographs." From the *British Journal of Aesthetics*, Vol. 32 No. 3 (1992) pp. 258-265. Reprinted by permission of Oxford University Press.

SECTION 5

Allen Carlson. "Appreciation and the Natural Environment." From the *Journal of Aesthetics and Art Criticism*, 37 (1979). Reprinted by permission of The American Society for Aesthetics.

Noël Carroll. "On Being Moved by Nature: Between Religion and Natural History." From *Landscape, Natural Beauty and the Arts*, edited by Salim Kemal and Ivan Gaskell. Copyright © Cambridge University Press 1993. Reprinted with the permission of Cambridge University Press.

SECTION 6

Gabriel García Márquez. From *One Hundred Years of Solitude*, by Gabriel García Márquez. English translation copyright © 1970 by Harper & Row Publishers, Inc. Reprinted by permission of HarperCollins Publishers, Inc.

Colin Radford. "How Can We Be Moved by the Fate of Anna Karenina?" From *The Proceedings of the Aristotelian Society*, Supplementary Volume 49, (1975). Reprinted by courtesy of the Editor of the Aristotelian Society: Copyright © 1975.

Alex Neill. "Fiction and the Emotions." From the *American Philosophical Quarterly*, Vol. 30 No. 1 (January 1993); pp. 1-13. Reprinted by permission of the *American Philosophical Quarterly*.

SECTION 7

David Hume. "Of Tragedy." Editorial notes by Eugene F. Miller. In *Essays Moral, Political and Literary*, by David Hume. Edited by Eugene F. Miller. Revised edition published in 1987 by Liberty Fund, Inc., 8335 Allison Pointe Trail, #300, Indianapolis, IN 46250-1687. Reprinted by permission of Eugene F. Miller and Liberty Fund, Inc.

Susan Feagin. "The Pleasures of Tragedy." From the *American Philosophical Quarterly*, Vol. 20 No. 1 (January 1983), pp. 95-104. Reprinted by permission of the *American Philosophical Quarterly*.

SECTION 8

Anthony Savile. "Sentimentality." From pp. 237-243 of *The Test of Time: An Essay in Philosophical Analysis*, by Anthony Savile. Copyright © Anthony Savile 1982. Reprinted by permission of the Oxford University Press.

Ira Newman. "The Alleged Unwholesomeness of Sentimentality." Previously unpublished. Published with the permission of the author.

SECTION 9

Rudolf Steiner. From "Music, the Astral World, and Devachan." In *The Inner Nature of Music and the Experience of Time*, by Rudolf Steiner. Reprinted by permission of the Anthroposophic Press, Inc., RR4, Box 94 A1, Hudson, NY 12534.

Peter Kivy. "The Profundity of Music." From *Music Alone: Philosophical Reflections on the Purely Musical Experience*, by Peter Kivy. Copyright © Cornell University Press, 1990. Reprinted with the permssion of Cornell University Press.

Jerrold Levinson. "Musical Profundity Misplaced." From the *Journal of Aesthetics and Art Criticism* 50 (1992). Reprinted by permission of The American Society for Aesthetics.

Aaron Ridley. "Profundity in Music." Previously unpublished. Published with the permission of the author.

SECTION 10

John Berger. From pp. 54, 63, 66 of *Ways of Seeing*, by John Berger. BBC/Penguin Books Ltd., 1972. Copyright ©1972 by Penguin Books Ltd. Reprinted by permission of Penguin Books Ltd. and Viking Penguin, a division of Penguin Books USA Inc.

Mary Devereaux. "Oppressive Texts, Resisting Readers and the Gendered Spectator: The *New Aesthetics*." From the *Journal of Aesthetics and Art Criticism*, 48 (1990). Reprinted by permission of The American Society for Aesthetics.

Curtis Brown. "Art, Oppression, and the Autonomy of Aesthetics." Previously unpublished. Published with the permission of the author.

SECTION 11

Robert Hughes. From *The Shock of the News*, by Robert Hughes. Copyright © 1980 by Robert Hughes. Reprinted by permission of Alfred A. Knopf, Inc. and BBC Enterprises Ltd.

John Dewey. "The Live Creature." From *Art As Experience,* by John Dewey. Copyright © 1934 by John Dewey, renewed © 1973 by The John Dewey Foundation. Copyright © 1962 by Roberta L. Dewey. Reprinted with the permission of The Putnam Publishing Group.

Albert William Levi. "The Art Museum as an Agency of Culture." From the *Journal of Aesthetic Education* Vol. 19 No. 2 (1985), pp. 23-40. Copyright © 1985 by the Board of Trustees of the University of Illinois. Used with the permission of the University of Illinois Press.

in one important sense of that term. Since originality is not an observable feature (you cannot tell whether a work is original simply by looking at it), lack of originality does not affect a forgery's aesthetic value. However, lack of originality does negatively affect its status as art.

One question we might ask here is whether Lessing's account of what is wrong with forgery is sufficiently specific. In essence, Lessing's suggestion seems to be that the trouble with forgeries is that they are unoriginal, derivative. However, it may be argued that a great deal of art—perhaps most of it—lacks originality in the sense that Lessing is concerned with. Indeed, this may be why most art is not *great* art. But don't the objections we have to forged art go beyond the objections that we have to unoriginal art? For one thing, aren't you likely to be *more* disappointed by the discovery that your drawing is a forgery, that it is not by Klee at all, than you would have been had you discovered that although the drawing is by Klee, it is one in which he is mimicking the style and subject matter of an earlier artist? We should consider, then, the possibility that Lessing's account is too broad; that it fails to explain how the offensiveness of forgery goes beyond the deficiencies of unoriginal art.

We might also ask whether Lessing's account is based on an overly restrictive view of what is relevant to aesthetic appreciation. In particular, is it true that only the observable features of a work are relevant to our aesthetic appreciation of it? In the second of the articles in this section, Denis Dutton argues against this view. Dutton suggests that all works of art can be seen as performances, and that a central part of what is involved in aesthetic appreciation is appreciation of what an artist has *achieved* in his or her performance. This achievement (or lack of it) may not be wholly observable. Understanding an artist's achievement, Dutton argues, depends on knowing something about the origins of the work and about the context in which it was produced. In Dutton's view, that is, nonobservable features of a work, and in particular facts about its origins, are relevant to our assessment of the achievement the work represents, and thus may well be relevant to our aesthetic appreciation of it. The problem with forgery, he suggests, is that "it misrepresents artistic achievement," by misleading us about the origins of the work in question. Although discovering that a work is a forgery may not lead us to notice any difference in its observable features, it does alter our understanding of its origins, and hence our assessment of the achievement it represents. Thus, if Dutton is right, discovering that a work is a forgery may legitimately affect our aesthetic appreciation of that work.

Clearly, discovering that your drawing is a forgery is likely to upset you. The articles in this section suggest, however, that it is not so clear whether your reasons for being upset can include aesthetic reasons. In essence the question is this: Can the fact of forgery matter to a person whose only concern is with aesthetic value? Answering this question is an important step toward understanding the nature of aesthetic experience.

What Is Wrong with a Forgery?

Alfred Lessing

This article attempts to answer the simple question: What is wrong with a forgery? It assumes, then, that something *is* wrong with a forgery. This is seen to be a reasonable assumption when one considers that the term *forgery* can be defined only in reference to a contrasting phenomenon which must somehow include the notion of genuineness or authenticity. When thus defined there can be little doubt that the concept of forgery is a normative one. It is clear, moreover, that it is a negative concept implying the absence or negation of value. But a problem arises when we ask what kind of value we are speaking of. It appears to be generally assumed that in the case of artistic forgeries we are dealing with the absence or negation of *aesthetic* value. If this were so, a forgery would be an aesthetically inferior work of art. But this, as I will show, is not the case. Pure aesthetics cannot explain forgery. Considering a work of art aesthetically superior because it is genuine, or inferior because it is forged, has little or nothing to do with aesthetic judgment or criticism. It is rather a piece of snobbery.[1]

It is difficult to make this position convincing to a person who is convinced that forgery *is* a matter of aesthetics. If a person insists that for him the aesthetic value (i.e., the beauty) of a work of art is affected by the knowledge that it is or is not genuine, there is little one can say to make that fact unreal for him. At most one can try to show that in the area of aesthetics and criticism we are easily confused and that his view, if carried through, leads to absurd or improbable conclusions. It is important that we do this because it is impossible to understand what is wrong with a forgery unless it be first made quite clear that the answer will not be in terms of its aesthetic worth.

Somehow critics have never understood this and have again and again allowed themselves to be forced into an embarrassing position upon the discovery of some forgery or other. Perhaps the classic, certainly the most celebrated case in point, was that of Han van Meegeren, who in 1945 disturbed the complacent tranquility of the world of art and art critics by confessing that he was the artist responsible for eight paintings, six of which had been sold as legitimate Vermeers and two as de Hooghs. It is not hard to imagine the discomfort felt by critics at that time, especially when we recall how thoroughly successful van Meegeren was in perpetrating his fraud. His *Disciples at Emmaus* was subjected to the very highest praise by the noted critic and scholar Abraham Bredius as one of

[1] Cf. Arthur Koestler, "The Anatomy of Snobbery," *The Anchor Review* 1 (Garden City: Doubleday Anchor Books, 1955): 1–25.

Vermeer's finest achievements, and it hung in the Boymans Museum for seven years. During that time thousands upon thousands admired and praised the painting. There was no doubt in anyone's mind that this was one of the greatest of Vermeer's paintings and, indeed, one of the most beautiful works of art in the world. It was undoubtedly this universal judgment of aesthetic excellence which accounts largely for the sensational effects of van Meegeren's confession in 1945.

It is of course embarrassing and irritating for an expert to make a mistake in his field. And it *was*, as it turned out, a mistake to identify the painting as a Vermeer. But it should be obvious from the words of Bredius that there is more involved here than a mere matter of misidentification. "The colors are magnificent," he writes. "The highest art . . . this magnificent painting . . . *the* masterpiece of Vermeer": this is more than identification. This clearly is aesthetic praise. And it is just the fact that the critics heaped such lavish praise on a picture which turned out to have been painted by a second-rate contemporary artist that made the van Meegeren case such a painful affair for them. To their way of thinking, which I am trying to show was not very logical, they were now apparently faced with the dilemma of either admitting that they had praised a worthless picture or continuing to do so.

This was, of course, precisely the trap that van Meegeren had laid for the critics. It was, in fact, the whole *raison d'être* of his perpetrating the fraud. He deliberately chose this extreme, perhaps pathological, way of exposing what he considered to be false aesthetic standards of art critics. In this respect his thinking was no more logical than that of the critics. His reasoning, at least about his first forgery, *The Disciples*, was in effect as follows: "Once my painting has been accepted and admired as a genuine Vermeer, I will confess publicly to the forgery and thus force the critics either to retract their earlier judgments of praise, thereby acknowledging their fallibility, or to recognize that I am as great an artist as Vermeer." The dilemma as stated contains a difficulty to which we shall return later. What is important historically is that the critics accepted van Meegeren's dilemma as a genuine one (thereby becoming the dupes of a logical forgery as well as an artistic one), although in the public outburst of indignation, condemnation, praise, blame, analysis, investigation, and discussion which followed van Meegeren's confession, it is difficult to determine which horn of this dilemma the critics actually chose to be impaled on.

There existed, in fact, a small group of critics who never for a moment accepted van Meegeren's claim to have painted *The Disciples at Emmaus*. They argued vehemently that whereas all the other paintings in question are easily shown to be forgeries, no convincing evidence had been produced to prove that *The Disciples* (as well as one other painting entitled *The Last Supper*) was not by Vermeer and that, in fact, all evidence pointed to the conclusion that it was a genuine Vermeer. Subsequent laboratory tests using more modern techniques have finally settled the issue against these critics, but that need not concern us.

What should concern us is the fact that aesthetically it would seem to make no difference whatever whether *The Disciples* is a Vermeer or a van Meegeren. Needless to say, this is not the view of the critics. To them apparently it makes all the difference in the world. Consider, for example, the words of J. Decoen, who was one of that aforementioned group of critics that held that *The Disciples* was a genuine Vermeer:

> I must recall that the moment of greatest anguish for me was when the verdict [of van Meegeren] was being considered. The Court might, according to an ancient Dutch Law, have ordered the destruction of *all* the pictures. One shudders at the thought that one could, officially, have destroyed two of the most moving works which Vermeer has created. During the trial, at the moment of his indictment, the Public Prosecutor stated that there was in Court a man who claimed that a number of the paintings were not by van Meegeren. He made this statement because, ever since 1945, he must have realized that my perseverance had not faltered, that my conviction was deep, and that I had never changed my original statements in any respect whatsoever. These words may possibly have influenced the decision of the Court with regard to the application of the Law. If this be so, I should consider myself amply repaid for my efforts and pains, for my tenacity may possibly have ultimately rescued two capital works of the Dutch school of the seventeenth century.[2]

But what does it matter that Decoen is wrong? Could he no longer take pride in having prevented the destruction of these "capital" paintings even though they are products of the twentieth instead of the seventeenth century? The answers, it seems to me, are almost self-evident. What, after all, makes these paintings "capital works"? Surely it is their purely aesthetic qualities, such as the ones mentioned by Bredius in his description of *The Disciples*. But if this is so, then why, even if this painting is a forgery, should Decoen not be justified in his actions, since he has preserved a painting which is aesthetically important for the only reason that a painting can be aesthetically important—namely, its beauty? Are we any more justified in destroying capital paintings of the twentieth century than those of the seventeenth? To this question we are usually given the answer that the one is after all a forgery while the other is genuine. But our question is precisely: What is the difference between a genuine Vermeer and a van Meegeren forgery? It is of no use to maintain that one need but look to see the difference. The fact that *The Disciples* is a forgery (if indeed it is) cannot, so to speak, be read off from its surface, but can finally be proved or disproved only by means of extensive scientific exper-

[2] J. Decoen, *Vermeer-Van Meegeren, Back to the Truth,* trans. E. J. Labarre (London: Donker, 1951), p. 60.

iments and analyses. Nor are the results of such scientific investigations of any help in answering our question, since they deal exclusively with non-aesthetic elements of the picture, such as its chemical composition, its hardness, its crackle, and so on. The truth is that the difference between a forgery and a genuine work of art is by no means as obvious as critics sometimes make out. In the case of *The Disciples,* at least, it is certainly not a matter of but needing to look in order to see. The actual history of *The Disciples* turns all such attempted *post facto* explanations into a kind of academic sour grapes.

The plain fact is that aesthetically it makes no difference whether a work of art is authentic or a forgery, and, instead of being embarrassed at having praised a forgery, critics should have the courage of their convictions and take pride in having praised a work of beauty. Perhaps if critics did respond in this way we should be less inclined to think that so often their judgments are historical, biographical, economical, or sociological instead of aesthetic. For in a sense, of course, van Meegeren proved his point. Perhaps it is a point for which such radical proof was not even necessary. We all know very well that it is just the preponderance in the art world of nonaesthetic criteria such as fame of the artist and the age or cost of the canvas which is largely responsible for the existence of artistic forgeries in the first place. We all know that a few authentic pen and ink scratches by Picasso are far more valuable than a fine landscape by an unknown artist. If we were offered a choice between an inferior (but genuine) Degas sketch and a beautiful Jones or Smith or X, how many of us would choose the latter? In a museum that did not label its paintings, how many of us would not feel uneasy lest we condemn one of the greats or praise an unknown? But, it may be argued, all this we know. It is simply a fact and, moreover, probably an unavoidable, understandable—even a necessary—fact. Is this so serious or regrettable? The answer, of course, is that it is indeed serious and regrettable that the realm of art should be so infested with nonaesthetic standards of judgment that it is often impossible to distinguish artistic from economic value, taste or fashion from true artistic excellence, and good artists from clever businessmen.

This brings us to the point of our discussion so far. The matter of genuineness versus forgery is but another nonaesthetic standard of judgment. The fact that a work of art is a forgery is an item of information about it on a level with such information as the age of the artist when he created it, the political situation in the time and place of its creation, the price it originally fetched, the kind of materials used in it, the stylistic influences discernible in it, the psychological state of the artist, his purpose in painting it, and so on. All such information belongs to areas of interest peripheral at best to the work of art as aesthetic object, areas such as biography, history of art, sociology, and psychology. I do not deny that such areas of interest may be important and that their study may even help us to become better art appreciators. But I do deny that the information which they provide is of the essence of the work of art or of the aesthetic experience which it engenders.

It would be merely foolish to assert that it is of no interest whatsoever to know that *The Disciples* is a forgery. But to the man who has never heard of either Vermeer or van Meegeren and who stands in front of *The Disciples* admiring it, it can make no difference whether he is told that it is a seventeenth-century Vermeer or a twentieth-century van Meegeren in the style of Vermeer. And when some deny this and argue vehemently that, indeed, it does make a great deal of difference, they are only admitting that *they* do know something about Vermeer and van Meegeren and the history of art and the value and reputation of certain masters. They are only admitting that *they* do not judge a work of art on purely aesthetic grounds but also take into account when it was created, by whom, and how great a reputation it or its creator has. And instead of seeking justification in the fact that in truth it is difficult to make a pure, aesthetic judgment, unbiased by all our knowledge of the history and criticism of art, they generally confuse matters of aesthetics even more by rationalizing that it is the complexity of the aesthetic experience which accounts for the difference made by the knowledge that a work of art is a forgery. That the aesthetic experience is complex I do not deny. But it is not so complex that such items of information as the place and date of creation or the name of the creator of a work of art have to be considered. The fact that *The Disciples* is a forgery is just that, a fact. It is a fact *about* the painting which stands entirely apart from it as an object for aesthetic contemplation. The knowledge of this fact can neither add anything to nor subtract anything from the aesthetic experience (as aesthetic), except insofar as preoccupation with it or disappointment on its account may in some degree prevent us from having an aesthetic experience at all. Whatever the reasons for the removal of *The Disciples* from the walls of the Boymans Museum in Rotterdam, they were assuredly not aesthetic.

And yet, we can all sympathize with, or at least understand, why *The Disciples* was removed. It was, after all, a forgery, and even if we grant that it is not a matter of aesthetics, it still seems self-evident that forgery remains a normative term implying a defect or absence in its object. In short, we still need to answer our question: What is wrong with a forgery?

The most obvious answer to this question, after the aesthetic one, is that forgery is a moral or legal normative concept, and that it thus refers to an object which, if not necessarily aesthetically inferior, is always morally offensive. Specifically, the reason forgery is a moral offense, according to this view, is of course that it involves *deception*. Reasonable as this view seems at first, it does not, as I will try to show, answer our question adequately.

Now it cannot be denied, I think, that we do in fact often intend little more than this moral connotation when we speak of forgery. Just because forgery is a normative concept we implicitly condemn any instance of it because we generally assume that it involves the breaking of a legal or moral code. But this assumption is only sometimes correct. It is important to note this because historically by far the majority of artistic fakes or forgeries have not been legal forgeries. Most often they have been the result of simple mistakes, misunderstandings, and lack of information about given works of art. We can, as a point of terminology, exclude all such instances from the category of forgery and restrict the term to those cases involving deliberate deception. There is, after all, a whole class of forgeries, including simple copies, misattributions, composites, and works "in the manner of" some reputable artist, which represent deliberate frauds. In these cases of forgery, which are undoubtedly the most notorious and disconcerting, someone, e.g., artist or art dealer, has passed off a work of art as being something which it is not. The motive for doing so is almost always economic, but occasionally, as with van Meegeren, there is involved also a psychological motive of personal prestige or revenge. In any case, it seems clear that—if we leave out of consideration the factor of financial loss, which can of course be considerable, as again the van Meegeren case proved—such deliberate forgeries are condemned by us on moral grounds, that is, because they involve conscious deception.

Yet as a final answer to our question as to what is wrong with a forgery, this definition fails. The reason is the following: Although to some extent it is true that passing *anything* off as *anything* that it is not constitutes deception and is thus an undesirable or morally repugnant act, the case of deception we have in mind when we define forgery in terms of it is that of passing off the inferior as the superior. Although, strictly speaking, passing off a genuine de Hoogh as a Vermeer is also an immoral act of deception, it is hard to think of it as a forgery at all, let alone a forgery in the same sense as passing off a van Meegeren as a Vermeer is. The reason is obviously that in the case of the de Hoogh a superior work is being passed off as a superior work (by another artist), while in the van Meegeren case a presumably inferior work is passed off as a superior work.

What is needed, then, to make our moral definition of forgery more accurate is the specification "passing off the inferior as the superior." But it is just at this point that this common-sense definition of artistic forgery in moral terms breaks down. For we are now faced with the question of what is meant by superior and inferior in art. The moral definition of forgery says in effect that a forgery is an inferior work passed off as a superior one. But what is meant here by inferior? We have already seen that the forgery is not necessarily *aesthetically* inferior. What, then, does it mean? Once again, what is wrong with a forgery?

The attempt to define forgery in moral terms fails because it inevitably already assumes that there exists a difference between genuine works of art and forgeries which makes passing off the latter as the former an offense against a moral or legal law. For only if such a difference does in fact exist can there be any rationale for the law. It is, of course, precisely this assumed real difference which we are trying to discover in this chapter.

It seems to me that the offense felt to be involved in forgery is not so much against the spirit of beauty (aesthetics) or the spirit of the law (morality) as against the spirit of art. Somehow, a work such as *The Disciples* lacks artistic integrity. Even if it is beautiful and even if van Meegeren had not forged Vermeer's signature, there would still be something wrong with *The Disciples. What?* is still our question.

We may approach this problem by considering the following interesting point. The concept of forgery seems to be peculiarly inapplicable to the performing arts. It would be quite nonsensical to say, for example, that the man who played the Bach suites for unaccompanied cello and whom at the time we took to be Pablo Casals was in fact a forger. Similarly, we should want to argue that the term *forgery* was misused if we should read in the newspaper that Margot Fonteyn's performance in *Swan Lake* last night was a forgery because as a matter of fact it was not Margot Fonteyn who danced last night, but rather some unknown person whom everyone mistook for Margot Fonteyn. Again, it is difficult to see in what sense a performance of, say, *Oedipus Rex* or *Hamlet* could be termed a forgery.

Here, however, we must immediately clarify our point, for it is easily misunderstood. There is, of course, a sense in which a performance of *Hamlet* or *Swan Lake* or the Bach suites could be called a forgery. If, for example, someone gave a performance of *Hamlet* in which every gesture, every movement, every vocal interpretation had been copied or imitated from the performance of *Hamlet* by Laurence Olivier, we could, I suppose, call the former a forgery of the latter. But notice that in that case we are interpreting the art of acting not as a performing art but as a creative art. For what is meant is that Olivier's interpretation and performance of *Hamlet* is itself an original and creative work of art which can be forged. Similar comments would apply to Margot Fonteyn's *Swan Lake* and Casals's Bach suites and, in fact, to every performance.

My point, is then, that the concept of forgery applies only to the creative and not to the performing arts. It can be denied, of course, that there is any such ultimate distinction between creative and performing arts. But we shall still have to admit, I think, that the duality on which it is based—the duality of creativity or originality on the one hand and reproduction or technique on the other—is real. We shall have to admit that originality and technique are two elements of all art; for it can be argued not only that a performance requires more than technique, namely originality, but also that the creation of a work of art requires more than originality, namely technique.

The truth of the matter is probably that both performances and works of art vary greatly and significantly in the degree to which they possess these elements. In fact, their relative presence in works of art and performances makes an interesting way of categorizing the latter. But it would be wrong to assert that these two elements are inseparable. I can assure the reader that a portrait painted by me would be technically almost totally incompetent, and yet even I would not deny that it might be original. On the other hand, a really skillful copy of, for example, a Rembrandt drawing may be technically perfect and yet lack all originality. These two examples establish the two extreme cases of a kind of continuum. The copy of Rembrandt is, of course, the forgery *par excellence.* My incompetent portrait is as far removed from being a forgery as any work can be. Somewhere in between lies the whole body of legitimate performances and works of art.

The implications of this long and devious argument are as follows: Forgery is a concept that can be made meaningful only by reference to the concept of originality, and hence only to art viewed as a *creative,* not as a reproductive or technical, activity. The element of performance or technique in art cannot be an object for forgery because technique is not the kind of thing that can be forged. Technique is, as it were, public. One does or does not possess it or one acquires it or learns it. One may even pretend to have it. But one cannot forge it because in order to forge it one must already possess it, in which case there is no need to forge it. It is not Vermeer's technique in painting light which van Meegeren forged. That technique is public and may be had by anyone who is able and willing to learn it. It is rather Vermeer's discovery of this technique and his use of it, that is, Vermeer's originality, which is forged. The light, as well as the composition, the color, and many other features, of course, were original with Vermeer. They are not original with van Meegeren. They are forged.

At this point our argument could conclude were it not for the fact that the case which we have used throughout as our chief example, *Christ and the Disciples at Emmaus,* is not in fact a skillful copy of a Vermeer but a novel painting in the style of Vermeer. This threatens our definition of forgery since this particular forgery (always assuming it *is* a forgery) obviously possesses originality in some sense of the word.

The problem of forgery, in other words, is a good deal more complex than might at first be supposed, and before we can rest content with our definition of forgery as the lack of originality in works of art, we must show that the concept of originality can indeed account for the meaning of forgery as an untrue or objectionable thing in all instances, including even such a bizarre case as van Meegeren's *Disciples at Emmaus.* It thus becomes important to examine the various possible meanings that the term *originality* may have in the context of art in order to determine in what sense *The Disciples* does and does not possess it, and hence in what sense it can meaningfully and justifiably be termed a forgery.

1. A work of art may be said to be original in the sense of being a

particular object not identical with any other object. But this originality is trivial since it is a quality possessed by all things. *Particularity* or *self-identity* would be better names for it.

2.   By originality in a work of art we may mean that it possesses a certain superficial individuality which serves to distinguish it from other works of art. Thus, for example, a certain subject matter in a particular arrangement painted in certain colors may serve to identify a painting and mark it as an original work of art in the sense that its subject matter is unique. Probably the term *individuality* specifies this quality more adequately than *originality*.

It seems safe to assert that this quality of individuality is a necessary condition for any work of art to be called original in any significant sense. It is, however, not a necessary condition for a work to be called beautiful or to be the object of an aesthetic experience. A good reproduction or copy of a painting may be the object of aesthetic contemplation yet lack all originality in the sense which we are here considering. Historically many forgeries are of this kind, i.e., more or less skillful copies of existing works of art. They may be described as being forgeries just because they lack this kind of originality and hence any other kind of originality as well. Notice that the quality which makes such a copy a forgery, i.e., its lack of individuality, is not a quality which exists in the work of art as such. It is a fact about the work of art which can be known only by placing the latter in the context of the history of art and observing whether any identical work predates it.

As we said above, it is not this kind of originality which is lacking in *The Disciples*.[3]

3. By originality in art we may mean the kind of imaginative novelty or spontaneity which is a mark of every good work of art. It is the kind of originality which attaches to individual works of art and which can be specified in formal or technical terms such as composition, balance, color intensity, perspective, harmony, rhythm, tempo, texture, rhyme, alliteration, suspense, character, plot, structure, choice of subject matter, and so on. Here again, however, in order for this quality to be meaningfully called originality, a reference must be made to a historical context in terms of which we are considering the particular work of art in question, e.g., this work of art is original because the artist has done something with the subject and its treatment which has never been done before, or this work is not original because many others just like it predate it.

In any case, *The Disciples* does, by common consent, possess this kind of originality and is therefore, in this sense at least, not a forgery.

---

[3] A slightly more complex case is offered by forgeries (including probably some of van Meegeren's less carefully executed Vermeer forgeries) which are not simple copies of other paintings but which are composites of other paintings. While such forgeries clearly have a measure of individuality totally lacking in the simple copy, I should want to maintain that they lack only superficially the kind of originality here discussed.

4. The term *originality* is sometimes used to refer to the great artistic achievement of a specific work of art. Thus we might say that whereas nearly all of Milton's works are good and original in the sense of (3) above, *Paradise Lost* has a particularly profound originality possessed only by really superlative works of art. It is hard to state precisely what is meant by this use of the term *originality*. In justifying it we should probably point to the scope, profundity, daring, and novelty of the conception of the work of art in question as well as to the excellence of its execution. No doubt this kind of originality differs from that discussed under (3) above only in degree.

It is to be noted that it cannot be the lack of this kind of originality which defines a forgery since, almost by definition, it is a quality lacking in many—maybe the majority of—legitimate works of art. Moreover, judging from the critical commentary with which *The Disciples* was received at the time of its discovery—commentary unbiased by the knowledge that it was a forgery—it seems reasonable to infer that the kind of originality meant here is in fact one which *The Disciples* very likely possesses.

5. Finally, it would seem that by originality in art we can and often do mean the artistic novelty and achievement not of one particular work of art but of the totality of artistic productions of one man or even one school. Thus we may speak of the originality of Vermeer or El Greco or Mozart or Dante or Impressionism or the Metaphysical Poets or even the Greeks or the Renaissance, always referring, I presume, to the artistic accomplishments achieved and embodied in the works of art belonging to the particular man, movement, or period. In the case of Vermeer we may speak of the originality of the artist's sense of design in the genre picture, the originality of his use of bright and pure colors, and of the originality of his treatment and execution of light.

We must note first of all that this meaning of originality, too, depends entirely on a historical context in which we are placing and considering the accomplishment of one man or one period. It would be meaningless to call Impressionism original, in the sense here considered, except in reference to the history of art which preceded it. Again, it is just because Vermeer's sense of pictorial design, his use of bright colors, and his mastery of the technique of painting light are not found in the history of art before him that we call these things original in Vermeer's work. Originality, even in this more profound sense, or rather especially in this more profound sense, is a quality definable only in terms of the history of art.

A second point of importance is that while originality as here considered is a quality which attaches to a whole corpus or style of works of art, it can be considered to exist in one particular work of art in the sense that that work of art is a typical example of the style or movement to which it belongs and therefore embodies the originality of that style or movement.

Thus we may say that Vermeer's *A Painter in His Studio* is original because in this painting (as well as in several others, of course) we recognize those characteristics mentioned earlier (light, design, color, etc.) which are so typical of Vermeer's work as a whole and which, when we consider the whole of Vermeer's work in the context of the history of art, allow us to ascribe originality to it.

Turning our attention once more to *The Disciples*, we are at last in a position to provide an adequate answer to our question as to the meaning of the term forgery when applied to a work of art such as *The Disciples*. We shall find, I think, that the fraudulent character of this painting is adequately defined by stating that it lacks originality in the fifth and final sense which we have here considered. Whatever kinds of originality it can claim—and we have seen that it possesses all the kinds previously discussed—it is *not* original in the sense of being the product of a style, period, or technique which, when considered in its appropriate historical context, can be said to represent a significant achievement. It is just this fact which differentiates this painting from a genuine Vermeer! The latter, when considered in its historical context, i.e., the seventeenth century, possesses the qualities of artistic or creative novelty which justify us in calling it original. *The Disciples*, on the other hand, in *its* historical context, i.e., the twentieth century, is not original, since it presents nothing new or creative to the history of art even though, as we have emphasized earlier, it may well be as beautiful as the genuine Vermeer pictures.

It is to be noted that in this definition of forgery the phrase "appropriate historical context" refers to the date of production of the particular work of art in question, not the date which in the history of art is appropriate to its style or subject matter.[4] In other words, what makes *The Disciples* a forgery is precisely the disparity or gap between its stylistically appropriate features and its actual date of production. It is simply this

---

[4] To avoid all ambiguity in my definition of forgery, I need to specify whether "actual date of production" refers to the completion of the finished, concrete work of art or only to the productive means of such works. This question bears on the legitimacy of certain works in art forms where the means of production and the finished product are separable. Such works include lithographs, etchings, wood-cuts, cast sculptures, etc. What, for example, are we to say of a modern bronze cast made from a mold taken directly from an ancient bronze cast or a modern print made from an eighteenth-century block? Are such art objects forgeries? The answer, it seems to me, is largely a matter of convenience and terminology. Assuming that there is no moral fraud, i.e., deception, involved, whether or not to call such cases instances of forgery becomes an academic question. It depends entirely on what we take to be "the work of art." In the case of lithography or etching there may be some ambiguity about this. I myself would define "the work of art" as the finished concrete product and hence I would indeed call modern prints from old litho stones forgeries, though, assuming no deception is involved, forgeries of a peculiarly amoral, nonoffensive sort. In other arts, such as music, there is little or no ambiguity on this point. Clearly, no one would want to label the first performance of a newly discovered Beethoven symphony a forgery. In still other, e.g., the literary, arts, due to the absolute inseparability of the concrete work of art and the means of its production, this problem cannot arise at all.

disparity which we have in mind when we say that forgeries such as *The Disciples* lack integrity.

It is interesting at this point to recall van Meegeren's reasoning in perpetrating the Vermeer forgeries. "Either," he reasoned, "the critics must admit their fallibility or else acknowledge that I am as great an artist as Vermeer." We can see now that this reasoning is not sound. For the notion of greatness involved in it depends on the same concept of historical originality which we have been considering. The only difference is that we are now thinking of it as an attribute of the artist rather than of the works of art. Van Meegeren's mistake was in thinking that Vermeer's reputation as a great artist depended on his ability to paint beautiful pictures. If this were so, the dilemma which van Meegeren posed to the critics would have been a real one, for his picture is undeniably beautiful. But, in fact, Vermeer is *not* a great artist only because he could paint beautiful pictures. He is great for that reason plus something else. And that something else is precisely the fact of his originality, i.e., the fact that he painted certain pictures in a certain manner *at a certain time in the history and development of art*. Vermeer's art represents a genuine creative achievement in the history of art. It is the work not merely of a master craftsman or technician but of a creative genius as well. And it is for the latter rather than for the former reason that we call Vermeer great.

Van Meegeren, on the other hand, possessed only craftsmanship or technique. His works lack the historical originality of Vermeer's and it is for this reason that we should not want to call him great as we call Vermeer great.[5] At the same time it must be recalled that van Meegeren's forgeries are not forgeries *par excellence. The Disciples,* though not original in the most important sense, possesses, as we have seen, degrees of originality generally lacking in forgeries.

In this connection it is interesting to speculate on the relations between originality and technique in the creative continuum which we came upon earlier. A totally original work is one which lacks all technique. A forgery *par excellence* represents the perfection of technique with the absence of all originality. True works of art are somewhere in between. Perhaps the really great works of art, such as Vermeer's, are those which embody a maximum of both originality and technique: van Meegeren's forgeries can never be in this last category, for, as we have seen, they lack the most important kind of originality.

Finally, the only question that remains is why originality is such a significant aspect of art. Now we need to note, of course, that the concern with originality is not a universal characteristic of art or artists. Yet the fact that the search for originality is perhaps typical only of modern Western art tends to strengthen the presumption of its fundamental rela-

---

[5] Unless it be argued that van Meegeren derives *his* greatness from the originality of his works when considered in the context not of the history of art but of the history of forgery!

tion to the concept of forgery. For it is also just in the modern Western tradition that the problem of forgery has taken on the kind of economic and aesthetic significance which warrants our concern with it here. But why, even in modern Western art, should the importance of originality be such that the concepts of greatness and forgery in art are ultimately definable only by reference to it? The answer is, I believe, not hard to find. It rests on the fact that art has and must have a history. If it did not, if artists were concerned only with making beautiful pictures, poems, symphonies, etc., the possibilities for the creation of aesthetically pleasing works of art would soon be exhausted. We would (perhaps) have a number of lovely paintings, but we should soon grow tired of them, for they would all be more or less alike. But artists do not seek merely to produce works of beauty. They seek to produce *original* works of beauty. And when they succeed in achieving this originality we call their works great not only because they are beautiful but because they have also unlocked, both to artists and to appreciators, unknown and unexplored realms of beauty. Men like Leonardo, Rembrandt, Haydn, Goethe, and Vermeer are great not merely because of the excellence of their works but also because of their creative originality which goes on to inspire other artists and leads through them to new and aesthetically valuable developments in the history of art. It is, in fact, this search for creative originality which insures the continuation and significance of such a history in the first place.

It is for this reason that the concept of originality has become inseparable from that of art. It is for this reason too that aesthetics has traditionally concerned itself with topics such as the inspiration of the artist, the mystery of the creative act, the intense and impassioned search of the artist, the artist as the prophet of his times, the artistic struggle after expression, art as the chronicle of the emotional life of a period in history, art as a product of its time, and so on. All such topics are relevant not to art as the production of works of beauty but to art as the production of *original* works of beauty, or, more accurately, works of original beauty. As such they are perfectly legitimate topics of discussion. But we must not forget that the search for originality is, or ought to be, but the means to an end. That end is, presumably, the production of aesthetically valuable or beautiful works of art; that is, works which are to become the object of an aesthetic experience. That experience is a wholly autonomous one. It does not and cannot take account of any entity or fact which is not aesthetically perceivable in the work of art itself. The historical context in which that work of art stands is just such a fact. It is wholly irrelevant to the pure aesthetic appreciation and judgment of the work of art. And because the fact of forgery—together with originality and greatness—can be ultimately defined only in terms of this historical context, it too is irrelevant to the aesthetic appreciation and judgment of *The Disciples at Emmaus* or any other work of art. The fact of forgery is important historically, biographically, perhaps legally, or, as the van Meegeren case proved, financially; but not, strictly speaking, aesthetically.

In conclusion, let us consider the following paradoxical result. We have seen in what sense Vermeer is considered to be a great artist. We have also seen that although *The Disciples* is indistinguishable from a genuine Vermeer, van Meegeren cannot be thus called great. And yet we would suppose that Vermeer's greatness is somehow embodied in his work, that his paintings are proof of and monuments to his artistic genius. What are we to say, then, of this van Meegeren forgery which hung in a museum for seven years as an embodiment and proof of Vermeer's genius? Are we to say that it now no longer embodies anything at all except van Meegeren's skillful forging technique? Or are we to grant after all that this painting proves van Meegeren's greatness as Vermeer's paintings do his? The answer is, I think, surprising but wholly appropriate. Paradoxically, *The Disciples at Emmaus* is as much a monument to the artistic genius of Vermeer as are Vermeer's own paintings. Even though it was painted by van Meegeren in the twentieth century, it embodies and bears witness to the greatness of the seventeenth-century art of Vermeer.

Artistic Crimes

Denis Dutton

The concept of forgery is a touchstone of criticism. If the existence of forgeries—and their occasional acceptance as authentic works of art—has been too often dismissed or ignored in the theory of criticism, it may be because of the forger's special power to make the critic look ridiculous. Awkward as it is, critics have heaped the most lavish praise on art objects that have turned out to be forged. The suspicion this arouses is, of course, that the critics were led to praise the forgery for the wrong reasons in the first place. Since the aesthetic object as perceived is no different after the revelation that it is forged, the implication to be drawn is that it had previously been critically valued not for its intrinsic aesthetic properties, but because it was believed to be the work of an esteemed artist.

Natural as this suspicion is, it represents a point of view I shall seek to discredit in the following discussion. Everyone recognizes that the proper identification of an art object as genuine or forged is crucial as regards monetary value, that forgery has moral implications, that there are important historical reasons for wanting to distinguish the genuine from the faked art object. But there are many who believe as well that when we come down to assessing the *aesthetic* merits of an art object, the question of authenticity is irrelevant. In this respect, the Han van Meegeren episode is an excellent test case. For van Meegeren's ambition went beyond merely monetary rewards: he wanted to wreak revenge on a critical establishment which he viewed as unjust in its assessment of his talents. And it must have been sweet, during the unveiling of the painting in 1937, to stand at the edge of a crowd in the Boymans Museum and hear one of the world's reigning experts on Dutch masters proclaim van Meegeren's own *Christ and the Disciples at Emmaus* as "perhaps *the* masterpiece of Johannes Vermeer." Not all of his subsequent forgeries received such unqualified acceptance, but it must be remembered that van Meegeren's activities did not come to light until he was arrested shortly after the war for having sold a Dutch national treasure (*The Adulteress*) to the enemy. (The buyer of that painting, Hermann Göring, was reportedly unbelieving when informed of the matter in jail, and there remained critics who continued to doubt van Meegeren's story, at least with regard to the *Emmaus*, for years.)

The van Meegeren episode is just one example of the general problem of forgery in the arts. I say "arts" in the plural because I believe that in one form or another the problem can arise in all of the arts. The problem may be stated quite simply thus: if an aesthetic object has been widely admired and it is discovered that it is a forgery, a copy, or a misattribution, why reject it? A painting has hung for years on a museum wall, giving delight to generations of art lovers. One day it is revealed to be a forgery, and is immediately removed from view. But why? The discovery that a work of art is forged, as, say, with a van Meegeren Vermeer, does not alter the perceived qualities of the work. Hence it can make no *aesthetic* difference whether a work is forged or not. At least this is how one approach to this question goes, an approach that has had such able defenders as Alfred Lessing and Arthur Koestler.[1] Koestler, for instance, insists that an object's status as original or forged is extraneous information, incidental to its intrinsic aesthetic properties. Thus the individual who pays an enormous sum for an original but who would have no interest in a reproduction which he could not tell from the original (perhaps a Picasso pen-and-ink drawing), or worse, who chooses an aesthetically inferior original over an excellent and superior forgery (or reproduction), is said to be at best confused and at worst a snob.

In a discussion largely in agreement with this, Lessing mentions that the possibility of forgery exists only in the "creative" but not the "performing" arts. While I will argue that in certain respects this distinction itself is dubious, as regards the possibility of forgery it is surely misleading. Consider for a moment Smith and Jones, who have just finished listening

---

[1] Arthur Koestler, "The Aesthetics of Snobbery," *Horizon* 8 (1965): 50–53; Alfred Lessing, "What Is Wrong with a Forgery?" reprinted in the present volume.

to a new recording of Liszt's *Transcendental Études.* Smith is transfixed. He says, "What beautiful artistry! The pianist's tone is superb, his control absolute, his speed and accuracy dazzling. Truly an electric performance!" Jones responds with a sigh. "Yeah, it was electrical all right. Or to be more precise, it was electronic. He recorded the music at practice tempo and the engineers speeded it up on a rotating head recorder." Poor Smith—his enthusiasm evaporates.

But really, ought it to? If Smith cannot with his ears discriminate the difference between the pianist's technical accomplishments and an engineer turning a knob, why *should* it make any difference to him? In fact, looking at the situation from Koestler's perspective, we will have to consider that Smith is a snob, or at least somehow confused. But surely there is something legitimate in Smith's response; surely there is more to this than can be accounted for by saying that Smith is simply letting extraaesthetic considerations influence his aesthetic response to the piano performance.

I raise this example in connection with Lessing's claim that "the concept of forgery applies only to the creative and not to the performing arts." The distinction between so-called creative and performing arts has certain obvious uses: we would not wish to confuse the actor and the playwright, the conductor and the composer, the dancer and the choreographer. And yet this distinction (often employed invidiously against the performer) can cause us to lose sight of the fact that in certain respects all arts are creative, and correlatively, all arts are performing. It is this latter fact which is of particular relevance to understanding what is wrong with forgeries. For it can be argued that every work of art—every painting, statue, novel, symphony, ballet, as well as every interpretation or rendition of a piece of music, every reading of a poem or production of a play—involves the element of performance.

When we speak of a performance we usually have in mind a human activity which stands in some sense complete in itself: we talk of the President's performance at a press conference, or a student's performance on an examination, with the intention of marking off these particular activities from the whole of a presidential administration or the quality of the student's work done throughout a course. Moreover, as these examples also indicate, performances are said to involve some sense of accomplishment, of achievement. As objects of contemplation, art works stand in differing relations to the performances of artists, depending on the art form in question. On the one hand, we have such arts as the dance, where the human activity involved in creating the object of contemplation and the object itself are one and the same thing. In such a case it would be odd to say that the object somehow represents the performance of the artist, because to perceive the object is to perceive the performance. On the other hand, we have painting, where we normally perceive the work of art without perceiving those actions which have brought it into being. Nevertheless, in cases such as the latter what we see is the end-product of human activity; the object of our perception can be understood as representative of a human performance. That arts differ with respect to how or whether we actually perceive at the moment of creation the artist's performance makes no difference to the relevance of the concept to understanding all of the arts. In fact, the concept of performance is internal to our whole notion of art.[2]

Every work of art is an artifact, the product of human skills and techniques. If we see an actor or a dancer or a violinist at work, we are constantly conscious of human agency. Less immediately apparent is the element of performance in a painting that has hung perhaps for generations in a museum, or a long-familiar musical composition. Yet we are no less in such cases confronted with the results of human agency. As performances, works of art represent the ways in which artists solve problems, overcome obstacles, make do with available materials. The ultimate product is designed for our contemplation, as an object of particular interest in its own right, perhaps in isolation from other art objects or from the activity of the artist. But this isolation which frequently characterizes our mode of attention to aesthetic objects ought not to blind us to a fact we may take for granted: that the work of art has a human origin, and must be understood as such.

We begin to see this more clearly when we consider our aesthetic response to natural beauty. In a passage in *Art as Experience*, John Dewey asks us to imagine that some object we had come to enjoy, believing it to be a primitive artifact, is revealed to us to be an "accidental natural product."[3] In Dewey's view, this revelation changes our "appreciative perception" of the object. His point is that aesthetic appreciation is "inherently connected with the experience of making." This is well taken; imagine, for instance, the sorts of things we might say of the object before and after the revelation of its natural origin. We could continue to appreciate those features from among the object's purely physical qualities which please us, such as shape and texture. But aspects of the object which we had previously assumed to be expressive will no longer be understood as such: it could still be called "angular" or "jagged" but not "energetic" or "restless"; it could still be "fragile," perhaps even "graceful," but no longer "economical" or "witty." It could in general still be described in terms of predicates indicating that it is agreeably shaped, but not in terms of predicates implying that it is well wrought. We could continue to enjoy the object, but we would no longer find ourselves admiring it in the same way: "to admire" usually means in part "to enjoy," but it also carries with it im-

---

[2] For a detailed discussion of the general relevance of the notion of performance to aesthetic criticism, see F. E. Sparshott, *The Concept of Criticism* (Oxford: Clarendon Press, 1967).
[3] John Dewey, *Art as Experience* (New York: Capricorn Books, 1958), pp. 48–49.

does not entail that they would be uninterested ever in distinguishing a copy from a newly invented composition, or a marvelously carved stone from one smoothed by the waters of a brook. To be sure, culture shapes and changes what various peoples believe about art and their attitudes toward it. This may be strikingly different from ours, as in the case of the elaborately carved *Malagan* of New Ireland, which is unceremoniously discarded after its one-time use. Anyone who concluded from this that the people of New Ireland had no concept of art would be open to ridicule; they may have different views about how art is to be treated—to that extent we could even say loosely that it is a "different conception of art from ours." But, limiting ourselves only to that consideration germane to the present discussion, it is a conception of art so long as according to it art is treated among other things as human performance, the work of art having implicit in it the possibility of achievement of some kind. Thus the concept of art is constituted a priori of certain essential properties. I do not propose to enumerate those features (the question of the contents of any such list lies at the heart of the philosophy of art); but I do insist that reference to origins and achievement must be included among these properties.[6] This whole issue is what gives the problem of forgery such central philosophical importance: theorists who claim that it ought to make no difference to appreciation whether a work is forged or not do not merely challenge a few dearly held cultural beliefs about what is important in art. To the contrary, they attack they very idea of art itself.

Let us take stock of what I have so far argued. I have claimed that in certain respects, differing according to the type of art in question, the concept of performance is intrinsic to our understanding of art; that works of art of whatever sort can be seen under the aspect of performance. In emphasizing the importance of the notion of performance in understanding art, I have centered attention on the extent to which works of art are the end-products of human activities, on the degree to which they represent things done by human agents. In this way, part of what constitutes our understanding of works of art involves grasping what sort of achievement the work itself represents. This takes us, then, to the question of the origins of the work: we cannot understand the work of art without some notion of its origins, who created it, the context in which the creator worked, and so forth. But now it must be stressed that our interest in origins, in the possibility or actuality of human achievement, always goes hand-in-hand with our interest in the work of art as visual, verbal, or aural surface. In its extreme forms, contextualism in critical theory has

---

[6] Cf. Leonard B. Meyer, "Forgery and the Anthropology of Art," in *Music, the Arts, and Ideas* (Chicago: University of Chicago Press, 1967). Meyer quotes Eliot's remark, "certain things have been done once and for all and cannot be achieved again." He then adds, "The crucial word here is 'achieved.' They can perhaps be done again, but they cannot be achieved again. Beethoven's late style is a discovery and an achievement. Someone coming later can only imitate it" (pp. 58–59).

tended to emphasize the origins of the work, its status as human achievement, at the expense of attention to the purely formal properties; in its exclusive concentration on formal properties, isolationism, or formalism,
has (by definition) tended to slight the importance of the human context,
the human origins, of art. Both of these positions in their more extreme
and dogmatic forms constitute a kind of philistinism. The more familiar
sort of philistinism (the sort against which Koestler and Lessing react) has
it that if a work of art is a forgery, then it must somehow be without value:
once we are told that these are van Meegerens before us, and not
Vermeers, we reject them, though their formal properties remain unchanged. The opposed sort of philistinism, which could well be called *aestheticist philistinism,* claims that formal properties are the only significant
properties of works of art; that since questions of origins are not important, it ought to make no difference to us at all whether we are confronted
with Vermeers or van Meegerens. Both positions are properly called
philistine because both fail to acknowledge a fundamental element of
artistic value.

In developing a view which finds the aesthetic significance of forgery
in the extent to which it misrepresents artistic achievement, I have hitherto avoided discussion of a concept often contrasted with the idea of
forgery: originality. It is of course easy to say that originality is a legitimate source of value in art, that forgeries lack it, and that they therefore
are to be discredited on that account. This seems true enough as far as it
goes, but the difficulty is that it does not go far enough. One problem centers on deciding what "original" means, or ought to mean, in contrast to
"forged." Originality is often associated with novelty in art, but this sense
alone will not do, since there are many fine works of art whose outstanding features have little to do with novelty. Stravinsky's musical ideas, or
Wagner's, were more novel in their respective epochs than Mozart's or
Bach's; yet it would be odd on that account to call the contributions of the
latter composers relatively unoriginal. Furthermore, even forgeries—
those putative paradigm cases of unoriginal effort—can have strikingly
original aspects. Not, perhaps, with those forgeries which are mere
copies; but indeed, the most interesting cases of forgery involve works
which are precisely not slavish copies, but pastiches, or works in the style
of another artist. Here there is room for originality. Consider the heavy-
lidded, sunken eyes of van Meegeren's faces: they may be insipid, but
they are certainly original, and not to be found in Vermeer. In fact, we
must remind ourselves that stripped of its pretensions, each of the van
Meegeren Vermeers is an original van Meegeren. For what it is worth,
each of these canvases is in that sense an original work of art: my point is
precisely that it may not be worth much.

A crux here is that an artistic performance can be perfectly original
and yet at the same time share with forgery the essential element of being
misrepresented in terms of its actual achievement. The concept of origi-

nality is important in this context because it emphasizes the importance of the origins of the work of art: part of what disturbs us about such cases as the van Meegeren episode is that aesthetically significant aspects of the paintings at issue did not have their origins with Vermeer but with an artist who lived some hundreds of years later. In that sense, we can call the van Meegeren fakes "unoriginal"; though they are original van Meegerens, elements which we especially value in them did not originate with Vermeer—and part of what would make those elements valuable is that they be the product of seventeenth-century Vermeer performances rather than twentieth-century van Meegeren performances. But even where all aspects of the performance in question did in fact originate with the single individual who is credited with it, even where the performance is in that sense pluperfectly original, it is possible for it to share with forgery the essential feature of misrepresentation of achievement. Consider an instrumental performer who announces he will play an improvisation and then proceeds to play a carefully premeditated composition of his own creation. What is performed originates entirely with the performer; it is in no sense a copy of the work of another, and one would not want to call it "unoriginal." But it is surely a performance that shares with forgery the fact that its true nature is misrepresented. (Still, even though its status as composition or improvisation is indifferent to the fact that the same person is performing, origins remain important: an improvisation is distinguished from a composition in that it is originated spontaneously, on the spur of the moment—it is heard as it is created.)

And just as there can be cases of misrepresentation of achievement which do not, strictly speaking, involve any misunderstanding of the identity of the individual with whom the art object originates, so there can be misattributions of origin which do not entail significant misrepresentation of achievement. There are stanzas counting as decent Keats which would not have to be radically reappraised in terms of the artistic achievement they represent if they were discovered to have actually been written by Shelley. The same might be said of certain canvases by Derain and Cézanne, or sonatas by Kuhlau and Telemann. (This is not to deny that there are crucial differences between these artists and many of their works: but to mistake Mozart for Haydn is not *always* a foolish or naive blunder.) In other cases, subtle and interesting shifts in our understanding of particular works might result: a piece of music perceived as run-of-the-mill Beethoven might be seen as outstanding Spohr. In such a case, however, our reassessment of the achievement involved is relative only to the career of the individual artist, and not to the historical achievement the work represents.

The significant opposition I find then is not between "forged" and "original," but between correctly represented artistic performance and misrepresented artistic performance. Originality remains a highly relevant concept here, however, insofar as it shows us that some notion of the origins of a work is always germane to appreciation. Without such concern, we cannot understand the full nature of the achievement a work represents, and such understanding is intrinsic to a proper grasp of the work of art. The predictable challenge to this involves the insistence that while I have been directing attention to human performances, what is really in question in appreciating works of art is aesthetic experience. On this account, aesthetic experience is said to refer to the visual or auditory experience of the sensuous surface of the work of art. Yet who is it who ever has these curious "aesthetic experiences"? In fact, I would suppose they are never had, except by infants perhaps—surely never by serious lovers of painting, music, or literature (the latter always a difficult case for aestheticians who like talking about "sensuous surface"). The encounter with a work of art does not consist in merely hearing a succession of pretty sounds or seeing an assemblage of pleasing shapes and colors. It is as much a matter of hearing a virtuoso perform a dazzling and original interpretation of a difficult piece of music or of experiencing a new vision of a familiar subject provided by a painter. Admittedly, there is an attraction in wanting to look past these thorny complexities to concentrate on the sensuous surface, and it is the same attraction that formalism in all its various guises has always had. It is a marvelously simple view, but (alas!) art itself is even more marvelously complex. Against those who insist that an object's status as forged is irrelevant to its artistic merit, I would hold that when we learn that the kind of achievement an art object involves has been radically misrepresented to us, it is not as though we have learned a new fact about some familiar object of aesthetic attention. To the contrary, insofar as its position as a work of art is concerned, it is no longer the same object.[7]

SUGGESTIONS FOR FURTHER READING

Bailey, George. "Amateurs Imitate, Professionals Steal." *Journal of Aesthetics and Art Criticism* 47 (1989): 221–27.

Battin, M. Pabst. "Exact Replication in the Visual Arts." *Journal of Aesthetics and Art Criticism* 37 (1979): 153–58.

Cahn, Steven M., and Griffel, L. Michael. "The Strange Case of John Shmarb: An Aesthetic Puzzle." *Journal of Aesthetics and Art Criticism* 34 (1975): 21–22.

Courtney, Neil. "The Strange Case of John Shmarb: An Epilogue and Further Reflections." *Journal of Aesthetics and Art Criticism* 34 (1975): 27–28.

Currie, Gregory. "Authenticity." Chapter 4 of his *An Ontology of Art.* New York: St. Martin's Press, 1989.

[7] Many friends and colleagues offered interesting suggestions and comments on various early drafts of this article. In particular, I thank Palko Lukacs, Edward Sayles, Alexander Sesonske, and Kendall Walton for their valuable advice.

Dutton, Denis, ed. *The Forger's Art: Forgery and the Philosophy of Art.* Berkeley: University of California Press, 1983. A very useful collection of articles on forgery. The first article, "Han van Meegeren *fecit*," by Hope B. Werness, tells the story of one of the most famous forgers in history.

Epperson, Gordon. "The Strange Case of John Shmarb: Some Further Thoughts." *Journal of Aesthetics and Art Criticism* 34 (1975): 23–25.

Gardner, Howard. "Illuminating Comparisons: Looking at Fakes and Forgeries." In his *Art, Mind and Brain.* New York: Basic Books, Inc., 1982.

Gerald, W. R., ed. *The Eye of the Beholder: Fakes, Replicas and Alterations in American Art.* New Haven: Yale University Press, 1977.

Goodman, Nelson. "Art and Authenticity." Chapter 3 of his *Languages of Art.* 2d ed. Indianapolis: Hackett, 1976.

Hoaglund, John. "Originality and Aesthetic Value." *British Journal of Aesthetics* 16 (1976): 46–55.

Koestler, Arthur. "The Anatomy of Snobbery." *Anchor Review* 1 (1955): 1–25.

Kulka, Thomas. "The Artistic and Aesthetic Status of Forgeries." *Leonardo* 15 (1982): 115–17.

Kurz, Otto. *Fakes: A Handbook for Collectors and Students.* 2d ed. New York: Dover, 1967.

Levinson, Jerrold. "Aesthetic Uniqueness." *Journal of Aesthetics and Art Criticism* 38 (1980): 435–50.

Levinson, Jerrold. "Allographic and Autographic Art Revisited." *Philosophical Studies* 38 (1980): 367–83.

McFee, Graham. "The Fraudulent in Art." *British Journal of Aesthetics* 20 (1980): 215–28.

Radford, Colin. "Fakes." *Mind* 87 (1978): 66–76.

Sagoff, Mark. The Aesthetic Status of Forgeries." *Journal of Aesthetics and Art Criticism* 35 (1976): 169–80.

Sagoff, Mark. "On Restoring and Reproducing Art." *Journal of Philosophy* 75 (1978): 453–70.

Sagoff, Mark. "On the Aesthetic and Economic Value of Art." *British Journal of Aesthetics* 21 (1981): 318–29.

Sartwell, Crispin. "Aesthetics of the Spurious." *British Journal of Aesthetics* 28 (1988): 360–67.

Steele, Hunter. "Fakes and Forgeries." *British Journal of Aesthetics* 17 (1977): 254–58.

2

COLORIZING MOVIES

I chose to shoot [*It's a Wonderful Life*] in black-and-white film. The lighting, the makeup for the actors and actresses, the camera and laboratory work, all were geared for black-and-white film, not color. I beseech you with all my heart and mind not to tamper with a classic in any form of the arts. Leave them alone. They are classics because they are superior. Do not help the quick-money makers who have delusions about taking possession of classics by smearing them with paint.

—Frank Capra, writing to the Copyright Office of the
Library of Congress
(quoted in *The New York Times*, August 5, 1986)

Ultimately, of course, the colorizers will lose this battle. If not immediately then future generations will surely discard these cheesy, artificial symbols of one society's greed. They will, of course, go back to the great originals. And if we are foolish enough to permit this monstrous practice to continue one can easily picture young men and women someday discussing us with disgust and saying, "They did this and nobody stopped them?"

"Well, there was a lot of money involved."

"But surely the people could see the deeper value to America of its film treasury, of its image among civilizations. Surely they understood the immorality of defacing an artist's work against his will. Don't tell me it was the kind of nation that adored profit at any cost and humiliation."

Here I will finish because it's too early to know how it turns out, but I hope dearly that I will not be part of a culture that is one day ridiculed and reviled.

—Woody Allen, "True Colors," *New York Review of Books,*
August 13, 1987

INTRODUCTION

As James O. Young remarks in the final reading in this section, "Colorization has been, perhaps, more reviled than any other development affecting the arts since the Visigoths and Vandals visited Rome." And he scarcely exaggerates. Movie buffs have been enraged at the thought that their favorite black-and-white movies might be tinted in new and lurid colors, courtesy of someone's computer paint pot. Famous directors have competed with one another in their expressions of fury and indignation. Colorization is condemned from every side. Or rather, it is condemned from every side but one: The great mass of ordinary movie-watchers seem to like it. People will now sit through movies which they may well otherwise not have seen. For large numbers of people, at any rate, colorization represents a distinct improvement. So what is all the fuss about? Why is colorizing found so objectionable by so many of those associated with the world of movies and film criticism?

It is useful here to distinguish between *moral* objections to colorization and *aesthetic* objections to it. A moral objection might go something like this: By colorizing a movie against a filmmaker's will, or without his or her permission, one misrepresents what the filmmaker set out to achieve, and so one is guilty of a kind of deception. Additionally, one prevents the filmmaker from expressing what he or she wished to express, and so one is guilty of a form of oppression. An aesthetic objection, by contrast, will have to go rather differently: Colorization is bad, it will have to claim, because it results in less beautiful movies, or in movies which are in some way aesthetically inferior to the black-and-white originals.

Notice that the aesthetic objection might be raised in a weaker or a stronger form. A weak version of the objection will claim only that colorized movies are, as it happens, usually inferior to their originals. And hence the weak version will claim only that colorization is *usually* aesthetically undesirable. But this might only be because of the relative crudity of the results which can at present be achieved by colorizing technology. The technology is in its infancy, after all, and it can presumably be expected to become less crude in the future. If it does improve, then the weak version of the aesthetic objection will lose much of its force.

The strong version of the aesthetic objection will claim more: that colorized versions of movies are *necessarily* aesthetically inferior to the black-and-white originals. Whatever improvements there might be in the colorizing process, a colorized movie will still, according to the strong version of the objection, be aesthetically less desirable than the original. The strong version of the objection will be plausible only if it restricts itself to condemning the colorization of aesthetically *successful* black-and-white movies. It may be true, for instance, that a black-and-white movie is aesthetically successful partly because it has certain features (features such as lighting and contrast) which would be lost if the film were colorized. When this is so, there will be good grounds for claiming that colorizing the movie must inevitably make the movie less aesthetically satisfying. But such an objection would clearly be implausible if it were raised against colorizing *in general.* For there is no reason to think that *every* black-and-white movie has aesthetically valuable features which would be lost if the movie were colorized. Therefore there can be no plausible reason for saying that every case of colorizing must be aesthetically objectionable.

What exactly is the relationship between moral objections to colorization and aesthetic objections to the process? It might be argued that moral objections are in principle completely independent of aesthetic considerations. That is, it might be argued, the charges that colorization involves oppression of artists or deception of audiences do not *depend* upon charges of aesthetic vandalism.

However, since a movie is, or can be, a work of art, it is reasonable to think that moral charges against colorization will gain force if they can be shown to be based on aesthetic considerations. For example, it seems likely that a moral objection to colorizing a black-and-white masterpiece which would be aesthetically destroyed in the process will be more effective than a moral objection to colorizing a movie that is actually *improved* by the process. Suppose that we have only one print of Woody Allen's movie *Manhattan* and only one print of the Laurel and Hardy comedy *Way Out West.* (Flo Leibowitz discusses these and other cases in the third reading in this section.) It seems clear that colorizing *Manhattan* would ruin it, while it is at least arguable that *Way Out West* would be improved by colorization. How do such considerations about the *aesthetic* consequences of colorization bear on whether we think it is *morally* acceptable to colorize? Would we take Woody Allen's tirades against colorization so seriously if, instead of being the creator of a masterpiece like *Manhattan,* he were a third-rate director of third-rate movies?

It is interesting, then, to consider ways in which moral objections and aesthetic objections to colorization are connected. And in the readings that follow, questions about the relationship between the moral and the aesthetic are never far from the surface. There are four readings in all, which form a kind of symposium. The first piece, by James O. Young, defends the practice of colorizing against its detractors. The next two pieces take issue with some aspect of his defense. And in the last piece, Young responds to his critics and clarifies his position.

Young's defense of colorization consists in a reply to the charge that "colorization is a limitation of a director's freedom of artistic expression," or that it is a way of oppressing artists. Colorization would only be such a limitation or form of oppression, Young argues, if a movie were the kind of art work which is "embodied in a single artifact"—as a particular painting is constituted, for example, by the brush strokes on just one canvas, or as a particular work of architecture is constituted by just one building. But each movie, of course, is actually "instantiated many times": There are many prints of each movie, and colorizing one of them leaves "just as many black and white prints of the films as there were before." Therefore, Young concludes, colorizing movies does "not restrict artists' freedom of expression since artifacts still exist which embody what they wished to express." Indeed, Young argues that it would actually be wrong to forbid colorization, for "the creative use of colorization could result in interesting works of art." Colorization, that is, may result in new works of art. And to forbid the creation of those would very definitely be to limit artistic freedom of expression.

Jerrold Levinson, in the second reading of this section, disagrees with Young. Levinson objects to colorization, not because it limits freedom of expression, but rather because it interferes with and distorts what the filmmaker has, in fact, succeeded in expressing. Colorization, he suggests, is a process which results in deception. It misleads us about the nature of an artist's achievement. In Levinson's view, despite the existence of uncolorized prints of the original movie, the commercial distribution of the colorized version cynically discounts "the capacity for aesthetic discipline on the part of the average viewer," and distorts the vision which the filmmaker expressed, and intended to express, in black-and-white. In the third reading, Flo Leibowitz explores and expands upon aspects of Levinson's argument. She concentrates especially on expressive features of movies which are intrinsic to the black-and-white medium, and which must inevitably be lost when a movie is colorized.

The positions taken by Leibowitz and Levinson appear to presuppose a strong version of the aesthetic objection to colorization, so we should ask to what extent the moral force of their positions depends upon their aesthetic presuppositions. Certainly the considerations raised in their arguments are taken seriously by Young. In the final reading, Young refines his position in the light of criticism and concludes that while the colorizer (the actual technician) is guilty of no misdemeanor, there *is* (after all) a villain of the piece, and it is "the entertainment industry," for which the colorizers work. But even so, he suggests, "It is better that films are seen in colorized versions than not at all." And so he maintains his defense—for as he says, "If even the Devil receives an advocate . . . surely colorization deserves one as well."

In Defense of Colorization

James O. Young

New technology makes it possible to convert black and white motion pictures into color films. The process of transformation is known as 'color conversion' or 'colorization.' A number of manufacturers are presently engaged in colorizing films made before the advent of color photography. The process of colorization has proved to be very controversial. There are many questions about the artistic merits of color conversion. Use of the process has also raised a number of moral issues. Both philosophers and several distinguished directors have denounced unauthorized use of colorization.[1] Legislation to control use of the process has been introduced. The source of the controversy is the suggestion that the unauthorized use of colorization is a violation of a director's rights as an artist. Directors have held that no one may (without its director's permission) colorize a film without unjustifiably interfering with an artist's freedom of expression. In this essay I will argue that colorization does not interfere with artists' prerogatives. There are no moral objections to color conversion.

Saying that colorizing films is not immoral is not equivalent to recommending that the process be carried out. On the contrary, there are many good artistic reasons why (at least some) films should not be colorized. Directors often take advantage of black and white photography to achieve particular effects. Colorization may very well obscure what the director wished to express. Woody Allen gives a good example from one of his own films. If 'Manhattan' were to be colorized, the feeling of nostalgia would be lost. The film would cease to express what Allen intended. No doubt there are many similar cases where colorization would be artistically unsuccessful. Moreover, we should be under no illusions as to why color conversion is being undertaken. Colorizers have pecuniary and not artistic motives. Still, even if there are artistic reasons why films should not be colorized, color conversion might still be perfectly moral.

Questions about colorization are quite distinct from questions raised by restoration. Few would deny that it is (at least sometimes) unobjectionable to restore a work of art. There are differences of opinion about the sort of steps restorers may take. But most people think that steps may be taken to ensure the preservation of art works as created by the original artists. The 'colorization' of Greek statues would be controversial (at least

---

[1] For a philosopher's view see John Fisher, Editorial, *Journal of Aesthetics and Art Criticism*, 45 (1987), 227–28. Woody Allen writes that it is 'sinful' to colorize a film against the wishes of its director. He holds that no one should ever be able to tamper with any artist's work in any medium against the artist's will. To do so is, he says, morally 'atrocious', *New York Review of Books*, Vol. 34, No. 13 (13 August 1987), p. 38. The late John Huston was another director who objected to the colorization of his films.

in part) because restorers do not know how to preserve the intentions of the original artists. The colorization of films is controversial for another reason. It is controversial just because the process involves the deliberate departure from what artists have intended. There is no question of simply preserving what artists have expressed. Rather, there is a deliberate attempt to change what is expressed.

A very strong intuition underlies the argument against the morality of colorization. It seems wrong to tamper with works of art without the permission of the artists who created them. Suppose the privatization of public resources continues and I am able to buy Leonardo da Vinci's painting of Ginevra de' Benci. Even if the painting were my property, most people's intuitions would suggest that it would be wrong for me to draw a moustache on the portrait. And it would still be wrong even if lots of people thought the portrait looked better with a moustache. Or suppose I discovered a previously unknown novel by Jane Austen. I would act wrongly if I rewrote some chapters, destroyed the manuscript and published the revised version. In both cases we would regard me as having interfered with an artist's freedom of expression. My act would be like preventing someone from speaking or like falsely reporting what someone had said in a speech. And this is surely wrong.

The opponents of colorization suggest that the unauthorized use of the process is exactly parallel to the cases just considered. Their argument could be formulated as follows. Artists express themselves in works of art. It is wrong to limit a person's artistic freedom of expression. Colorization involves altering a work of art. Therefore, colorization is a limitation of a director's artistic freedom of expression. Altering a work of art always limits an artist's freedom of expression. Therefore, colorization is wrong. This is a plausible argument but unsound since its third premiss is false. Altering a work of art does not always limit an artist's freedom of expression.

In order to see why altering a work of art is not always objectionable it is necessary to distinguish between two sorts of art work. This distinction can be drawn without entering into any of the debates about what works of art are. There is a distinction between art works embodied in a single artefact and works instantiated many times. Into the first class of work fall many paintings, sculptures and works of architecture. Perhaps not all such works fall into this class. Two statues from the same mould perhaps instantiate the same work of art. But the portrait of Ginevra de' Benci clearly either is, or is instantiated in (depending on one's ontology), a single artefact. The second class consists of art works such as novels, poems, musical compositions and ballets. Again, not all such works fall into the second class. Most novels, for example, have at one time existed in only one copy. At this time they may be said to belong to the first class. But *Pride and Prejudice* clearly is instantiated in many different artefacts.

Only altering art works with a single instantiation is objectionable. Only tampering with the first sort of art work constitutes an infringement of artistic freedom of expression. Once such a work has been modified it is no longer able to express what its creator or creators intended. Not even all altering of the first sort of art work is always objectionable. The cathedrals of the Middle Ages were constantly altered. Each generation would modify and add to the efforts of earlier generations. There was nothing objectionable in these alterations. Indeed, much of the beauty of mediaeval cathedrals is due to the fact that they are the cumulative work of an era. Still, there can be no doubt that it would be wrong for us to tamper with the cathedrals. To do so would be to prevent an era, and not just an individual, from expressing itself. And it is equally clear that, in general, where artists' ability to express themselves depends on the continued integrity of one artefact, it is wrong to tamper with it.

There is nothing wrong with modifying works of art of the second sort. Or, at any rate, there is nothing wrong with such modification so long as at least some unmodified instantiations of the work survive. Not only is the modification of art unobjectionable but it is done every day. Musicians perform compositions on instruments other than their composers intended. Compositions are arranged, transcribed or borrowed from. Poems are translated into different languages or set to music. Novels are adapted for the stage and screen. Even films are constantly subject to alteration. Sub-titles are added or their sound tracks are dubbed. Many of these modifications modify what artists wish to express. But they do not restrict artists' freedom of expression since artefacts still exist which embody what they wished to express.

Now the question to be asked is whether films belong to the first or second class of art works. They are not, perhaps, such paradigms of the second class of work as are musical compositions. There can be no doubt, however, that films are art works of the second sort. Typically there are many prints of a film. Furthermore, the color conversion of a film does not destroy the instantiation of an art work. After a film has been colorized there are just as many black and white prints of the film as there were before. These black and white prints continue to express what the director intended. Since films belong to the second class of art work, and since the modification of such works is unobjectionable, there is nothing wrong about colorization. If there were only one print of a film and colorizing modified its original state, then color conversion would be objectionable. But this is not what happens.

Not only is there nothing wrong with colorization but there is also a strong case to be made against forbidding use of the process. To forbid the unauthorized use of color conversion would, arguably, be to limit artistic freedom. There is every reason to suppose that the creative use of colorization could result in interesting works of art. These would be different works of art than the original artist created. A prohibition against unauthorized colorization would be, in effect, a ban on creating the new art work. Perhaps some directors do not or, because of death, cannot consent to the colorization of their films. Their cases are no different than dramatists or novelists whose works have been adapted. Jane Austen cannot, and likely would not, consent to the dramatization of her novels for television. Handel would probably be outraged to see one of his operas performed on modern instruments and by singers in spacesuits. But such alteration of works of art cannot be forbidden without limiting artistic freedom of expression.

An insistence on the inviolability of films would not only limit artistic freedom. It might deny the world important works of art. Not all modification of art works is bowdlerization. Some of the greatest artists of the past thrived on the modification of their predecessors' works. Bach, Handel and, indeed, most baroque composers modified the works of other musicians. Even Beethoven was not above borrowing. Shakespeare, of course, regularly modified the works of other playwrights. The result was great art. It is possible that an artist will create important works of art by colorizing or otherwise modifying films.

Opposition to colorization is motivated by a mistaken view of art and artists. Underlying the argument against color conversion is the assumption that artists are heroic individuals who create works of art in isolation. In fact, however, works of art are, in an important sense, social products. They always owe much to a tradition, even if they are reactions against it. Artists must work in co-operation with others. Even the solitary novelist had teachers, read other works, and has editors and readers. Film is, of course, a paradigm of a socially produced art work. It is the result of the co-operative efforts of many individuals. If art works were the work of single individuals, it might make some sense to allow them complete control over their fate. But art works are not produced by isolated individuals. At the very least we should say that actors, screen play writers, cinematographers and camera operators should be consulted about the alteration of a film. But it is better to recognize that the art work becomes part of a tradition. And members of the artistic tradition may do what they like with art works, so long as they do not prevent others from expressing themselves.[2]

It is easy to sympathize with directors who see their films being colorized. Even if the choice of color film was not available to them, they directed their films in a way that, in their view, best exploited the medium. The fact that most colorization is done for mercenary reasons and without aesthetic justification must be particularly galling. Some directors

---

[2] R. G. Collingwood scorned the idea that works of art were the inviolable products of a single individual: 'I will only say that this fooling about personal property must cease. Let painters and writers and musicians steal with both hands whatever they can use, wherever they can find it', *The Principles of Art* (Oxford U.P., 1958), p. 320.

may be in a legal position to stop unauthorized color conversion. There are, however, no moral reasons why it cannot be undertaken, even against a director's wishes. And there are good artistic reasons why some alteration of art works should be permitted to proceed unfettered.[3]

[3] In the course of writing this essay I profited from the comments of Christopher Cordner, Stephen Davies and Barry Taylor.

Colorization Ill-Defended

Jerrold Levinson

I

James Young has offered a short and easily grasped defence of the now increasingly widespread practice of colorization of classic films. Unfortunately, his defence of this regrettable practice seems to me to almost entirely miss the point, and I will try in this note briefly to explain why.

Young begins by suggesting that what might be wrong with colorizing—the conversion of a black and white film into necessarily arbitrary colored form—is that it is in some way a limitation on the cinematic artist's freedom of artistic expression. He then endeavours to show that it is not, in fact, such a limitation. But immediately, this is an odd way to put the matter. For it would seem that a film maker has artistically expressed himself, roughly speaking, if he has gotten his film made, pretty much as he wanted to, with at least some of the artistic aims he had in view satisfied. Can freedom to express really be the problem? Colorizers are not, after all, maliciously poised to tint the daylights out of films as they are being made.

The issue, I suggest, is more transparently put as follows: given a film artist who has managed to express himself by creating an expressive cinematic object, will the expressiveness now inherent in his creation be adequately preserved for, and conveyed to, his intended audience? The question, in other words, is whether the potential communication from artist to audience, of the expressiveness (or other sort of meaning) that has been achieved, is threatened by the prevalence of colorization. Being permitted to express oneself in a medium is not the artistic bargain it would appear to be if the results of one's expressive activity are regularly in peril of being colored over, with the sickly cast of commerce, by any subsequent middleman. Freedom of expression through art, in the narrow sense, is not all an artist has a right to—in addition, he would seem to have a right not to have his expression interfered with in subsequent transmission.

I will assume that Young would grant the above—that what centrally concerns us is the effective preservation of an artist's expression, its possibility of transmission intact, and not the mere fact of such expression having once been allowed. (We could count this as part of 'freedom of expression' in a broad sense.) So the issue is really one of our continuing and undistorted access, epistemically and experientially, to what an artist has expressed in a work.

But now we come to the crux of Young's defense. Films, he claims, along with sonnets and sonatas, have a different status from paintings and (most) sculptures with respect to the aesthetic rights at hand, because they exist in multiple instantiations—prints, copies, performances— whereas the latter are, ontologically, unique objects. Thus, if you alter the Arnolfini 'Marriage' in the National Gallery, London you have altered, possibly irrevocably, Van Eyck's painting, but if you tear up your copy of Eliot's *Wasteland,* or disrupt a performance of Beethoven's *Hammerklavier,* or colorize a few prints of Huston's *Asphalt Jungle,* you have done nothing untoward to those works of art themselves. You have not really altered the expressiveness of poem, sonata, or film, assuming that undoctored instances of each continue to exist to carry on the work's original structure and appearance. '. . . [T]here is nothing wrong with such modification so long as at least some unmodified instantiations of the work survive.' The rights of Eliot, Beethoven and Huston to sustain their works in the expressive condition in which they were created, and thus to provide for the possibility of their continued experience have not, it appears, been infringed, since harm to one instance does no harm to other instances, representative of the original state of the work. Metaphysics does, for once, make a difference!

Thus, as long as we don't fool with the master print of a film, and take care to see that some good second-generation prints are around as well as insurance, no one—surely not the film maker—can complain. Directors' artistic expressions, and the communicability of such to an audience, have not been threatened 'since artefacts still exist which embody what they [directors] wished to express.'

II

Whatever may be true of the innocuousness of disposing of a few copies of a famous poem, or crashing a performance here and there of a celebrated sonata, the speciousness of this analysis in regard to classic black and white film is glaring.

In the first place, our access to film is controlled, more than with any other art, by the commercial world and the channels of media distribution. It's easy for individuals to make additional copies of a poem, correcting for misprints if need be, and not hard to secure, with the co-operation of musicians, various sorts of performances of a sonata, but for the most part we must rely on the entertainment industry and its outlets to supply us with instances of films. If colorized versions of a film are what are predominantly available—in video stores, on television, in movie halls—then the film as a social entity turns into a colored object, willy-nilly. The colorized film has a tendency to displace the original, in consciousness as on the shelves. It is hard to overestimate the likelihood of this happening, once a colorized version acquires an economic foothold, especially in our present culturally complacent environment. Access to the original becomes more and more strictly notional, or theoretical, anchored only by unaltered prints remaining in existence somewhere, rarely screened. 'Freedom of choice' for the majority is all but inevitably purchased at the price of a drastically reduced avenue to an artist's original expression for those legitimately interested in it.

Secondly, colorizing is often minimally acknowledged, if at all, in the prefatory material provided with the new version, and this, together with the fact that viewers generally pay scant attention to such material, leads inevitably to false impressions and opinions of the nature of a director's work and the quality of his achievement. Although colorizations are obviously not forgeries, in practice they will have many of the same ill effects through misrepresenting, to all but connoisseurs, what the films subjected to this treatment, and bearing the very same titles afterwards, are really about, aesthetically and expressively. The reputations of both films and film makers are at stake here, and this is not a negligible thing. As Thomas Nagel and others have stressed, one can be harmed after one's death; having one's expressly black and white films wilfully colorized forty years later seems a particularly gratuitous example of this. More broadly, the image of the history of film as art is in danger of wholesale distortion and disintegration if colorizations, often minimally flagged as such, become rampant.[1]

A third point, related to the preceding, is this. A film artist would

---

[1] The situation of a film colorized 'against its will', and yet left to enjoy a parallel existence in its original state, is almost precisely analogous to that of Titular Councillor Golyadkin in Dostoyevsky's satirical novel *The Double*. No one puts Golyadkin in jail, or threatens him with liquidation, but meanwhile another, 'false' Golyadkin, a dashing and scurrilous fellow, obviously somewhat different from the original in matters of appearance and behaviour, is everywhere seen in his stead and taken for him, and—most maddening of all—gladly so. Though Golyadkin could of course lull himself with the knowledge that he was still who he was, unchanged—that perhaps his mother, at least, would acknowledge him—this was of little solace given the fact that his 'double' was running around town, out of Golyadkin's control, ruining his good name.

seem to be entitled to a fair shot at displaying his oeuvre as he created it—of having it come across as it is—to a broad range of well-meaning spectators, and not just those who are serious and dedicated scholars of the art form, who can be expected to make the often considerable efforts required to view works as they were meant to be viewed, and to get everything straight as regards appreciative context. It is unfair to older cinematic artists to so stack the deck against them with regard to less conscientious viewers, as the practice of widespread colorization would in effect do, despite the existence of original prints in film archives and a sprinkling of undoctored tapes in the odd video salon here and there.[2]

Consider such a viewer in front of a colorized version of Hitchcock's *Sabotage* (1936). Is he likely to be keeping in mind that this is not really how the film was conceived, and not really how the film looks? Not too likely, but let us suppose for argument's sake that he is. The viewing over, is he likely to feel that he has seen Hitchcock's film, and is in a position to take its measure? Of course. What are the chances he will ever feel he ought to see the original? Very slim. To the casual filmgoer or renter-of-videos, *Sabotage* will unfairly begin to take on whatever look and resonance, however enjoyable, it has in its colorized version, and certain aesthetic qualities of the original, though safe in vaults, and at film festivals, will in a real sense be on the way to disappearance.

Fourthly, we might note that colorizing is done for a number of reasons, but at least one seems central. Modern viewers, especially those whose earliest viewing years postdate the widespread adoption of color film, are assumed to be too lazy or spoiled to interest themselves in products of an earlier cinematographic age, or simply incapable of sustaining what interest they may actually muster throughout the course of a film. Colorizing is the only way to get them, and hold them, where antiques such as Hitchcock, Lang, and Welles are concerned. If this is part of the rationale, as seems likely, then we have grounds for another moral complaint against the procedure. If we grant that experience of the arts—including the art of cinema—has a profound value, and that realizing this value presupposes adequate appreciation of objects and structures for what they are,[3] then we are implicitly cheating the aesthetically unformed

---

[2] Young's discussion gives the impression that colorized versions of classic films would be no more harmful than postcard or connect-the-dots versions of famous paintings, transcriptions of piano works for full orchestra, or translations of poems into foreign languages. But no one will take these to be the works they are derived from—no one is likely to conflate the two—whereas there is a real danger of viewers assuming an identity between colorized versions and the (unknown) films themselves.

[3] If this premise seems too sweeping for the purpose, then we need only agree, more narrowly, that experience of the original is aesthetically superior to that of a random colorization. If so, then we do a disservice to the general viewer, ultimately, by pandering to a weakness for the easy and familiar.

by seducing them with substitutes, perhaps even assisting them to become indeed more and more incapable of comprehending the originals on their own terms. The cynical discounting of the capacity for aesthetic discipline on the part of the average viewer, which is part of the justification for going ahead with colorization, not surprisingly tends to be self-confirming. And this is a bad thing. It is a bad thing to foster degradation of taste in the general populace, since this leads, at least for viewers who are not literally constitutionally unable to deal with black and white film, to lives intrinsically worse than they might otherwise be.

III

Young argues, finally, that not only is there nothing morally wrong about colorizing, but it would be morally wrong to forbid it, because of the damper this would place on artistic creativity. 'There is every reason to suppose that the creative use of colorization could result in interesting works of art. . . . A prohibition against unauthorized colorization would be, in effect, a ban on creating . . . new art work.'

But the analogies that Young intends with artists' appreciative adaptations of earlier works, or even ones he does not invoke directly, with dadaistic acts of symbolic defacement, are misleading. For colorizers are not making artistic statements, are not coming up with synthetic fusions, to which they contribute some substantial material or perspective, are not engaged in the ongoing dialectic of reaction and counter-reaction that makes up the history of art. Instead they are out merely to 'improve' the original and still—paradoxically though actually hypocritically—pass it off as 'the same thing'. Colorizations, in the sense that is commercially at issue, are not homages to, or variations on, or even creative repudiations of,[4] the films they masquerade as, and it is dishonest to try to give them legitimacy by this kind of suggested assimilation. Surely it cannot be impossible to distinguish, either in moral assessment or in the legal code, between current efforts at colorization and certain artistically interesting modes thereof that we may envisage.

Of course, if it were not standard colorization, of familiar intent, that was involved, but instead post-modernist appropriation, or inventive re-use, or ironic commentary—akin, say, to what Woody Allen, one of the most outspoken opponents of standard colorization, did with an obscure Japanese spy film in his entirely distinct work of art, *What's Up, Tiger Lily?*—then my objections would vanish. But that would be changing the subject. The subject is the activities envisaged by present-day commercial

---

[4] See Noël Carroll, 'Art, Practice, and Narrative', *The Monist,* 71 (1988), 140–56.

colorizers, and there are indeed moral objections to them. Neither Young's metaphysical observation as to a film's persistence despite the colorizing of some of its offspring, nor his laudable concern to prevent roadblocks for future artistic experimentation in film, shows that there aren't.[5]

We might, finally, turn this last argument of Young's around, and use it to our own account. Even were it the case that forbidding colorization of the sort in question could have as a consequence the inhibiting of certain forms of creative adaptation or appropriation, this would be more than offset by the dampening effect on future film artists of permitting such. If artists do not feel their works will generally be disseminated without significant alteration, their incentives to take the utmost pains to express themselves adequately, or to bring the maximum of beauty into existence they can, will have been seriously weakened.[6] And thus we would all be aesthetically impoverished down the line. This is a much greater danger than the one Young claims to espy.

Young frames his defence, recall, in terms of freedom of expression, in terms of artists being able to say what they want to say. I will revert in closing to that formulation of the issue. There are a manifold of ways, some more subtle than others, in which this freedom can be abridged. To be sure, an artist's materials can be taken away as he is clapped in irons and forcibly muzzled. Or, less crudely, he can be completely deprived of effective outlets of distribution. But more insidiously, even if his work is left intact and limited access to it ensured, an artist's right of expression—in the broad sense Young must be understood as invoking—can be undercut. For as noted earlier, it is not enough to be allowed merely to 'say' something, there must be a reasonable chance of its being correctly 'heard' by others. Suppressing an utterer, or modifying his output at the source, is a direct way to interfere with artistic 'saying'. But drowning out his voice in a sea of imitations, distorting the context which his utterance needs in order to be properly construed, and subverting his potential audience's capacity of comprehension, is only another, if more indirect, method of sabotage. It is the one with which the filmic 'sayings' of Hitchcock, Lang, Welles, and all the other 'marketable' directors of classic

---

[5] I should add at this point that I do not believe I have touched on all, or even all the most important, moral objections to the currently threatening practice of colorization. I have attempted only to establish that Young's considerations fall far short of showing that the moral ground for today's colorizers is clear. (And there are angles to this issue which neither Young's remarks nor my own even broach; one concerns cases where there is strong evidence that a director working in black and white on a given film would have wanted to employ color stock if it had been available. But that angle opens onto another paper.)

[6] The fact that current film makers do not regularly work in black and white is irrelevant. They will take the message, with transposition to some other feature of their films they regard as important, but which may some day prove economically or socially inconvenient.

cinema are now menaced.[7] If philosophers wish to give rationales for colorization then they, at least, have a duty to see that such rationales are more substantial than those thin films which are, in the last analysis, the object of everyone's concern.

[7] Thus, thankfully, Bresson, Antonioni, Godard, and Bergman are probably not endangered—though early Fellini and Truffaut might have more to worry about.

Movie Colorization and the Expression of Mood

Flo Leibowitz

To colorize a black and white movie is to apply to it a specific technology: a videotape copy is made of the movie and color is added to it with a computer paintpot. In this sense, colorizing is a technology for electronic image making and might provide interesting art if used creatively. For example, filmmakers might design colorizing into the production of new films because they like the effect of it. They might use colorized film footage as part of an installation, in performance art or in music theater.[1] Still, to colorize a movie has come to mean applying this technology for a particular end: one takes an old black and white movie which the audience will perceive as dated or unexciting (or so it is believed) and colorize it on the theory that the audience will find it more engaging. It is colorizing in this sense that has provoked opposition, and this is how I will understand "colorization" (and "colorizing") in what follows.[2]

In his defense of colorization, James Young argued that colorizing a movie does not require the destruction of already-existing prints, and (he argued), since there are typically many prints of a particular movie in existence colorizing movies is not objectionable.[3] This argument is appealing because it directly addresses the kind of object a movie is. Yet it

[1] The dancer Kathy Rose made a dance in which she performed in front of a projected animated film and appeared to be part of it. The film in this case was not colorized, but it could have been.

[2] I have deliberately not posed the issue as a matter of colorizing old movies for commercial purposes. The commercial nature of the motivation is a secondary consideration if it is relevant at all. At most, the commercial motivation adds insult to injury, and I want to concentrate on the injury.

[3] James O. Young, "In Defence of Colorization." David James makes a similar argument; David James, "On Colorizing: A Venture into Applied Aesthetics," *Metaphilosophy* 20 (1989): 332–340. See the "Integrity of the Artwork Argument," 335–337.

doesn't address the kind of expressive object it is, and if the issue is whether colorization obscures or changes what the uncolorized movie expresses, the multiplicity of copies is less relevant.

Jerrold Levinson argued that colorizing a black and white movie interferes with the expressiveness which movie-makers build into the cinematic objects that have made (an art theory claim),[4] and thereby interferes with a movie-maker's freedom of expression (a claim about ethics). The present discussion elaborates Levinson's art-theory claim: it maintains that colorizing a black and white movie affects a particular property of it—its mood—and mood makes a significant contribution to what a movie expresses.[5] Thereby, further support is given to the art-theory claim. Young argued that opposition to colorization is based on a myth about art and its production. He held that opponents of colorization fail to recognize that art is a social product, and that their opposition is based on assuming that "artists are heroic individuals who create works of art in isolation."[6] But the case against colorization made in these remarks does not rest on that assumption. It assumes that movies employ characteristic expressive practices; accordingly, the movie-maker may be a single individual or a film collective or other corporate entity.

Colorizing the film *It's a Wonderful Life* was supposed to have ruined the somber mood of the suicide-contemplation scenes, and thereby to have ruined their emotional contrast with the reassuring scenes of reunion which follow. Yet Vincent Canby thought that in the colorized *Way Out West* (a Laurel and Hardy comedy) the mood was enhanced, because "the tinting process effectively complements the mock-historical period of the film and the dainty archaic mannerisms of its two stars."[7] It is my contention that both these judgments could be right, because the moods of the two films are different.

This raises a further question: Since colorizing only changes something about the way a movie looks, how could colorizing have had either effect? The reply is that the "only" is a mistake: a movie is not just a narrative, it is a pictorial narrative. That is, it is a story told by means of an ordered sequence of pictures. Expressive work is done by the way the pictures look and changing their look can change what is expressed. One reason for this is that the mood of a movie is not only a result of the

---

[4] Jerrold Levinson, "Colorization Ill-Defended."

[5] A corollary is that a movie's mood is something which ordinary filmgoers routinely perceive, or are expected to perceive. To put it another way, perceiving a movie's mood is part of cinematic competence.

[6] Young, "In Defence of Colorization."

[7] Quoted in David James, "On Colorizing Films," note 3, p. 338. It might be said as well that the opening credits of *It's a Wonderful Life* are improved by colorization in that the cheerful tinting complements the greeting card motif with which the credits are presented. However, the mood of the movie as a whole is not "cheerful," it's more serious than that.

movie's narrative line, but is also dependent on the narrative's pictorialization. Alternatively put, the mood of a movie appears to come partly from its picturing strategies, and not exclusively from its narrative strategies. If you colorize a movie, you may change it in more profound ways than regarding a movie as a narrative simpliciter makes it appear.

It is well-accepted that the mood of a movie made in color is affected by the way color is used in it. For example, Stanley Cavell has observed that the Technicolor in the 1938 *Robin Hood* gave the movie an air of youthful fantasy (he said it reminded him of the tissue-covered illustrations in children's books).[8] *The Wizard of Oz* contrasted color and black and white—color Oz looked exotic; black and white Kansas looked ordinary. In the end, the fantasy land had more presence than the real land, which was presumably the intended effect. In these movies, color gave the objects pictured a presence of a fantastic type. Maybe that's why Woody Allen, in narrating *Manhattan*, said that "New York City was a city that still existed in black and white."[9]

A black and white palette also contributes to a movie's mood. The film noir genre provides dramatic, and by now familiar, examples of the contribution to a movie's mood which is made by the use of black and white pictures. A black and white palette contributes to mood in other types of movies also. If Ingmar Bergman had made *The Virgin Spring* in color, it might have appeared less like a meditative religious fable and more like a titillating revenge fantasy. Consider, for example, *Death Wish* and its sequels. *Citizen Kane* contains many striking compositions and juxtapositions, and seems to have been made with much attention to how particular scenes would look. Had it been made in color, Xanadu might have looked more like a luxurious estate and less like a cage. In black and white, its dual (or ambiguous) nature is apparent; in color it might not have been. And according to an often-repeated story, the director of the movie of *Billy Budd* once said that he made it in black and white in order to make it seem "real." I take this to mean the director wanted an air of seriousness in the movie rather than one of fantasy.[10]

Palette is not the only picturing device that contributes to a movie's mood. Slow motion is used to suggest a moment of portent or gravity. (*Bonnie and Clyde, The Wild Bunch*). Grainy images are used to suggest seriousness, too, by intimating (falsely or otherwise) of low budget purity, a device which has already been adopted by music videos that wish to

---

[8] Stanley Cavell, *The World Viewed* (Viking, 1971), p. 81.

[9] For additional examples of the expressive use of color, see Thomas Elsaesser's suggestive remarks about *Written on the Wind* and other films of the 1950s. Elsaesser, "Tales of Sound and Fury: Observations on the Family Melodrama" in *Film Genre Reader*, ed. Barry Keith Grant (University of Texas Press, 1986), pp. 278–308.

[10] Quoted in Jurij Lotman, "The Illusion of Reality" in *Film Theory and Criticism*, 2d ed., eds. Gerald Mast and Marshall Cohen (Oxford University Press, 1979), p. 65. This is an excerpt from Lotman's *Semiotics of the Cinema*. Reference to this story is also made by Francis E. Sparshott (Mast and Cohen, p. 325); reprinted from *Journal of Aesthetic Education* 5 (1971).

seem "arty."[11] Zooms can be used to enhance the surprise created by the revelation of a surprising detail.

Does colorizing a movie produce a new movie? After all, colorizing a movie affects its mood, and mood is important to a movie. The answer is that colorizing a movie does not produce a new mood because it isn't making the right kind of change. Joseph Cornell made the film *Rose Hobart* by cutting up a print of a movie named *East of Borneo*, which starred Rose Hobart, and rearranging some of the pieces. Despite this relationship to *Borneo*, *Rose Hobart* is a different movie than *Borneo*; this is because it consists of a different picture sequence than *Borneo* does. In 1985, Nina Gilberti made a film called *Life Is A Bitch And Then You Die* by re-editing footage from Joris Ivens' *The Bridge* and adding narration and music. The mood of *Life* is different from the mood of *The Bridge* (in fact, appreciating the difference is much of the fun of watching Gilberti's film). But this isn't why they are different movies. They are different movies because of the structural difference described above; the mood difference is a consequence of this more basic difference.[12]

Does colorizing a black and white movie present visual information that was implicit in that movie? It does not, because the original movie was in black and white. This is not the simple-minded comment it may appear to be. Rather, it reflects an aspect of movie identity which has been described by John Fisher: In movies, as in photographs and paintings, "visual information that is not in the original look of the work is not a part of the piece."[13] By this principle, the visual information added to a black and white movie by colorizing one of the prints is *not* part of the movie, because it is not part of the black and white movie's "look." Accordingly, what colorization adds to a movie print is extraneous to the embodied movie.[14]

From this perspective, a colorized movie is not comparable to a new arrangement of a musical composition, for example, a familiar string

---

[11] The notion of mood seems to have many uses in describing responses to movies and other movie-like depictions. There is a television advertisement in which the famous aria from *Pagliacci* is played over a scene of a car's finish being ruined for lack of a proper waxing. It's played for comical effect, and it is comical because the mood of the music (its sadness) is only superficially like the mood of the situation in the picture. In short, the advertisement is comical because its parts don't match, and the parts don't match because their moods don't match.

[12] A description of *Rose Hobart* may be found in P. Adams Sitney, *Visionary Film* (Oxford University Press, 1979), pp. 348–349. Gilberti's film is described in the 1986 *Canyon Cinema Update* (the film catalogue of Canyon Cinema, Inc., 2325 Third Street, San Francisco CA 94107), p. 19. Ken Jacobs' film *Tom, Tom the Piper's Son* is another experiment of this kind; see Sitney, *Visionary Film*, pp. 365–368.

[13] John Fisher, "Vandalism at the Movies—Is Colorization a Question of Preservation?," American Society of Aesthetics (Pacific Division) Annual Meeting (April 1989) note 5, p. 11.

[14] In speaking of an "embodiment" in this way, I am intending to follow Joseph Margolis "The Ontological Peculiarity of Works of Art," *Journal of Aesthetics and Art Criticism* 36 (1977): 45–50.

quartet. The information in the new arrangement belongs to the string quartet of which it is an arrangement, but the information added by colorization does not belong to the movie which is being colorized. This is not entirely surprising, because different things are done with string quartets than are done with movies—string quartets are "performed" but movies are "shown." The existence of movie remakes might have suggested that movies are like string quartets, but it should not suggest this. A movie remake is a new movie for the same kinds of reasons that *Life* and *Rose Hobart* were new movies, but a new arrangement of a string quartet is not a new string quartet. The separate identity of a movie remake is sometimes emphasized by giving the remake its own title; for example, *His Girl Friday* is a remake of *The Front Page.*

Thus, colorizing a movie does not produce a new movie, the information which colorizing adds is extraneous to the movie being colorized, and colorizing affects the mood of a movie. Such reasons provide support for Levinson's claim that colorization interferes with a movie's expressiveness.

Still More in Defense of Colorization

James O. Young

Colorization has been, perhaps, more reviled than any other development affecting the arts since the Visigoths and Vandals visited Rome. If even the Devil receives an advocate, however, surely colorization deserves one as well. Such an advocate is particularly desirable in view of the rather weak arguments sometimes advanced against the use of the process. When I wrote "In Defence of Colorization," I hoped that my defense would, at least, lead others to sharpen the arguments against the color conversion of black and white films. This hope has been largely fulfilled. Three thoughtful responses to my short essay have now appeared in print and, as a result, we have a much clearer understanding of the aesthetic and moral consequences of colorization.[1] While I am persuaded by much of what the authors of these replies have to say, I am still not convinced that every instance of colorization is aesthetically or morally objectionable.

In my original essay I maintained that colorization does not involve a morally objectionable restriction of film makers' freedom of expression. I distinguished between works of art, such as paintings, which are instanti-

---

[1] Charles B. Daniels, "Note on Colorization," *British Journal of Aesthetics* 30 (1990): 68–70; Jerrold Levinson, "Colorization Ill-Defended," and Flo Leibowitz, "Movie Colorization and the Expression of Mood."

ated in one material object, and works, such as novels and films, which are instantiated in many. Tampering with works in the latter class does unjustifiably limit an artist's freedom of expression, I conceded, but works of the latter sort are fair game. So long as there exists a number of copies of an artwork, and more can be made at will, there is nothing wrong with altering one copy of the work. I went on to suggest that many aesthetically successful works of art result from the modification of earlier works. Similarly, I suggested, there is no reason to doubt that the innovative use of colorization could produce aesthetically successful works. Consequently, it would be unwise to discourage the use of the process.

The position I adopted has been subjected to three principal objections. The first of these objections, developed most fully by Flo Leibowitz, reinforces the claim that colorization does, indeed, result in an artifact which is no longer able to convey what the original film makers wished to express. This claim must be established for the moral case against color conversion to proceed. The second line of argument is designed to distinguish between the objectionable modification of an artwork which occurs during colorization and the creative and unobjectionable appropriation of elements of earlier artworks. The suggestion is that colorization is somehow relevantly different from, say, Woody Allen's addition of a new sound track to an existing movie when he made *What's Up, Tiger Lily* or from what composers do when they arrange the works of other musicians. The third objection to my article, developed in some detail by Jerrold Levinson, takes issue with the suggestion that colorization can be defended by means of the distinction I draw between artworks which are and are not instantiated in a single artifact. Artists' freedom of expression can be wrongly constrained, Levinson claims, even if examples of their works are preserved unaltered.

I have nothing to say against the first objection. Leibowitz is undoubtedly correct when she argues that the mood of a film can be dramatically altered by colorization. Neither can there be any doubt that this alteration of mood can stop a film from expressing what its makers wished to express. This matter was never at issue: the moral issue only arises because colorized films are unable to express what the original film makers wished to express. My critics and I differ on the question of whether this inability to express what was originally intended is enough to make colorization morally objectionable. There is, however, no disagreement about the source of the controversy.

The second sort of objection to my essay is the source of more controversy. While Leibowitz and Levinson hold that colorization is objectionable, they want to allow that some tampering with artworks is permissible and even aesthetically successful. Both writers argue that there is a distinction to be drawn between colorizing and an artistic process which gives rise to a new artwork. Levinson writes that he sees no objection to the modification of a film which involves "post-modernist appropriation, or inventive re-use, or ironic commentary." Allen engaged in such a process when he made *What's Up, Tiger Lily* and produced an "entirely distinct work of art." Colorizers, on the other hand, "are not making artistic statements."[2] Similarly, Leibowitz holds that "colorizing a movie does not produce a new movie." On the other hand, when Joseph Cornell re-arranges some sequences from *East of Borneo* to produce *Rose Hobart*, Leibowitz has no complaint. The difference is that Cornell produced "a different movie."[3] The complaint against colorization is that it obscures what is expressed in a prior work of art without creating a new work able to express something new.

For the sake of argument, grant that colorization, unlike some other means of modifying films, does not normally create a new work of art. This concession is difficult to avoid since it is by no means clear how we are to individuate works of art. It seems clear that artworks can undergo some modification without becoming new works. A performance of Beethoven's *Eroica Symphony* which adds, as many do, a few trumpet flourishes, is plausibly still a performance of Beethoven's composition. An edition of *Hamlet* which modernizes the spelling is still the Bard's work. Plainly, however, there is some threshold at which the play is not Shakespeare's or the symphony not Beethoven's. Tom Stoppard's *Fifteen Minute Hamlet* has clearly crossed the line. I am prepared to grant, however, that no such threshold has been crossed in any colorization hitherto undertaken. Such a threshold could be crossed: a surrealist reading of *Casa Blanca*, in which Bogart appears in a variety of jackets, each a differ-ent, rather striking, fluorescent hue, may have crossed the line. This may count as an example of post-modernist appropriation, inventive re-use or ironic commentary. Certainly, colorizing *Citizen Kane* in soft pastels would count as an example of ironic commentary. I would not want to be the person drawing the line between colorization and the surrealist's un-objectionable revision. Nothing turns, however, on colorizers being on the wrong side of the line.

Most colorization is more akin to musical transcription than it is to the creation of a new work of art. Stephen Davies has characterized transcrip-tion as the interpretation of a composer's score. He holds that a transcrip-tion can be valued as "enriching our understanding and appreciation of the merits (and demerits) of their models."[4] Colorizers can similarly be re-garded as interpreters of already existing movies. Leibowitz quotes Vincent Canby, who gives an example of precisely this: the colorization of Laurel and Hardy's *Way Out West* "effectively compliments the mock-his-torical period of the film and the dainty archaic mannerisms of its two stars."[5] If there is a close analogy between color conversion and transcrip-

---

[2] Levinson, "Colorization Ill-Defended."
[3] Leibowitz, "Movie Colorization."
[4] Stephen Davies, "Transcription, Authenticity and Performance," *British Journal of Aesthetics* 28 (1988): p. 221.
[5] Leibowitz, "Movie Colorization."

tion, a moral case against colorization will prove elusive. There is nothing wrong with transcription, so there ought to be nothing wrong with colorization.

Two objections to this line of argument immediately present themselves. According to one objection the analogy between color conversion and transcription fails because colorization changes a work more than does transcription. According to the second objection, just the opposite is the case: transcriptions alter compositions so dramatically that they give rise to new works (which, of course, are unobjectionable). Leibowitz offers the first objection. She claims that the information in an arrangement of a composition "belongs" to the composition of which it is an arrangement but "the information added by colorization does not belong to the movie which is being colorized."[6] Leibowitz underestimates the metamorphosis involved in transcription. Colorization certainly introduces tones which are not present in the black and white original but transcription similarly introduces elements foreign to the original score. Consider, for example, the changes involved in transcribing a Bach lute suite for guitar. The key is changed, notes outside the compass of the guitar are eliminated and new ones introduced in their places. Perhaps most importantly, tone color is dramatically altered. The difference between the warm, mellow tone of the lute and the silvery tone of the guitar is as marked as the contrast between color and black and white. The analogy does not break down because transcription leaves a work unaltered. Those who object to the analogy are better advised to try the second objection. They could argue that transcriptions are new works and, thus, as we have seen, immune to the sort of objection which plagues colorized films. There seems, however, to be no way of characterizing transcriptions as new works which would not also apply to colorized films and make them count as new artworks with the immunity possessed by such works.

Consider the following scenario, where there is no question of transcription giving rise to a new composition. Imagine that, as actually happened, people come to think of the clavichord as—to use Leibowitz' words—"dated or unexciting." People are still interested in the music written for the clavichord, however, and musicians begin playing music written for the instrument on the pianoforte. There is no question about creating a new work of art, a new composition. Precisely the same notes are played on the piano as were once played on the clavichord. Even though the same notes are played, even though no "information" is added, tone color (not spectral color in this case) is dramatically changed. The tone of the composition becomes brighter and more lively as the contemplative clavichord is superseded. As the tone changes, the mood of the erstwhile clavichord compositions is altered and the music is no longer able to express what its composer intended. A melancholy piece is now more cheerful. There seems, however, to be nothing morally wrong in this

[6] Ibid.

scenario. Perhaps there are aesthetic grounds for objecting to the performance of clavichord music on the piano. Perhaps, however, some compositions can make the transition quite effectively and audiences are able to see new beauties in them. Such aesthetic decisions must be made on a case by case basis, just as aesthetic decisions about the value of colorization must be made one at a time. In any case, there seems to be nothing morally wrong with performing clavichord music on the piano and, by analogy, nothing wrong with colorized films.

It is at this point that Levinson's objections become worrisome. He maintains that there is a significant difference between films and other artworks. We can go to a library or a bookstore if we are unhappy with a revised edition of Shakespeare but we depend for our access to films "on the entertainment industry and its outlets."[7] Revising Shakespeare, that is, does not hinder access to the unrevised editions or performances but colorizing a film will restrict access to the original black and white version. This becomes morally important because freedom of expression involves more than freedom to create expressive items. It also involves the freedom to distribute these items. This point seems to undercut the defense of color conversion which depends on the distinction between works which are and are not instantiated in a single artifact. An artist's freedom of expression can be constrained even though there are dozens of original prints of a film in a vault somewhere. Any restriction of freedom of expression is wrong in itself but, as Levinson notes, it has further negative consequences. The "reputations of both films and film makers are at stake." Film makers, it seems, may be harmed by the bowdlerization of colorizers. A film maker, Levinson adds, is "entitled to a fair shot at displaying his oeuvre as he created it."[8]

Levinson's objections are genuinely worrisome. Directors whose work is available only in colorized form are denied what they may reasonably expect: public access to their works as they were created. And the reputations of film makers may, indeed, suffer if restrictions are placed on the distribution of their work. If wrong is done to film makers in these ways, however, it is not the colorizers who harm them. Levinson has himself identified the real villain of the piece: the entertainment industry. It is true that colorizers are often working at the behest of the industry. But the colorizer is still no more at fault than pianists who perform a clavichord composition in the full knowledge that impresarios are no longer engaging clavichordists. Access to clavichord music is itself rather tightly controlled. Not everyone has access to or can play the clavichord. In the nineteenth century, it would have been much harder to hear a clavichord recital than it is to see a black and white movie today. And yet pianists did no wrong when they played clavichord music. Indeed, likely it was better

---

[7] Levinson, "Colorization Ill-Defended."
[8] Ibid.

that the music was played on an inappropriate instrument than not heard at all. Perhaps, likewise, it is better that films are seen in colorized versions than not at all.

SUGGESTIONS FOR FURTHER READING

Allen, Woody. "True Colors." *New York Review of Books* 34 No. 13 (August 13, 1987): 38.

Blum, David. "Emotion Pictures." *The New Republic* 196 (February 9, 1987): 13–15.

Daniels, Charles B. "A Note on Colorization." *British Journal of Aesthetics* 30 (1990): 68–70.

Dempsey, Michael. "Colorization." *Film Quarterly* 40 (1986–87): 2–3.

Fisher, John. Editorial. *Journal of Aesthetics and Art Criticism* 45 (1987): 227–28.

James, David. "On Colorizing Films: A Venture into Applied Aesthetics." *Metaphilosophy* 20 (1989): 332–40.

Klawans, Stuart. "Colorization: Rose-Tinted Spectacles." In *Seeing Through Movies*, edited by Mark Crispin Miller. New York: Pantheon Books, 1990.

Linfield, Susan. "The Color of Money." *American Film* 12 (1987): 29–35, 52.

Saito, Yuriko. "Contemporary Aesthetic Issues: The Colorization Controversy." *Journal of Aesthetic Education* 23 (1989): 21–31.

U.S. Congress. Senate. Committee on the Judiciary. Subcommittee on Technology and the Law. *Hearing on legal issues that arise when color is added to films originally produced, sold, and distributed in black and white.* 100th Congress, 1st session, 1987. Washington, D.C.: U.S. Government Printing Office, 1988.

U.S. Congress. House. Committee on the Judiciary. Subcommittee on Courts, Intellectual Property and the Administration of Justice. *Hearing on Moral Rights and the Motion Picture Industry.* 101st Congress, 2d session, 1990. Washington, D.C.: U.S. Government Printing Office, 1991.

3

THE "AUTHENTIC" PERFORMANCE OF MUSIC

Please request Herr von Seyfried to conduct my opera today; I myself want to see and hear it at a distance; by that means, at any rate, my patience will not be so severely tried, as when close by I hear my music murdered. I cannot help thinking that it is done purposely.

—Ludwig van Beethoven, in a letter to Meyer

Beethoven's Violin Concerto is a lesson in the correct attitude of a composer towards a player. It was written for a virtuoso of the name of Clement, and is inscribed to him with a vile pun on his "clemency" towards the poor composer. The score assigns four staves to the violin solo, in order to leave room for alterations; and in many places all the four staves have been filled. The violinist whose criticism Beethoven took so much pains to meet produced (or, as he called it, "created") the concerto under conditions of his own making that were not considered unusual in those days. The first movement was played in the first part of the programme, the slow movement and the finale in the second part. Among the items which took place between these divisions was a sonata of Clement's own composing, to be played on one string with the violin upside down. Clement survived this performance for many years.

—Donald Francis Tovey, *Concertos and Choral Works*, pp. 70–71

INTRODUCTION

Much of the music which fills our concert halls, our record shops, and the airwaves was composed during periods when the instruments available were very different from those we have grown used to since. The modern grand piano, for instance, with its steel strings and its sturdy iron frame, only came into existence in the last century, which means that much of the music now performed on the modern piano was originally conceived for a very different instrument. Mozart's and Beethoven's "piano" music, for instance, was composed with the forte-piano in mind—a gut-stringed, wood-framed instrument, with a distinctive light sound all its own. And Bach's keyboard music was composed for organs, harpsichords, and other instruments of the early eighteenth century, none of which sounds even remotely like a modern concert grand. All of the main kinds of instruments have undergone similar evolutionary changes, and these changes have brought in their train successively different approaches to the interpretation of earlier music.

What we hear when we listen to a Mozart piano concerto, then, performed on a modern piano and with modern orchestral instruments, is quite different from what we would have heard had we attended a concert given by Mozart himself, a little more than two centuries ago. The sound is different, and the style of performance is different. Indeed, it is one of the triumphs of recent musicological scholarship to have established just how large these differences are. And it is a consequence of such scholarship that many musicians, over the last three decades, have been attempting to give performances of old music on historically appropriate instruments, played in historically appropriate ways. These musicians—advocates of "authentic" performance practices—try to let us hear in the music of earlier ages something that more closely resembles the sounds which were originally conceived.

By themselves, of course, such efforts might represent no more than exercises in archaeological reconstruction: attempts to understand how, as a matter of fact, things were actually done. But combined, as they frequently are, with the evaluative claim that "authentic" performances are in some way *preferable* to "inauthentic" ones, these efforts raise a variety of important philosophical questions. For example, what precisely must a performance be like if it is to count as "authentic"? Must it be identical to some earlier performance, perhaps one approved by the composer? Must it be a performance which allows the work to be experienced in a way similar to that in which the composer's contemporaries might have experienced it? If we can answer these questions, and so decide what we *mean* by "authentic" performance, a further question arises. Do such performances have *aesthetic* advantages not possessed by "inauthentic" performances—and if so, which aesthetic advantages, and why? In answering this question, we will in effect be making a practical recommendation. We will be advocating, or refusing to advocate, the adoption by musicians of some particular set of performance practices, perhaps rather narrow ones. Philosophical and musicianly considerations come together here, and the answers we give will clearly need to be informed by both kinds.

Stephen Davies, in the first of the readings in this section, is a determined defender of authentic performance practices. A performance "will be more rather than less authentic," he argues, "if it successfully (re)creates the sound of a performance of the work in question as could be given by good musicians playing good instruments under good conditions." What Davies means by "good" here is good compared to "the best of what was known by the composer to be available at the time, whether or not those resources were available for the composer's use." Thus, for Davies, authenticity represents an *ideal* to be aimed at, rather than an attempt to reproduce any *actual* past performance. For instance, an authentic performance does not necessarily attempt to recreate a performance witnessed and approved by the composer or by his contemporaries.

But why ought a performer to aim at such an ideal? What aesthetic benefits might result from doing so? It might be suggested that aesthetic benefits arise from faithfulness to the intentions of the composer—that aesthetically successful performances are performances which do justice to what the composer *wanted.* But there are difficulties involved in this suggestion. For one thing, we often don't know what a composer did want. And for another thing, some composers may have wanted perverse or unrealizable things. Davies argues instead that authenticity in performance is an ideal worth aiming at because aesthetic value arises from the creative contribution made by musicians in attempting to realize the composer's musical conception. "It is the creative skill required of the performer in faithfully interpreting the composer's score which is valued in praising the authenticity of performances of that score."

James O. Young takes a very different view. In the second of the readings, he argues that "authentic performance cannot be characterized in such a way that it represents an artistic ideal which is both attainable and worth attaining." He considers five possible answers to the question, What is an authentic performance? The third of these answers is very similar to the answer give by Davies, and Young rejects it for two reasons. The first is that, because we are listening from an entirely different historical perspective, and our experience is colored by our knowledge of all the music that has been written in the meantime, an authentic *experience* of an authentic performance is impossible for us to have. So why bother trying to give such a performance? And second, Young argues, even if an authentic experience of an authentic performance *were* attainable, there is no reason to think that it would be worth having. Much of the music which we value today appeared graceless and ugly to its contemporaries. Why would we want to regain *that* experience? Young's conclusion is that the concept of authentic performance "is not a useful one." If musicians wedded to the ideal of authenticity have enriched our musical experience, he says, then they have done so "not by giving authentic performances but by giving successful ones."

The controversy here is a rich one. On the face of it, the suggestion that we should perform music of the past in certain historically appropriate ways might seem unproblematic. But it turns out to be difficult to say just what is meant by "historically appropriate," and no easier to explain what the aesthetic justification for seeking such appropriateness might be. Do we need to refer to the composer's original intentions? Are we aiming at a certain kind of *sound?* Or are we aiming at a certain way of *experiencing* sounds?

These are intriguing questions—and not only to those who are concerned with classical music. For closely analogous questions arise elsewhere. Paul Simon conceived "Bridge over Troubled Water," for example, with the voice of Art Garfunkel in mind. Does this mean that Simon's ballad is only "authentically" performed when Garfunkel sings it? What about "Bridge over Troubled Water" sung by a woman, or indeed by Paul Simon himself? Are cover versions or remakes inevitably worse than the originals? Again, consider theater. The kinds of performance which are given today of Shakespeare's plays are very different from those which could have been witnessed by his contemporaries. Modern productions often employ modern technology for stage effects, for instance. Certain productions include such un-Elizabethan props as motorbikes and automatic weapons. And sometimes the plays are performed as a kind of political or social commentary on questions important to us today, but which could not have been asked by an audience of the late sixteenth century. What should we think about these cases? The arguments advanced by Davies and Young in the present section can be translated directly into terms appropriate for the discussion of such questions. And they allow us to see just how important the issues surrounding "authenticity" are both for our understanding of the performing arts in general, and for our understanding of particular performances *of* those arts.

Authenticity in Musical Performance

Stephen Davies

In this paper I discuss musical performances and their authenticity with respect to the independently identifiable musical pieces of which they are performances.[1] I intend my account to be descriptive rather than prescriptive (but I appreciate that, where intuitions clash, it is the location of the border between description and prescription which is at issue).

The adjective 'authentic' has a number of meanings which no doubt are related. But I am not here interested in the unity of the concept, nor with the relative primacy of these different meanings. Nor shall I discuss one familiar notion of musical authenticity—that in which a performance is authentic with respect to a style or *genre*. My limited interest is in the authenticity of musical performances *as* performances of particular compositions (which are independently identified with event-specifications which, in the case of the Western cultural tradition on which I shall concentrate, take the form of musical scores). That is, if I talk of the authenticity of a performance of Beethoven's Fifth Symphony, I am interested in its authenticity as a member of the class of performances recognizable as performances of Beethoven's Fifth Symphony and not with it as a member of other classes of performances to which it may also belong, such as nineteenth-century symphony.

The view for which I argue characterizes authenticity in musical performance as follows: a performance which aims to realize the composer's score faithfully in sound may be judged for authenticity. A performance of X is more rather than less authentic the more faithful it is to the intentions publicly expressed in the score by the composer (where those intentions are determinative and not merely recommendatory of performance practice). Because the composer's score under-determines the sound of a faithful performance, the authenticity of any particular performance is judged against (the appropriate member/s of) a set of ideally faithful performances. As a commendatory term 'authentic' is used to acknowledge the creative role of the performer in realizing faithfully the composer's specifications.

The paper is divided into six sections. The first four sections concentrate on the aim of faithfulness in securing authenticity; as well as an attempt to define authenticity these sections contain a characterization of what is involved in faithfully realizing a composer's intentions. In the penultimate section I discuss why authenticity in musical performance is value-conferring. In the final section I emphasize the creative nature of the performer's role.

---

[1] Although it might be argued, for example, that rehearsals are not performances, this is a subtlety I shall attempt to ignore.

I

In this first section I argue that the pursuit of authenticity involves the attempt to produce musical *sounds* as opposed to the social *milieu* within which those sounds originally were created.

Over the past fifty years there has been a growing interest in authenticity in musical performance. The same period also has seen a developing interest in the performance of pre-modern music. These parallel developments probably are related. Where modern music is written for modern instruments and notated in the standard fashion, a high degree of authenticity will be achieved in performance by a competent musician. But the more foreign the styles of performance and the more unfamiliar the instruments employed, the harder will it be for musicians to produce authentic performances without the benefit of scholarly advice and instruction.

A moment's reflection shows that the pursuit of authenticity in musical performance has been highly selective. The price of admission, the dress of the audience, the method by which the programme is printed— each of these and much else in the context in which music is performed is decidedly modern. The search for musical authenticity takes a very particular direction. A highly authentic performance is likely to be one in which instruments contemporary to the period of composition (or replicas of such instruments) are used in its performance, in which the score is interpreted in the light of stylistic practices and performance conventions of the time when the work was composed, in which ensembles of the same size and disposition as accord with the composer's specification are employed, and so forth.

The selectivity displayed in the search for authenticity in musical performance has been systematic in a way which suggests that the quest may be characterized as aiming at the production of a particular *sound*, rather than at the production of, for example, the social ambience within which the music would or could be presented by the composer's contemporaries. This point is effectively illustrated as follows: orchestral music composed in the latter half of the eighteenth century might standardly have been performed in wood-panelled rooms. Nowadays such works would be performed in concert halls. Modern concert halls are designed with modifiable acoustics, the adjustments being made by the use of baffles etc. In performing music of the period in question, the acoustics of the concert hall would be set with a reverberation period such as one might find in a wood-panelled room containing a small audience. Although the music now is performed in a large hall in front of a large audience, the acoustic properties of the modern building are so arranged that they duplicate the acoustic properties of the sort of room in which the music would have been performed in the composer's day. Now, whilst one might prefer the intimacy of music performed in salons I take it that it will be accepted that the use of concert halls which reproduce the acoustic properties of wood-panelled rooms would be considered not *merely* as an adequate compromise between the demands of authenticity and, say, economic considerations, but, instead, would be accepted as a full-blooded attempt at authentic performance.[2] That modern acoustic technology might serve the aim of authenticity in this way suggests strongly that musical authenticity aims at the creation of a particular sound and not at the production of a particular visual, social, or other effect.

Some performances are less authentic for being given in buildings other than that for which the work was written, but this is true only of performances of works written with an ear to the unique acoustic properties of a particular building. That is, it is true of performances of Stravinsky's *Canticum Sacrum* and of many works by Andrea and Giovanni Gabrieli which were written for San Marco in Venice, and it is not true of Verdi's *Aïda* which was written for the opera house in Cairo, because, whereas the acoustics of the opera house in Cairo are not distinctively different from those of other opera houses, the acoustics of San Marco are unlike those of other buildings. These examples do not count against the point that a concern with the authenticity of a performance is a concern with its sound.

II

In this second section I suggest that one might best hope to make a performance authentic by recreating the musical sound of a performance which might have been heard by the composer's contemporaries. (Why this is a formula for success is a matter considered in the next section.) I also argue that the sound to which an authentic performance aspires is that of a possible, rather than an actual, performance; that is, authenticity in musical performance is judged against an ideal.

So far I have said that a performance is more or less authentic in a way which depends upon its sound. One might ask—the sound of what? A musical work comprises notes and relationships between them, so an authentic performance of a given work must be a performance which concerns itself with producing the notes which comprise the work. The sound of an authentic performance will be the sound of those notes.

But it is not easy to specify the set of notes which comprise a given work.[3] The notes recorded in the score often are not the notes which the

---

[2] As implied here, the desirability of musical authenticity may sometimes be outweighed by other factors—musical, pragmatic or even moral. (I assume that arguments against the use of trained *castrati* in *opera seria* are of the latter kind.) Of course, where the choice is between no performance at all and a less than ideally authentic performance, the latter may be preferable.

[3] Some of the considerations I mention are discussed also by Paul Ziff in 'The Cow on the Roof', *The Journal of Philosophy*, Vol. 70 (1973), pp. 713–23. Guy Sircello (in 'Various Variants', pp. 723–4) and Kendall L. Walton (in 'Not a Leg to Stand On', pp. 725–6) reply to Ziff in the same volume.

performer should play; frequently there are conventions known both to composers and performers governing the ways in which the written notes are to be modified (for example by accidentals or embellishment). So an interest in discrepancies between that which is written and that which is conventionally to be played is of practical and not merely scholarly significance. Debates about the problems of *musica ficta* in music written pre-1600 reflect strongly a desire to achieve authentic performances of the music in question.

Even where the conventions by which the score is to be read are known, it is not a straightforward matter always to say which notes should be played. Consider music written at about the end of the seventeenth century when pitches were as much as a minor third lower than now. The modern performer might play the work at the modern pitch level, but vocal and wind parts will then sound strained even if sung or played brilliantly and correctly.[4] Or the performer might tune down modern instruments, as a result of which their tone will suffer, or transpose orchestral parts, in which case the sound is affected by alterations in fingerings and *embouchure*, by changes in register, by shifts to harmonics etc. In view of such difficulties it is understandable that performers have turned to the use of instruments from the period of composition, or to replicas of such instruments, so that vocal and instrumental parts 'lie' comfortably to the voice and hands. The use of such instruments is justified ultimately by the resulting sound of the performance.

However, despite the use of instruments and the appeal to musical conventions from the time of composition, clearly it is inadequate to characterize authenticity in musical performance in terms of the sound heard by the composer's contemporaries. His or her contemporaries could perform the work in question in ways which were relatively inauthentic.[5] Typically this would occur where the performance contained wrong notes or where the composer's specifications were misrepresented in some other way. Probably the musicians who sight-read the overture to *Don Giovanni* from orchestral parts on which the ink was still wet gave a performance which was not as authentic as it could have been. Since the

---

[4] Competent musicians do not usually stumble over fast passages, lose the tempo or produce gross tonal contrasts but, despite this, hard music sounds hard to play. Thomas Carson Mark makes this clear in 'On Works of Virtuosity', *The Journal of Philosophy*, Vol. 77 (1980), pp. 28–45.

[5] It might be objected to what I have said that judgements of authenticity apply only to performances which are historically removed from the period of composition or culturally removed from the place or style of composition, or in some other way distanced from the composition. On my view judgements of authenticity tend to reduce to judgements of accuracy. But this does not mean that a performance by the composer's contemporaries (for whom the score is 'transparent' to the conventions by which it is to be read) are not distanced from the work in a way that leaves room for judgements of authenticity. Performance involves a creative element which is integral and not merely appended to the faithfulness of the performance. This creative element distances *any* particular performance from the work of which it is a performance.

performances heard by the composer's contemporaries often were less authentic than was possible, authenticity in musical performance cannot be defined in terms of the sounds actually heard by the composer's contemporaries. This suggests that, in striving for authenticity, the performer aims at an *ideal* sound rather than at the sound of some actual, former performance.

III

In this third section I consider the relevance of the composer's intentions in an assessment of the authenticity of a performance of the composer's work. I suggest that only those intentions which conventionally are accepted as determinative are relevant to judgements of authenticity; other of the composer's intentions or wishes might be ignored in an ideally authentic performance. Because the composer's determinative intentions under-determine the sound of an ideally authentic performance of his or her work, there is a set of ideal performances (and not any single ideal performance) in terms of which the relative authenticity of actual performances is judged.

There are conventions in terms of which musical scores are to be read. The composer is able to express his or her intentions in a musical notation only because the conventions for realizing in sound that notation are known both to the composer and to the performer of the day. Those conventions provide not only a vehicle for, but also a limitation on, the intentions which may be expressed in the score. Not all of the intentions which the conventions allow to be expressed are determinative of that which can be required in the name of authenticity. Non-determinative intentions (as expressed in the score or in other ways) have the status of recommendations. I take it that exact metronome indications are non-determinative in that tempo may be varied to suit the performance conditions. Both the composer and the performing musician who is his or her contemporary are familiar with the conventions usually and know which of the expressed intentions are determinative and which are not determinative of that at which an authentic performance must aim.

The conventions by which musical scores are to be read change over time in ways which affect that which the composer may determine with respect to the performer's attempt to produce an authentic performance. Phrasing was not notationally determined in the early seventeenth century, but was notationally determined by the nineteenth century. At some time, before the convention was established, composers notated phrasings which would have been understood rightly as recommendations for, rather than as determinative of, what should be played. At that time the composer's indications of phrasing might be disregarded without any diminution in the authenticity of the performance (although the performance may have been less good as a result on other grounds). (Sometimes these changes in convention arise from composers' rebelling against the existing conventions, but such rebellions reject only a few conventions at any one time and do so against a wider background of accepted conventions.) Because conventions of determinativeness change through time, the conventions appropriate to the authentic performance of a score are those with which the composer would have taken musicians *of the day* to be familiar. It is this fact which explains that which I have emphasized in the previous section—that an attempt at an authentic performance is likely to be successful by aiming to recreate the sound of an accurate performance by the composer's contemporaries.[6]

Sometimes it is possible to infer from what is written in the score that the composer would have preferred to write something else had the instruments or the performers been capable of accommodating his or her intentions. For example, a sequential pattern might be interrupted by an octave transposition where a continuation of the pattern would have exceeded the singer's or the instrument's range. In these cases it is appropriate to talk of the composer's wishes (rather than intentions). Sometimes nowadays, with the wider range of some instruments and the greater proficiency of many musicians, these wishes could be realized and there would be a musical point to doing so. However, such wishes have no more a bearing on the authenticity of a performance than do the composer's non-determinative intentions. Both the work and the performance may be better for the modification, but not because the alteration makes the performance more authentic. If it were accepted that mere wishes could set the standards of authenticity, it would also be accepted that many works could not have been performed authentically by the composer's contemporaries and some could not be performed authentically at all.

Clearly, in taking the line that I have, I must deny that authenticity in musical performance is judged against the *sound* of some particular performance which was envisaged by the composer. I have said that not all of the composer's expressed intentions are determinative of that which must be accurately rendered in an ideally authentic performance, in which case

[6] The claim that the conventions of score-reading and/or performance practice establish which of the composer's publicly expressed intentions are determinative may be defeated where there are grounds for believing that the composer was not familiar with the conventions or that the composer believed that the musicians who would perform the piece were not familiar with all the relevant conventions. These double-take and triple-take situations are unusual. An example: If the composer had only ever heard violins with a thin and reedy tone and by the indication 'violin' on the score meant to designate instruments of that type, then the fact that Guaneri's violins were extant as the time would not license their use in performances of the composer's works in the name of authenticity, not even if the composer had *wished* that the instruments which he or she knew as violins had a richer, fruitier tone. (To avoid such problem cases I should relativize all claims about the role of the relevant conventions to the composer's knowledge of those conventions and beliefs about the performers' knowledge of those conventions.)

I must also hold that the sound of an ideally authentic performance is under-determined by the intentions in terms of which its authenticity is judged. The way in which we talk of authenticity favours my view, I claim, rather than the view that authenticity is measured against the *sound* of a performance which the composer had in mind. First, in reaching judgments about the authenticity of performances we do not seem to face the epistemological difficulties which would inevitably arise if the standard for authenticity was a sound which may never have been realized. Second, rather than taking composer's performances as definitive models which performers are obliged to copy slavishly, we take them to be revealing of what we expect to be an interesting interpretation. In a performance the composer may make his or her intentions as regards the *sound* of a performance more explicit than could be done in the score, but that which is made explicit is not thereby made definitive. Other performers are left with the job of interpreting the score for themselves.[7] Third, we would not (as we do) accept that *different-sounding* performances of a single work might be equally and ideally authentic if authenticity were judged against the sound of a *particular* performance imagined by the composer. It is (a member of) a *set* of ideal performances against which the authenticity of an actual performance is judged.

This last point deserves emphasis. Because an ideally authentic performance faithfully preserves the composer's determinative intentions, and because those intentions under-determine the sound of a faithful performance, different-sounding performances may be equally and ideally authentic. For example, many combinations of vocal and instrumental resources are compatible with that which is determinative in the score of Guillaume de Machaut's *Messe de Notre-Dame*. Even if the composer wrote for a particular combination of singers and instruments (such as were to be assembled for the coronation of Charles V in 1364, perhaps) the conventions of the day allow that performances by quite different combinations would be no less authentic. As long as two performances are faithful to the score and are consistent with the performance practices in terms of which it is to be rendered, they may be equally authentic whilst sounding different. Compare, for example, performances of Beethoven's symphonies as conducted by Klemperer and Toscanini, both of whom have been praised as interpreters of the works. Klemperer tends to take the pieces at the slowest tempo consistent with Beethoven's instructions and

---

[7] A pertinent discussion of musical authenticity and the relevance of composers' intentions may be found in Richard Taruskin's 'On Letting the Music Speak for Itself: Some Reflections on Musicology and Performance' in *The Journal of Musicology*, Vol. 1 (1982), pp. 338–49. The status of the composer's intentions are discussed interestingly by Randall R. Dipert in 'The Composer's Intentions: An Examination of Their Relevance for Performance', *The Music Quarterly*, Vol. 66 (1980), pp. 205–18. The philosophical literature on the subject of artist's intentions is immense. Two of my own papers bear on our topic: 'The Relevance of Authors' and Painters' Intentions', *The Journal of Aesthetics and Art Criticism*, Vol. 40 (1982), pp. 65–76 and 'Attributing Significance to Unobvious Musical Relationships', *The Journal of Music Theory*, Vol. 27 (1983), pp. 203–13.

he emphasizes the structural qualities of the music so that, for example, climaxes at relatively weak structural points receive less weight than do those in structurally important places, even where the dynamics are the same in both places. Toscanini takes the works at a brisk tempo and concentrates on the drama or beauty of each individual passage, investing every note and phrase with its full potential of power. Without Klemperer's staid approach, the grandeur and architectonic qualities of Beethoven's music could not be presented. Without Toscanini's volatile approach, the dynamism and verve of Beethoven's music could not be appreciated. So, the ideally authentic performance has no *particular* sound because it is no *particular* performance. Rather, the standard against which the authenticity of performances of a work is judged comprises a *set* of performance each of which is faithful to the composer's determinative intentions.

In view of the above I offer the following account: a performance will be more rather than less authentic if it successfully (re)creates the sound of a performance of the work in question as could be given by good musicians playing good instruments under good conditions (of rehearsal time etc.), where 'good' is relativized to the best of what was known by the composer to be available at the time, whether or not those resources were available for the composer's use.

IV

In this fourth section I analyze musical performance as involving both certain intentions on the part of the performer and a relationship of invariance between the composer's sound-specification and the performer's realization of that score. Performing is contrasted briefly with improvising and fantasizing. The point of authenticity is said to be the faithful realization of the composer's score in sound.

The notion of performance must be analysed in terms of the performer's intentions. If the production of some set of sounds is to be a performance of X, then it must be the intention of the producer of the sounds to generate a sound faithful to an X-specification. However, the intention to perform X is defeasible; where the sound produced is not recognizable as a realization of the X-specification the attempt at performance has failed. The notion of authenticity operates *within* the range set on the one hand by performances which are barely recognizable as such and on the other hand by performances which are ideally accurate. The closer comes a performance recognizable as such to the sound of an ideal performance of the work in question, the more authentic is that performance.[8]

---

[8] It is controversial, I realize, to regard a barely recognizable performance as authentic. Of course, the level of authenticity expected in a *competent* performance is far higher than the minimum at which a performance is barely recognizable as such. A minimally recognizable performance is inauthentic when authenticity is relativized to a standard of acceptability at the level of a competent performance.

I have suggested that there must be, as well as the appropriate intentions, an invariant relationship between the composer's specification and a performance of that specification as a necessary condition of the success of the attempt at performance. There must be some common factor (or tolerance across a range of features) necessary for a performance's being a performance of X rather than of Y, and necessary for different sounding performances all to be performances of the same X. Now, clearly the standard by which an attempted performance is minimally recognizable as such falls far short of a standard which identifies the work with the totality of notes which comprise it. By this standard only a perfectly accurate performance could count as a performance of the work in question, yet we all know that the school orchestra may play wrong notes, play out of tune, and fail to play together while performing what is unmistakably Beethoven's Fifth Symphony. Clearly it is because musical works comprise large numbers of notes, not all of which contribute equally to the overall effect, that the identity of the work survives the performance of wrong notes. So what is invariant between performances of the same work is *patterns* of notes (or aspects, gestalts, emergent properties, functions of notes) plus a tolerance for deviation from these patterns. Musical works are so complex that there are patterns of notes within patterns of notes and these various patterns may remain recognizable despite changes in or omissions of individual notes. The standard of adequacy which must be met in a successful attempt to perform the composer's score need not be one that requires a high degree of accuracy.[9] It is within the gap between a set of ideally faithful interpretations of a work and of barely recognizable performances of that work that the notion of authenticity operates. A performance is the more authentic the further beyond the minimum standard of adequacy it falls. The more faithful is a musical performance to the work's specification the more authentic is that performance.

The difference between a *performance* of X, an *improvisation* on X and an X-inspired *fantasia* lies in the musician's intentions, the aim being to realize a higher level of invariance with respect to the work's specification in performance than in improvisation and in improvisation than in fantasizing. Whereas authenticity is appropriately predicated of performances of particular works, it is not appropriately predicated of improvisations or fantasias inspired by particular works; that is, authenticity applies only

---

[9] The same kind of point may be made with respect to other musical parameters. A performance on the piano of J. S. Bach's Concerto in D Minor for Harpsichord, BWV 1052, *is* a performance of it, despite the change of instrument, and not the performance of a *transcription* of Bach's work. Conventions in Bach's time allowed quite free interchange between keyboard instruments and, in view of this, merely changing the solo instrument does not transform the work enough for the performance to count as that of a transcription. (One does not transcribe a musical work merely by altering a word in its *title*, which, in effect, is what happens here.)

where there is intended to be more rather than less invariance between the specification of the work and its rendition in sound. This suggests that the notion of authenticity applies where a text (usually a written score in literate music cultures and a model rendition in oral music cultures) is interpreted by a mediator who stands between the composer and his or her audience, and where the point of the interpretation is to render faithfully to the audience that which is determined of the sound of the performance in the work's specification. Ultimately a concern with the authenticity of performances of particular works takes it interest from a more fundamental concern with the authority of authorship.

A shift of focus to music which is primarily improvisational (i.e., most jazz, a substantial amount of non-western music and some recent 'classical' music) helps to bring out the point. In such music, where the composer creates a cipher which lends itself to improvisational manipulation, we are more likely to be concerned with the authenticity of the *style* of the performance of any given work than with its authenticity as a performance of that particular work. The less the sound of the performance is determined in a faithful realization of the composer's specification, the less we are concerned with the type of authenticity in performance which I have been discussing (and the more the musicians are rated above composers). The less the composer has a hand in the final outcome the less is a concern with musical authenticity a concern with the authority of authorship.

V

In this fifth section I consider the way in which authenticity in musical performance is valued. I suggest that, although such authenticity would not be valued were it not a means to an independently valued end—the end of presenting the composer's interesting musical ideas—nevertheless, authenticity in musical performance is not valued *as* a means to this end.

Beyond the level of an acceptably competent performance, authenticity is value-conferring. That is, a musical performance is better for its being more authentic (other things being equal). Because we have an aesthetic concern with the musical interest of the composer's ideas, and because those musical ideas must be mediated by performance, we value authenticity in performance for the degree of faithfulness with which the performance realizes the composer's musical conception as recorded in the score. I am not maintaining that authenticity in performance takes its value from the worth of the musical content contributed by the composer. Rather, my point is this: were it not for the fact that composers set out to write aesthetically rewarding works, and were it not for the fact that they are usually successful in this, we would not value authenticity in musical performances as we do. But, in any particular instance, authenticity in performance is valued independently and irrespective of the aesthetic value of the work itself. A performance is better for a higher degree of authenticity (other things being equal) *whatever* the merits of the composition itself. A performance praiseworthy for its authenticity may make evident that the composer wrote a work with little musical interest or merit. It is the creative skill required of the performer in faithfully interpreting the composer's score which is valued in praising the authenticity of performances of that score.[10]

Of course, authenticity is not the only quality for which a performance might be valued. Where a relatively inauthentic performance is highly valued, it is valued *in spite of* its inauthenticity. Thus Schnabel's recorded performances of the Beethoven sonatas are well regarded despite the wrong notes that they contain.

VI

In this final section I emphasize how creative is the role of the performer in realizing faithfully the composer's specification. In developing the point a contrast is drawn between performing and copying.

The performance transforms the notes-as-written into the notes-as-sounds. In talking casually of the notes of a piece, and so obscuring this distinction, one might easily lose sight of the creativity of the role enacted by the performer in faithfully converting the one into the other. The sounded notes created by the performer go far beyond the bare peg which the composer provides and on which the musicians hang their art. An authentic performance concerns itself with the production of the notes which comprise the piece and which the composer specified, but the notes-as-sounds produced by the performer involve subtleties of attack, decay, dynamics, tone and so on which cannot be captured in any notation that composers are likely to use. The written notes and the way in which they are played come together inseparably in the notes-as-sounds, and it is in no way to under-value the role of the composer as the specifier of the notes-as-written to acknowledge that the musician brings something original to the notes-as-written in rendering them into sound.[11] The creative role of the performer, rather than involving a departure from the concern to realize faithfully the composer's intentions, is integral to the execution of that concern.

---

[10] Indulging in some armchair socio-biology: it is perhaps not surprising in a social species such as ours—which is concerned with successful communication and for which there can be no guarantee that any particular attempt at communication will not fail—that that which facilitates communication becomes valued for its own sake and apart from the worth of the contents which it helps to communicate. (Not that I think that music can usefully be compared to a language with respect to its meaning—see 'Is Music a Language of the Emotions?', *The British Journal of Aesthetics*, Vol. 23 (1983), pp. 222–33.)

[11] For a similar view see the end of Nigel Harrison's 'Creativity in Musical Performance', *The British Journal of Aesthetics*, Vol. 18 (1978), pp. 300–6.

What is more, rather than consisting of mere aggregations of notes, music comprises themes, chords, subjects, answers, sequences, recapitulations, developments, motifs, accompaniments, and so forth. These are gestalts (or aspects etc.) and not mere successions of notes. Because their articulation in sound owes as much or more to the performer as to the composer, it can be seen how extensive and important is the creative role of the performer.

One way of bringing out the creative role of the performer as a necessary intermediary between the composer and the audience is by contrasting performing and copying. Copying need not be intentional; copying may be a mechanical process performed by a machine. And where copying is intentional, the aim of faithfulness is to be contrasted with that of creativity. By contrast, performance always is intentional, because the performer must bring more than is supplied by the composer to a performance which is faithful to the composer's ideas. Performing must go beyond that which is given in order to present accurately that which is given. But nothing not present in the original needs to be brought to copying. A machine might copy a performance (for example, by recording it on tape), but performing is done only by agents.[12] And copies are authentic only in the sense contrasted with forgery or fakery, whereas performances are authentic in the sense which here has been under discussion. Authenticity is an attribute acknowledging the way in which the interpretation of a musical score is both necessary in the presentation of the music-as-sounds and is also inherently creative. Authenticity, as a praiseworthy attribute, acknowledges the ineliminability of the performer's contribution to the sound of the performance.[13]

[12] I do not deny that copying by hand an illuminated manuscript might require patience, skill, etc. in a way that suggests that copying is anything but mechanical in this instance. Nor do I wish to deny that there are imaginable cases in which computers are programmed to produce sounds where we would be tempted to say a machine performs. (Just as there are cases in which the musician performs *on* a violin without our saying the violin performs, so there are cases in which musicians perform *on* computers—but the example to be imagined is not of this type.) But if there were such computers, talk of them as machines would begin to look inapposite; at such a point one begins thinking in terms of intelligent or agent-like 'machines'.

[13] A number of people have commented helpfully on versions of this paper. In particular, I owe thanks to Denis Dutton and Graham Oddie and a special debt to Denis Robinson and Jan Crosthwaite.

The Concept of Authentic Performance

James O. Young

If you feel the seriousness of a tune, what are you perceiving?—Nothing that could be conveyed by reproducing what you heard.
                                                  Wittgenstein, *Investigations*, p. 210e.

Interest in early music has increased dramatically in recent years. Anyone at all cognizant of music is aware of a constant stream of books, journals, concerts, workshops, conferences and recordings devoted to early music. The extent of interest in early music is indicated by the fact that in Britain alone there are well over one-hundred professional ensembles engaged in the performance of early music.[1] The early music movement is not so much concerned with a period of music as with an artistic ideal. Within the movement's purlieu falls the music of all periods from classical antiquity through the middle ages, the renaissance, the baroque, classical and romantic periods to the early twentieth century. 'Modern' musicians, however, interpret much of this same repertoire. What distinguishes the advocates of early music is that they aim at 'authentic performance'.[2]

There can be no doubt that the early music movement has been of enormous value. Members of the movement have, however, been insufficiently reflective about the concept of authentic performance.[3] They believe that it is possible to give performances which are 'authentic'. These performances have, moreover, more than antiquarian interest. Authentic performance is supposed to represent an attractive artistic ideal. That is, an authentic performance is an artistically successful interpretation of a composition. However, had advocates of early music paused to reflect, they would have realized that authentic performance cannot be characterized in such a way that it represents an ideal which is both attainable and worth attaining. There are principled, not merely practical, reasons why authentic performance is not a realizable artistic ideal. Reflection on these reasons will provide insight into the nature of music and the experience of music.

Members of the early music movement tend to regard the quest for

---

[1] See the *Directory of British Early Music Groups* (London: Early Music Centre, 1981).

[2] Robert Donington, a distinguished authority on early music, writes, for example, that 'if you want the best that any music has to offer, you do well to go at it in the authentic way'. 'Why early music?' *Early Music*, 11 (1983), p. 45.

[3] But see three recent articles, one by a musician, one by a music critic and one by a philosopher. Ton Koopman, 'Some Thoughts on Authenticity', *Musick*, Vol. 8, No. 3 (1987), pp. 2–6; Will Crutchfield, 'The Meanings of "Authenticity"', *Oberlin Alumni Magazine*, Vol. 82, No. 4 (1986), pp. 4–9; and Stephen Davies, 'Authenticity in Musical Performance', reprinted in this book.

authentic performance as a process of solving musicological difficulties of a practical nature. They begin by compiling scores which are faithful to composers' manuscripts or to early editions. Performers of early music pay particular attention to scoring. They perform on authentic instruments and do so with an ensemble of the authentic size. Having determined a score and selected their instruments, performers of early music proceed to perform in accordance with authentic performance techniques, the techniques contemporary with a piece's composition. They also ensure that their instruments are tuned as they would have been at the time of composition. So, for example, a Beethoven piano concerto will be performed on a fortepiano (either an 'original instrument' or an authentic copy) and not on a modern concert grand. The stringed instruments will be strung in gut and the wind instruments will have fewer keys and otherwise differ from modern instruments. The orchestra will be much smaller than is now common and there will be a greater balance between the strings and winds. The fast movements will be played at a tempo slower than is now common and the slow movements will be rather faster. The A above middle C will be tuned to 435 cycles per second and not to the now-standard 440. If all practical questions of score, instrumentation, tuning, and performance techniques could be resolved, performers of early music believe, authentic performance is possible.

Of course, as advocates of authentic performance recognize, some practical obstacles to authentic performance will never be overcome. We will never know precisely how bowed instruments were used to accompany mediaeval songs. No scores have survived since the accompaniment was improvised. There are insurmountable practical obstacles to giving an authentic performance of even such a familiar piece as Mozart's Clarinet Concerto. As is well known, the piece was written for Anton Stadler. What is less known is that he did not play a clarinet at all but a basset clarinet. Precisely what sort of instrument Stadler would have played is unknown and, in all probability, will remain unknown. Moreover, the manuscript of Mozart's concerto does not survive. In the first printed edition of the concerto, published ten years after Mozart's death, the basset clarinet part is rewritten so as to be playable on a clarinet. It is possible to reconstruct the original score but not with complete accuracy. But the concept of authentic performance is not problematic for practical reasons. Imagine that there is an Omniscient Musicologist, a musicologist than whom no greater can be conceived. Such a musicologist would know everything about original scores, instruments, performance techniques and tuning. But the concept of authentic performance would still be problematic.

Suppose that, with the aid of the Omniscient Musicologist, all of the practical difficulties of the early music movement are overcome. It would then be possible to give the first characterization of authentic performance:

(1) An authentic performance is a performance which reproduces music
as it was heard at the time of its composition.

There are good reasons to suppose that authentic performances, so characterized, could not be given. But it should be apparent that, when conceived of in this manner, authentic performance does not even represent
an artistic ideal worth attaining.[4]
    The first point worth noting is that there are moral obstacles which
should prevent the authentic performance of certain compositions.
Consider the authentic performance of eighteenth-century opera.[5] Many
of the parts were written for, and performed by, castrati. Now, the tone
colour of a castrato's voice differs from that of a female alto or soprano.
But not even the most committed advocate of early music will think that
the ideal of authentic performance would justify the mutilation of pre-
pubescent boys. This is, perhaps, an extreme example but it serves to
demonstrate that there are moral constraints which should prohibit the
realization of the ideal of the authentic performance of all music.
    There are, however, no moral obstacles facing the authentic perfor-
mance of many compositions. These compositions, it might be thought,
could be heard as they were at the time of their composition. A problem,
however, immediately presents itself. If (1) is accepted, there will be a
question about how to give an authentic performance of pieces which
were not performed at the time of their composition. And there certainly
are pieces which were not so performed. The performance of such pieces
cannot reproduce how the music sounded at the period of their composition. Or, rather, the only authentic performance is non-performance—
which is scarcely an attractive artistic ideal. But most compositions were
heard within a short time of their composition. It is not clear, however,
why anyone would want to hear them that way again.
    Music must often have sounded perfectly atrocious at the time of its
composition. The instruments on which music was performed were often
in very bad repair. While in the service of Esterházy, Haydn had to contend with oboes in rotten condition.[6] In 1770 Charles Burney travelled
throughout France and Italy collecting material for his history of music.
He wrote that 'All the keyed instruments I have yet heard on the conti-
nent, except some of the organs[,] are very bad'. Of the spinets he heard in
Italy he wrote that 'the keys are so noisy and tone so feeble one hears
more wood than wire'.[7] If authentic performance is to reproduce music as
it was originally heard, performers of early music are committed to play-

---

[4] Davies reaches this conclusion for reasons similar to those given here.
[5] This same example is used by Davies, note 2.
[6] This is reported in Christopher Hogwood, *Music at Court* (London: The Folio Society, 1977),
p. 112.
[7] Charles Burney, *Music, Men, and Manners in France and Italy 1770* (London: The Folio
Society, 1969), p. 69.

ing Haydn's early symphonies on rotten oboes and to performing eighteenth-century Italian domestic music on decrepit harpsichords. Surely this is enough to render unappealing authentic performance as characterized in (1).

But it gets worse. Not only were the instruments of the eighteenth century often of a poor quality, but often the musicians were as well. Many of the best-known pieces of the eighteenth century were originally performed by amateurs. Handel's Chandos Anthems were first played by the Duke of Chandos' domestic staff. One of the players was recommended because 'He shaves very well & hath an excellent hand on the violin & all necessary languages'.[8] However good his hand may have been on the violin, it is unlikely that he played as well as a modern professional. Even the professional musicians of the period were not up to present standards. The difficulties which Mozart had with his players were, of course, legion. Mind you, he often did not make things easy for them. He often provided them with scores only a few days or even a few hours before a performance. So, if we accept (1) as the characterization of authentic performance, it seems that performers of early music must not allow themselves to become too accomplished and must, in some cases, take care not to rehearse their parts.

Of course, not every original performance was given by poor musicians on bad instruments. But the fact that many were is enough to render (1) untenable. Authentic performance should be characterized in such a way that artistically attractive authentic performances can be given of any piece, regardless of how it may originally have sounded. Moreover, it should be clear that (1) is not in accord with the actual practices of performers of early music. In deciding how to play a composition they do not attempt to determine whether the piece was played well or poorly. Rather, they attempt to decide how the composition *should* sound. Talk about how early music should sound suggests another account of authentic performance.

Recognizing that standards of musicianship and of instrument making have not always been what they now are, one might characterize authentic performance in terms of the intentions of composers.[9] One might adopt the following account of authentic performance.

(2) An authentic performance is one in which a composition sounds the way its composer intended it to sound.

This characterization will avoid many of the objections to which (1) is subject. Unfortunately, if authentic performance is so characterized, there is

---

[8] Quoted in Christopher Hogwood, *Handel* (London: Thames and Hudson, 1984), p. 73.
[9] The harpsichordist Ralph Kirkpatrick reports that his aim is to perform 'harpsichord and clavichord music in a manner as close as possible to what could be ascertained of the intentions of the composers'. 'Fifty years of harpsichord playing', *Early Music*, 11 (1983), p. 31.

no way to determine which performances are authentic. And it is not even clear that (2) represents an ideal worth attaining.

The second account of authentic performance fails because of our inability to determine all of a composer's intentions. Certainly it is possible to know with a fair degree of certainty what some of a composer's intentions were. No doubt he intended that his compositions should sound as they do when played on the instruments available at the time of composition. And, no doubt, he intended that the instruments should be tuned as was customary in the period. The Omniscient Musicologist will be able to tell us a great deal about how a composer intended his works to sound. But there is a great deal that not even an Omniscient Musicologist can know. The totality of possible musicological evidence will underdetermine the selection of one performance as more authentic than another.

There is no possible evidence which will determine precisely what a composer's intentions were with respect to all aspects of the interpretation of a piece. The possible evidence could take one of two forms. Musicologists could discover a composer's instructions about how to play a piece and reports may survive about how he actually performed one of his compositions. In practice, of course, even this evidence is often unavailable. But if it were available to an Omniscient Musicologist, it would still not determine which performances are authentic. Even complete reports of a composer's own performance of a solo piece would not be decisive evidence. There is no guarantee that even a composer's own performance realized his intentions. Not even a composer's own reports would be decisive evidence. The knowledge of how a piece is to be interpreted is, in large measure, practical knowledge, a knowledge of how something is to be done. Such knowledge, like the knowledge of how to ride a bicycle, cannot be fully captured in propositional terms. Not even the composer will be able to describe precisely what his intentions were. If we cannot know what a composer's intentions were, we cannot determine which performances are authentic and which are not and (2) is unsatisfactory.

Even if authentic performance could be characterized in terms of composers' intentions, it is not clear that, so characterized, it would be an attractive artistic ideal. Composers may not be the best interpreters of their own compositions. Once a piece has been composed, the composer's views on how it is best performed are no better than those of any qualified musician. And they may be worse. Frescobaldi left very detailed instructions on how to perform his keyboard compositions.[10] These instructions do not, of course, determine the choice of authentic performances. But even if they did, performers might be wise to disregard them. Many musicians, including those interested in authentic performance, disregard

---

[10] Selections from Frescobaldi's instructions are found in *Composers on Music*, ed. Sam Morgenstern (New York: Pantheon, 1956), pp. 24–6.

but also express the painter's thoughts of Washington as benevolent and fatherly.

By contrast, Scruton argues, the relation between a photograph and its subject is a *causal* relationship. And by this he means that a photograph is merely a record of how its subject looked at the time the photograph was taken. In Scruton's view, photography (unlike painting) is an essentially *mechanical* process. (This point comes out especially clearly when you think about vacation snapshots. Indeed, camera manufacturers often emphasize the causal and mechanical simplicity of photography when advertising their products: "Auto focus! Just point and shoot!") Because of its causal and mechanical nature, a photograph can express no thoughts about its subject—it "is not interesting as the realization of an intention." Representations are essentially intentional—they express thoughts. Given that photographs are not intentional—they cannot express thoughts—photography cannot be a representational art. This is one of Scruton's conclusions.

Another conclusion, closely related to the first, is that photographs do not invite the kind of aesthetic interest that paintings characteristically do. An aesthetic interest in representation, he claims, is an "interest not in representation for the sake of its subject but in representation for its own sake." To be interested in a portrait solely as a record of what its subject looked like is not to be aesthetically interested in the portrait as a representation. It is to treat the portrait as a *surrogate* for its subject, to ignore "the way the painting presents its subject" and therefore to ignore the thoughts about the subject expressed by the painter. So we may be interested in a painting either as a surrogate for its subject *or* as a representation. By contrast, we can *only* be interested in a photograph as a surrogate. "If one finds a photograph beautiful, it is because one finds something beautiful in its subject. A painting may be beautiful, on the other hand, even when it represents an ugly thing." If we have an aesthetic interest in photographs, then, it is not the same as our aesthetic interest in paintings. The reasons we have for looking at photographs are different from the reasons we have for looking at paintings. Indeed, Scruton goes so far as to suggest that "the medium of photography . . . is inherently pornographic."

Given his conclusions, it is hardly surprising that Scruton's essay has provoked responses from other writers. In the second reading in this section, William L. King takes issue with Scruton's claim that photographs, being surrogates for their subjects, do not invite the kind of aesthetic interest that paintings characteristically do. King accepts that much of our interest in many photographs is interest in their subjects. Indeed, he distinguishes two sorts of interest that we may have in a photograph's subject: We may be interested in "how the subject appears," or in the "evocative power of the subject." We may also be interested in "the formal appearance of the photograph," or in the cause of that appearance. Most important, however, King contends that at least some photographs can be interesting in the way that paintings can be, "namely, aesthetically interesting by virtue of the manner of representation." He attempts to rebut Scruton's conclusion by showing that our reasons for looking at a photograph will often be different from our reasons for looking at its subject: In looking at a photograph, he argues, we may be interested in *"the manner of representing the subject."*

King does establish how varied an aesthetic engagement with photography can be. But does he establish all that he wants? The examples he offers certainly cast serious doubts on Scruton's claim that photographs must be treated merely as surrogates for their subjects (and hence on the claim that photography is inherently pornographic). But does it follow from this that photographs can be representations? Furthermore, does it follow that our aesthetic interest in photographs, even if they *are* representations, is an interest in them *as* representations? Another possibility is that photography, though representational, is not representational in the way that painting is. If that were true, then our aesthetic interest in photographs as representations might not be at all similar to our aesthetic interest in paintings as representations.

So the attempt to understand photography in terms derived from painting has left us with a hatful of questions. Is it true that representation is essentially intentional? Is it true that photography is essentially causal, and thus that photography cannot represent things? Is an interest in a photograph *always* an interest in its subject, and never an interest in the way the subject is presented. Do we always treat photographs as surrogates for their subjects? Whatever the answers we give to these questions, the point is that in thinking hard about representation (as Scruton invites us to do), and about the nature of our aesthetic interest in photographs (as King invites us to do), we are forced to ask exactly *what* kind of an art photography is. Is it an entirely new art form? Or is it just like painting, only less so?

Photography and Representation

Roger Scruton

Critics and philosophers have occasionally been troubled by the question whether the cinema is an independent art form—independent, that is, of the theatre, from which it borrows so many conventions.[1] This question can be traced back to a more basic one, the question whether photography is capable of representing anything. I shall argue that it is not and that, insofar as there is representation in film, its origin is not photographic. A film is a photograph of a dramatic representation; it is not, because it cannot be, a photographic representation. It follows that if there is such a thing as a cinematic masterpiece it will be so because—like *Wild Strawberries* and *Le règle du jeu*—it is in the first place a dramatic masterpiece.

It seems odd to say that photography is not a mode of representation. For a photograph has in common with a painting the property by which the painting represents the world, the property of sharing, in some sense, the appearance of its subject. Indeed, it is sometimes thought that since a photograph more effectively shares the appearance of its subject than a typical painting, photography is a better mode of representation. Photography might even be thought to have *replaced* painting as a mode of visual representation. Painters have felt that if the aim of painting is really to reproduce the appearances of things, then painting must give way to whatever means are available to reproduce an appearance more accurately. It has therefore been said that painting aims to record the appearances of things only so as to capture the experience of observing them (the *impression*) and that the accurate copying of appearances will normally be at variance with this aim. Here we have the seeds of expressionism and the origin of the view (a view which not only is mistaken but which has also proved disastrous for the history of modern art) that painting is somehow purer when it is abstract and closer to its essence as an art.

Let us first dismiss the word 'representation'. Of course this word can be applied to photography. We wish to know whether there is some feature, suitably called representation, common to painting and photography. And we wish to know whether that feature has in each case a comparable aesthetic value, so that we can speak not only of representation but also of representational art. (There is an important feature—sound—in common to music and to fountains, but only the first of these is properly described as an *art* of sound.)

---

[1] See for example, the discussions in Allardyce Nicoll, *Film and Theatre* (London, 1936; New York, 1972).

1

In order to understand what I mean by saying that photography is not a representational art, it is important to separate painting and photography as much as possible, so as to discuss not actual painting and actual photography but an ideal form of each, an ideal which represents the essential differences between them. Ideal photography differs from actual photography as indeed ideal painting differs from actual painting. Actual photography is the result of the attempt by photographers to pollute the ideal of their craft with the aims and methods of painting.

By an 'ideal' I mean a logical ideal. The ideal of photography is not an ideal at which photography aims or ought to aim. On the contrary, it is a logical fiction, designed merely to capture what is distinctive in the photographic relation and in our interest in it. It will be clear from this discussion that there need be no such thing as an ideal photograph in my sense, and the reader should not be deterred if I begin by describing photography in terms that seem to be exaggerated or false.

The ideal painting stands in a certain 'intentional' relation to a subject.[2] In other words, if a painting represents a subject, it does not follow that the subject exists nor, if it does exist, that the painting represents the subject as it is. Moreover, if x is a painting of a man, it does not follow that there is some *particular* man of which x is the painting. Furthermore, the painting stands in this intentional relation to its subject because of a representational act, the artist's act, and in characterizing the relation between a painting and its subject we are also describing the artist's intention. The successful realization of that intention lies in the creation of an appearance, an appearance which in some way leads the spectator to recognize the subject.

The ideal photograph also stands in a certain relation to a subject: a photograph is a photograph *of* something. But the relation is here causal and not intentional.[3] In other words, if a photograph is a photograph of a subject, it follows that the subject exists, and if x is a photograph of a man, there is a particular man of whom x is the photograph. It also follows, though for different reasons, that the subject is, roughly, as it appears in the photograph. In characterizing the relation between the ideal photograph and its subject, one is characterizing not an intention but a causal process, and while there is, as a rule, an intentional act involved, this is not an essential part of the photographic relation. The ideal photograph also yields an appearance, but the appearance is not interesting as the re-

---

[2] See Franz Clemens Brentano, *Psychology from an Empirical Standpoint*, ed. Linda McAlister (London and New York, 1973); Roderick M. Chisholm, *Perceiving* (London and Ithaca, NY, 1957), chapter 11; and G. E. M. Anscombe, 'The Intentionality of Sensation', in R. J. Butler (ed.), *Analytical Philosophy*, Second Series (Oxford, 1965).

[3] I think that in this area nonextensionality (intensionality) and intentionality should be sharply distinguished, so that the claim is not affected by any argument to the effect that causal relations are nonextensional.

alization of an intention but rather as a record of how an actual object looked.

Since the end point of the two processes is, or can be, so similar, it is tempting to think that the intentionality of the one relation and the causality of the other are quite irrelevant to the standing of the finished product. In both cases, it seems, the important part of representation lies in the fact that the spectator can see the subject *in* the picture. The appreciation of photographs and the appreciation of paintings both involve the exercise of the capacity to 'see as', in the quite special sense in which one may see *x* as *y* without believing or being tempted to believe that *x* is *y*.

2

Now, it would be a simple matter to define 'representation' so that '*x* represents *y*' is true only if *x* expresses a thought about *y*, or if *x* is designed to remind one of *y*, or whatever, in which case a relation that was *merely* causal (a relation that was not characterized in terms of any thought, intention, or other mental act) would never be sufficient for representation. We need to be clear, however, why we should wish to define representation in one way rather than in another. What hangs on the decision? In particular, why should it matter that the relation between a painting and its subject is an intentional relation while the photographic relation is merely causal? I shall therefore begin by considering our experience of painting and the effect on that experience of the intentionality of the relation between a painting and its subject.

When I appreciate a painting as a representation, I see it as what it represents, but I do not take it for what it represents. Nor do I necessarily believe that what is represented in the painting exists nor, if it does exist, that it has the appearance of the object that I see *in* the painting. Suppose that a certain painting represents a warrior. I may in fact see it not as a warrior but as a god. Here three 'objects' of interest may be distinguished:

1 The intentional object of sight: a god (defined by my experience).
2 The represented object: a warrior (defined, to put it rather crudely, by the painter's intention).[4]
3 The material object of sight: the painting.[5]

The distinction between 1 and 2 is not as clear-cut as it might seem: it would become so only if we could separate the 'pure appearance' of the painting from the sense of intention with which it is endowed. We cannot do this, not only because we can never separate our experience of human activity from our understanding of intention but also because in the case of a picture we are dealing with an object that is manifestly the expression

---

[4] I pass over the problem here of selecting and describing the appropriate intention.
[5] For the material/intentional distinction, I rely on Anscombe.

of thought. Hence we will look for clues as to how the painting is intended to be seen and—such being the nature of 'seeing as'—our sense of what is intended will determine our experience of what is there.

The 'inference' view of perception, the view that there are certain things that we *basically* see (sense-data, etc) from which we then *infer* the existence of other things, is wrong both as a matter of philosophical psychology, since there is no criterion for distinguishing datum and inference, and as a matter of epistemology, since it is only if we sometimes have knowledge of the 'inferred' entities that we can have knowledge of the experience.[6] The point applies also to intention: we do not see the gestures and movements of another man and then infer from them the existence of intentions; rather, we see the gestures as intentional, and that is the correct description of what we see. But of course we cannot choose to see just what we will as a manifestation of intention. Our ability to see intention depends on our ability to interpret an activity as characteristically human, and here, in the case of representational art, it involves our understanding the dimensions and conventions of the medium. Art manifests the 'common knowledge' of a culture;[7] as E. H. Gombrich has made clear, to understand art is to be familiar with the constraints imposed by the medium and to be able to separate that which is due to the medium from that which is due to the man. Such facts lead us to speak of understanding or misunderstanding representational painting.

Although there is not space to discuss fully the concept of 'understanding' that is involved here, it is worth mentioning the following point: to understand a painting involves understanding thoughts. These thoughts are, in a sense, communicated by the painting. They underlie the painter's intention, and at the same time they inform our way of seeing the canvas. Such thoughts determine the perception of the man who sees with understanding, and it is at least partly in terms of our apprehension of thoughts that we must describe what we see in the picture. We see not only a man on a horse but a man of a certain character and bearing. And *what* we see is determined not by independent properties of the subject but by our understanding of the painting. It is the way the eyes are painted that gives that sense of authority, the particular lie of the arm that reveals the arrogant character, and so on. In other words, properties of the medium influence not only what is seen in the picture but also the way it is seen. Moreover, they present to us a vision that we attribute not to ourselves but to another man; we think of ourselves as sharing in the vision

---

[6] The most famous arguments for this conclusion occur in Kant's *Critique of Pure Reason* (in particular in the 'Transcendental Deduction') and in Wittgenstein's *Philosophical Investigations*, part I.

[7] The importance of 'common knowledge', its complexity as a phenomenon, and its natural co-existence with conventions has been recognized in the philosophy of language; see especially the interesting discussion in David K. Lewis, *Convention: a Philosophical Study* (Cambridge, Mass., 1969; Oxford, 1972).

of the artist, and the omnipresence of intention changes our experience from something private into something shared. The picture presents us not merely with the perception of a man but with a thought about him, a thought embodied in perceptual form.[8] And here, just as in the case of language, thought has that character of objectivity and publicity upon which Frege commented.[9] It is precisely when we have the communication of thoughts about a subject that the concept of representation becomes applicable; and therefore literature and painting are representational in the same sense.

3

The ideal painting has no particular need for an identity of appearance with its subject. In order to present a visual account of the Duke of Wellington, it is not necessary for an artist to strive to present an exact copy of the Duke's appearance.[10] Indeed, it is tempting here to dispense with the notion of appearance altogether, to construe the painting as a conventional or even quasi-linguistic act which stands in a semantic relation—a relation of reference—to its subject, and which presents a visual appearance only as a means of fulfilling a referential function. Such a view would explain, perhaps better than all rival theories of representation, the role of intention in our understanding of art.[11]

I do not know how far those philosophers influenced by Gombrich's arguments—arguments emphasizing the place of convention in our understanding of visual art—would wish to take the analogy with language. I do not know, for example, whether a convention according to which colours were to be represented by their complements—a red object by a patch of green, a yellow object by a patch of blue—would be conceivable for such philosophers, conceivable, that is, as a mode of pictorial representation. It is undeniable, however, that such a painting would convey to someone who understood the convention as much information about its subject as another painting in which the colours copy the original. More bizarre conventions could also be imagined: a painting could be constructed entirely out of dashes and circles, arranged according to the grammar of a visual code. Given the right conventions, such a painting would count, according to the reference theory, as an extremely faithful representation of its subject. It would be read as a kind of scrambled mes-

---

[8] I have discussed elsewhere what I mean by the 'embodiment' of thought in perception; see my *Art and Imagination*, chapters 7 and 8.

[9] G. Frege, *Translations from the Philosophical Writings*, p. 79.

[10] There is a problem here about 'identity of appearance' on which I touch again, pp. 116–17.

[11] Nelson Goodman, the most important exponent of a semantic theory of art, manages to reconcile his approach with a view of photographs as representational; see his *Languages of Art*, p. 9n.

sage which had to be decoded in order to permit an understanding of what it says.

However, we cannot treat the visual connection between a painting and its subject as an entirely accidental matter, accidental, that is, to any process of representation that the painting may display. For we cannot deny that representational painting interests us primarily because of the visual connection with its subject. We are interested in the visual relation between painting and subject because it is by means of this relation that the painting represents. The artist presents us with a way of seeing (and not just any way of thinking of) his subject. (Hence the revolutionary character of such painters as Caravaggio and de la Tour.) It is this visual relation which seems to require elucidation. We cannot explain pictorial representation independently of the visual aspect of paintings and still expect our explanation to cast light upon the problem of the visual relation between a picture and its subject-matter. And yet it is that relation which is understood by the appreciative spectator.

That objection is of course not conclusive. It also seems to assume that a semantic theory of art (a theory which sees representation in terms of reference) must necessarily also be a linguistic theory. Surely there could be relations of reference that do not reflect the conventions of language, even relations that need to be understood in essentially visual terms. Let us, then, consider what such a conception of reference might be like.

It is no accident that language has a grammar. The existence of grammar is a necessary part of language and part of the all-important connection between language and truth. But there is a further significance in grammar, at least as grammar is now conceived. For the contemporary logician, grammar is primarily a 'generative' function, a means of building complex sentences from the finite number of linguistic parts. Taken in conjunction with a theory of interpretation, a proper grammar will explain how speakers of a language understand an indefinite number of sentences on the basis of understanding only a finite number of words.[12] In this way we can show how the truth or falsehood of a sentence depends upon the reference of its parts, and the concept of reference in language becomes inextricably bound up with the idea that from the references of words we may derive the truth conditions of sentences. This 'generative connection' between reference and truth is part of the intuitive understanding of reference which is common to all speakers of a language.

It is here, I think, that we find a striking difference between language and painting. While there may be repertoires and conventions in painting, there is nothing approaching grammar as we understand it. For one thing,

---

[12] I draw here on the now familiar arguments given by Donald Davidson in 'Truth and Meaning,' which originate with Frege and which were given full mathematical elaboration in Alfred Tarski's theory of truth.

the requirement of finitude is not obviously met. It is clearly true that we understand the representational meaning of, say, a Carpaccio through understanding the representational meaning of its parts. But the parts themselves are understood in *precisely the same way;* that is, they too have parts, each of which is potentially divisible into significant components, and so on ad infinitum. Moreover, there seems to be no way in which we can divide the painting into grammatically significant parts—no way in which we can provide a syntax which isolates those parts of the painting that have a particular semantic role. For in advance of seeing the painting, we have no rule which will decide the point, and thus the idea of syntactic or semantic rules becomes inapplicable. The means whereby we understand the total representation are identical with the means whereby we understand the parts. Understanding is not secured either by rules or by conventions but seems to be, on the contrary, a natural function of the normal eye. As we see the meaning of the painting, so do we see the meaning of its parts. This contrasts sharply with the case of reference in language, where we *construct* the meaning of the sentence from the reference of its parts, and where the parts themselves have reference in a way that is ultimately conventional.

There seems to be no justification, then, for thinking of representation in terms of reference. We could, however, insist that the relation of a painting to its subject is one of reference only by removing from 'reference' that feature which leads us to think that an account of reference is also an account of understanding. To speak of the connection between a word and a thing as one of reference is to show how we understand the word, for it is to show how the truth conditions of sentences containing the word are determined. If we speak of reference in describing paintings, therefore, we should not think that we thereby cast any light on the *understanding* of representation. What representation is, how we understand it, and how it affects us—those questions seem to remain as obscure as ever. The only thing that remains to support the invocation of reference is the fact that paintings may be true or false. It is that fact which we must now consider.

4

The fact that a painting may be true or false plays a vital role in visual appreciation. We could not explain realism, for example, either in painting or in literature, unless we invoked the concept of truth. Again we must emphasize information (and therefore the concept of reference) in our understanding of the painter's art; or at least we are obliged to find some feature of the painting that can be substituted for reference and which will show how the connection with truth is established.

Such a feature, as a matter of fact, has already been described: we may describe realism in terms of what we see *in* the painting. We therefore analyse truth not in terms of a relation between the painting and the world but in terms of a relation between what we see in the painting and the world. Goya's portrait of the Duke of Wellington is realistic because the figure we see in the painting resembles the Duke of Wellington.[13] The truth of the painting amounts to the truth of the viewer's perception; in other words, the 'intentional object of sight' corresponds to the nature of the subject. Those thoughts which animate our perception when we see the realistic painting with understanding are true thoughts.[14] Truth is not a property of the painting in the direct way in which it is the property of a sentence, and the possibility of predicating the truth of a painting does not open the way to a semantic theory of art any more than it opens the way to a semantic theory of, for example, clouds, or of any other phenomenon in which aspects may be seen.

Although distinctions may be made between true and false pictures, an aesthetic appreciation remains in one sense indifferent to the truth of its object. A person who has an aesthetic interest in the *Odyssey* is not concerned with the literal truth of the narrative. Certainly it is important to him that the *Odyssey* be lifelike, but the existence of Odysseus and the reality of the scenes described are matters of aesthetic indifference. Indeed, it is characteristic of aesthetic interest that most of its objects in representation are imaginary. For unless it were possible to represent imaginary things, representation could hardly be very important to us. It is important because it enables the presentation of scenes and characters toward which we have only contemplative attitudes: scenes and characters which, being unreal, allow our practical natures to remain unengaged.

If the concept of representation is to be of aesthetic importance, it must be possible to describe an aesthetic interest in representation. Only if there is such a thing as aesthetic interest which has representation as its object can there be representational art (as opposed to art that happens to be representational). It is commonly said that an aesthetic interest in something is an interest in it for its own sake: the object is not treated as a surrogate for another; it is *itself* the principal object of attention. It follows that an aesthetic interest in the representational properties of a picture must also involve a kind of interest in the picture and not merely in the thing represented.[15]

Now, *one* difference between an aesthetic interest in a picture, and an interest in the picture as a surrogate for its subject, lies in the kind of reason that might be given for the interest. (And to give the reasons for an interest is to give an account of its intentional object and therefore of the interest itself.) If I ask a man why he is looking at a picture, there are several

[13] That is, provided the painting is independently *of* the Duke of Wellington.

[14] See n. 8, above.

[15] Hence the tradition in philosophy, which begins with Kant, according to which representation constitutes a threat to the autonomy of art.

kinds of reply that he might give. In one case his reasons will be reasons for an interest only in the things depicted: they will describe properties of the subject which make it interesting. Here the interest in the picture is derivative: it lies in the fact that the picture reveals properties of its subject. The picture is being treated as a means of access to the subject, and it is therefore dispensable to the extent that there is a better means to hand (say, the subject itself). With that case one may contrast two others. First, there is the case where the man's reasons refer only to properties of the picture—to pictorial properties, such as colour, shape, and line—and do not mention the subject. For such a man the picture has interest as an abstract composition, and its representational nature is wholly irrelevant to him. Second, there is the case where the reasons for the interest are reasons for an interest in the *picture* (in the way it looks) even though they make essential reference to the subject and can be understood as reasons only by someone who understands the reference to the subject. For example, the observer may refer to a particular gesture of a certain figure, and a particular way of painting that gesture, as revelatory of the subject's character (for example, the barmaid's hands on the counter in Manet's *Bar aux Folies-Bergère*). Clearly, that is a reason not only for an interest in the subject but also (and primarily) for an interest in the picture, since it gives a reason for an interest in something which can be understood only by looking at the picture. Such an interest leads naturally to another, to an interest in the use of the medium—in the way the painting presents its subject and therefore in the way in which the subject is seen by the painter. Here it could not be said that the painting is being treated as a surrogate for its subject: it is *itself* the object of interest and irreplaceable by the thing depicted. The interest is not in representation for the sake of its subject but in representation for its own sake. And it is such an interest that forms the core of the aesthetic experience of pictorial art, and which—if analysed more fully—would explain not only the value of that experience but also the nature and value of the art which is its object. We see at once that such an interest it not, and cannot be, an interest in the literal truth of the picture.

5

If I were to describe, then, *what I see* in a picture, I would be bound not merely to describe the visual properties of the subject but also to provide an interpretation of the subject, a way of seeing it. The description under which the subject is seen is given by the total thought in terms of which I understand the picture. In the case of portraiture, this interpretive thought need not be a thought about the momentary appearance of the subject: it need not be the thought 'He looked like that'. The thought may relate to the subject not as he appeared at any one moment but as he was or, rather, as the artist saw him to be. The appearance may be presented only because it embodies the reality, in which case it will be the reality that is understood (or misunderstood) by the spectator.

One of the most important differences between photography and portraiture as traditionally practised lies in the relation of each to time. It is characteristic of photography that, being understood in terms of a causal relation to its subject, it is thought of as revealing something momentary about its subject—how the subject looked at a particular moment. And that sense of the moment is seldom lost in photography, for reasons that will shortly be apparent. Portrait painting, however, aims to capture the sense of time and to represent its subject as extended in time, even in the process of displaying a particular moment of its existence. Portraiture is not an art of the momentary, and its aim is not merely to capture fleeting appearances. The aim of painting is to give insight, and the creation of an appearance is important mainly as the expression of thought. While a causal relation is a relation between events, there is no such narrow restriction on the subject-matter of a thought. This perhaps partially explains the frequently made comment that the true art of portraiture died with the advent of photography and that representational art, insofar as it still pursues an ideal of realism, is unable to capture, as the realist ought to capture, the sense of the passage of time.[16]

Of course a photographer can aim to capture that fleeting appearance which gives the most reliable indication of his subject's character. He may attempt to find in the momentary some *sign* of what is permanent. But there is a great difference between an image which is a sign of something permanent and an image which is an expression of it. To express the permanent is to give voice to a thought about its nature. To give a sign of the permanent is to create something from which its properties may be inferred. A man may remain silent when asked to defend his friend, and from that silence I infer his friend's guilt. Yet the man has certainly not expressed the thought that his friend is guilty. Similarly a photograph may give signs of what is permanent despite the fact that it is incapable of expressing it.

6

The ideal photograph, as I mentioned earlier, stands in a causal relation to its subject and 'represents' its subject by reproducing its appearance. In understanding something as an ideal photograph, we understand it as exemplifying this causal process, a process which originates in the subject

---

[16] I am thinking of recent exercises in 'photographic' realism by such painters as Ken Danby and Alex Colville. More traditional styles of realism have also emerged in open opposition to both the clinical lines of the photographic school and the contentless images of abstract expressionism. Witness here the paintings of David Inshaw and Robert Lowe.

'represented' and which has as its end point the production of a copy of an appearance. By a 'copy' of an appearance I mean an object such that what is seen in it by a man with normal eyes and understanding (the intentional object of sight) resembles as nearly as possible what is seen when such a man observes the subject itself from a certain angle at a certain point in its history. A person studying an ideal photograph is given a very good idea of *how something looked.* The result is that, from studying a photograph he may come to know how something looked in the way that he might know it if he had actually seen it.

With an ideal photograph it is neither necessary nor even possible that the photographer's intention should enter as a serious factor in determining how the picture is seen. It is recognized at once for what it is—not as an interpretation of reality but as a presentation of how something looked. In some sense, looking at a photograph is a substitute for looking at the thing itself. Consider, for example, the most 'realistic' of all photographic media, the television. It seems scarcely more contentious to say that I saw someone on the television—that is, that in watching the television I saw *him*—than to say that I saw him in a mirror. Television is like a mirror: it does not so much destroy as embellish that elaborate causal chain which is the natural process of visual perception.

Of course it is not necessary to define the subject of a photograph in terms of this causal process, for the subject could be identified in some other way. But the fact remains that when we say that x is a photograph of y we *are* referring to this causal relation, and it is in terms of the causal relation that the subject of a photograph is normally understood. Let us at least say that the subject is so defined for my logical ideal of photography: that premise is all that my argument requires.

It follows, first, that the subject of the ideal photograph must exist; secondly, that it must appear roughly as it appears in the photograph; and thirdly, that its appearance in the photograph is its appearance at a particular moment of its existence.

The first of those features is an immediate consequence of the fact that the relation between a photograph and its subject is a causal relation. If a is the cause of b, then the existence of b is sufficient for the existence of a. The photograph lacks that quality of 'intentional inexistence' which is characteristic of painting. The ideal photograph, therefore, is incapable of representing anything unreal; if a photograph is a photograph of a man, then there is some particular man of whom it is a photograph.

Of course I may take a photograph of a draped nude and call it *Venus,* but insofar as this can be understood as an exercise in fiction, it should not be thought of as a photographic representation of Venus but rather as the photograph of a representation of Venus. In other words, the process of fictional representation occurs not in the photograph but in the subject: it is the *subject* which represents Venus; the photograph does no more than disseminate its visual character to other eyes. This is not to say that the model is (unknown to herself) acting Venus. It is not she who is representing Venus but the photographer, who uses her in his representation. But the representational act, the act which embodies the representational thought, is completed before the photograph is even taken. As we shall see, this fictional incompetence of photography is of great importance in our understanding of the cinema; but it also severely limits the aesthetic significance of 'representation' in photography. As we saw earlier, representation in art has a special significance precisely because of the possibility that we can understand it—in the sense of understanding its content—while being indifferent to, or unconcerned with, its literal truth. That is why fictional representation is not merely an important form of representational art but in fact the primary form of it, the form through which the aesthetic understanding finds its principal mode of expression.

One may wish to argue that my example is a special one, that there are other ways of creating fictional representations which are essentially photographic. In other words, it is not necessary for the photographer to create an independent representation in order for his photograph to be fictional. Suppose he were to take a photograph of a drunken tramp and label it *Silenus.* Would that not be a fictional photograph, comparable, indeed, to a painting of Silenus in which a drunken tramp was used as a model?

This example, which I owe to Richard Wollheim, is an interesting one, but it does not, I think, establish what it claims. Consider a parallel case: finding a drunken tramp in the street I point to him and say 'Silenus'. It is arguable that my gesture makes the tramp into a representation; but if it does, it is because I am inviting you to think of him in that way. I have expressed a representational thought: imagine this person as Silenus. And I have completed the thought by an act of ostension toward its dozing subject. The act of ostension might on some other occasion be accomplished by a camera (or a frame, or a mirror, or any other device which isolates what it shows).

The camera, then, is being used not to represent something but to point to it. The subject, once located, plays its own special part in an independent process of representation. The camera is not essential to that process: a gesturing finger would have served just as well. If the example shows that photographs can be representations, then it shows the same of fingers. To accept that conclusion is to fail to distinguish between what is accidental and what is essential in the expression of a representational thought. It is to open the way toward the theory that everything which plays a part in the expression of thought is itself a representation. Such a view does not account for the aesthetic significance of representations. It also, however, and far more seriously, implies that there is no distinction between representational and nonrepresentational art. The concept of representation that I am assuming makes such a distinction, and it makes it for very good reasons. I am not tempted by such dubious examples to abandon it. One might put the point by saying that a painting, like a sentence, is a *complete* expression of the thought which it contains. Painting is a sufficient vehicle of representational thought, and there may be no better way of expressing what a painting says. That is why representation can be thought of as an intrinsic property of a painting and not just as a property of some process of which the painting forms a part.

Consider also the second feature mentioned above: the subject of an ideal photograph must appear roughly as it appears in the photograph. By its very nature, photography can 'represent' only through resemblance. It is only because the photograph acts as a visual reminder of its subject that we are tempted to say that it represents its subject. If it were not for this resemblance, it would be impossible to see from the photograph how the subject appeared, except by means of scientific knowledge that would be irrelevant to any interest in the visual aspect of the photograph. Contrast here the case of an electron microscope, which punches out on a ticker tape a codified indication of a crystal's atomic structure. Is that a representation of the atomic structure? If it is, then why not say that any causal relation which enables us to infer the nature of the cause from the properties of its effect provides us with a representation of the cause in the effect? Such a concept of representation would be uninteresting indeed. It is impossible, therefore, that the ideal photograph should represent an object except by showing how it appeared at a certain moment in its history and still *represent* it in the way ideal photography represents anything. How indeed could we make sense of an ideal photograph representing its subject *as* other than it appeared? We could do so only if we could also say that a photograph sometimes represents its subject as it appears; that is, if we could say that representation here is 'representation as'. But consider this sentence: x is an ideal photograph of y as z. It seems that we have no means of filling out the description 'z', no means, that is, of filling it out by reference only to the photographic process and not, say, to some independent act of representation that precedes or follows it. One might say that the medium in photography has lost all importance: it can present us with what we see, but it cannot tell us how to see it.

We *must* be aware of the three features mentioned above if we are to appreciate the characteristic effects of photography. In looking at an ideal photograph, we know that we are seeing something which actually occurred and seeing it as it appeared. Typically, therefore, our attitude toward photography will be one of curiosity, not curiosity about the photograph but rather about its subject. The photograph addresses itself to our desire for knowledge of the world, knowledge of how things look or seem. The photograph is a means to the end of seeing its subject; in painting, on the other hand, the subject is the means to the end of its own representation. The photograph is transparent to its subject, and if it holds our interest it does so because it acts as a surrogate for the thing which it shows. Thus if one finds a photograph beautiful, it is because one finds something beautiful in its subject. A painting may be beautiful, on the other hand, even when it represents an ugly thing.

7

Someone might accept the general difference I have indicated between an aesthetic interest and an attitude of curiosity, and accept too the implication that something is a representation only if it is capable of carrying a reference to its subject without merely standing as a surrogate for it. He still might argue, however, that is possible to be interested in a photograph *as* a photograph and find it, and not just its subject, beautiful.

But what is it to be interested in a photograph as a photograph? Of course one might have a purely abstract aesthetic interest in a photograph—an interest in the photograph as a construction of lines and shapes (as one is intended to appreciate Man Ray's Rayogrammes, for example). One can have a purely abstract aesthetic interest in anything; photography is only a representational art if our interest in a photograph as a photographic 'representation' is a type of aesthetic interest.

Let us return to the previous discussion of representation in painting. It appears that there is a prima facie contradiction between saying that I am interested in a thing for its own sake and saying that I am interested in it as a representation of something else. In attempting to reconcile these two interests, it is necessary first to restrict the place of truth in aesthetic interest. Truth is aesthetically relevant only insofar as it may be construed as truth to the situation presented rather than 'truth to the facts'. From the point of view of aesthetic interest, it is always irrelevant that there should be a particular object which is the object represented or, if there is such an object, that it should exist as portrayed. That is not to say, of course, that an aesthetic interest does not require things to be in general roughly as they are shown; but that is another matter.

As I have already said, this conflicts with the typical way in which we are interested in photographs. Knowing what we know about photographs, it is at least natural that we should be interested in them both because they are true to the facts and because they tell us useful things about their subject-matter. It seems, therefore, that the emotional or 'aesthetic' qualities of a photograph tend to derive directly from the qualities of what it 'represents': if the photograph is sad, it is usually because its subject is sad; if the photograph is touching, it is because its subject is touching, and so on. It is worth reflecting on why there could not be a photograph of a martyrdom that was other than horrifying. One's curiosity here would be no different from one's curiosity in the act itself. Hence it would be as difficult (and perhaps also as corrupt) to have an aesthetic interest in the photograph as it would be in the real situation. By contrast, a painting of a martyrdom may be serene, as is Mantegna's great *Crucifixion* in the Louvre. The painting has emotional qualities in defiance of the qualities of its subject. In the case of a photograph—say of the victim of some accident—one's attitude is determined by the knowledge that this is how things are. One's attitude is made practical by the knowledge of the causal relation between photograph and object. This is not to deny that one might be interested in a photograph for its own sake and at the same time maintain a proper distance from its subject, even when it depicts a scene of agony or death. But the real question is, Can we have such an interest in a photograph without having the same interest in its subject? Can I have an aesthetic interest in the photograph of a dying soldier which is not also an aesthetic interest in the soldier's death? Or, rather, can I maintain that separation of interests and still be interested in the 'representational' aspect of the photograph? If we are distanced from the photograph only because we are distanced from its subject, then the important distinction that I wish to emphasize, between interest in the representation and interest in the subject, has still not been made. It seems necessary to show that photography *can*—by itself—create that sharp separation of interests which is everywhere apparent in serious painting. Consider too the photographs of old London. How is it possible to detach one's interest in their beauty from an interest in the beauty of London as it was? Regret is here the appropriate reaction to the photograph (as it is not—or at least not normally—an appropriate reaction to a Canaletto). 'That is how it looked!' is the central index of one's emotion.

Consider, then, the reasons that may be given in answer to the question, 'Why are you looking at that?' With a photograph, one mentions the features of the subject; with a painting, one mentions only the observable aspect captured in the picture. This essentially is what distinguishes an interest in a representation as a surrogate from an interest in a representation for its own sake. Suppose now that someone wishes to argue that it is *not* inevitable that we treat photographs, even ideal photographs, as I have described. Let us see what the consequences of such a position might be.

8

Imagine that we treat photographs as representations in just the same way that we treat paintings, so that their representational natures are themselves the objects of an aesthetic interest. What are the consequences if we study photography in such a way that it does not matter whether its subject actually existed or actually looked like the thing we see in the picture? Here we are interested not in the subject but in its manner of presentation. If there *can* be such an interest in a photograph, it suggests that a photograph may sometimes be the expression of a representational thought and not merely a simulacrum of its subject.

An interest in an object for its own sake, in the object as a whole, must encompass an interest in detail. For if there is nothing *for* which one contemplates an object, as has frequently been argued, there is no way of determining in advance of looking at it which features are, and which are not, relevant to one's interest.[17] It is for this reason that we cannot rest satisfied with nature but must have works of art as the objects of aesthetic judgment. Art provides a medium transparent to human intention, a medium for which the question, Why? can be asked of every observable feature, even if it may sometimes prove impossible to answer. Art is an expression of precisely the same rational impulses that find an outlet in aesthetic interest; it is therefore the only object which satisfies that interest completely.

The photographer, then, who aims for an aesthetically significant representation must also aim to control detail: 'detail' being here understood in the wide sense of 'any observable fact or feature'. But here lies a fresh difficulty. The causal process of which the photographer is a victim puts almost every detail outside of his control. Even if he does, say, intentionally arrange each fold of his subject's dress and meticulously construct, as studio photographers once used to do, the appropriate scenario, that would still hardly be relevant, since there seem to be few ways in which such intentions can be revealed in the photograph. For one thing, we lack all except the grossest features of style in photography; and yet it is style that persuades us that the question, Why this and not that? admits such fruitful exploration in the case of painting. Style enables us to answer that question by referring solely to aspects of the painting rather than to features which are aesthetically irrelevant, or in no way *manifest* in what is seen.[18] The search for meaning in a photograph is therefore curtailed or thwarted: there is no point in an interest in detail since there is nothing that detail can show. Detail, like the photograph itself, is transparent to its subject. If the photograph is interesting, it is only because what it portrays is interesting, and not because of the manner in which the portrayal is effected.

Let us assume, however, that the photographer could intentionally exert over his image just the kind of control that is exercised in the other representational arts. The question is, How far can this control be extended? Certainly there will be an infinite number of things that lie outside his control. Dust on a sleeve, freckles on a face, wrinkles on a hand: such minutiae will always depend initially upon the prior situation of the subject. When the photographer sees the photographic plate, he may still wish to assert his control, choosing just this colour here, just that number of wrinkles or that texture of skin. He can proceed to paint things out or in, to touch up, alter, or *pasticher* as he pleases. But of course he has now become a painter, precisely through taking representation seriously. The

[17] See for example, Stuart Hampshire, 'Logic and Appreciation' in William Elton (ed.), *Aesthetics and Language* (Oxford, 1954; New Jersey, 1970).
[18] See Richard Wollheim's interesting discussion 'Style now' in Bernard William Smith (ed.), *Concerning Contemporary Art* (Oxford and New York, 1975).

photograph has been reduced to a kind of frame around which he paints, a frame that imposes upon him largely unnecessary constraints.[19]

In other words, when the photographer strives towards representational art, he inevitably seems to move away from that ideal of photography which I have been describing toward the ideal of painting. This can be seen most clearly if we consider exactly what has to be the case if photography is to be a wholly representational art—if it is to manifest all those aspects of representation that distinguish it from mere copying and which endow it with its unique aesthetic appeal. No one could deny that from its origins photography has set itself artistic ideals and attempted to establish itself as a representational art. The culmination of that process— which can be seen in such photographs as Henry Peach Robinson's 'Autumn'—is to be found in the techniques of photo-montage used by the surrealists and futurists (and in particular, by such artists as László Moholy-Nagy and Hannah Höch). Here our interest in the result can be entirely indifferent to the existence and nature of the original subject. But that is precisely because the photographic figures have been so cut up and rearranged in the final product that it could not be said in any normal sense to be a *photograph* of its subject. Suppose that I were to take figures from a photograph of, say, Jane, Philip, and Paul, and, having cut them out, I were to arrange them in a montage, touching them up and adjusting them until the final result is to my mind satisfactory. It could very well be said that the final result represents, say, a lovers' quarrel; but it is not a photograph of one. It represents a quarrel because it stands in precisely the same intentional relation to a quarrel that a painting might have exhibited. Indeed, it is, to all intents and purposes, a painting, except that it happens to have employed photographic techniques in the derivation of its figures. Insofar as the figures can still be considered to be photographs, they are photographs of Jane, Philip, and Paul and not photographs of a lovers' quarrel. (Of course the fact of their *being* photographs might be aesthetically important. Some ironical comment, for example, may be intended in using figures cut from a medium of mass production.)

The history of the art of photography is the history of successive attempts to break the causal chain by which the photographer is imprisoned, to impose a human intention between subject and appearance, so that the subject can be both defined by that intention and seen in terms of it.[20] It is the history of an attempt to turn a mere simulacrum into the expression of a representational thought, an attempt to discover through techniques (from the combination print to the soft-focus lens) what was in fact already known.[21] Occasionally, it is true, photographers have at-

---

[19] This argument is hinted at in B. Croce, *Estetica*, 10th edn (Bari, 1958), p. 20.

[20] See for example, Aaron Scharf, *Creative Photography* (London, 1975) and Rudolf Arnheim, *Film as Art* (California, 1957; London, 1958).

[21] See especially Henry Peach Robinson, *The Elements of a Pictorial Photograph* (London, 1896).

tempted to create entirely fictional scenes through photography and have arranged their models and surroundings, as one might on the stage, in order to produce a narrative scene with a representational meaning. But, as I have argued, the resulting photograph would not be a representation. The process of representation was effected even before the photograph was taken. A photograph of a representation is no more a representation than a picture of a man is a man.

9

It might be felt that I have begged the question in allowing only one way in which photography may acquire representational meaning, a way which inevitably leads photography to subject itself to the aims of painting. One may argue that a photographer does not choose his subject at random, nor is he indifferent to the point of view from which he photographs it or to the composition in which it is set. The act of photography may be just as circumscribed by aesthetic intentions as the act of painting. A photograph will be designed to show its subject in a particular light and from a particular point of view, and by so doing it may reveal things about it that we do not normally observe and, perhaps, that we might not have observed but for the photograph. Such an enterprise leads to effects which are wholly proper to the art of photography, which therefore has its own peculiar way of showing the world. Why is that not enough to give to photography the status of a representational art?

I do not think that such an objection need cause me to revise my argument. For exactly the same might be said of a mirror. When I see someone in a mirror I see *him,* not his representation. This remains so even if the mirror is a distorting mirror and even if the mirror is placed where it is intentionally. This intention might even be similar to the intention in photography: to give a unique and remarkable view of an object, a view which reveals a 'truth' about it that might otherwise have gone unobserved. One could even imagine an art of mirrors, an art which involves holding a mirror aloft in such a way that what is seen in the mirror is rendered by that process interesting or beautiful.

This art of mirrors may, like the art of photography, sometimes involve representation. It may, for example, involve a representation of Venus or of Silenus in the manner of the two types of 'fictional' photographs considered earlier. But representation will not be a property of the *mirror.* It is impossible that I could, simply by holding a mirror before someone, make him into a representation of himself. For after all, whether I look at him or at the mirror, in either case it is *him* that I see. If the mirror is to become the expression of a representational thought, it too must be denatured; like the photomontage, it must be freed from the causal chain which links it to its subject. One can perhaps begin to see the truth in Oliver Wendell Holmes's description of the daguerreotype as a 'mirror with a memory'.[22] It was just such a mirror that led to the downfall of Lord Lambton.

It does not matter, therefore, how many aesthetic intentions underlie the act of photography. It does not matter that the subject, its environment, activity, or light are all consciously arranged. The real question is, What has to be done to make the resulting image into a representation? There are images which are representations (paintings) and images which are not (mirrors). To which class does the photograph belong? I have argued that it naturally belongs to the latter class. Photography can be *made* to belong to the former class by being made into the principal vehicle of the representational thought. But one must then so interfere with the relation between the photograph and its subject that it ceases to be a *photograph* of its subject. Is that not enough to show that it is not just my ideal of photography which fails to be a mode of representation, but also that representation can never be achieved through photography alone?

A final comparison: I mark out a certain spot from which a particular view of a street may be obtained. I then place a frame before that spot. I move the frame so that, from the chosen spot, only certain parts of the street are visible, others are cut off. I do this with all the skill available to me, so that what is seen in the frame is as pleasing as it might be: the buildings within the frame seem to harmonize, the ugly tower that dominates the street is cut off from view, the centre of the composition is the little lane between two classical façades which might otherwise have gone unnoticed, and so on. There I have described an activity which is as circumscribed by aesthetic intentions as anything within the experience of the normal photographer. But how could it be argued that what I see in the frame is not the street itself but a representation of it? The very suggestion is absurd.

10

Here one might object that representation is not, after all, an intrinsic property either of a painting or of a description. Representation is a relation; an object can be described as a representation only if one person uses it to represent something to another. On this view, there is no such thing as 'being a representation'; there is only 'having a representational use.' And if this were the case, my arguments would be in vain. Photographs are as much, and as little, representations as paintings, as gestures, as mirrors, as labels, and as anything else that can play its part in the process of communication.

The objection is more serious, and reflects a well-known dispute in the theory of meaning. Meaning, some say, is a property of a sentence;

---

[22] Holmes, quoted in Beaumont Newhall, *History of Photography* (New York, 1964; London, 1972), p. 22.

others, for instance, H. Paul Grice, argue that meaning is primarily a relation between utterance and speaker.[23] Now, even for Grice, there remains a distinction between utterances which are articulate and utterances which are not. Sentences are to be distinguished from nods of the head in that they participate in and exemplify a grammar, and through that grammar they can be understood independently of the context of their use. By being articulate, the sentence can stand alone as the principal expression of a thought. There arises a kind of interest in the sentence (and in its content) which is independent of any direct involvement in the act of communication. Meaning can be read *in* the sentence and need not be inferred from surrounding circumstances.

Similarly, painting, being fully articulate, can attract attention as the principal expression of a process of thought. It can be understood in isolation from the special circumstances of its creation, because each and every feature of a painting can be both the upshot of an intentional act and at the same time the creation of an intentional object. The interest in the intentional object becomes an interest in the thought which it conveys. A painter can fill his canvas with meaning in just the way that a writer may fill his prose. This is what makes painting and literature into representational arts: they are arts which can be appreciated as they are in themselves and at the same time understood in terms of a descriptive thought which they articulate.

In photography we may have the deliberate creation of an image. Moreover, I may use a photograph as a representation: I may use a photograph of Lenin as a representation of him, in the way that I might have used a clenched fist or a potato or a photograph of Hitler. The question is, What makes the image *itself* into the principal vehicle of representational thought? I wish to argue that an image can be deliberate without being properly articulate. The image becomes articulate when (a) the maker of the image can seriously address himself to the task of communicating thought through the image alone, and (b) when the spectator can see and understand the image in terms of the process of thought which it expresses. To satisfy (a) we require a painterly approach to detail; to satisfy (b) we must distract the spectator's attention from the causal relation which is the distinguishing feature of photography. Either way, the persistence of that relation—in other words, the persistence of the *photographic* image—can only hinder representation. It can contribute nothing to its achievement. This is perhaps what James Joyce meant when he wrote the following in his Paris notebooks of 1904:

> Question: Can a photograph be a work of art? Answer: A photograph is a disposition of sensible matter and may be so disposed for an aesthetic end, but it is not a human disposition of sensible matter. Therefore it is not a work of art.

[23] 'Meaning', *Philosophical Review*, LXVI (1957), pp. 377–88.

If Joyce meant by 'work of art' what I mean by 'representation', then he was clearly getting at the same point. The property of representation, as I have characterized it, is the upshot of a complex pattern of intentional activity and the object of highly specialized responses. How can a photograph acquire that property? My answer is that it can do so only by changing in precisely those respects which distinguish photography from painting. For it is only if photography changes in those respects that the photographer can seriously address himself to the thoughts and responses of his spectators. It is only then, therefore, that the photograph becomes a proper *vehicle* of representational thought.

11

Photography is not representation; nor is it representation when used in the cinema. A film is a photograph of a dramatic representation, and whatever representational properties belong to it belong by virtue of the representation that is effected in the dramatic action, that is, by virtue of the words and activities of the actors in the film. *Ivan the Terrible* represents the life of Ivan, not because the camera was directed at *him*, but because it was directed at an actor who *played the part of* Ivan. Certainly the camera has its role in presenting the action, much as the apparatus of production has its role on the stage. It directs the audience's attention to this or that feature and creates, too, its own peculiar effects of atmosphere. Proper use of the camera may create an interest in situations that could not be portrayed on the stage. Hence photography permits the extension of dramatic representation into areas where previously it would not have been possible, just as music, which is not a representational art, enabled Wagner to create for the first time a theatrical representation of a cosmic theme.[24] (Consider, for example, the camera in Bergman's *Persona*, where it is used to create a dramatic situation between two characters, one of whom never speaks. Such mastery is perhaps rare, but it has existed as an ideal since the earliest days of cinema.) Nonetheless, the process of photography does not, because it cannot, *create* the representation. Thus documentary films are in no sense representations of their subject-matter. (Which is not to say that they cannot involve the realization of elaborate aesthetic ideas: it is hardly necessary to mention Leni Riefenstahl's film of the Berlin Olympics.) A cinematic record of an occurrence is not a representation of it, any more than a recording of a concert is a representation of its sound. As all must agree, representation in the cinema involves an *action,* in just the way that a play involves an action. The action is understood when the audience realizes that the figure photographed is attempting to portray adventures, actions, and feelings which are not his own, and yet which are nevertheless the proper subject-matter of aes-

[24] See my 'Representation in Music', in *The Aesthetic Understanding* (London, 1983).

thetic interest. It follows that the fundamental constraints which the cinema must obey as an art form—those constraints which are integral to its very nature as a representational art—are dramatic ones, involving the representation of character and action. ('Dramatic' here does not mean 'theatrical', but is applied in the sense which Henry James gave to it when he spoke of the novel as a form of dramatic art.) To succeed as cinema, a film must have true characters, and it must be true to them; the director can no more sentimentalize with impunity than can the novelist or the playwright. The true source of the badness of most cinema lies, of course, in the fact that the gorgeous irrelevancies of photography obscure the sentimentality of the dramatic aim.

Photography, far from making dramatic representation more easy, in fact makes it more difficult. Indeed, the possibility of dramatic success in the cinema is a remote one, for which there are two reasons. The first, and somewhat shallow, reason is that the film director is photographing something which either is or purports to be a part of the actual world. It follows that he can only with the greatest difficulty convey to his audience an appropriate sense of detail. Typically the audience is given no criterion of relevance, no criterion which settles what must be attended to. Was the audience meant to notice the man on the street corner, the movement of the eyebrow, the colour of the macintosh, the make of the car? In every cinematographic image, countless such questions remain unanswered. There are various reasons for this. For one thing, a film is fixed with respect to all its details; although it is a dramatic representation, it cannot exist in more than one performance. Therefore features of interpretation cannot be separated from features of the action: there is no such distinction. It is only in understanding the representation as a whole that I come to see what I should be attending to. Furthermore, the cameraman operates under a permanent difficulty in making any visual comment on the action. The difficulty can be solved, but its solution is perforce crude in comparison with the simpler devices of the stage; crude because it must both create irrelevancies and at the same time persuade us to ignore them. (Consider, for example, the ritualized expressionism of *Der blaue Engel* or *The Cabinet of Doctor Caligari*. Even Fritz Lang's *Siegfried* contains reminiscences of this *commedia dell'arte* mannerism, whereby the actor attempts to divert the audience's attention from the infinite irrelevance of detail, toward the dramatic meaning of the whole. Of course more recent directors have emancipated themselves from the theatrical constraints of expressionism; as a result they have at least felt happy to ignore the problem, even if they could not solve it.)

In the theatre the situation is different. The necessary limitations of the stage and the conventions of stage performance, which derive from the fact that the play exists independently of its performance, provide a strong representational medium through which the dramatic action is filtered. Someone with a knowledge of the conventions will see at once what is relevant and what is not. Symbolism in the theatre is therefore clear and immediate, whereas on the screen it is too often vague, portentous, and psychologically remote. Consider, for example, *L'Eclisse,* where the camera, striving again and again to make a comment, succeeds only in inflating the importance of the material surroundings out of all proportion to the sentiments of the characters. The effect is to render the image all-engrossing, while at the same time impoverishing the psychology.

It is for this reason that what often passes for photographic comment in the cinema ought more properly to be described as photographic effect. The camera may create an atmosphere—it may be an instrument of expression—but it is unable to make any precise or cogent analysis of what is shows. Consider the techniques of montage, used to such effect by the Russians. Eisenstein argues that there is a precise parallel between the technique of montage and the sequential structure of verse.[25] For example, each image that Milton presents in the following passage corresponds to a precise and unambiguous shot:

> ... at last
> Farr in th'Horizon to the North appeer'd
> From skirt to skirt a fierie Region, stretcht
> In battailous aspect, and neerer view
> Bristl'd with upright beams innumerable
> Of rigid Spears, and Helmets throng'd, and Shields
> Various, with boastful Argument portraid,
> The banded Powers of *Satan* hasting on
> With furious expedition ...

(One may note the cinematographic device 'and neerer view' and the very Eisensteinian quality of the image that follows it.) The contention is that for each of Milton's images one may find a cinematic shot that somehow 'says the same thing'; the total montage would form a dramatic unity in precisely the same sense, and for the same reason, as Milton's lines. The director will be doing something analogous to the poet: he will be focusing attention on carefully chosen details with a view to creating a unified expression of the prevailing mood.

It should be noted, however, that each shot in the montage will also present infinitely many details that are *not* designed as objects of attention. The shot corresponding to 'Helmets throng'd' will capture that idea among others, but it will also say much more that is irrelevant. It will not be able to avoid showing the *kind* of helmet, for example, the material, size, and shape of it. By so concretizing the thought, the camera leaves nothing to the imagination. As a result the detail that really matters—the thronging of Satanic helmets—is in danger of being lost. It was for this reason that Eisenstein developed techniques of contrast and composition

[25] See Sergei Eisenstein, 'Word and Image', *The Film Sense* (London, 1943; New York, 1969).

in order to control more effectively the attention of his audience. It is a testimony to his genius that the poetry of *Ivan the Terrible* has rarely been re-
discovered by subsequent directors. Even in Eisenstein, however, comment comes primarily through drama rather than through image. The
whole effort of photography lies in expression and effect. And interestingly enough the clearest examples of photographic comment in the cinema come when once again the causal relation between image and subject
is replaced by an intentional one. Consider the following sequence from
The Battleship Potemkin:

1 Title: 'And the rebel battleship answered the brutality of the tyrant
   with a shell upon the town.'
2 A slowly and deliberately turning gun-turret.
3 Title: 'Objective—the Odessa Theatre.'
4 Marble group at the top of the theatre building.
5 Title: 'On the general's headquarters.'
6 Shot from the gun.
7 Two very short shots of a marble figure of Cupid above the gates of the
   building.
8 A mighty explosion; the gates totter.
9 Three short shots: a stone lion asleep;

> a stone lion with open eyes;
> a rampant stone lion.

10 New explosion, shattering the gates.[26]

Here we have one of Eisenstein's most striking visual metaphors. A stone
lion rises to its feet and roars. This amazing image (impossible, incidentally, outside the limitations of the silent screen) acts as a powerful comment on the impotence of imperial splendour precisely because it startles
us into a recognition of the underlying thought. But we know that this
cannot be a photograph of a stone lion roaring. It is, rather, the intentional
juxtaposition of unconnected images; it is the intention that we see and
which determines our understanding of the sequence. It is of course
lamentable that such art should have subjected itself to the inane myth-
making revealed in the titles to this script; that does not alter the fact that,
if there is art here, it is an art which is essentially photographic.

The second and deeper point I wish to mention is extremely difficult
to express in terms that would be acceptable to the contemporary analytical philosopher. I shall try not to be too deterred by that.[27] Photography,
precisely because it does not represent but at best can only distort, remains inescapably wedded to the creation of illusions, to the creation of
lifelike *semblances* of things in the world. Such an art, like the art of the

---

[26] Discussed by V. I. Pudovkin, *Writings,* trans. I. Montagu (London, 1954), p. 88.

[27] The point is made at greater length, and more rigorously, in 'Fantasy, Imagination and the
Screen' in *The Aesthetic Understanding* (London, 1983).

waxworks, is an art that provides a ready gratification for fantasy, and in so doing defeats the aims of artistic expression. A dramatic art can be significant only if it is, at some level, realistic; but to be realistic it must first forbid expression to those habits of unseriousness and wish fulfilment that play such an important part in our lives. Unless it can do that, the greatest effects of drama—such as we observe in the tragedies of the Greeks, of Racine, and of Shakespeare—will be denied to it. Art is fundamentally serious; it cannot rest content with the gratification of fantasy, nor can it dwell on what fascinates us while avoiding altogether the question of its meaning. As Freud put it in another context, art provides the path from fantasy back to reality. By creating a representation of something unreal, it persuades us to consider again those aspects of reality which, in the urgency of everyday existence, we have such strong motives for avoiding.[28] Convention in art, as Freud saw, is the great destroyer of fantasies. It prevents the ready *realization* of scenes that fascinate us, and substitutes for the creation of mere semblance the elaboration of reflective thought.

The cinema has been devoted from its outset to the creation of fantasies. It has created worlds so utterly like our own in their smallest details that we are lulled into an acceptance of their reality, and persuaded to overlook all that is banal, grotesque, or vulgar in the situations which they represent. The cinema has proved too persuasive at the level of mere realization and so has had little motive to explore the significance of its subject. It is entirely beguiling in its immediacy, so that even serious critics of literature can be duped into thinking that a film like *Sunset Boulevard* expresses an aesthetic idea, instead of simply preying on the stereotyped fantasies of its audience.

Moreover, the cinema, like the waxworks, provides us with a ready means of realizing situations which fascinate us. It can address itself to our fantasy directly, without depending upon any intermediate process of thought. This is surely what distinguishes the scenes of violence which are so popular in the cinema from the conventionalized death throes of the theatre. And surely it is this too which makes photography incapable of being an erotic art, in that it presents us with the object of lust rather than a symbol of it: it therefore gratifies the fantasy of desires long before it has succeeded in understanding or expressing the fact of it. The medium of photography, one might say, is inherently pornographic.[29]

---

[28] See *The Standard Edition of the Complete Psychological Works of Sigmund Freud,* ed. James Strachey, 24 vols. (London, 1953–74; New York, 1976), IX, p. 153; XI, p. 50; XII, p. 224; XIII, pp. 187–8; XIV, pp. 375–7; XX, p. 64.

[29] I have benefited greatly from discussions with Richard Wollheim, Mark Platts, John Casey, Peter Suschitzky, and Ruby Meager, as well as from the criticisms of Robert A. Sharpe and Rickie Dammann, my fellow symposiasts at a conference organized in Bristol by Stephen Körner, to whom I am grateful for the opportunity to reflect on the nature of photography.

Scruton and Reasons for Looking at Photographs

William L. King

I

In a provocative essay on the nature of photography,[1] Roger Scruton claims that photographs cannot be interesting in a way that paintings[2] can be. Paintings, because of their manner of representation, can possess qualities and evoke emotions not possessed by or evoked by their subjects. Thus Mantegna's *Crucifixion* in the Louvre evokes serenity, although the scene it portrays—a martyrdom—normally evokes horror: 'The painting has emotional qualities in defiance of the subject'.[3] Photographs, by contrast, seemingly lacking any manner of representation, can possess only the qualities and evoke the emotions possessed by and evoked by their subjects: 'The photograph is transparent to its subject, and if it holds our interest it does so because it acts as a surrogate for the represented thing. Thus if one finds a photograph beautiful, it is because one finds something beautiful in its subject'.[4] Photographs of old London are beautiful because old London was itself beautiful.[5]

Is this an accurate account of photographs? I shall argue that, at best, Scruton's account is applicable to photographs made as records, and to one way of seeing photographs. Otherwise, it is a distortion stemming from his initial claim that all photographs, since caused by their subjects, are copies of their subjects,[6] and his inclination to ignore the diversity of photographic practice.[7]

A way of testing his account is to develop one of its implications: that *the reasons we may give for looking at a photograph are the same reasons we may give for looking at the subject.*

Consider, then, the reasons that may be given in answer to the question, 'Why are you looking at that?' With a photograph, one mentions the features of the subject; with a painting, one mentions only the observable

[1] Roger Scruton, 'Photography and Representation', reprinted in this book.

[2] For these comparative claims, and apparently by interest, Scruton's remarks about painting are restricted to representational paintings.

[3] Ibid., pp. 102–103.

[4] Ibid., pp. 101–102.

[5] Ibid., p. 103.

[6] Ibid., pp. 98–99.

[7] Apart from the old London photographs his examples are few in number and similar in nature (hypothetical documentary).

aspect captured in the picture. This essentially is what distinguishes an interest in a representation as a surrogate from an interest in a representation for its own sake.[8]

If one assumes that these reasons are the reasons *actually* given by viewers, then Scruton is off the mark in both cases. What is happening here, I suggest, is that he is employing specific, disparate models of the viewer for both paintings and photographs. The painting model constitutes relatively complex seeing, the seeing of mature viewers, including the seeing of representational painters in their non-technical moments. The photograph model constitutes relatively simple seeing, a seeing directed by historical or scientific concerns, certainly not the seeing of serious photographers, except in their historical or scientific moments.

II

To reveal the distortion in Scruton's monistic account of photographs—that the reasons for looking are all about the subject—I propose *assembling examples of reasons actually given by viewers*. Some of these reasons I have given myself; others I report from conversations with other viewers. Consider the following examples:

(1) Here is an 1860 photograph of Abraham Lincoln. Now look at this 1865 photograph. The man was undergoing accelerated aging. The war.

(2) Look at this satellite photograph of Hurricane Hugo (17 September 1989). You can see that Hugo is like a gigantic disc, spinning slowly counter-clockwise over the Caribbean. Awesome.

(3) Want to see how some painters, for example, Géricault, misrepresented galloping horses? Look at Muybridge's photographs of Stanford's horse. All four hoofs *are* off the ground at one point, but never in the painter's 'flying-gallop' position.

These remarks, functioning as reasons for looking at photographs, are consistent obviously with Scruton's account. And, of course, the list can be extended far beyond these representative cases. The interests are *cognitive;* they are interests in what the subjects looked, or look, like. Who would deny that these reasons are a dominant type of reason for looking at photographs?

Now consider another example similar to but different from the above:

(4) Can you believe that I have been staring at this photograph of Paris's Notre Dame island, Ile de la Cité, for twenty minutes? It isn't that I

---

[8] Scruton, op. cit., p. 103.

don't remember what it looks like. I do. It's that sitting here alone, lingering over the details, I relive a pleasant May of wandering about the island, sunning along the river.

The dominant interest here is not in knowing the appearance of the subject. One remembers that. The interest is in memories that are stirred, feelings that are evoked. Again, as Scruton argues, the interest is in the subject, and—we add—*its emotional impact*, not in the photograph itself.
But there are other examples, different in another, significant way:

(5) Students—look—here is what happens when you make a print from an overexposed, overdeveloped negative: a contrasty, grainy print. You may like that result; you may not.
(6) This (colour) print has a weird look, yes? Look here by the window— it is faint pink all over. The exposing light is too green; that's the cause. Change the filter pack.

Here, of course, no subject is mentioned. The remarks are about the photograph—how it looks—and the causes. These reasons are clear-cut cognitive, but *technical* reasons: look at these photographs in order to learn about photographic processes, *not* about some subject. Such reasons constitute a type of counter-example to Scruton's viewer-model. Thus his phrase 'reasons that may be given' excludes one type of actual reason, and his phrase 'with a photograph, one mentions' excludes one type of viewer, namely, the photographer concerned about technical issues. However, these exclusions, while providing some evidence for the charge of distortion in Scruton's account, are relatively peripheral.

The exclusion that is central, and that is deliberate, is another type of reason, characterized by him as *aesthetic:* 'It is commonly said that an aesthetic interest in something is an interest in it for its own sake: the object is not treated as a surrogate for another; it is itself the principal object of attention'.[9] By restricting the reasons for looking at photographs to remarks about the subject, Scruton denies that photographs can be interesting in themselves or interesting aesthetically. His starting point—that photographs are caused by their subjects, and thus are copies of their subjects—is decisive here. Should it be? What about additional reasons actually given by viewers? To what extent are the following remarks *not* about the photograph itself?

(7) You know why I'm still looking at that pink print? Well, I'm no longer looking to decide about a change; I'm looking because I like the bloody thing. That overall colour—rather subtle—in an otherwise almost black and white photograph seems to enhance the feeling of unity.
(8) You just can't beat large format black and white for rich tonal values.

---

[9] Ibid., p. 96.

Look at this 8 X 10 contact print, 'Dunes, Oceano, 1936', by Edward Weston. The whites are gleaming, the blacks compelling, the greys vibrant. The thing really glows. Stunning.

The interest here is in the photographs themselves, in the way they look, in part or overall. Traditionally, the features noted by these remarks—colour, luminosity—have been characterized as formal features or elements, and an interest in them has been called an *aesthetic* interest. Of course, some theorists, notably Clive Bell, have judged such an interest the *only* aesthetic interest. Do we have another set of counter-examples? Well, yes indeed, assuming Scruton's explicit reason-giving model for photographs, namely, that the reasons for looking are monistic, all about the subject. But—close by and unexpectedly—he admits that photographs *can* elicit this aesthetic interest since one can have a purely abstract aesthetic interest in anything.[10] The implication here is that some reasons for looking *can* be aesthetic, namely those reasons about purely abstract features of a photograph. While annoying, and providing further evidence for Scruton's temptation to present a simplistic account, this problem should be distinguished from the following, main issue.

III

Can photographs elicit a *second type of aesthetic interest,* a non-formal interest that would involve an interest in manners of representation? Scruton's position on this issue is clear: repeatedly, photographs are denied the power to elicit this type of interest. A manner of representation presupposes an ability to control detail. The photographer, contrary to the painter, lacks this ability if the photograph is caused by the subject. Scruton's example of a picture that does elicit this interest is Manet's painting *Bar aux Folies-Bergère.* The barmaid's hands allegedly express Manet's way of seeing the subject.[11] This comment isn't developed, but any viewer can observe that the hands are almost invisible, gripping the back edge of the counter and extending down behind it. What is visible are rather long arms, extending to near the counter's edge. A point needing stress here, Scruton might say, is that Manet's ability to represent the barmaid in a certain manner presupposes his ability to control detail in the painting. Supposedly, the photographer's situation differs: 'The causal process of which the photographer is a victim puts almost[12] every detail outside of his control'.[13] A difference in kind? Or merely a difference in degree?

---

[10] Ibid., p. 103.
[11] Ibid., p. 97.
[12] This qualification, potentially significant for Scruton's position, is pushed aside, undeveloped.
[13] Ibid., p. 104.

IV

Among the reasons given for looking at photographs we have distinguished several types: remarks about how the subject appears (examples 1–3); remarks about an evocative power of the subject (example 4); remarks about the cause of the photograph's formal appearance (examples 5–6); and remarks simply about the formal appearance of the photograph (examples 7–8). Contrary to Scruton, can one distinguish yet another type consisting of *remarks about the manner of representing the subject?* These remarks must be about observable features of the photograph which are controlled by the photographer, hence, are caused by the photographer, not by the subject.

Caution is needed in choosing examples, since some controls employed can pose a question about the nature of the result, namely, whether it remains a *photograph.* The techniques of photo-montage and multiple printing, Scruton argues, pose this question.[14] The results of employing these techniques, he concludes, are more accurately described as paintings and stand as evidence for the pollution of photography by photo-painters. Of course, *some* photography—traditionally called 'Pictorialism'—has sought painterly qualities, frequently by employing non-photographic, even painterly, methods. We are seeking counter-examples that involve photographic controls only.

Must a photographer avoid the aims of painting also? Much painting, especially during the last century, has sought to be expressive. Is this aim forbidden for photographers? Forbidding expression—if photography *can* be expressive—must be purely arbitrary, since sculpture, architecture, literature, music, even weaving, share this aim with painting. To be sure, the solitary aim of what Scruton calls 'ideal photography'—a logical construct allegedly capturing the 'essential nature' of the medium—is recording, since nothing else is possible. Assume that the 'ideal photograph' is a copy of the subject, assume that it is caused altogether by light reflected from the subject, assume that the photographer is a victim of this causal process, unable to control detail; assume all this, and of course, nothing else *is* possible.[15] But is the photographer so victimized? Does an expressive aim compel him to become a painter? As a matter of fact, some actual photography, while remaining photography, does aim at and succeed in being expressive. This is polluted photography? *That* is dogma.

Consider now these further examples of what one may see when looking at photographs:

(9) Want to see a compelling photograph? Look here: William Klein's 'Entrance to Beach, Ostia, Italy, 1956'. I say 'compelling'; I mean that it pulls me back repeatedly. Part of the explanation, of course, is the

[14] Ibid., p. 105.

[15] For an argument that something else is possible, that even Scruton's 'ideal photograph' may serve an expressive purpose, see Robert Wicks, 'Photography as a Representational Art', *British Journal of Aesthetics*, Vol. 29, No. 1 (Winter 1989), pp. 1–9.

faces—three young male adults close up, unsmiling, staring directly at the camera. Curiosity? Hostility? Another factor, clearly, is the composition. The middle face is farther back, peering from between two uprights, one eye in shadow; two more young male faces, much farther back, peer around from the right. Additional glass door uprights contribute to a rectangular framing of the figures. Finally, the photograph is contrasty and grainy, enough in fact to impose a 'photographic' texture throughout. This grain effect, especially, is most apparent in the light objects—a white shirt, human skin. These objects look like what they are, having the appropriate shapes; yet, in another respect, they don't look like what they are, lacking any visual clue suggesting smoothness. This texture—clusters of tiny black specks—can be interesting in itself. Furthermore, it causes a slight distancing of the subject, seeming to contribute to an overall enigmatic, rather than threatening, quality.

(10) Are you moonstruck? I am; and some photographers are, too. Ansel Adams was. Look here at his 'Moon and Half Dome'. A gibbous moon, showing surface detail, and appearing larger than normal in a darker than normal sky, has been placed slightly above a deep shadow on the top left edge of Half Dome, a massive granite cliff which occupies most of the picture space. This shadow is repeated by a much larger, equally dark, shadow on the right side and base of Half Dome. On the left edge of the photograph, a closer, smaller cliff is in total, almost featureless, shadow. Portions of the Dome's face, including snow patches, are gleaming in light from a low winter sun. The resultant contrast of rich blacks and whites, combined with a sense that the objects are closer than normal because larger than normal, gives the photograph a quality of unreality.

(11) This photograph, 'The Priest', by Ralph Gibson, is not the everyday head and shoulders photographic portrait. Look. The head above the chin, including the mouth, is missing; simply cut off. Perhaps *that* is enough to rivet one's glance; but there is more. One-half of his clerical collar, in direct sunlight, is an intense white, contrasting with his very dark, almost solid black vest and coat. The shadow cast by his chin forms a small, gleaming triangle at the front, widest portion of the collar. Most of the neck is in featureless shadow. Only the chin-shape and its skin-like texture suggest the presence of a living human. *Is* it a portrait, or merely a study in black and white? What is going on here?

Certainly, subjects are mentioned, even described, in these examples. And there are remarks about formal elements and relationships. What is new here are *remarks about the photographer's manner of representing the subject:* Klein has imposed a photographic texture, transforming the look of fabric and of human skin: Adams has juxtaposed, magnified, and heightened the contrast in monumental geologic forms; and Gibson has obliterated part of the subject—normally an important part—as well as obliterating shadow detail in the remainder. One would be hard pressed to understand how these examples differ *in kind* from Manet's handling of the barmaid's hands. Furthermore, the methods employed were altogether photographic.

Klein's transformation of values, but especially texture detail, is like a stylistic device, evident in the extensive body of his work focused on urban life.

Adams is recognized as the developer of a system of exposure called the 'Zone System'. Applying this system for the sake of an expressive purpose—his own purpose generally—entails deciding how we want the subject in a photograph to look *before* the subject is recorded on photographic film. He calls this act 'visualizing'; it is the important initial step which guides exposing, developing, and printing. What is noteworthy here is that the photographer *systematically* becomes an additional causal agent of the photograph. The result, while an approximation of visual reality, is not a copy, nor is it intended to be: 'Many consider my photographs to be in the "realistic" category. Actually, what reality they have is in their optical-image accuracy; their *values* are definitely departures from reality . . . if it were possible to make direct visual comparison with the subjects, the differences would be startling'.[16] In 'Moon and Half Dome' Adams visualized the objects larger than in normal vision, as if the viewer were closer, even above the valley floor looking straight on, rather than up, at Half Dome; and he visualized the shadows and sky much darker, seeking a heightened contrast. This rather radical transformation of reality was effected by using only photographic controls: a telephoto lens, an orange filter, longer-than-normal development, and burning-dodging manipulation during printing.[17]

That the photographer is doing something with the subject is most evident, perhaps, in the case of Gibson. His commentary: 'My primary concern in the photograph of the priest was to formalize the composition as rigidly as possible . . . [he] was posed in bright sun so that the geometric division of his collar would be intense . . . Of course I wanted to make a statement, both religious and photographic, in a tight structural way'.[18] Is the photographer trying to do something here that is photographically impossible? Saying this is baffling since a hidden half-head is more puzzling visually than hidden hands. If the latter is evidence for a manner of representing the subject, then the former, in conjunction with other details, seems to be even stronger evidence. Surely Gibson effects a manner of representation without becoming a photo-painter.

---

[16] Ansel Adams, *The Negative* (Little, Brown and Company, 1981), p. ix.

[17] Ansel Adams, *Examples: The Making of 40 Photographs* (Little, Brown and Company, 1983), pp. 133–5.

[18] 'Ralph Gibson: High Contrast Printing', *Darkroom*, E. Lewis, ed. (Lustrum Press, 1977), p. 68.

My conclusion, then, is that attention to detail in a photograph isn't necessarily attention to the subject as such. On the contrary, it may be attention to a manner of representing the subject. In other words, it can be attention to a quality possessed by the photograph that is *not* possessed by the subject. Commonplace subjects that are threatening can be made enigmatic (Klein), that are dramatically real can be made unreal (Adams), that are formally human can be made non-human (Gibson). Consequently, some photographs can be interesting in one way that paintings can be, namely, aesthetically interesting by virtue of the manner of representation.

SUGGESTIONS FOR FURTHER READING

Arnheim, Rudolf. "On the Nature of Photography." *Critical Inquiry* 1 (1974): 149–61.

Barthes, Roland. *Camera Lucida.* New York: Hill and Wang, 1981.

Bazin, André. "The Ontology of the Photographic Image." In his *What is Cinema?* trans. by Hugh Grey. Berkeley: University of California Press, 1967.

Blocker, Gene. "Pictures and Photographs." *Journal of Aesthetics and Art Criticism* 36 (1977): 155–62.

Brook, Donald. "On the Alleged Transparency of Photographs." *British Journal of Aesthetics* 26 (1986): 277–82.

Brook, Donald. "Painting, Photography and Representation." *Journal of Aesthetics and Art Criticism* 42 (1983): 171–80.

Cavell, Stanley. *The World Viewed.* Enlarged ed. Cambridge: Harvard University Press, 1979.

Currie, Gregory. "Photography, Painting and Perception." *Journal of Aesthetics and Art Criticism* 49 (1991): 23–29.

Maynard, Patrick. "The Secular Icon: Photography and the Functions of Images." *Journal of Aesthetics and Art Criticism* 42 (1983): 155–70.

Ross, Stephanie. "What Photographs Can't Do." *Journal of Aesthetics and Art Criticism* 41 (1982): 5–17.

Savedoff, Barbara. "Transforming Images: Photographs of Representations." *Journal of Aesthetics and Art Criticism* 50 (1992): 93–106.

Scharf, Aaron. *Art and Photography.* London: Allen Lane, 1968.

Snyder, Joel, and Allen, Neil Walsh: "Photography, Vision, and Representation." *Critical Inquiry* 2 (1975): 143–69.

Sontag, Susan. *On Photography.* New York: Farrar, Straus and Giroux, 1977.

Sontag, Susan. "Photography." *New York Review of Books* 20, October 18, 1973: 59ff.

Szarkowski, John. "Photography—A Different Kind of Art." *New York Times Magazine,* April 13, 1975: 16–19ff.

Walton, Kendall L. "Transparent Pictures: On the Nature of Photographic Realism." *Critical Inquiry* 11 (1984): 246–77.

Warburton, Nigel. "Photographic Communication." *British Journal of Aesthetics* 28 (1988): 173–81.

Wicks, Robert. "Photography as a Representational Art." *British Journal of Aesthetics* 29 (1989): 1–9.

5

APPRECIATION, UNDERSTANDING, AND NATURE

The face of the water, in time, became a wonderful book—a book that was a dead language to the uneducated passenger, but which told its mind to me without reserve, delivering its most cherished secrets as clearly as if it uttered them with a voice. . . . In truth, the passenger who could not read this book saw nothing but all manner of pretty pictures in it, painted by the sun and shaded by the clouds, whereas to the trained eye these were not pictures at all, but the grimmest and most dead-earnest of reading matter.

Now when I had mastered the language of this water and had come to know every trifling feature that bordered the great river as familiarly as I knew the letters of the alphabet, I had made a valuable acquisition. But I had lost something, too. I had lost something which could never be restored to me while I lived. All the grace, the beauty, the poetry had gone out of the majestic river: I still keep in mind a certain wonderful sunset which I witnessed when steamboating was new to me. A broad expanse of the river was turned to blood; in the middle distance the red hue brightened into gold, through which a solitary log came floating, black and conspicuous; in one place a long, slanting mark lay sparkling upon the water; in another the surface was broken by boiling, tumbling rings, that were as many-tinted as an opal; where the ruddy flush was faintest, was a smooth spot that was covered with graceful circles and radiating lines, ever so delicately traced; the shore on our left was densely wooded, and the sombre shadow that fell from this forest was broken in one place by a long, ruffled trail that shone like silver; and high above the forest wall a clean-stemmed dead tree waved a single leafy bough that glowed like a flame in the unobstructed splendor that was flowing from the sun. There were graceful curves, reflected images, woody heights, soft distances; and over the whole scene, far and near, the dissolving lights drifted steadily, enriching it, every passing moment, with new marvels of coloring.

I stood like one bewitched. I drank it in, in a speechless rapture. . . . But as I have said, a day came when . . . if that sunset scene had been repeated, I should have looked upon it without rapture, and should have commented upon it, inwardly, after this fashion: The sun means that we are going to have wind to-morrow; that floating log means that the river is rising, small thanks to it; that slanting mark on the water refers to a bluff reef which is going to kill somebody's steamboat one of these nights, if it keeps on stretching out like that; those tumbling "boils" show a dissolving bar and a changing channel there; . . . that tall dead tree, with a single living branch, is not going to last long, and then how is a body ever going to get through this blind place at night without the friendly old landmark?

No, the romance and the beauty were all gone from the river. . . . Since those days, I have pitied doctors from my heart. What does the lovely flush in a beauty's cheek mean to a doctor but a "break" that ripples above some deadly disease? . . . Does he ever see her beauty at all, or doesn't he simply comment upon her unwholesome condition all to himself? And doesn't he sometimes wonder whether he has gained most or lost most by learning his trade?

—Mark Twain, *Life on the Mississippi*

INTRODUCTION

A large part of our aesthetic experience and enjoyment is experience and enjoyment of nature. Think of the ways in which we talk about and respond to things as various as pieces of driftwood and uncut quartz, patches of wildflowers growing by the highway, sunsets, rainbows, rain forests, glacier plains, mountain ranges. It seems clear that we often regard these and other natural objects and natural environments not only as aspects of our world that give us pleasure, but as aspects of our world that are *aesthetically* important. Gazelles as well as Brancusi's sculpture *Bird in Space* are "delicately graceful," birdsong as well as music can be "melodious," and the Grand Tetons as well as Chartres Cathedral are "majestic." Indeed, it might be said that we first learn about beauty through our engagement with the natural world. Children are likely to find rainbows beautiful long before they appreciate poetry, and the art that children learn to appreciate first is likely to be art which represents aspects of the natural world. (Consider how many picture books for babies and infants are picture books about animals.)

So it seems clear that natural objects and natural environments are aspects of the world which we can appreciate aesthetically. But although this may be clear, it is not so clear just what is *involved* in aesthetic appreciation of the natural world. In particular, we may wonder how similar aesthetic appreciation of the natural world is to aesthetic appreciation of works of art. Is coming to see that the Grand Tetons are majestic the same sort of process as coming to see that Chartres Cathedral is majestic? There are certain features of our experience that are clearly involved in and relevant to our appreciation of art: Are the same features involved in and relevant to our appreciation of the natural world?

In the first of the readings in this section, Allen Carlson explores the differences and similarities between aesthetically appreciating art and aesthetically appreciating nature. He examines two models of aesthetic appreciation, two ways in which we might aesthetically appreciate works of art, which he calls the "object model" and the "landscape model." He argues that these models do not carry over to our aesthetic appreciation of nature, and thus that we need a new model of aesthetic appreciation if we are to understand our aesthetic responses to nature. Carlson calls the model that he presents the "environmental model." On this model, in order to aesthetically appreciate a natural environment, "We must experience our background setting in all those ways in which we normally experience it, by sight, smell, touch and whatever. However, we must experience it not as unobtrusive background, but as obtrusive foreground!" If we are to appreciate nature aesthetically, he suggests, we must appreciate it *as* natural—not as an isolated "object" or piece of scenery, but as a dynamic and organic whole of which we, the appreciators, are a part.

However, Carlson suggests that there is also an important similarity between the aesthetic appreciation of art and the aesthetic appreciation of nature. Both modes of appreciation, he suggests, are fundamentally *cognitive*. In responding to art, our appreciation and understanding is based on knowledge of cultural history and conventions. Some knowledge of this sort is crucial if there is to be even the possibility of understanding and hence appreciating works of art. For example, if we think of Stravinsky's *The Rite of Spring* or The Rolling Stones's song "Brown Sugar" as lullabies, then we are not likely to think much of them—as lullabies, they are simply not very good! In order to appreciate these pieces, we have to know something about the *categories* that they belong to. (This idea is developed by Kendall Walton in an extremely influential article entitled "Categories of Art.") If we are to make sensible judgments about "Brown Sugar," we have to see it in the category of "rock and roll music" or perhaps that of "rhythm and blues music." Once we do see the song in the right category, we can see that some of the features which make it a terrible lullaby (its raucous, abrasive tone, for example) may be part of what makes it a *good* rock song. Seeing a work in the appropriate category does not guarantee that all our judgments about that work will be true. But it does make it likely that our judgments about the work will at least be "in the right ballpark."

Carlson suggests that just as our aesthetic appreciation of art is based on our knowledge of cultural history and artistic conventions, so our aesthetic appreciation of nature is based on knowledge—but in this case, knowledge of science and *natural* history rather than cultural history. For example, how we appreciate an environment composed of a wide expanse of sand and mud will depend on whether we see it as a beach or a seabed or a tidal basin. If our knowledge of natural history is so poor that we think of whales as big fish rather than as mammals, we will be unable to aesthetically appreciate whales as fully as a person who has some knowledge of the kind of creatures that they are. As Carlson says, "To aesthetically appreciate nature we must have knowledge of the different environments of nature and of the systems and elements within those environments. In the way in which the art critic and the art historian are well equipped to aesthetically appreciate art, the naturalist and the ecologist are well equipped to aesthetically appreciate nature."

In Carlson's view, then, some knowledge of natural history is essential if we are to appreciate nature aesthetically. One question we might ask in considering this view is how *much* knowledge is essential to appreciation? Mark Twain suggests in the opening reading in this section that too much knowledge may be a hindrance rather than a help to aesthetic appreciation. As Twain says, once he had learned "the language of the river"—once he had some scientific understanding of the Mississippi—he found that he had lost something: "All the grace, the beauty, the poetry had gone out of the majestic river." Are the naturalist and the botanist better equipped to appreciate nature aesthetically than those of us who lack scientific knowledge of the natural world, as Carlson argues? Or is the naturalist's and the ecologist's knowledge rather an obstacle to their appreciation of nature, as Twain suggests?

If Carlson's conclusion is that only scientifically trained people—botanists, ecologists, zoologists, and the like—can fully appreciate nature (and, analogously, that only artists, art critics, and art historians can fully appreciate art), does this suggest that his position is unacceptably restrictive or exclusive? In the second reading in this section, Noël Carroll argues that Carlson's view *is* too narrow. It leaves out, Carroll suggests, "certain very common appreciative responses to nature—responses of a less intellectual, more visceral sort, which we might refer to as 'being moved by nature.'" Carroll does not deny that Carlson's "environmental model" captures *one* of the ways in which we may aesthetically appreciate nature, but he holds that it is not the *only* way of doing so. As Carroll says, "We may appreciate nature by opening ourselves to its stimulus, and to being put in a certain emotional state by attending to its aspects." For example, being excited by the grandeur of a waterfall may be a way of aesthetically appreciating that waterfall. On Carroll's view, that is, aesthetic appreciation of nature may be less cognitive, less dependent on knowledge of science and natural history, than Carlson suggests. Indeed, he implies, the same may be true of our aesthetic appreciation of works of art: For example, "One may find certain Surrealist paintings haunting without knowing the metaphysical, psychological and political aims of the Surrealist movement."

If we may aesthetically appreciate a work of art or a natural environment by being emotionally moved by it, does this suggest that our judgments about art and nature must be purely *subjective* judgments? Carroll argues that this is not so. He holds that emotional experience—and hence aesthetic appreciation—may be assessed as rational or irrational, appropriate or inappropriate, by reference to the beliefs that the emotional experience is grounded on. Does Carroll's insistence on the role of belief in emotional experience strengthen or weaken his position? In particular, does it leave him open to the charge that his position, like Carlson's, presents an overly cognitive view of emotion?

As these readings suggest, reflection on our aesthetic experience of and engagement with the natural world gives rise to a number of questions that are central to the philosophy of art. What exactly is it to appreciate something aesthetically? How are appreciation and understanding connected? Is aesthetic appreciation and judgment fundamentally subjective, or is it open to assessment in terms of rationality and truth? These are questions which we cannot ignore if we are to understand the importance to us of both art and nature.

Appreciation and the Natural Environment

Allen Carlson

I

With art objects there is a straightforward sense in which we know both what and how to aesthetically appreciate. We know *what* to appreciate in that, first, we can distinguish a work and its parts from that which is not it nor a part of it. And, second, we can distinguish its aesthetically relevant aspects from its aspects without such relevance. We know that we are to appreciate the sound of the piano in the concert hall and not the coughing which interrupts it; we know that we are to appreciate that a painting is graceful, but not that it happens to hang in the Louvre. In a similar vein, we know *how* to appreciate in that we know what "acts of aspection" to perform in regard to different works. Ziff says:

> . . . to contemplate a painting is to perform one act of aspection; to scan it is to perform another; to study, observe, survey, inspect, examine, scrutinise, etc., are still other acts of aspection.
> . . . I survey a Tintoretto, while I can an H. Bosch. Thus I step back to look at the Tintoretto, up to look at the Bosch. Different actions are involved. Do you drink brandy in the way you drink beer?[1]

It is clear that we have such knowledge of what and how to aesthetically appreciate. It is, I believe, also clear what the grounds are for this knowledge. Works of art are our own creations; it is for this reason that we know what is and what is not a part of a work, which of its aspects are of aesthetic significance, and how to appreciate them. We have made them for the purpose of aesthetic appreciation; in order for them to fulfill this purpose this knowledge must be accessible. In making an object we know what we make and thus its parts and its purpose. Hence in knowing what we make we know what to do with that which we make. In the more general cases the point is clear enough: In creating a painting, we know that what we make is a painting. In knowing this we know that it ends at its frame, that its colors are aesthetically important, but where it hangs is not, and that we are to look at it rather than, say, listen to it. All this is involved in what it is to be a painting. Moreover, this point holds for more particular cases as well. Works of different particular types have different kinds of boundaries, have different foci of aesthetic significance,

---

[1] Paul Ziff, "Reasons in Art Criticism," *Philosophy and Education*, ed., I. Scheffler (Boston, 1958). Reprinted in *Art and Philosophy*, ed., W. E. Kennick (New York, 1964). p. 620.

and perhaps most important demand different acts of aspection. In knowing the type we know what and how to appreciate. Ziff again:

> Generally speaking, a different act of aspection is performed in connection with works belonging to different schools of art, which is why the classification of style is of the essence. Venetian paintings lend themselves to an act of aspection involving attention to balanced masses: contours are of no importance, for they are scarcely to be found. The Florentine school demands attention to contours, the linear style predominates. Look for light in a Claude, for color in a Bonnard, for contoured volume in a Signorelli.[2]

I take the above to be essentially beyond serious dispute, except as to the details of the complete account. If it were not the case, our complementary institutions of art and of the aesthetic appreciation of art would not be as they are. We would not have the artworld which we do. But the subject of this paper is not art nor the artworld. Rather: it is the aesthetic appreciation of nature. The question I wish to investigate is the question of what and how to aesthetically appreciate in respect to natural environment. It is of interest since the account which is implicit in the above remarks and which I believe to be the correct account for art cannot be applied to the natural environment without at least some modification. Thus initially the questions of what and how to appreciate in respect to nature appear to be open questions.

II

In this section I consider some paradigms of aesthetic appreciation which prima facie seem applicable as models for the appreciation of the natural environment. In this I follow tradition to some extent in that these paradigms are ones which have been offered as or assumed to be appropriate models for the appreciation of nature. However, I think we will discover that these models are not as promising as they may initially appear to be.

The first such paradigm I call the object model. In the artworld nonrepresentational sculpture best fits this model of appreciation. When we appreciate such sculpture we appreciate it as the actual physical object which it is. The qualities to be aesthetically appreciated are the sensuous and design qualities of the actual object and perhaps certain abstract expressive qualities. The sculpture need not represent anything external to itself; it need not lead the appreciator beyond itself: it may be a self-con-

---

[2] Ibid. Ziff is mainly concerned with the way in which knowledge of types yields different acts of aspection. For an elaboration of this point and its ramifications concerning what is and is not aesthetically significant in a work, see K. Walton, "Categories of Art," *Philosophical Review* (1970), 334–67. How our knowledge of art (and the artworld) yields the boundaries between art and the rest of reality is interestingly discussed in A. Danto, "The Artistic Enfranchisement of Real Objects: the Artworld," *Journal of Philosophy* (1964), 571–84.

tained aesthetic unit. Consider a Brancusi sculpture, for example, the famous *Bird In Space* (1919). It has no representational connections with the rest of reality and no relational connections with its immediate surroundings and yet it has significant aesthetic qualities. It glistens, has balance and grace, and expresses flight itself.

Clearly it is possible to aesthetically appreciate an object of nature in the way indicated by this model. For example, we may appreciate a rock or a piece of driftwood in the same way as we appreciate a Brancusi sculpture: we actually or contemplatively remove the object from its surroundings and dwell on its sensuous and design qualities and its possible expressive qualities. Moreover, there are considerations which support the plausibility of this model for appreciation of the natural environment. First, natural objects are in fact often appreciated in precisely this way: mantel pieces are littered with pieces of rock and driftwood. Second, the model fits well with one feature of natural objects: such objects, like the Brancusi sculpture, do not have representational ties to the rest of reality. Third and most important, the model involves an accepted, traditional aesthetic approach. As Sparshott notes, "When one talks of the aesthetic this or that, one is usually thinking of it as entering into a subject/object relation."[3]

In spite of these considerations, however, I think there are aspects of the object model which make it inappropriate for nature. Santayana, in discussing the aesthetic appreciation of nature (which he calls the love of nature) notes that certain problems arise because the natural landscape has "indeterminate form." He then observes that although the landscape contains many objects which have determinate forms, "if the attention is directed specifically to them, we have no longer what, by a curious limitation of the world, is called the love of nature."[4] I think this limitation is not as curious as Santayana seems to think it is. The limitation marks the distinction between appreciating nature and appreciating the objects of nature. The importance of this distinction is seen by realizing the difficulty of appreciating nature by means of the object model. For example, on one understanding of the object model, the objects of nature when so appreciated become "ready-mades" or "found art." The artworld grants "artistic enfranchisement" to a piece of driftwood just as it has to Duchamp's urinal or to the real Brillo cartons discussed by Danto.[5] If this magic is successful the result is art. Questions of what and how to aesthetically appreciate are answered, of course, but in respect to art rather than nature; the appreciation of nature is lost in the shuffle. Appreciating sculpture which

---

[3] F. E. Sparshott, "Figuring the Ground: Notes on Some Theoretical Problems of the Aesthetic Environment," *Journal of Aesthetic Education* (1972), 13.

[4] George Santayana, *The Sense of Beauty* (New York, 1961), p. 100.

[5] Danto, op. cit., p. 579.

was once driftwood is no closer to appreciating nature than is appreciating a totem pole which was once a tree or a purse which was once a sow's ear. In all such cases the conversion from nature to art (or artifact) is complete; only the means of conversion are different.

There is, however, another understanding of how the object model applies to the objects of nature. On this understanding natural objects are simply (actually or contemplatively) removed from their surroundings, but they do not become art, they remain natural objects. Here we do not appreciate the objects *qua* art objects, but rather *qua* natural objects. We do not consider the rock on our mantel a ready-made sculpture, we consider it only an aesthetically pleasing rock. In such a case, as the example of non-representational sculpture suggests, our appreciation is limited to the sensuous and design qualities of the natural object and perhaps a few abstract expressive qualities: Our rock has a wonderfully smooth and gracefully curved surface and expresses solidity.

The above suggests that, even when it does not require natural objects to be seen as art objects, the object model imposes a certain limitation on our appreciation of natural objects. The limitation is the result of the removal of the object from its surroundings which the object model requires in order even to begin to provide answers to questions of what and how to appreciate. But in requiring such a removal the object model becomes problematic. The object model is most appropriate for those art objects which are self-contained aesthetic units. These objects are such that neither the environment of their creation nor the environment of their display are aesthetically relevant: the removal of a self-contained art object from its environment of creation will not vary its aesthetic qualities and the environment of display of such an object should not affect its aesthetic qualities. However, natural objects possess what we might call an organic unity with their environment of creation: such objects are a part of and have developed out of the elements of their environments by means of the forces at work within those environments. Thus the environments of creation are aesthetically relevant to natural objects. And for this reason the environments of display are equally relevant in virtue of the fact that these environments will be either the same as or different from the environments of creation. In either case the aesthetic qualities of natural objects will be affected. Consider again our rock: on the mantel it may seem wonderfully smooth and gracefully curved and expressive of solidity, but in its environment of creation it will have more and different aesthetic qualities—qualities which are the product of the relationship between it and its environment. It is here expressive of the particular forces which shaped and continue to shape it and displays for aesthetic appreciation its place in and its relation to its environment. Moreover, depending upon its place in that environment it may not express many of those qualities, for example, solidity, which it appears to express when on the mantel.

I conclude that the object model, even without changing nature into art, faces a problem as a paradigm for the aesthetic appreciation of nature.

The problem is a dilemma: either we remove the object from its environment or we leave it where it is. If the object is removed, the model applies to the object and suggests answers to the questions of what and how to appreciate. But the result is the appreciation of a comparatively limited set of aesthetic qualities. On the other hand if the object is not removed, the model seemingly does not constitute an adequate model for a very large part of the appreciation which is possible. Thus it makes little headway with the what and how questions. In either case the object model does not provide a successful paradigm for the aesthetic appreciation of nature. It appears after all not a very "curious limitation" that when our attention is directed specifically toward the objects in the environment it is not called the love of nature.

The second paradigm for the aesthetic appreciation of nature I call the scenery or landscape model. In the artworld this model of appreciation is illustrated by landscape painting; in fact the model probably owes its existence to this art form. In one of its favored senses "landscape" means a prospect—usually a grandiose prospect—seen from a specific standpoint and distance; a landscape painting is traditionally a representation of such a prospect.[6] When aesthetically appreciating landscape paintings (or any representative paintings, for that matter) the emphasis is not on the actual object (the painting) nor on the object represented (the actual prospect); rather it is on the representation of the object and its represented features. Thus in landscape painting the appreciative emphasis is on those qualities which play an essential role in representing a prospect: visual qualities related to coloration and overall design. These are the qualities which are traditionally significant in landscape painting and which are the focus of the landscape model of appreciation. We thus have a model of appreciation which encourages perceiving and appreciating nature as if it were a landscape painting, as a grandiose prospect seen from a specific standpoint and distance. It is a model which centers attention on those aesthetic qualities of color and design which are seen and seen at a distance.

It is quite evident that the scenery or landscape model has been historically significant in our aesthetic appreciation of nature.[7] For example,

---

[6] This favored sense of "landscape" is brought out by Yi-Fu Tuan. See *Topophilia: A Study of Environmental Perception, Attitudes, and Values* (Englewood Cliffs, 1974), pp. 132–33, or "Man and Nature: An Eclectic Reading," *Landscape*, 15 (1966), 30.

[7] For a good, brief discussion of this point, see R. Rees, "The Scenery Cult: Changing Landscape Tastes over Three Centuries," *Landscape*, 19 (1975). Note the following remarks by E. H. Gombrich in "The Renaissance Theory of Art and the Rise of Landscape," *Norm and Form: Studies in the Art of the Renaissance* (London, 1971), pp. 117–18: ". . . I believe that the idea of natural beauty as an inspiration of art . . . is, to say the least, a very dangerous oversimplification. Perhaps it even reverses the actual process by which man discovers the beauty of nature. We call a scenery 'picturesque' . . . if it reminds us of paintings we have seen. . . . Similarly, so it seems, the discovery of Alpine scenery does not precede but follows the spread of prints and paintings with mountain panoramas."

this model was evident in the eighteenth and nineteenth centuries in the use of the "Claude-glass," a small, tinted, convex mirror with which tourists viewed the landscape. Thomas West's popular guidebook to the Lake District (first published in 1778) says of the glass:

> . . . where the objects are great and near, it removes them to a due distance, and shews them in the soft colours of nature, and most regular perspective the eye can perceive, art teach, or science demonstrate . . . to the glass is reserved the finished picture, in highest colouring, and just perspective.[8]

In a somewhat similar fashion, the modern tourist reveals his preference for this model of appreciation by frequenting "scenic viewpoints" where the actual space between the tourist and the prescribed "view" often constitutes "a due distance" which aids the impression of "soft colours of nature, and the most regular perspective the eye can perceive, art teach, or science demonstrate." And the "regularity" of the perspective is often enhanced by the positioning of the viewpoint itself. Moreover, the modern tourist also desires "the finished picture, in highest colouring, and just perspective"; whether this be the "scene" framed and balanced in his camera's viewfinder, the result of this in the form of a kodachrome slide, and/or the "artistically" composed postcard and calendar reproductions of the "scene" which often attract more appreciation than that which they "reproduce." R. Rees has described the situation as follows:

> . . . the taste has been for a view, for scenery, not for landscape in the original Dutch—and present geographical—meaning of the term, which denotes our ordinary, everyday surroundings. The average modern sightseer, unlike many of the Romantic poets and painters who were accomplished naturalists, is interested *not* in natural forms and processes, but in a prospect.[9]

It is clear that in addition to being historically important, the landscape model, like the object model, gives us at least initial guidelines as to what and how to appreciate in regard to nature. We appreciate the natural environment as if it were a landscape painting. The model requires dividing the environment into scenes or blocks of scenery, each of which is to be viewed from a particular point by a viewer who is separated by the appropriate spatial (and emotional?) distance. A drive through the country is not unlike a walk through a gallery of landscape paintings. When seen in this light, this model of appreciation causes a certain uneasiness in a number of thinkers. Some, such as ecologist Paul Shepard, seemingly believe this kind of appreciation of the natural environment so misguided that they entertain doubts about the wisdom of *any* aesthetic

---

[8] Thomas West, *Guide to the Lakes* (London, 1778) as quoted in J. T. Ogden, "From Spatial to Aesthetic Distance in the Eighteenth Century," *Journal of the History of Ideas*, 35 (1974), 66–67.
[9] R. Rees, "The Taste for Mountain Scenery," *History Today*, 25 (1975), 312.

approach to nature.[10] Others find the model to be ethically suspect. For example, after pointing out that the modern sightseer is interested only in a prospect, Rees concludes:

> In this respect the Romantic Movement was a mixed blessing. In certain phases of its development it stimulated the movement for the protection of nature, but in its picturesque phase it simply confirmed our anthropocentism by suggesting that nature exists to please as well as to serve us. Our ethics, if the word can be used to describe our attitudes and behaviour toward the environment, have lagged behind our aesthetics. It is an unfortunate lapse which allows us to abuse our local environments and venerate the Alps and the Rockies.[11]

What has not been as generally noted, however, is that this model of appreciation is suspect not only on ethical grounds, but also on aesthetic grounds. The model requires us to view the environment as if it were a static representation which is essentially "two dimensional." It requires the reduction of the environment to a scene or view. But what must be kept in mind is that the environment is not a scene, not a representation, not static, and not two dimensional. The point is that the model requires the appreciation of the environment not as what it is and with the qualities it has, but rather as something which it is not and with qualities it does not have. The model is in fact inappropriate to the actual nature of the object of appreciation. Consequently it not only, as the object model, unduly limits our appreciation—in this case to visual qualities related to coloration and overall design, it also misleads it. Hepburn puts this point in a general way:

> Supposing that a person's aesthetic education . . . instills in him the attitudes, the tactics of approach, the expectations proper to the appreciation of art works only, such a person will either pay very little aesthetic heed to natural objects or else heed them in the wrong way. He will look—and of course look in vain—for what can be found and enjoyed only in art.[12]

---

[10] Paul Shepard, *The Tender Carnivore and the Sacred Game* (New York, 1973), pp. 147–48. Shepard made this position more explicit at a lecture at Athabasca University, Edmonton, Alberta, November 16, 1974.

[11] Rees, "Mountain Scenery," op. cit., p. 312. Ethical worries are also expressed by Tuan, *Topophilia*, op. cit., Chapter 8, and R. A. Smith and C. M. Smith, "Aesthetics and Environmental Education," *Journal of Aesthetic Education* (1970), 131–32. Smith and Smith put the point as follows: "Perhaps there is a special form of arrogance in experiencing nature strictly in the categories of art, for the attitude involved here implies an acceptance, though perhaps only momentarily, of the notion that natural elements have been arranged for the sake of the man's aesthetic pleasure. It is possible that this is what Kant had in mind when he said that in the appreciation of natural beauty one ought not assume that nature has fashioned its forms for our delight and that, instead, 'it is we who receive nature with favour, and not nature that does us a favour.'"

[12] R. W. Hepburn, "Aesthetic Appreciation of Nature," *Aesthetics and the Modern World*, ed. H. Osborne (London, 1968), p. 53. Hepburn implicitly argues that our aesthetic appreciation of nature is enhanced by our "realizing" that an object is what it is and has the qualities which it has. See pp. 60–65.

III

I conclude that the landscape model, as the object model, is inadequate as a paradigm for the aesthetic appreciation of nature. However, the reason for its inadequacy is instructive. The landscape model is inadequate because it is inappropriate to the nature of the natural environment. Perhaps to see what and how to appreciate in respect to the natural environment, we must consider the nature of that environment more carefully. In this regard there are two rather obvious points which I wish to emphasize. The first is that the natural environment is an environment; the second is that it is natural.

When we conceptualize the natural environment as "nature" I think we are tempted to think of it as an object. When we conceptualize it as "landscape" we are certainly led to thinking of its as scenery. Consequently perhaps the concept of the "natural environment" is somewhat preferable. At least it makes explicit that it is an environment which is under consideration. The object model and the landscape model each in its own way fail to take account of this. But what is involved in taking this into account? Here I wish initially to follow up some remarks made by Sparshott. He suggests that to consider something environmentally is primarily to consider it in regard to the relation of "self to setting," rather than "subject to object" or "traveler to scene."[13] An environment is the setting in which we exist as a "sentient part"; it is our surroundings. Sparshott points out that, as our surroundings, our setting, the environment is that which we take for granted, that which we hardly notice—it is necessarily unobtrusive. If any one part of it becomes obtrusive, it is in danger of being seen as an object or a scene, not as our environment. As Sparshott says, "When a man starts talking about 'environmental values' we usually take him to be talking about aesthetic values of a background sort."[14]

The aesthetic values of the environment being primarily background values has obvious ramifications for the questions of what and how to appreciate. In regard to what to appreciate this suggests the answer "everything," for in an essentially unobtrusive setting there seems little basis for including and excluding. I will return to this shortly. In regard to how to appreciate, the answer suggested is in terms of all those ways in which we normally are aware of and experience our surroundings. Sparshott notes that "if environmental aspects are background aspects, eye and ear lost part of their privilege" and goes on to mention smell, touch, and taste, and even warmth and coolness, barometric pressure and humidity as pos-

---

[13] Sparshott, op. cit., pp. 12–13. Sparshott also considers other possible relations which are not directly relevant here. Moreover, I suspect he considers the "traveler to scene" relation to be more significant than I do.
[14] Ibid., pp. 17–18.

sibly relevant.[15] This points in the right direction, but as Sparshott also notes, it seems to involve a difficulty: that "the concept of the aesthetic tugs in a different direction"—the direction of the subject/object relation involving primarily the visual scrutiny of an aesthetic object.[16] However, I do not think this difficulty need be as serious as Sparshott seems to think. I suspect the apparent tension here is not due to the concept of the aesthetic being necessarily tied to the subject/object relation or to the visual, but rather is due to its being antithetical to the appreciation of anything only as unobtrusive background. To confirm this we need to consider the concept of the aesthetic as it is elaborated by John Dewey in *Art as Experience*.[17] Dewey's concept is such that anything which is aesthetically appreciated must be obtrusive, it must be foreground, but it need not be an object and it need not be seen (or only seen). Moreover, to assume that that which is aesthetically appreciated need be an object or only seen is to confine aesthetic appreciation to either the object model or the landscape model, which, as we have noted, impose unacceptable limitations on the aesthetic appreciation of the natural environment.

I suggest then that the beginning of an answer to the question of *how* to aesthetically appreciate an environment is something like the following: We must experience our background setting in all those ways in which we normally experience it, by sight, smell, touch, and whatever. However, we must experience it not as unobtrusive background, but as obtrusive foreground! What is involved in such an "act of aspection" is not completely clear. Dewey gives us an idea in remarks such as:

> To grasp the sources of esthetic experience it is . . . necessary to have recourse to animal life below the human scale. . . . The live animal is fully present, all there, in all of its actions: in its wary glances, its sharp sniffing, its abrupt cocking of ears. All senses are equally on the *qui vive*.[18]

And perhaps the following description by Yi-Fu Tuan gives some further indication:

> An adult must learn to be yielding and careless like a child if he were to enjoy nature polymorphously. He needs to slip into old clothes so that he could feel free to stretch out on the hay beside the brook and bathe in a meld of physical sensations: the smell of the hay and of horse dung; the warmth of the ground, its hard and soft contours; the warmth of the sun tempered by breeze; the tickling of an ant making its way up the calf of his leg; the play of shifting leaf shadows on his face; the sound of water over the pebbles and boulders, the sound of cicadas and distant traffic. Such an environment might break all the formal rules of euphony and

---

[15] Ibid., p. 21.
[16] Ibid., pp. 13–14, 21.
[17] John Dewey, *Art as Experience* (New York, 1958), especially chapters 1–3.
[18] Ibid., pp. 18–19.

aesthetics, substituting confusion for order, and yet be wholly satisfying.[19]

Tuan's account as to how to appreciate fits well with our earlier answer to the question of what to appreciate, viz. everything. This answer, of course, will not do. We cannot appreciate everything; there must be limits and emphasis in our aesthetic appreciation of nature as there are in our appreciation of art. Without such limits and emphases our experience of the natural environment would be *only* "a meld of physical sensations" without any meaning or significance. It would be a Jamesian "blooming buzzing confusion" which truly substituted "confusion for order" and which, I suspect contra to Tuan, would not be wholly satisfying. Such experience would be too far removed from our aesthetic appreciation of art to merit the label "aesthetic" or even the label "appreciation." Consider again the case of art. In this case, as noted in Section I, the boundaries and foci of aesthetic significance of works of art are a function of the type of art in question, e.g., paintings end at their frames and their colors are significant. Moreover, I suggested that our knowledge of such matters is due to art works being our creations. Here it is relevant to note the second point which I wish to emphasize about natural environments: they are natural. The natural environment is not a work of art. As such it has no boundaries or foci of aesthetic significance which are given as a result of our creation nor of which we have knowledge because of our involvement in such creation.

The fact that nature is natural—not our creation—does not mean, however, that we must be without knowledge of it. Natural objects are such that we can discover things about them which are independent of any involvement by us in their creation. Thus although we have not created nature, we yet know a great deal about it. This knowledge, essentially common sense/scientific knowledge, seems to me the only viable candidate for playing the role in regard to the appreciation of nature which our knowledge of types of art, artistic traditions, and the like plays in regard to the appreciation of art. Consider the aesthetic appreciation of an environment such as that described by Tuan. We experience the environment as obtrusive foreground—the smell of the hay and of the horse dung, the feel of the ant, the sound of the cicadas and of the distant traffic all force themselves upon us. We experience a "meld of sensations" but, as noted, if our state is to be aesthetic appreciation rather than just the having of raw experience, the meld cannot be simply a "blooming buzzing confusion." Rather it must be what Dewey called a consummatory experience: one in which knowledge and intelligence transform raw experience by making it determinate, harmonious, and meaningful. For example, in order for there to be aesthetic appreciation we must recognize

[19] Tuan, *Topophilia*, op. cit., p. 96.

the smell of the hay and that of the horse dung and perhaps distinguish between them; we must feel the ant at least as an insect rather than as, say, a twitch. Such recognizing and distinguishing results in certain aspects of the obtrusive foreground becoming foci of aesthetic significance. Moreover, they are natural foci appropriate to the particular natural environment we are appreciating. Likewise our knowledge of the environment may yield certain appropriate boundaries or limits to the experience. For example, since we are aesthetically appreciating a certain kind of environment, the sound of cicadas may be appreciated as a proper part of the setting, while the sound of the distant traffic is excluded much as we ignore the coughing in the concert hall.

What I am suggesting is that the question of *what* to aesthetically appreciate in the natural environment is to be answered in a way analogous to the similar question about art. The difference is that in the case of the natural environment the relevant knowledge is the common sense/scientific knowledge which we have discovered about the environment in question. This knowledge gives us the appropriate foci of aesthetic significance and the appropriate boundaries of the setting so that our experience becomes one of aesthetic appreciation. If to aesthetically appreciate art we must have knowledge of artistic traditions and styles within those traditions, to aesthetically appreciate nature we must have knowledge of the different environments of nature and of the systems and elements within those environments. In the way in which the art critic and the art historian are well equipped to aesthetically appreciate art, the naturalist and the ecologist are well equipped to aesthetically appreciate nature.[20]

The point I have now made about what to appreciate in nature also has ramifications for how to appreciate nature. When discussing the nature of an environment, I suggested that Tuan's description seems to indicate a general act of aspection appropriate for any environment. However, since natural environments differ in type it seems that within this general act of aspection there might be differences which should be noted. To aesthetically appreciate an environment we experience our surroundings as obtrusive foreground allowing our knowledge of that environment to select certain foci of aesthetic significance and perhaps exclude others, thereby limiting the experience. But certainly there are also different kinds of appropriate acts of aspection which can likewise be selected by our knowledge of environments. Ziff tells us to look for contours in the Florentine school and for color in a Bonnard, to survey a Tintoretto and to scan a Bosch. Consider different natural environments. It seems that we must survey a prairie environment, looking at the subtle contours of the land, feeling the wind blowing across the open space, and

---

[20] I have in mind here individuals such as John Muir and Aldo Leopold. See, for example, Leopold's *A Sand County Almanac*.

smelling the mix of prairie grasses and flowers. But such an act of aspection has little place in a dense forest environment. Here we must examine and scrutinize, inspecting the detail of the forest floor, listening carefully for the sounds of birds and smelling carefully for the scent of spruce and pine. Likewise, the description of environmental appreciation given by Tuan, in addition to being a model for environmental acts of aspection in general, is also a description of the act of aspection appropriate for a particular kind of environment—one perhaps best described as pastoral. Different natural environments require different acts of aspection; and as in the case of what to appreciate, our knowledge of the environment in question indicates how to appreciate, that is, indicates the appropriate act of aspection.

The model I am thus presenting for the aesthetic appreciation of nature might be termed the environmental model. It involves recognizing that nature is an environment and thus a setting within which we exist and which we normally experience with our complete range of senses as our unobtrusive background. But our experience being aesthetic requires unobtrusive background to be experienced as obtrusive foreground. The result is the experience of a "blooming, buzzing confusion" which in order to be appreciated must be tempered by the knowledge which we have discovered about the natural environment so experienced. Our knowledge of the nature of the particular environments yields the appropriate boundaries of appreciation, the particular foci of aesthetic significance, and the relevant act or acts of aspection for that type of environment. We thus have a model which begins to give answers to the questions of what and how to appreciate in respect to the natural environment and which seems to do so with due regard for the nature of that environment. And this is important not only for aesthetic but also for moral and ecological reasons.

IV

In this paper I have attempted to open discussion on the questions of what and how to aesthetically appreciate in regard to nature. In doing so I have argued that two traditional approaches, each of which more or less assimilates the appreciation of nature to the appreciation of certain art forms, leave much to be desired. However, the approach which I have suggested, the environmental model, yet follows closely the general structure of our aesthetic appreciation of art. This approach does not depend on an assimilation of natural objects to art objects or of landscapes to scenery, but rather on an application of the general structure of aesthetic appreciation of art to something which is not art. What is important is to recognize that nature is an environment and is natural, and to make that recognition central to our aesthetic appreciation. Thereby we will aesthetically appreciate nature for what it is and for the qualities it has. And we will avoid being the person described by Hepburn who "will either pay very little aesthetic heed to natural objects or else heed them in the wrong way," who "will look—and of course look in vain—for what can be found and enjoyed only in art."[21]

[21] Hepburn, op. cit., p. 53.

On Being Moved by Nature: Between Religion and Natural History

Noël Carroll

I. Introduction

For the last two and a half decades—perhaps spurred onwards by R. W. Hepburn's seminal, wonderfully sensitive and astute essay "Contemporary Aesthetics and the Neglect of Natural Beauty"[1]—philosophical interest in the aesthetic appreciation of nature has been gaining momentum. One of the most coherent, powerfully argued, thorough, and philosophically compelling theories to emerge from this evolving arena of debate has been developed over a series of articles by Allen Carlson.[2] The sophistication of Carlson's approach—especially in terms of his careful style of argumentation—has raised the level of philosophical discussion concerning the aesthetic appreciation of nature immensely and it has taught us all what is at stake, logically and epistemologically, in advancing a theory of nature appreciation. Carlson has not only presented a bold theory of the aesthetic appreciation of nature; he has also refined a methodological framework and a set of constraints that every researcher in the field must address.

[1] R. W. Hepburn, "Contemporary Aesthetics and the Neglect of Natural Beauty," in his *Wonder and Other Essays* (Edinburgh University Press, 1984). This essay appeared earlier in *British Analytical Philosophy*, eds. B. Williams and A. Montefiore (London: Routledge and Kegan Paul, 1966).
[2] See especially: Allen Carlson, "Appreciation and the Natural Environment," reprinted in this book. "Formal Qualities in the Natural Environment," *Journal of Aesthetic Education* 13 (July, 1979); "Nature, Aesthetic Judgment and Objectivity," *Journal of Aesthetics and Art Criticism* 40 (autumn, 1981); "Saito on the Correct Aesthetic Appreciation of Nature," *Journal of Aesthetic Education* 20 (summer, 1986); "On Appreciating Agricultural Landscapes," *Journal of Aesthetics and Art Criticism* (spring, 1985); "Appreciating Art and Appreciating Nature," in this volume; Barry Sadler and Allen Carlson, "Environmental Aesthetics in Interdisciplinary Perspective," in *Environmental Aesthetics: Essays in Interpretation*, eds. Barry Sadler and Allen Carlson (Victoria, British Columbia: University of Victoria, 1982); and Allen Carlson and Barry Sadler, "Towards Models of Environmental Appreciation," in *Environmental Aesthetics*.

Stated summarily, Carlson's view of the appreciation of nature is that it is a matter of scientific understanding; that is, the correct or appropriate form that the appreciation of nature—properly so called—should take is a species of natural history; appreciating nature is a matter of understanding nature under the suitable scientific categories. In appreciating an expanse of modern farm land, for example, we appreciate it by coming to understand the way in which the shaping of such a landscape is a function of the purposes of large-scale agriculture.[3] Likewise, the appreciation of flora and fauna is said to require an understanding of evolutionary theory.[4]

Carlson calls his framework for nature appreciation the natural environmental model.[5] He believes that the strength of this model is that it regards nature as (a) an environment (rather than, say, a view) and (b) as natural. Moreover, the significance of (b) is that it implies that the appreciation of nature should be in terms of the qualities nature has (and these, in turn, are the qualities natural science identifies). Carlson writes "for significant appreciation of nature, something like the knowledge and experience of the naturalist is essential."[6]

My major worry about Carlson's stance is that it excludes certain very common appreciative responses to nature—responses of a less intellective, more visceral sort, which we might refer to as "being moved by nature." For example, we may find ourselves standing under a thundering waterfall and be excited by its grandeur; or standing barefooted amidst a silent arbor, softly carpeted with layers of decaying leaves, a sense of repose and homeyness may be aroused in us. Such responses to nature are quite frequent and even sought out by those of us who are not naturalists. They are a matter of being emotionally moved by nature. This, of course, does not imply that they are noncognitive, since emotional arousal has a cognitive dimension.[7] However, it is far from clear that all the emotions appropriately aroused in us by nature are rooted in cognitions of the sort derived from natural history.

Appreciating nature for many of us, I submit, often involves being moved or emotionally aroused by nature. We may appreciate nature by opening ourselves to its stimulus, and to being put in a certain emotional state by attending to its aspects. Experiencing nature, in this mode, just is a manner of appreciating it. That is not to say that this is the only way in which we can appreciate nature. The approach of the naturalist that Carlson advocates is another way. Nor do I wish to deny that naturalists

---

[3] See Carlson, "Appreciating Agricultural Landscapes."

[4] Carlson, "Appreciating Art," in *Landscape, Natural Beauty and the Arts* ed. by Ivan Gaskell and Salim Kemal (Cambridge University Press, 1993).

[5] Carlson, Appreciation and the Natural Environment," p. 134.

[6] Carlson, "Nature, Aesthetic Judgment," p. 25.

[7] See, for example, William Lyons, *Emotion* (Cambridge University Press, 1980), especially ch. 4.

can be moved by nature or even to deny that something like our nonscientific arousal by nature might be augmented, in some cases, by the kind of knowledge naturalists possess. It is only to claim that sometimes we can be moved by nature—*sans* guidance by scientific categories—and that such experiences have a genuine claim to be counted among the ways in which nature may be (legitimately) appreciated.

Carlson's approach to the appreciation of nature is reformist. His point is that a number of the best-known frameworks for appreciating nature—which one finds in the literature—are wrongheaded *and* that the model of appreciation informed by naturalism which he endorses is the least problematic and most reasonable picture of what nature appreciation should involve. In contrast, I wish to argue that there is at least one frequently indulged way of appreciating nature which Carlson has not examined adequately and that it need not be abjured on the basis of the kinds of arguments and considerations Carlson has adduced. It is hard to read Carlson's conclusions without surmising that he believes that he has identified *the* appropriate model of nature appreciation. Instead, I believe that there is one form of nature appreciation—call it being emotionally moved by nature—that (a) is a longstanding practice, (b) remains untouched by Carlson's arguments, and (c) need not be abandoned in the face of Carlson's natural environmental model.

In defending this alternative mode of nature appreciation, I am not offering it in place of Carlson's environmental model. Being moved by nature in certain ways is one way of appreciating nature; Carlson's environmental model is another. I'm for coexistence. I am specifically *not* arguing that, given certain traditional conceptions of the *aesthetic,* being moved by nature has better claims to the title of *aesthetic* appreciation whereas the environmental model, insofar as it involves the subsumption of particulars under scientific categories and laws, is not an *aesthetic* mode of appreciation at all. Such an objection to Carlson's environmental model might be raised, but it will not be raised by me. I am willing to accept that the natural environmental model provides *an* aesthetic mode of appreciating nature for the reasons Carlson gives.

Though I wish to resist Carlson's environmental model of nature appreciation as an exclusive, comprehensive one, and, thereby, wish to defend a space for the traditional practice of being moved by nature, I also wish to block any reductionist account—of the kind suggested by T. J. Diffey[8]—that regards our being moved by nature as a residue of religious feeling. Diffey says, "In a secular society it is not surprising that there will be a hostility towards any religious veneration of natural beauty and at the same time nature will become a refuge for displaced religious emotions."[9] But I want to stress that the emotions aroused by nature that con-

---

[8] T. J. Diffey, "Natural Beauty without Metaphysics," in *Landscape, Natural Beauty and the Arts* ed. by Ivan Gaskell and Salim Kemal (Cambridge University Press, 1993).
[9] *Ibid.*

cern me can be fully secular and have no call to be demystified as displaced religious sentiment. That is, being moved by nature is a mode of nature appreciation that is available between science and religion.

In what follows I will try to show that the kinds of considerations that Carlson raises do not preclude being moved by nature as a respectable form of nature appreciation. In order to do this, I will review Carlson's major arguments—which I call, respectively: science by elimination, the claims of objectivist epistemology and the order argument. In the course of disputing these arguments, I will also attempt to introduce a positive characterization of what being moved by nature involves in a way that deflects the suspicion that it should be reduced to displaced religious feeling.

II. Science by Elimination

Following Paul Ziff, Carlson points out that in the appreciation of works of art, we know what to appreciate—in that we can distinguish an artwork from what it is not—and we know which of its aspects to appreciate—since in knowing the type of art it is, we know how it is to be appreciated.[10] We have this knowledge, as Vico would have agreed, because artworks are our creations. That is, since we have made them to be objects of aesthetic attention, we understand what is involved in appreciating them.[11]

However we explain this feature of artistic appreciation, it seems clear that classifying the kind and style of an artwork is crucial to appreciating it. But with nature—something which in large measure it is often the case that we have not made—the question arises as to how we can appreciate it. By what principles will we isolate the appreciable from what it is not, and how will we select the appropriate aspects of the nature so circumscribed to appreciate? In order to answer this question, Carlson explores alternative models for appreciating nature: the object paradigm, the landscape or scenery model, and the environmental paradigm.[12]

The object paradigm of nature appreciation treats an expanse in nature as analogous to an artwork such as a nonrepresentational sculpture; as in the case of such a sculpture, we appreciate its sensuous properties, its salient patterns and perhaps even its expressive qualities.[13] That is, the object model guides our attention to certain aspects of nature—such as

---

[10] Carlson, "Appreciation and the Natural Environment," p. 127.

[11] *Ibid.*

[12] This is the way that the argument is set up in "Appreciation and the Natural Environment." In "Formal Qualities in the Natural Environment," the object paradigm and the scenery model, it seems to me, both get assimilated under what might be called the formal-qualities model.

[13] Carlson, "Appreciation and the Natural Environment," pp. 128–129.

patterned configurations—which are deemed relevant for appreciation. This is clearly a possible way of attending to nature, but Carlson wants to know whether it is an aesthetically appropriate way.[14]

Carlson thinks not; for there are systematically daunting disanalogies between natural expanses and works of fine art. For example, a natural object is said to be an indeterminate form. Where it stops is putatively ambiguous.[15] But with artworks, there are frames or framelike devices (like the ropes and spaces around sculptures) that tell you where the focus of artistic attention ends. Moreover, the formal qualities of such artworks are generally contingent on such framings.[16]

Of course, we can impose frames on nature. We can take a rock from its natural abode and put it on a mantlepiece. Or, we can discipline our glance in such a way as to frame a natural expanse so that we appreciate the visual patterns that emerge from our own exercise in perceptual composition. But in doing this, we work against the organic unity in the natural expanse, sacrificing many of those real aesthetic features that are not made salient by our exercises in visual framing, *especially* the physical forces that make the environment what it is.[17] And in this sense, the object paradigm is too exclusive; it offends through aesthetic omission.

Thus, Carlson confronts the object paradigm with a dilemma. Under its aegis, either we frame—literally or figuratively—a part of nature, thereby removing it from its organic environment (and distracting our attention from its interplay with many real and fascinating ecological forces) OR we leave it where it is, unframed, indeterminate, and bereft of the fixed visual patterns and qualities (that emerge from acts of framing). In the first case, the object model is insensitive; in the second, it is, putatively, inoperable.

A second paradigm for nature appreciation is the landscape or scenery model. This also looks to fine art as a precedent; it invites us to contemplate a landscape as if it were a landscape painting. Perhaps this approach gained appeal historically in the guidebooks of the eighteenth century which recommended this or that natural prospect as affording a view reminiscent of this or that painter (such as Salvator Rosa).[18] In appreciating a landscape as a piece of scenery painting, we attend to features it might share with a landscape painting, such as its coloration and design.

But this, like the object model, also impedes comprehensive attention to the actual landscape. It directs our attention to the visual; but the full

---

[14] *Ibid.*

[15] *Ibid.*

[16] Carlson, "Formal Qualities," p. 108–9.

[17] Carlson, "Appreciation and the Natural Environment," p. 130.

[18] See for example, Peter Bicknell, *Beauty, Horror and Immensity: Picturesque Landscape in Britain 1750–1850* (Cambridge University Press, 1981).

appreciation of nature comprises smells, textures and temperatures. And landscape painting typically sets us at a distance from nature. Yet often we appreciate nature for our being amidst it.[19] Paintings are two-dimensional, but nature has three dimensions; it offers a participatory space, not simply a space that we apprehend from outside.

Likewise, the picture frame excludes us whereas characteristically we are included as a self in a setting in the natural expanses we appreciate.[20] Thus, as with the object model of nature appreciation, the problem with the scenery model is that it is too restrictive to accommodate all the aspects of nature that might serve as genuine objects of aesthetic attention.

Lastly, Carlson offers us the natural environment model of appreciation. The key to this model is that it regards nature as nature. It overcomes the limitations of the object model by taking as *essential* the organic relation of natural expanses and items to their larger environmental contexts. The interplay of natural forces like winds are as significant as the sensuous shapes of the rock formations that are subject to them. On this view, appreciating nature involves attending to the organic interaction of natural forces. *Pace* the scenery model, the totality of natural forces, not just those that are salient to vision, are comprehended. Whereas the scenery paradigm *proposes* nature as a static array, the natural environment approach acknowledges the dynamism of nature.

Undoubtedly the inclusiveness of the natural environment model sounds promising. But the question still remains concerning which natural categories and relations are relevant to attending to nature as nature. It is Carlson's view that natural science provides us with the kind of knowledge that guides us to the appropriate *foci* of aesthetic significance and to the pertinent relations within their boundaries.

In order to aesthetically appreciate art, we must have knowledge of the artistic traditions that yield the relevant classificatory schemes for artists and audiences; in order to aesthetically appreciate nature, we need comparable knowledge of different environments and of their relevant systems and elements.[21] This knowledge comes from science and natural history, including that which is embodied in common sense. Where else could it come from? What else could understanding nature as nature amount to? The knowledge we derive from art criticism and art history for the purpose of art appreciation come from ecology and natural history with respect to nature appreciation.

Carlson writes: "What I am suggesting is that the question of *what* to aesthetically appreciate in the natural environment is to be answered in a way analogous to the similar question about art. The difference is that in

---

[19] Carlson, "Appreciation and the Natural Environment," p. 133.
[20] Carlson, "Formal Qualities," p. 110.
[21] Carlson, "Appreciation and the Natural Environment," pp. 137–138.

the case of the natural environment the relevant knowledge is the commonsense/scientific knowledge which we have discovered about the environment in question."[22]

The structure of Carlson's argument is motivated by the pressure to discover some guidance with respect to nature appreciation that is analogous to the guidance that the fixing of artistic categories does with works of art. Three possibilities are explored: the object paradigm, the scenery paradigm and the natural environment paradigm. The first two are rejected because they fail to comprehensively track all the qualities and relations we would expect a suitable framework for the appreciation of nature to track. On the other hand, the natural environment model is advanced not only because it does not occlude the kind of attentiveness that the alternative models block, but also because it has the advantage of supplying us with classificatory frameworks which play the role that things like genres do with respect to art, while at the same time these categories are natural (derived from natural history).

Stated formally, Carlson's argument is basically a disjunctive syllogism:

(1) All aesthetic appreciation requires a way of fixing the appropriate *loci* of appreciative acts.
(2) Since nature appreciation is aesthetic appreciation, then nature appreciation must have a means of fixing the appropriate *loci* of appreciative acts.
(3) With nature appreciation, the ways of fixing the appropriate *loci* of appreciative acts are the object model, the scenic model and the natural environment model.
(4) Neither the object model nor the scenic model suit nature appreciation.
(5) Therefore, the natural environment model (using science as its source of knowledge) is the means for fixing the *loci* of appreciative acts with respect to nature appreciation.

Of course, the most obvious line of attack to take with arguments of this sort is to ask whether it has captured the relevant field of alternatives. I want to suggest that Carlson's argument has not. Specifically, I maintain that he has not countenanced our being moved by nature as a mode of appreciating nature and that he has not explored the possibility that the *loci* of such appreciation can be fixed in the process of our being emotionally aroused by nature.

Earlier I conjured up a scene where standing near a towering cascade, our ears reverberating with the roar of falling water, we are overwhelmed and excited by its grandeur. People quite standardly seek out such experiences. They are, pretheoretically, a form of appreciating nature.

[22] *Ibid.*

Moreover, when caught up in such experiences our attention is fixed on certain aspects of the natural expanse rather than others—the palpable force of the cascade, its height, the volume of water, the way it alters the surrounding atmosphere, etc.

This does not require any special scientific knowledge. Perhaps it only requires being human, equipped with the senses we have, being small and able to intuit the immense force, relative to creatures like us, of the roaring tons of water. Nor need the common sense of our culture come into play. Conceivably humans from other planets bereft of waterfalls could share our sense of grandeur. This is not to say that all emotional responses to nature are culture-free, but only that the pertinent dimensions of some such arousals may be.

That is, we may be aroused emotionally by nature, and our arousal may be a function of our human nature in response to a natural expanse. I may savor a winding footpath because it raises a tolerable sense of mystery in me. Unlike the scenery model of nature appreciation, what we might call the arousal model does not necessarily put us at a distance from the object of our appreciation; it may be the manner in which we are amidst nature that has moved us to the state in which we find ourselves. Nor does the arousal model of nature restrict our response to only the visual aspects of nature. The cascade moves us through its sound, and weight, and temperature, and force. The sense of mystery awakened by the winding path is linked to the process of moving through it.

Perhaps the arousal model seems to raise the problem of framing, mentioned earlier, in a new way. Just as the object model and the scenery model appeared to impose a frame on an otherwise indeterminate nature, similarly the arousal model may appear to involve us in imposing emotional gestalts upon indeterminate natural expanses. Nevertheless, there are features of nature, especially in relation to human organisms, which, though they are admittedly "selected," are difficult to think of as "impositions."

Certain natural expanses have natural frames or what I prefer to call natural closure: caves, copses, grottoes, clearings, arbors, valleys, etc. And other natural expanses, though lacking frames, have features that are naturally salient for human organisms—i.e., they have features such as moving water, bright illumination, etc. that draw our attention instinctually toward them. And where our emotional arousal is predicated on either natural closure or natural salience, it makes little sense to say that our emotional responses, focused on said features, are impositions.

An emotional response to nature will involve some sort of selective attention to the natural expanse. If I am overwhelmed by the grandeur of a waterfall, then certain things and not others are in the forefront of my attention. Presumably since I am struck emotionally by the grandness of the waterfall, the features that are relevant to my response have to do with those that satisfy interests in scale, notably large scale. But my arousal does not come from nowhere. The human perceptual system is already keyed to noticing salient scale differentials and the fact that I batten on striking examples of the large scale is hardly an imposition from the human point of view.

Suppose, then, that I am exhilarated by the grandeur of the waterfall. That I am exhilarated by grandeur is not an inappropriate response, since the object of my emotional arousal is grand—i.e., meets the criteria of scale appropriate to grandeur, where grandeur, in turn, is one of the appropriate sources of exhilaration. In this case, our perceptual make-up initially focuses our attention on certain features of the natural expanse, which attention generates a state of emotional arousal, which state, in turn, issues in reinforcing feedback that consolidates the initial selective gestalt of the emotional arousement experience. The arousal model of nature appreciation has an account of how we isolate certain aspects of nature and why these are appropriate aspects to focus upon; that is, they are *emotionally* appropriate.

Perhaps Carlson's response to this is that emotional responses to nature of the sort that I envision are not responses to nature as nature. This route seems inadvisable since Carlson, like Sparshott, wants us to think of the appreciator of nature as a self in a setting which I understand as, in part, a warning not to divorce human nature from nature.[23] Admittedly, not all of our emotional arousals in the face of nature should be ascribed to our common human nature, rather than to what is sectarian in our cultures, but there is no reason to preclude the possibility that some of our emotional arousals to nature are bred in the bone.

Conceding that we are only talking about *some* of our appreciative responses to nature here may seem to open another line of criticism. Implicit in Carlson's manner of argument seems to be the presupposition that what he is about is identifying the one and only form of nature appreciation. His candidate, of course, is the environmental model which relies heavily on natural science.

I have already argued that this model is not the only respectable alternative. But another point also bears emphasis here, namely, why presume that there is only one model for appreciating nature and one source of knowledge—such as natural history—relevant to fixing our appreciative categories? Why are we supposing that there is just one model, applying to all cases, for the appropriate appreciation of nature?

That the appreciation of nature sometimes may involve emotional arousal, divorced from scientific or commonsense ecological knowledge, does not disallow that at other times appreciation is generated by the nat-

[23] Francis Sparshott, "Figuring the Ground: Notes on Some Theoretical Problems of the Aesthetic Environment," *Journal of Aesthetic Education*, 6.3 (July 1972).

ural environment model. Certainly a similar situation obtains in artistic appreciation. Sometimes we may be emotionally aroused—indeed, appropriately emotionally moved—without knowing the genre or style of the artwork that induces this state. Think of children amused by capers of *Commedia dell'arte* but who know nothing of its tradition or its place among other artistic genres, styles and categories. Yet the existence of this sort of appreciative response in no way compromises the fact that there is another kind of appreciation—that of the informed connoisseur—which involves situating the features of the artwork with respect to its relevant artistic categories.

I want to say that the same is true of nature appreciation. Appreciation may sometimes follow the arousal model or the natural environment model. Sometimes the two models may overlap—for our emotions may be aroused on the basis of our ecological knowledge. But, equally, there will be clear cases where they do not. Moreover, I see no reason to assume that these are the only models for the appropriate response to nature. In some cases—given the natural closure and salience of arrays in nature—the object model may not be out of place for, given our limited perceptual capacities, structured as they are, nature may not strike us as formally indeterminate.

My basic objection to Carlson is that emotional arousal in response to nature can be an appropriate form of nature appreciation and that the cognitive component of our emotional response does the job of fixing the aspects of nature that are relevant to appreciation. Here, I have been assuming that emotional arousal, though cognitive, need not rely on categories derived from science. But Carlson sometimes describes his preferred source of knowledge as issuing from common sense/science. So perhaps the way out of my objection is to say that with my cases of being moved by nature, the operative cognitions are rooted in commonsense knowledge of nature.

A lot depends here on what is included in commonsense knowledge of nature. I take it that for Carlson this is a matter of knowing in some degree how nature works; it involves, for example, some prescientific, perhaps folk, understanding of things like ecological systems. That I know, in my waterfall example, that the stuff that is falling down is water is not commonsense knowledge of nature in the way that Carlson seems to intend with phrases like common sense/science. For the knowledge in my case need not involve any systematic knowledge of nature's working of either a folk or scientific origin. And if this is so, then we can say that we are emotionally moved by nature where the operative cognitions that play a constitutive role in our response do not rely on the kind of commonsense systemic knowledge of natural processes that Carlson believes is requisite for the aesthetic appreciation of nature. And, perhaps even more clearly, we can be moved by nature where our cognitions do not mobilize the far more formal and recondite systemic knowledge found in natural history and science.

III. The Claims of Objectivist Epistemology

One reason, as we have just seen, that prompts Carlson to endorse natural history as the appropriate guide to nature appreciation is that it appears to provide us with our only satisfactory alternative. I have disputed this. But Carlson has other compelling motives for the type of nature appreciation he advocates. One of these is epistemological. It has already been suggested; now is the time to bring it centerstage.

Echoing Hume's "Of the Standard of Taste," Carlson's impressive "Nature, Aesthetic Judgment and Objectivity" begins with the conviction that certain of the aesthetic judgments that we issue with respect to nature—such as "The Grand Tetons are majestic"—are or can be appropriate, correct or true. That is, certain aesthetic judgments of nature are objective. Were someone to assert that "The Grand Tetons are paltry," without further explanation, our response would converge on the consensus that the latter assertion is false.

However, though the conviction that aesthetic judgments of nature can be objective is firm, it is nevertheless difficult to square with the best available models we possess for elucidating the way in which aesthetic judgments of art are objective. Indeed, given our best models of the way that aesthetic judgments of art are objective, we may feel forced to conclude that aesthetic judgments of nature are relativistic or subjective, despite our initial conviction that aesthetic judgments of nature can be objective.

So the question becomes a matter of explaining how our aesthetic judgments of nature can be objective. This is a problem because, as just mentioned, reigning accounts of how aesthetic judgments of art are objective have been taken to imply that aesthetic judgments of nature cannot be objective.

In order to get a handle on this problem, we need, of course, to understand the relevant theory of art appreciation which ostensibly renders nature appreciation subjective or relative. The particular theory that Carlson has in mind is Kendall Walton's notion of categories of art. This theory is an example of a broader class of theories—that would include institutional theories of art—which can be usefully thought of as cultural theories. Roughly speaking, cultural theories of art supply the wherewithal to ground aesthetic judgments of art objectively by basing such judgments on the cultural practice and forms—such as artistic genres, styles and movements—in which and through which artworks are created and disseminated.

On Walton's account, for example, an aesthetic judgment concerning an artwork can be assessed as true or false. The truth value of such judgments is a function of two factors, specifically: the non-aesthetic perceptual properties of the artwork (e.g., dots of paint), and the status of said properties when the artwork is situated in its correct artistic category (e.g., pointillism). Psychologically speaking, all aesthetic judgments of art, whether they are subjective or objective, require that we locate the perceived, nonaesthetic properties of the artwork in *some* category. For example, if an uninformed viewer finds the image in a cubist painting woefully confused, it is likely that that viewer regards the work in terms of the (albeit wrong) category of a realistic, perspectival representation.

However, logically speaking, if an aesthetic judgment is true (or appropriate), then that is a function of the perceived, nonaesthetic properties of the artwork being comprehended within the context of the *correct* category of art. In terms of preceding example, it is a matter of viewing the painting in question under the category of cubism. Consequently, the objectivity of aesthetic judgments of art depends upon identifying the correct category for the artwork in question.

A number of circumstances can count in determining the category of art that is relevant to the aesthetic judgment of an artwork. But some of the most conclusive depend on features relating to the origin of the work: such as which category (genre, style, movement) the artist intended for the artwork, as well as cultural factors, such as whether the category in question is a recognized or well-entrenched one. These are not the only considerations that we use in fixing the relevant category of an artwork; but they are, nevertheless, fairly decisive ones.

However, if these sorts of considerations are crucial in fixing the relevant categories of artworks, it should be clear that they are of little moment when it comes to nature. For nature is not produced by creators whose intentions can be used to isolate the *correct* categories for appreciating a given natural expanse *nor* is nature produced with regard for recognized cultural categories. But if we cannot ascertain the correct category upon which to ground our aesthetic judgments of nature, then those judgments cannot be either true or false. Moreover, since the way in which we fix the category of a natural object or expanse appears to be fairly open, our aesthetic judgments of nature appear to gravitate towards subjectivity. That is, they do not seem as though they can be objective judgments, despite our starting intuition that some of them are.

The structure of Carlson's argument revolves around a paradox. We start with the conviction that some aesthetic judgments of nature can be objective, but then the attempt to explain this by the lights of our best model of aesthetic objectivity with respect to the arts, indicates that no aesthetic judgment of nature can be objective (because there are no *correct* categories for nature). Carlson wants to dissolve this paradox by removing the worry that there are no objective, aesthetic judgments of nature.

He does this by arguing that we do have the means for identifying the relevant, *correct* categories that are operative in genuine aesthetic judgments of nature. These are the ones *discovered* by natural history and science.

For example, we know that the relevant category for aesthetically appreciating whales is that of the mammal rather than that of fish as a result of scientific research. Moreover, these scientific categories function formally or logically in the same way in nature appreciation that art historical categories function in art appreciation. Thus, the logical form, though not the content, of nature appreciation corresponds to that of art appreciation. *And* insofar as the latter can be objective in virtue of its form, the former can be as well.

Another way to characterize Carlson's argument is to regard it as a transcendental argument. It begins by assuming as given that nature appreciation can be objective and then goes on to ask how this is possible—especially since there does not seem to be anything like correct categories of art to ground objectivity when it comes to nature appreciation. But, then, the possibility of the objectivity of nature appreciation is explained by maintaining that the categories discovered by natural history and science are available to play the role in securing the objectivity of aesthetic judgments of nature in a way that is analogous to the service performed by art historical categories for art.

Thus, for epistemological reasons, we are driven to the view of nature appreciation as a species of natural history. Effectively, it is advanced as the only way to support our initial intuitions that some aesthetic judgments of nature can be objective. Moreover, any competing picture of nature appreciation, if it is to be taken seriously, must have comparable means to those of the natural environment model for solving the problem of the objectivity of nature appreciation.

Of course, I do not wish to advance the "being moved by nature" view as competing with the natural environment approach. Rather, I prefer to think of it as a coexisting model. But even as a coexisting model, it must be able to solve the problem of objectivity. However, the solution to the problem is quite straightforward when it comes to being emotionally moved by nature.

For, being emotionally moved by nature is just a subclass of being emotionally moved. And on the view of the emotions that I, among many others, hold, an emotion can be assessed as either appropriate or inappropriate. In order to be afraid, I must be afraid of *something,* say an oncoming tank. My emotion—fear in this case—is directed; it takes a particular object. Moreover, if my fear in a given case is appropriate, then the particular object of my emotional state must meet certain criteria, or what are called "formal objects" in various philosophical idioms.

For example, the formal object of fear is the dangerous. Or, to put the point in less stilted language: if my fear of the tank (the particular object of my emotion) is appropriate, then it must satisfy the criterion that I believe the tank to be dangerous to me. If, for instance, I say that I am afraid of chicken soup, but also that I do not believe that chicken soup is dangerous, then my fear of chicken soup is inappropriate. C. D. Broad writes: "It is appropriate to cognize what one takes to be a threatening object with some degree of fear. It is inappropriate to cognize what one takes to be a fellow man in undeserved pain or distress with satisfaction or with amusement."[24]

Of course, if emotions can be assessed with respect to appropriateness and inappropriateness, then they are open to cognitive appraisal. Ronald deSousa says, for example, that "appropriateness is the truth of the emotions."[25] We can assess the appropriateness of the emotion of fear for an emoter in terms of whether or not she believes that the particular object of her emotion is dangerous. We can, furthermore, assess whether the appropriateness of her fear ought to be shared by others by asking whether the beliefs, thoughts or patterns of attention that underpin her emotions are the sorts of beliefs, thoughts or patterns of attention that it is reasonable for others to share. Thus we can determine whether her fear of the tank is objective in virtue of whether her beliefs about the dangerousness of the tank, in the case at hand, is a reasonable belief for the rest of us to hold.

Turning from tanks to nature, we may be emotionally moved by a natural expanse—excited, for instance, by the grandeur of a towering waterfall. All things being equal, being excited by the grandeur of something that one believes to be of a large scale is an appropriate emotional response. Moreover, if the belief in the large scale of the cascade is one that is true for others as well, then the emotional response of being excited by the grandeur of the waterfall is an objective one. It is not subjective, distorted, or wayward. If someone denies being moved by the waterfall, but agrees that the waterfall is large scale and says nothing else, we are apt to suspect that his response, as well as any judgments issued on the basis of that response, are inappropriate. If he does not agree that the waterfall is of a large scale, and does not say why, we will suspect him either of not understanding how to use the notion of large scale, or of irrationality. If he disagrees that the waterfall is of a large scale because the galaxy is much much larger, then we will try to convince him that he has the wrong comparison class—urging, perhaps, that he should gauge the scale of the waterfall in relation to human scale.

---

[24] C. D. Broad, "Emotion and Sentiment," in his *Critical Essays in Moral Philosophy* (London: Allen and Unwin, 1971), p. 293.

[25] Ronald deSousa, "Self-Deceptive Emotions," in *Explaining Emotions* ed. Amelie Okesenberg Rorty (Berkeley: University of California Press, 1980), p. 285.

In introducing the notion of the "wrong comparison class," it may seem that I have opened the door to Carlson's arguments. But I do not think that I have. For it is not clear that in order to establish the relevant comparison class for an emotional response to nature one must resort to scientific categories. For example, we may be excited by the grandeur of a blue whale. I may be moved by its size, its force, the amount of water it displaces, etc., but I may think that it is a fish. Nevertheless, my being moved by the grandeur of the blue whale is not inappropriate. Indeed, we may be moved by the skeleton of a *Tyrannosaurus rex* without knowing whether it is the skeleton of a reptile, a bird, or a mammal. We can be moved by such encounters, without knowing the natural history of the thing encountered, on the basis of its scale, along with other things, relative to ourselves.

Such arousals may or may not be appropriate for us and for others. Moreover, judgments based on such emotional responses—like "that whale excites grandeur" or "The Grand Tetons are majestic"—can be objective. Insofar as being moved by nature is a customary form of appreciating nature, then it can account for the objectivity of some of our aesthetic judgments of nature. Thus, it satisfies the epistemological challenge whose solution Carlson appears to believe favors only his natural environment model for the aesthetic appreciation of nature. Or, to put it another way, being moved by nature remains *a* way of appreciating nature that may coexist with the natural environment model.

At one point, Carlson concedes that we can simply enjoy nature—"we can, of course, approach nature as we sometimes approach art, that is, we can simply *enjoy* its forms and colors or *enjoy* perceiving it however we may happen to."[26] But this is not a very deep level of appreciation for Carlson, for, on his view, depth would appear to require objectivity. Perhaps what Carlson would say about my defense of being moved by nature is that being emotionally aroused by nature falls into the category of *merely* enjoying nature and, as an instance of that category, it isn't really very deep.

Undoubtedly, being moved by nature may be a way of enjoying nature. However, insofar as being moved by nature is a matter of being moved by appropriate objects, it is not dismissable as enjoying nature in whatever way we please. Furthermore, if the test of whether our appreciation of nature is deep is whether the corresponding judgments are susceptible to objective, cognitive appraisal, I think I have shown that some cases can pass this test. Is there any reason to think that being moved by nature must be any less deep a response than attending to nature with the eyes of the naturalist?

[26] Carlson, "Nature, Aesthetic Judgment," p. 25.

I would be very suspicious of an affirmative answer to this question. Of course, part of the problem is that what makes an appreciative response to nature shallow or deep is obscure. Obviously, a naturalist's appreciation of nature could be deep in the sense that it might go on and on as the naturalist learns more and more about nature, whereas a case of emotional arousal with respect to nature might be more consummatory. Is the former case deeper than the latter? Are the two cases even commensurable? Clearly, time alone cannot be a measure of depth. But how exactly are we to compare appreciative stances with respect to depth?

Maybe there is no way. But if the depth of a response is figured in terms of our intensity of involvement and its "thorough-goingness,"[27] then there is no reason to suppose that being moved by nature constitutes a shallower form of appreciation than does appreciating nature scientifically. The Kantian apprehension of sublimity[28]—and its corresponding aesthetic judgment—though it may last for a delimited duration, need not be any less deep than a protracted teleological judgment.

Again, it is not my intention to dispute the kind of appreciation that Carlson defends under the title of the natural environment model. It is only to defend the legitimacy of an already well-entrenched mode of nature appreciation that I call being moved by nature. This mode of nature appreciation can pay the epistemological bill that Carlson presupposes any adequate model of nature appreciation should accommodate. It need not be reducible to scientific appreciation, nor must it be regarded as any less deep than appreciation informed by natural history.

Of course, it may seem odd that we can appreciate nature objectively this way when it seems that a comparable form of appreciation is not available to art. But the oddity here vanishes when we realize that to a certain extent we are able to appreciate art and render objective aesthetic judgments of artworks without reference to precise art historical categories. One may find a fanfare in a piece of music stirring and objectively assert that it is stirring without any knowledge of music history and its categories. Being emotionally aroused by nature in at least certain cases need be no different.

Carlson may be disposed to question whether being emotionally moved by nature is really a matter of responding to nature as nature. Perhaps he takes it to be something like a conceptual truth that, given the culture we inhabit, attending to nature as nature can only involve attending to it scientifically. However, if I am taken with the grace of a group of deer vaulting a stream, I see no reason to suppose that I am not respond-

---

[27] A test suggested by Robert Solomon in his "On Kitsch and Sentimentality," *Journal of Aesthetics and Art Criticism,* 49.1 (winter, 1981): 9.

[28] See Immanuel Kant, *The Critique of Judgement,* trans. James Creed Meredith (Oxford: Clarendon Press, 1952), especially the "Analytic of the Sublime."

ing to nature as nature. Moreover, any attempt to regiment the notion of responding to nature as nature so that it only strictly applies to scientific understanding appears to me to beg the question.

IV. Order Appreciation

The most recent argument that Carlson has advanced in favor of the natural environmental model of nature appreciation is what might be called the order argument.[29] In certain respects, it is reminiscent of his earlier arguments, but it does add certain new considerations that are worth our attention. Like his previous arguments, Carlson's order argument proceeds by carefully comparing the form of nature appreciation with that of art appreciation.

One paradigmatic form of art appreciation is design appreciation. Design appreciation presupposes that the artwork has a creator who embodies the design in an object or a performance, and that the design embodied in the artwork indicates how we are to take it. However, this model of appreciation is clearly inappropriate for nature appreciation since nature lacks a designer.

Nevertheless, there is another sort of art appreciation which has been devised in order to negotiate much of the *avant-garde* art of the twentieth century. Carlson calls this type of appreciation order appreciation. When, for example, we are confronted by something like Duchamp's *Fountain*, the design of the object does not tell us how to take it or appreciate it. Instead, we rely on certain stories about how the object came to be selected by Duchamp in order to make a point. These stories inform us of the ideas and beliefs that lead an *avant-garde* artist to produce or to select (in the case of a found object) the artwork.

These stories direct us in the appropriate manner of appreciating the object; they guide us in our selection of the relevant features of the work for the purposes of appreciation. They do the work with unconventional, experimental art that design does with more traditional art. For example, our knowledge, given a certain art historical narrative, of Surrealism's commitment to revealing the unconscious, alerts us to the importance of incongruous, dreamlike juxtapositions in paintings by Dali.

For Carlson, design appreciation is obviously ill-suited to nature appreciation. On the other hand, something like order appreciation appears to fit the case of nature appreciation. We can appreciate nature in terms of the forces that bring natural configurations about, and we can be guided to the relevant features of nature by stories. But where do these stories come from? At an earlier stage in our culture, they may have come from

---

[29] See Carlson, "Appreciating Art."

mythology. But at this late date, they come from the sciences, including astronomy, physics, chemistry, biology, genetics, meteorology, geology and so on. These sciences, and the natural histories they afford, guide our attention to the relevant forces that account for the features of nature worthy of attention.

Basically, Carlson's most recent argument is that art appreciation affords two possible models for nature appreciation: design appreciation and order appreciation. Design appreciation, however, is clearly inadmissible. That leaves us with order appreciation. However, the source of the guiding stories pertinent to the order appreciation of nature differ from those that shape order appreciation with respect to art. The source of the latter is art history while the source of the former is natural history.

But once again Carlson's argument is open to the charge that he has not canvased all of the actual alternatives. One's appreciation of art need not fall into either the category of design appreciation or order appreciation. We can sometimes appreciate art appropriately by being moved by it. Moreover, this is true of the *avant-garde* art that Carlson suggests requires order appreciation as well as of more traditional art.

For example, Man Ray's *The Gift* is an ordinary iron with pointed nails affixed to its smooth bottom. Even if one does not know that it is a specimen of Dada, and even if one lacks the art-historical story that tells one the ideology of Dada, reflecting on *The Gift* one may readily surmise that the object is at odds with itself—you cannot press trousers with it—in a way that is brutally sardonic and that arouses dark amusement. Similarly, one can detect the insult in Duchamp's *Fountain* without knowing the intricate dialectics of art history, just as one may find certain Surrealist paintings haunting without knowing the metaphysical, psychological and political aims of the Surrealist movement.

As it is sometimes with art, so is it with nature. In both cases, we may be emotionally moved by what we encounter without any really detailed background in art history or natural history. With respect to both art and nature, emotional arousal can be a mode of appreciation, and it is possible, in a large number of cases, to determine whether the emotional arousal is appropriate or inappropriate without reference to any particularly specific stories of either the art-historical or the natural-history varieties.

A parade or a sunset may move us, and this level of response, though traditionally well-known, need not be reduced to either design appreciation or order appreciation, nor must it be guided by art history or by natural history. Insofar as Carlson's approach to both art and nature appears wedded to certain types of "professional" knowledge as requisite for appreciation, he seems to be unduly hasty in closing off certain common forms of aesthetic appreciation. This is not said in order to reject the sort of informed appreciation Carlson advocates, but only to suggest that certain more naive forms of emotive, appreciative responses may be legitimate as well.[30]

I have argued that one form of nature appreciation is a matter of being aroused emotionally by the appropriate natural objects. This talk of the emotions, however, may seem suspicious to some. Does it really seem reasonable to be emotionally moved by nature? If we feel a sense of security when we scan a natural expanse, doesn't that sound just too mystical? Perhaps, our feeling, as Diffey has suggested, is some form of displaced religious sentiment. Maybe being moved by nature is some sort of delusional state worthy of psychoanalysis or demystification.

Of course, many emotional responses to nature—such as being frightened by a tiger—are anything but mystical. But it may seem that others—particularly those that are traditionally exemplary of aesthetic appreciation, like finding a landscape to be serene—are more unfathomable and perhaps shaped by repressed religious associations. However, I think that there is reliable evidence that many of our emotional responses to nature have a straightforwardly secular basis.

For example, in his classic *The Experience of Landscape*,[31] and in subsequent articles,[32] Jay Appleton has defended the view that our responses to landscape are connected to certain broadly evolutionary interests that we take in landscapes. Appleton singles out two significant variables in our attention to landscape—what he calls prospect (a landscape opportunity for keeping open the channels of perception) and refuge (a landscape opportunity for achieving concealment).

That is, given that we are the kind of animal we are, we take a survival interest in certain features of landscapes: open vistas give us a sense of security insofar as we can see there is no threat approaching, while en-

---

[30] Toward the end of "Appreciating Art," Carlson does refer to certain responses to nature, such as awe and wonder, which sound like the type of emotional responses I have been discussing. He thinks that even armed with the natural environment model, we may become aware that nature is still mysterious to us and *other*. And, in consequence, we feel awe and wonder. I do not want to deny that we may come to feel awe and wonder at nature through the process Carlson describes. However, I do not think that this is the only way that we can be overwhelmed with awe in the face of nature. We may, for example, be struck by the scale of nature, without any reference to scientific categories, and be overwhelmed by awe. Thus, though there may be a route to awe through the natural environment model, it is not the only route. There are still other ways in which we may be moved to awe by nature *sans* natural history. Consequently, the account of awe that Carlson offers does not eliminate the more naive model of emotional arousal that I have been defending.

[31] Jay Appleton, *The Experience of Landscape* (New York: Wiley, 1975).

[32] Jay Appleton, "Prospects and refuges revisited," in *Environmental Aesthetics: Theory, Research & Applications,* ed. Jack L. Nasar (Cambridge University Press, 1988); and Jay Appleton, "Pleasure and the Perception of Habitat: A Conceptual Framework," in *Environmental Aesthetics: Essays in Interpretation.*

closed spaces reassure us that there are places in which to hide. We need not be as theoretically restrictive as Appleton is and maintain that these are the major foci of our attention to landscape. But we can agree that features of landscape like prospect and refuge may cause our humanly emotional responses to natural expanses in terms of the way they address our deep-seated, perhaps tacit, interests in the environment as a potential theatre of survival.

Thus, when we find a natural environment serene, part of the cause of that sense of serenity might be its openness—the fact that nothing can approach us unexpectedly across its terrain. And such a response need not be thought to be mystical nor a matter of displaced religion, if it is connected to information processing molded by our long-term evolution as animals.

Other researchers have tried to isolate further features of landscape—such as mystery and legibility[33]—that shape our responses to natural expanses in terms of a sense, however intuitive and unconscious, of the sorts of experiences we would have—such as ease of locomotion, of orientation, of exploration and so on—in the environment viewed. That is, our perhaps instinctive sense of how it would be to function in a given natural environment may be part of the cause of our emotional arousal with respect to it. A landscape that is very legible—articulated throughout with neat subdivisions—may strike us as hospitable and attractive in part because it imparts such a strong sense of how we might move around and orient ourselves inside of it.

Earlier I sketched a scene in which we found ourselves in an arbor, carpeted by layers of decaying foliage and moss. I imagined that in such a situation we might feel a sense of solace, repose, and homeyness. And such an emotional state might be caused by our tacit recognition of its refuge potential. On this view, I am not saying that we consciously realize that the arbor is a suitable refuge and appreciate it as such. Rather the fact that it is a suitable refuge acts to causally trigger our emotional response which takes the arbor as its particular object and responds to it with a feeling of repose and homeyness, focusing on such features as its enclosure and softness, which features are appropriate to the feeling of solace and homeyness.

Our feeling is not a matter of residual mysticism or religious sentiment, but is perhaps instinctually grounded. Moreover, if such a scenario is plausible for at least some of our emotional responses to nature, then it is not the case that being aroused by nature is always a repressed religious response. Some responses of some observers may be responses rooted in associations of nature with the handiwork of the gods. But other emo-

---

[33] Stephen Kaplan, "Perception and landscape: conceptions and misconceptions," in *Environmental Aesthetics: Theory*, pp. 49–51. See also Kaplan's "Where cognition and affect meet: a theoretical analysis of preference," in the same volume.

tional responses, appropriate ones, may have perfectly secular, naturalistic explanations which derive from the kinds of insights that Appleton and others have begun to enumerate.

Admitting that our emotional responses to nature have naturalistic explanations, of course, does not entail a reversion to the natural environmental model of nature appreciation. For such explanations pertain to how our emotional responses may be caused. And when I appreciate a natural expanse by being emotionally aroused by it, the object of my emotional state need not be the recognition of my instinctual response to, for example, prospects. Perhaps one could appreciate nature *à la* Carlson from an evolutionary point-of-view in which the focus of our attention is the interaction of our emotions with the environment as that interaction is understood to be shaped by the forces of evolution. But this is not typically what one has in mind with the notion of being moved by nature.

In conclusion: to be moved by nature is to respond to the features of natural expanses—such as scale and texture—with the appropriate emotions. This is one traditional way of appreciating nature. It need not rely upon natural history nor is it a residual form of mysticism. It is one of our characteristic forms of nature appreciation—not reducible without remainder to either science nor religion.

SUGGESTIONS FOR FURTHER READING

Appleton, Jay. *The Experience of Landscape.* London: John Wiley and Sons, 1975.

Berleant, Arnold. *The Aesthetics of Environment.* Philadelphia: Temple University Press, 1992.

Boursassa, Steven C. *The Aesthetics of Landscape.* London: Belhaven Press, 1991.

Callicott, J. Baird. "The Land Aesthetic." *Environmental Review* 7 (1983): 345–58.

Carlson, Allen. "Formal Qualities in the Natural Environment." *Journal of Aesthetic Education* 13 (1979): 99–114.

Carlson, Allen. "Nature, Aesthetic Judgment and Objectivity." *Journal of Aesthetics and Art Criticism* 40 (1981): 15–27.

Carlson, Allen. "On Appreciating Agricultural Landscapes." *Journal of Aesthetics and Art Criticism* 43 (1985): 301–12.

Carlson, Allen. "Saito on the Correct Aesthetic Appreciation of Nature." *Journal of Aesthetic Education* 20 (1986): 85–93.

Crawford, Donald. "Nature and Art: Some Dialectical Relationships." *Journal of Aesthetics and Art Criticism* 42 (1983): 49–58.

Eaton, Marcia M. *Aesthetics and the Good Life.* Rutherford, N.J.: Farleigh Dickinson University Press, 1989. Chapter 4.

Hepburn, R. W. "Contemporary Aesthetics and the Neglect of Natural Beauty." In his *Wonder and Other Essays.* Edinburgh University Press, 1984.

Kemal, Salim, and Gaskell, Ivan, eds. *Landscape, Natural Beauty and the Arts.* Cambridge: Cambridge University Press, 1993.

Leopold, Aldo. *A Sand County Almanac.* New York: Oxford University Press, 1949.

Muir, John. *The Mountains of California.* New York: Penguin, 1985.

Nasar, Jack L., ed. *Environmental Aesthetics: Theory, Research and Applications.* Cambridge: Cambridge University Press, 1988.

Sadler, Barry, and Carlson, Allen, eds. *Environmental Aesthetics: Essays in Interpretation.* Victoria, B.C.: University of Victoria, 1982.

Saito, Yuriko. "Is There a Correct Aesthetic Appreciation of Nature?" *Journal of Aesthetic Education* 18 (1984): 35–46.

Sepanmaa, Yrjo. *The Beauty of Environment.* Helsinki: Suomalainen Tiedeakatemia, 1986.

Sparshott, Francis. "Figuring the Ground: Notes on Some Theoretical Problems of the Aesthetic Environment." *Journal of Aesthetic Education* 6 (1972): 11–23.

Thoreau, Henry David. "Walking." In *The Portable Thoreau,* ed. by Carl Bode. New York: The Viking Press, 1947.

Tuan, Yi-Fu. *Topophilia: A Study of Environmental Perception, Attitudes and Values.* Englewood Cliffs, N.J.: Prentice-Hall, 1974.

Walton, Kendall L. "Categories of Art." *Philosophical Review* 79 (1970): 334–67.

6

FEELINGS AND FICTIONS

Dazzled by so many and such marvellous inventions, the people of Macondo did not know where their amazement began. . . . They became indignant over the living images that the prosperous merchant Bruno Crespi projected in the theater with the lion-head ticket windows, for a character who had died and was buried in one film and for whose misfortune tears of affliction had been shed would reappear alive and transformed into an Arab in the next one. The audience, who paid two cents apiece to share the difficulties of the actors, would not tolerate that outlandish fraud and they broke up the seats. The mayor, at the urging of Bruno Crespi, explained in a proclamation that the cinema was a machine of illusions that did not merit the emotional outbursts of the audience. With that discouraging explanation many felt that they had been the victims of some new and showy gypsy business and they decided not to return to the movies, considering that they already had too many troubles of their own to weep over the acted-out misfortunes of imaginary beings. . . . It was as if God had decided to put to the test every capacity for surprise and was keeping the inhabitants of Macondo in a permanent alternation between excitement and disappointment, doubt and revelation, to such an extreme that no one knew for certain where the limits of reality lay.

—Gabriel Garcia Marquez, *One Hundred Years of Solitude*, pp. 185–86

INTRODUCTION

We often respond to novels and plays and movies in ways that go beyond the purely intellectual. They make us laugh and cry; we feel sorry for their characters, we fear for them, and sometimes even say that we are afraid *of* them. Indeed, Aristotle suggests in the *Poetics* that the arousal of pity and fear in the audience is the very point of one sort of fiction, namely tragedy.

However, there is something puzzling about the fact that we are so often moved emotionally by characters and events that we come across in works of fiction. For these are characters who never existed as persons and events that never actually took place! And typically we are well aware that this is so as we read or watch such works. After all, most of us would not think of climbing onto the stage during a performance of *Othello* in an attempt to save Desdemona from Othello's clutches. And a person who tried to find the original copy of Tom Sawyer's birth certificate in the Missouri State Archives would simply have misunderstood the sort of things that Mark Twain's novels are. If we are to appreciate and respond appropriately to works of fiction, we have to appreciate and respond to them *as* fiction.

But why does knowing that a work of fiction *is* fiction make our emotional responses to it puzzling? In the first reading of this section, Colin Radford argues that it is largely because in everyday circumstances beliefs and judgments appear to play a crucial role in our emotional responses. Part of what it is to be afraid for oneself, for example, is to *judge* the situation one is in to be dangerous or threatening. Similarly, I cannot feel pity for others unless I *believe* them to be victims of misfortune. And beliefs of this sort would appear to depend on beliefs in the existence of the objects in question. For example, it will be difficult to make sense of my claim to be afraid of the burglar in the kitchen if I know that there is no such burglar. If I know that there is no burglar, how can I believe that a burglar (what burglar?) threatens me?

So there is something puzzling about the fact that we so often respond emotionally to what we know to be purely fictional characters and events. On the one hand, it seems that in many circumstances, at least, emotional response is in one way or another dependent on belief in the existence of what we are responding to: You cannot feel sorry for my sister if you know that I do not *have* a sister. On the other hand, it seems that we are often moved emotionally by what happens to fictional characters, knowing full well that they do not and never did exist.

Our emotional responses to fictional characters and events give rise to a number of interrelated questions. Two of these questions are discussed in the readings that follow. First, is it *rational* for us to respond emotionally to, to care about, what we know to be ("merely") fictional? Second, what *sort* of responses are our emotional responses to fiction?

Colin Radford takes the problem which arises here to concern the rationality of our responses to fiction. Radford argues that when we respond to novels by experiencing emotions such as pity for their characters, we are being *inconsistent*. In everyday life, he argues, we are not moved by what we know is not real; however, in responding to fiction we are moved by fictional characters and events which we know do not exist. After considering a number of possible "solutions" to the problem he raises, Radford concludes that our emotional responses to fictional characters and events are irrational. Many people have found Radford's view extremely implausible, and a good number of articles have been written attempting to show that it is mistaken. (Some of these are listed among the Suggestions for Further Reading in this section.) However, it is interesting and useful to think about what follows if Radford is right. If caring about the creatures of fiction and what happens to them is irrational, should we try harder *not* to care about them? If Radford is right, would that give those of us who are easily moved reason to avoid fiction, or even to try to ban it, as Plato advocated in Book 10 of the *Republic*? Or would it rather force us to reconsider the scope of reason and the importance of the irrational in human life? These are questions which touch on deep and ancient themes in aesthetics, and Radford's essay encourages us to reconsider these themes from an unusual and even disturbing perspective.

A different way of understanding the problem is pursued by Alex Neill, in the second reading in this section. Neill suggests that the real question to be answered here concerns the nature rather than the rationality of our emotional responses to fiction: Just what *sort* of responses are they? Do they really constitute *emotions* at all? Some have suggested that while the emotions we feel in response to fiction *are* genuine emotions, they are not "directed at" fictional characters and events, but rather at real people who are more or less like them. Fictions move us, as Dr. Johnson put it, because they "bring realities to mind." Perhaps it is reality and real people, then, rather than fictional characters and events, who are the "targets" of our emotional responses to fiction. (Different versions of this kind of view are defended by Paskins and by Charlton, in their articles listed in the bibliography to this section.) Some of our emotional responses to fiction may well be of this sort. But Neill suggests that it would be a mistake to assume that all of them must be. He argues that our beliefs about what is fictionally the case, despite the fact that they are not beliefs about real or actual things, may nevertheless be sufficient to ground genuine and rational emotions which are directed at fictional characters and events. Certain emotions, he suggests, depend on the adoption of a certain sort of perspective—they depend on *"seeing things from another's point of view"*— and this perspective is one that readers may take on fiction, and indeed which fiction may demand of its readers.

But Neill holds that in thinking about these issues it is important to bear in mind the *variety* of our emotional responses. For they are far from being all of a kind. For example, he suggests, fearing for oneself and being jealous are very different sorts of emotional states from fearing for others and pitying them. Again, think of how different are the responses that Harlequin Romances aim at from the responses that a good horror movie can evoke in us. It may be that not all of the emotional responses that we can have to fiction are to be explained in the same way. Indeed, Neill suggests, not every sort of emotion can be experienced in response to fictional characters and events: For example, he claims that we cannot really be *afraid* of fictional characters.

Neill's remarks about "seeing things from another's point of view," and about the ways in which our focus of attention can shift as we respond and come to understand a fiction, as well as Radford's discussion of some of the possible "solutions" to the problem he is concerned with, raise questions about the role played by the imagination in our responses to fiction. Clearly, it would be hard to understand a work of fiction adequately, or to respond to it fully, if we were not prepared to engage with that work imaginatively. But what exactly *is* it to be imaginatively engaged with a work of fiction? Is an imaginative mode of engagement with something *opposed* to a rational mode of engagement with it? Or is imaginative activity *essential* to a rational engagement with the world? If, as many would suggest, the answer to this last question is "yes," then Radford's concern with the rationality of our responses to fiction and Neill's concern with the imaginative basis of those responses may be more closely related than they at first appear.

A number of intriguing and difficult questions arise when we begin to think closely about the nature of our emotional engagement with the worlds of fiction. They are questions which bear directly on the wider issue of what it is to understand and appreciate fiction. And in addressing them, we also broach deep and important questions in the philosophy of mind and metaphysics. In exploring the relations between mind and world, and between reason and imagination, aesthetics here as elsewhere can be seen to bear directly on some of the oldest concerns of philosophy itself.

How Can We Be Moved by the Fate of Anna Karenina?

Colin Radford

'What's Hecuba to him, or he to Hecuba,
That he should weep for her?'
            Hamlet Act 2 Sc. 2.

1. That men feel concern for the fate of others, that they have some interest, and a warm and benevolent one in what happens to at least some other men, may be simply a brute fact about men, though a happy one. By this I mean that we can conceive that men might have been different in this respect, and so it is possible for us to be puzzled by the fact that they are not different. In a situation where men did not feel concern for others, children might be nurtured only because mothers could not stand the pain of not feeding them, or because it gave them pleasure to do this and to play with them, or because they were a source of pride. So that if a child died, a mother might have the kind of feeling the owner of a car has if his car is stolen and wrecked. He doesn't feel anything for the car, unless he is a sentimentalist, and yet he is sorry and depressed when it happens.

Of course there may be good biological reasons why men should have concern for each other, or at least some other men, but that is not to the point. The present point, a conceptual one, is that we can conceive that all men might have been as some men are, *viz.,* devoid of any feeling for anyone but themselves, whereas we cannot conceive, *e.g.,* that all men might be what some men are, chronic liars.

2. So concern and related feelings are in this sense brute. But what are they? What is it to be moved by something's happening to someone?

Anything like a complete story here is a very long one, and in any case I have a particular interest. Suppose then that you read an account of the terrible sufferings of a group of people. If you are at all humane, you are unlikely to be unmoved by what you read. The account is likely to awaken or reawaken feelings of anger, horror, dismay or outrage and, if you are tender-hearted, you may well be moved to tears. You may even grieve.

But now suppose you discover that the account is false. If the account had caused you to grieve, you could not continue to grieve. If as the account sank in, you were told and believed that it was false this would make tears impossible, unless they were tears of rage. If you learned later that the account was false, you would feel that in being moved to tears you had been fooled, duped.

It would seem then that I can only be moved by someone's plight if I believe that something terrible has happened to him. If I do not believe that he has not and is not suffering or whatever, I cannot grieve or be moved to tears.

It is not only seeing a man's torment that torments us, it is also, as we say, the thought of his torment which torments, or upsets or moves us. But here thought implies belief. We have to believe in his torment to be tormented by it. When we say that the thought of his plight moves us to tears or grieves us, it is thinking of or contemplating suffering which we believe to be actual or likely that does it.

3. The direction of my argument should now be fairly clear. Moving closer to its goal: suppose that you have a drink with a man who proceeds to tell you a harrowing story about his sister and you are harrowed. After enjoying your reaction he then tells you that he doesn't have a sister, that he has invented the story. In his case, unlike the previous one, we might say that the 'heroine' of the account is fictitious. Nonetheless, and again, once you have been told this you can no longer feel harrowed. Indeed it is possible that you may be embarrassed by your reaction precisely because it so clearly indicates that you were taken in—and you may also feel embarrassed for the storyteller that he could behave in such a way. But the possibility of your being harrowed again seems to require that you believe that someone suffered.

Of course, if the man tells you in advance that he is going to tell you a story, you may reach for your hat, but you may stay and be moved. But this is too quick.

Moving closer still: an actor friend invites you to watch him simulate extreme pain, agony. He writhes about and moans. Knowing that he is only acting, could you be moved to tears? Surely not. Of course you may be embarrassed, and after some time you may even get faintly worried, 'Is he really acting, or is he really in pain? Is he off his head?' But as long as you are convinced that he is only acting and is not really suffering, you cannot be moved by his suffering, and it seems unlikely as well as—as it were—unintelligible that you might be moved to tears by his portrayal of agony. It seems that you could only perhaps applaud it if it were realistic or convincing, and criticise if it were not.

But now suppose, horribly, that he acts or re-enacts the death agonies of a friend, or a Vietcong that he killed and tells you this. Then you might be horrified.

4. If this account is correct, there is no problem about being moved by historical novels or plays, documentary films, *etc.* For these works depict and forcibly remind us of the real plight and of the real sufferings of real people, and it is for these persons that we feel.[1]

---

[1] Not for the performance which elicits this feeling or for the actor—for those we feel admiration, are impressed and so on. This may help to explain how we can enjoy tragedy. Besides the actor's skill and the producer's we also enjoy the skill of the writer. What is difficult is that we weep. This turns the usual problem upside down. People are more often puzzled about how we can enjoy a tragedy, not how it can harrow us, *cf.* Hume's essay, 'On Tragedy', reprinted in this book.

What seems unintelligible is how we could have a similar reaction to the fate of Anna Karenina, the plight of Madame Bovary or the death of Mercutio. Yet we do. We weep, we pity Anna Karenina, we blink hard when Mercutio is dying and absurdly wish that he had not been so impetuous.

5. Or do we? If we are seized by this problem, it is tempting for us to argue that, since we cannot be anguished or moved by what happens to Anna Karenina, since we cannot pity Madame Bovary and since we cannot grieve at the marvellous Mercutio's death, we do not do so.

This is a tempting thesis especially because, having arrived at it, we have then to think more carefully about our reactions to and feelings about, *e.g.*, the death of Mercutio, and these investigations reveal—how could they do otherwise?—that our response to Mercutio's death differs massively from our response to the untimely death of someone we know. As we watch Mercutio die the tears run down our cheeks, but as O.K. Bouwsma has pointed out,[2] the cigarettes and chocolates go in our mouths too, and we may mutter, if not to each other, then to ourselves, 'How marvellous! How sublime!' and even 'How moving!'

'Now', one might say, 'if one is *moved*, one surely cannot comment on this and in admiring tones? Surely being moved to tears is a massive response which tends to interfere with saying much, even to oneself? And surely the nature of the response is such that any comments made that do not advert to what gives rise to the feeling but to the person experiencing it tend to suggest that the response isn't really felt? Compare this with leaning over to a friend in a theatre and saying "I am completely absorbed (enchanted, spellbound) by this!"'

But although we cannot truly grieve for Mercutio, we can be moved by his death, and are. If and when one says 'How moving' in an admiring tone, one can be moved at the theatre. One's admiration is for the play or the performance, and one can admire or be impressed by this and avow this while being moved by it.

6. So we cannot say that we do not feel for fictional characters, that we are not sometimes moved by what happens to them. We shed real tears for Mercutio. They are not crocodile tears, they are dragged from us and they are not the sort of tears that are produced by cigarette smoke in the theatre. There is a lump in our throats, and it's not the sort of lump that is produced by swallowing a fishbone. We are appalled when we realise what may happen, and are horrified when it does. Indeed, we may be so appalled at the prospect of what we think is going to happen to a character in a novel or a play that some of us can't go on. We avert the impending tragedy in the only way we can, by closing the book, or leaving the theatre.

This may be an inadequate response, and we may also feel silly or

---

[2] In 'The Expression Theory of Art', collected in his Philosophical Essays. Cf. p. 29.

shamefaced at our tears. But this is not because they are always inappropriate and sentimental, as, *e.g.*, is giving one's dog a birthday party, but rather because we feel them to be unmanly. They may be excusable though still embarrassing on the occasion of a real death, but should be contained for anything less.

Of course we are not only moved by fictional tragedies but impressed and even delighted by them. But I have tried to explain this, and that we are other things does not seem to the point. What is worrying is that we are moved by the death of Mercutio and we weep while knowing that no one has really died, that no young man has been cut off in the flower of his youth.[3]

7. So if we can be and if some of us are indeed moved to tears at Mercutio's untimely death, feel pity for Anna Karenina and so on, how can this be explained? How can the seeming incongruity of our doing this be explained and explained away?

First Solution

When we read the book, or better when we watch the play and it works, we are 'caught up' and respond and we 'forget' or are no longer aware that we are only reading a book or watching a play. In particular, we forget that Anna Karenina, Madame Bovary, Mercutio and so on are not real persons.

But this won't do. It turns adults into children. It is true that, *e.g.*, when children are first taken to pantomimes they are unclear about what is going on. The young ones are genuinely and unambiguously terrified when the giant comes to kill Jack. The bolder ones shout 'Look Out!' and even try to get on the stage to interfere.

But do we do this? Do we shout and try to get on the stage when, watching *Romeo and Juliet*, we see that Tybalt is going to kill Mercutio? We do not. Or if we do, this is extravagant and unnecessary for our being moved. If we really did think someone was really being slain, either a person called Mercutio or the actor playing that rôle, we would try to do

---

[3] Though why that should worry us in another worry. There may be some who still feel that there really is no problem, so consider the following case. A man has a genre painting. It shows a young man being slain in battle (but it is not an historical picture, that is, of the death of some particular real young man who was killed in a particular battle). He says that he finds the picture moving and we understand, even if we do not agree. But then he says that, when he looks at the picture, he feels pity, sorrow, *etc.*, for *the young man in the picture*. Surely this very odd response would be extremely puzzling? How *can* he feel sorry for the young man in the painting? But now suppose that the picture is a moving picture, *i.e.*, a movie, and it tells a story. In this case we *do* say that we feel sorry for the young man in the film who is killed. But is there a difference between these two cases which not only explains but justifies our differing responses? Is it, perhaps, simply because most of us do respond in this way to films that we do not find our doing so puzzling?

something or think that we should. We would, if you like, be genuinely appalled.[4]

So we are not unaware that we are 'only' watching a play involving fictional characters, and the problem remains.

Second Solution

Of course we don't ever forget that Mercutio is only a character in a play, but we 'suspend our disbelief' in his reality. The theatre management and the producer connive at this. They dim the lights and try to find good actors. They, and we, frown on other members of the audience who draw attention to themselves and distract us by coughing, and if, during a scene, say a stage hand steals on, picks up a chair that should have been removed and sheepishly departs, our response is destroyed. The 'illusion' is shattered.

All this is true but the paradox remains. When we watch a play we do not direct our thoughts to it's only being a play. We don't continually remind ourselves of this—unless we are trying to reduce the effect of the work on us. Nonetheless, and as we have seen, we are never unaware that we are watching a play, and one about fictional characters even at the most exciting and moving moments. So the paradox is not solved by invoking 'suspension of disbelief', though it occurs and is connived at.

Third Solution

It's just another brute fact about human beings that they can be moved by stories about fictional characters and events. *I.e.,* human beings might not have been like this (and a lot of them are not. A lot of people do not read books or go to the theatre, and are bored if they do).

But our problem is that people *can* be moved by fictional suffering given their brute behaviour in other contexts where belief in the reality of the suffering described or witnessed is necessary for the response.

Fourth Solution

But this thesis about behaviour in non-fictional contexts is too strong. The paradox arises only because my examples are handpicked ones in which there is this requirement. But there are plenty of situations in which we can be moved to tears or feel a lump in the throat without thinking that anyone will, or that anyone is even likely to suffer or die an untimely death, or whatever.

---

[4] *Cf.* 'The delight of tragedy proceeds from our consciousness of fiction; if we thought murders and treasons real, they would please no more.' Johnson, *Preface to Shakespeare.*

But are there? A mother hears that one of her friend's children has been killed in a street accident. When her own children return from school she grabs them in relief and hugs them, almost with a kind of anger. (Is it because they have frightened her?) Their reaction is 'What's wrong with you?' They won't get a coherent answer perhaps, but surely the explanation is obvious. The death of the friend's child 'brings home', 'makes real', and perhaps strengthens the mother's awareness of the likelihood of her own children being maimed or killed. We must try another case. A man's attention wanders from the paper he is reading in his study. He thinks of his sister and, with a jolt, realises that she will soon be flying to the States. Perhaps because he is terrified of flying he thinks of her flying and of her 'plane crashing and shudders. He imagines how this would affect their mother. She would be desolated, inconsolable. Tears prick his eyes. His wife enters and wants to know what's up. He looks upset. Our man is embarrassed but says truthfully, 'I was thinking about Jean's flying to the States and, well, I thought how awful it would be if there were an accident—how awful it would be for my mother.' Wife: 'Don't be silly! How maudlin! And had you nearly reduced yourself to tears thinking about all this? Really, I don't know what's got into you, *etc, etc.*'

In this case the man's response to his thoughts, his being appalled at the thought of his sister's crashing, *is* silly and maudlin, but it is intelligible and non-problematic. For it would be neither silly nor maudlin if flying were a more dangerous business than we are prone to think it is. Proof: change the example and suppose that the sister is seriously ill. She is not suffering yet, but she had cancer and her brother thinks about her dying and how her death will affect their mother. If that were the situation his wife would do well to offer comfort as well as advice.

So a man can be moved not only by what has happened to someone, by actual suffering and death, but by their prospect and the greater the probability of the awful thing's happening, the more likely are we to sympathise, *i.e.*, to understand his response and even share it. The lesser the probability the more likely we are not to feel this way. And if what moves a man to tears is the contemplation of something that is most unlikely to happen, *e.g.*, the shooting of his sister, the more likely are we to find his behaviour worrying and puzzling. However, we can explain his divergent behaviour, and in various ways. We can do this in terms of his having false beliefs. He thinks a 'plane crash or a shooting is more likely than it is, which itself needs and can have an explanation. Or his threshold for worry is lower than average, and again this is non-problematic, *i.e.*, we understand what's going on. Or lastly, we may decide he gets some kind of pleasure from dwelling on such contingencies and appalling himself. Now this is, logically, puzzling, for how can a man get pleasure from pain? But if only because traces of masochism are present in many of us, we are more likely to find it simply offensive.

The point is that our man's behaviour is only more or less psychologically odd or morally worrying. There is no logical difficulty here, and the reason for this is that the suffering and anguish that he contemplates, however unlikely, is pain that some real person may really experience.

Testing this, let us suppose first that our man when asked 'What's up' says, 'I was thinking how awful it would have been if Jean had been unable to have children—she wanted them so much.' Wife: 'But she's got them. Six!' Man: 'Yes, I know, but suppose she hadn't?' 'My God! Yes it would have been but it didn't happen. How can you sit there and weep over the dreadful thing that didn't happen, and now cannot happen.' (She's getting philosophical. Sneeringly) 'What are you doing? Grieving for her? Feeling sorry for her?' Man: 'All right! But thinking about it, it was so vivid I could imagine just how it would have been.' Wife: 'You began to snivel!' Man: 'Yes'.

It is by making the man a sort of Walter Mitty, a man whose imagination is so powerful and vivid that, for a moment anyway, what he imagines seems real, that his tears are made intelligible, though of course not excusable.

So now suppose that the man thinks not of his sister but of a woman . . . that is, he makes up a story about a woman who flies to the States and is killed and whose mother grieves, and so on, and that this gives him a lump in his throat. It might appear that, if my thesis is correct, the man's response to the story he invents should be even more puzzling than his being moved by the thought of his sister's not having children. 'Yet', one who was not seized by the philosophical problem might say, 'this case is really not puzzling. After all he might be a writer who first gets some of his stories in this manner!'

But that is precisely why this example does not help. It is too close, too like what gives rise to the problem.[5]

Fifth Solution

A solution suggested by an earlier remark: if and when we weep for Anna Karenina, we weep for the pain and anguish that a real person might suffer and which real persons have suffered, and if her situation were not of that sort we should not be moved.

There is something in this, but not enough to make it a solution. For we do not really weep for the pain that a real person might suffer, and which real persons have suffered, when we weep for Anna Karenina, even if we should not be moved by her story if it were not of that sort. We

[5] Incidentally, and to avoid misunderstanding, I do not have a monolithic view about aesthetic response. I am not saying, for example, that we must believe a story about Harold Wilson to find it *funny*. I am saying that, with the paradoxical exception of watching plays, films, *etc.*, including those about Harold Wilson, we need to believe the story to weep for him, to feel pity for him.

weep for *her*. We are moved by what happens to her, by the situation she gets into, and which is a pitiful one, but we do not feel pity for her state or fate, or her history or her situation, or even for others, *i.e.*, for real persons who might have or even have had such a history. We pity her, feel for her and our tears are shed for her. This thesis is even more compelling, perhaps, if we think about the death of Mercutio.

But all over again, how can we do this knowing that neither she nor Mercutio ever existed, that all their sufferings do not add one bit to the sufferings of the world?

Sixth Solution

Perhaps there really is no problem. In non-fictional situations it may be necessary that in order for a person to be moved, he must believe in the reality of what he sees or is told, or at least he must believe that such a thing may indeed happen to someone. But, as I concede, being moved when reading a novel or watching a play is not exactly like being moved by what one believes happens in real life and, indeed, it is very different. So there are two sorts of being moved and, perhaps, two senses of 'being moved'. There is being moved (Sense 1) in real life and 'being moved' (Sense 2) by what happens to fictional characters. But since there are these two sorts and senses, it does not follow from the necessity of belief in the reality of the agony or whatever it is, for being moved (S. 1), that belief in its reality is, or ought to be necessary for 'being moved' (S. 2). So I have not shown that there is a genuine problem, which perhaps explains why I can find no solution.

But although being moved by what one believes is really happening is not exactly the same as being moved by what one believes is happening to fictional characters, it is not wholly different. And it is what is common to being moved in either situation which makes problematic one of the differences, *viz.*, the fact that belief is not necessary in the fictional situation. As for the hesitant claim that there is a different sense here, this clearly does not follow from the fact that being moved by what happens in real life is different from being moved in the theatre or cinema or when reading a novel, and I find it counterintuitive.[6] But even if the phrase did have different senses for the different cases, it would not follow that there was no problem. It may be that 'being moved' (S. 2) is an incoherent notion so that we and our behaviour are incoherent, when we are 'moved' (S. 2).

When, as we say, Mercutio's death moves us, it appears to do so in very much the same way as the unnecessary death of a young man moves

---

[6] Does 'killed' have a different sense in 'Nixon has been killed' and 'Mercutio has been killed'?

us and for the same reason. We see the death as a waste, though of course it is really only a waste in the real case, and as a 'tragedy', and we are, unambiguously—though problematically as I see it in the case of fiction—saddened by the death. As we watch the play and realise that Mercutio may die or, knowing the play, that he is about to die, we may nonetheless and in either case say to ourselves 'Oh! No! Don't let it happen!' (It seems *absurd* to say this, especially when we know the play, and yet we do. This is part of what I see as the problem.) When he is run through we wince and gasp and catch our breath, and as he dies the more labile of us weep.

How would our behaviour differ if we believed that we were watching the death of a real young man, perhaps of the actor playing the part of Mercutio? First, seeing or fearing that the actor playing the part of Tybalt is bent on killing the other actor, we might try to intervene or, if we did not, we might reproach ourselves for not doing so. When he has been run through we might try to get help. But if we are convinced that we can do nothing, as we are when we watch the death of Mercutio or read about Anna, and if we thought that our watching was not improper, these irrelevant differences in our behaviour would disappear. Once again, we would say to ourselves—and, in this case also to each other since there is no question of aesthetic pleasure—'My God! How terrible!' And as the actor lay dying, perhaps delivering Mercutio's lines, either because he felt them to be appropriate or because, unaware that he was actually dying, he felt that the show must go on, we should again weep for the dying man and the pity of it. Secondly, but this is not irrelevant, our response to the real death is likely to be more massive, more intense and longer in duration for, after all, a real young man has been killed, and it will not be alloyed—or allayed—by aesthetic pleasure. But such differences do not destroy the similarity of the response and may even be said to require it.

So a similarity exists, and the essential similarity seems to be that we are saddened. But this is my difficulty. For we are saddened, but how can we be? What are we sad *about*? How can we feel genuinely and involuntarily sad, and weep, as we do, knowing as we do that no one has suffered or died?

To insist that there is this similarity between being moved and 'being moved' is not to deny that there are other differences between them besides the necessary presence of belief in the one case and its puzzling absence in the other. Yet, as I have already indicated, some of the peculiar features of 'being moved' add to the problem it presents. Not *any* difference between being moved and 'being moved', over and above the difference in belief, has the effect of reducing the conceptual problem presented by the latter, as is suggested by this sixth solution. *E.g.*, when we hope that Mercutio will not get killed, we may realise, knowing the play, that he must be killed, unless the play is altered or the performance is interrupted and we may not wish for that. So not only is our hope vain, for he must die and we know this,[7] but it exists alongside a wish that he will die. After the death, in retrospect, our behaviour differs. In the case of the real man, we should continue to be moved and to regret that happened. With Mercutio we are unlikely to do this and, in talking about his death later, we might only be moved say 'How moving it was!' For we are no longer at the performance or responding directly to it. We do not so much realise later as appropriately remind ourselves later that Mercutio is only a character and that, being a character, he will, as it were, be born again to die again at the next performance. Mercutio is not lost to us, when he dies, as the actor is when he dies.

Our response to Mercutio's death is, then, different from our response to the death of the actor. We do not entirely or simply hope that it will not happen, our response is partly aesthetic, the anguish at his death is not perhaps as intense, and it tends not to survive the performance.

Perhaps we are and can be moved by the death of Mercutio only to the extent that, at the time of the performance, we are 'caught up' in the play, and see the characters as persons, real persons, though to see them as real persons is not to believe that they are real persons. If we wholly believe, our response is indistinguishable from our response to the real thing, for we believe it to be the real thing. If we are always and fully aware that these are only actors mouthing rehearsed lines, we are not caught up in the play at all and can only respond to the beauty and tragedy of the poetry and not to the death of the character. The difficulty is, however—and it remains—that the belief, to say the least, is never complete. Or, better, even when we are caught up, we are still aware that we are watching a play and that Mercutio is 'only' a character. We may become like children, but this is not necessary for our tears.

So the problem remains. The strength of our response may be proportionate to, *inter alia,* our 'belief' in Mercutio. But we do not and need not at any time believe that he is a real person to weep for him. So that what is necessary in other contexts, *viz.,* belief, for being moved, is not necessary here and, all over again, how can we be saddened by and cry over Mercutio's death knowing as we do that when he dies no one really dies?

8. I am left with the conclusion that our being moved in certain ways by works of art, though very 'natural' to us and in that way only too intelligible, involves us in inconsistency and so incoherence.

It may be some sort of comfort, as well as support for my thesis, to realise that there are other sorts of situation in which we are similarly inconsistent, *i.e.,* in which, while knowing that something is or is not so, we

---

[7] Of course, seeing a clip from the newsreel of Kennedy's assassination may elicit the same response, 'Don't let him get killed!', and here we do realise that our response is silly, is incompatible with our knowledge that he is dead and we are watching a film of his death. But there is in the theatre nothing analogous to actually witnessing Kennedy's death. The death of a character is always irrevocable, out of reach, and out of our control.

spontaneously behave, or even may be unable to stop ourselves behaving, as if we believed the contrary. Thus, a tennis player who sees his shot going into the net will often give a little involuntary jump to lift it over. Because he knows that this can have no effect it is tempting to say that the jump is purely expressive. But almost anyone who has played tennis will know that this is not true. Or again, though men have increasingly come to think of death as a dreamless sleep, it was pointed out long ago—was it by Dr. Johnson or David Hume?[8]—that they still fear it. Some may say that this fear is not incoherent, for what appals such men is not their also thinking of death as an unpleasant state, but the prospect of their non-existence. But how can this appal? There is, literally, nothing to fear. The incoherence of fearing the sleep of death for all that it will cause one to miss is even clearer. We do not participate in life when we are dead, but we are not then endlessly wishing to do so. Nonetheless, men fear the endless, dreamless sleep of death and fear it for all that they will miss.

[8] Either could have made such an observation, though Hume regarded death with phlegm, Johnson with horror. But in fact it was a contemporary, Miss Seward, 'There is one mode of the fear of death which is certainly absurd; and that is the dread of annihilation, which is only a pleasing sleep without a dream.' Boswell, *Life of Johnson*, for 1778.

Fiction and the Emotions

Alex Neill

I

It is a fact about many of us that we can be moved by what we know to be fictional. But it is a fact that has been seen by philosophers as problematic in a variety of ways. Plato worried about the effect that responses of this sort have on our cognitive and moral development; Dr. Johnson wondered "how the drama moves, if it is not credited"; and more recently Colin Radford has started a small industry in philosophical aesthetics with a series of articles arguing that our emotional responses to what we know to be fictional are inconsistent, incoherent, and irrational.[1] In this article, I wish to focus on a question related to but nonetheless different from those raised by Johnson and by Radford: the question of what it is that we are moved *to* when we are moved by fiction. What *kind* of re-

[1] See Plato's *Republic,* Books III and X. Johnson's remarks on this issue are in his *Preface to Shakespeare's Plays* (Menston, England: The Scolar Press, 1969), pp. 26–28. Radford's first article on the topic was "How Can We Be Moved by the Fate of Anna Karenina?" reprinted in this book.

sponses are our affective responses to what we know to be fictional characters and events?

This question is related to Dr. Johnson's "causal" question (*how*, or *why*, are we moved by what we know to be fiction?) and to Radford's question (is it *rational* to be so moved?) not least inasmuch as all three are motivated by the same thought—the thought that standardly, at least, we are moved by what we *do* "credit," that our emotional responses are typically founded on *belief*. This thought is central to the "cognitive theory" of emotion, which takes beliefs and judgments to be central to the emotions.[2] This theory of emotion has puzzling consequences with respect to our affective engagement with fiction. Given that I do not believe that Nosferatu the Vampire exists, I cannot believe that he poses any threat to me. And if such a belief is a necessary element of fear for oneself, as the cognitive theory of emotion holds that it is, it would appear to follow that I cannot be afraid of Nosferatu. Similarly, although what I feel for Conrad's character Winnie Verloc may *feel* very much like pity, I do not believe that Winnie ever existed, and hence do not believe that she underwent any suffering. And if pity conceptually involves a belief of this sort, as the cognitive theory suggests that it does, it would appear that I cannot properly be described as pitying Winnie. It is important to notice that, *pace* Radford, the problem here does not, or at least does not initially, concern the *rationality* of our affective responses to fiction. If I lack the relevant beliefs, the question is not whether my "pity" for Winnie is *rational* or not, but rather whether my response is one of *pity* at all.

Several philosophers have come to the conclusion that my response cannot properly be described as one of pity, or at any rate not as pity for *Winnie*. Ryle, for example, wrote that "novel readers and theater-goers feel real pangs and real liftings of the heart, just as they may shed real tears and scowl unfeigned scowls. But their distresses and indignation are feigned."[3] And more recently Malcolm Budd has suggested that "it cannot be literally true that we pity Desdemona, or are horrified by Oedipus's self-blinding, or are envious of Orpheus's musical talent, or are distressed by the death of Anna Karenina—even if there should be tears in our eyes when we read the account of her suicide. For, as we know, these people never existed."[4] But if this conclusion is right, then how *are* we to describe those of our affective responses that appear to be "directed" at fictional characters and events? A number of strategies have been proposed in response to this question. One of the most popular involves attempting to redescribe what we are prereflectively inclined to

---

[2] Recent versions of this theory (which goes back to Aristotle's *Rhetoric*) can be fond in Anthony Kenny's *Action, Emotion and Will* (London: Routledge and Kegan Paul, 1963) and in William Lyon's *Emotion* (Cambridge University Press, 1980).

[3] Gilbert Ryle, *The Concept of Mind* (Harmondsworth: Penguin Books, 1963), p. 103.

[4] Malcolm Budd, *Music and the Emotions* (London: Routledge and Kegan Paul, 1985), p. 128. Similar conclusions are reached by Kenny in *Action, Emotion and Will*, p. 49, and by Kendall L. Walton in "Fearing Fictions," *Journal of Philosophy* 75 (1978), p. 6.

describe as pity for Winnie Verloc (for example) as pity for real people who are brought to mind by Conrad's novel, about whom we do have the relevant beliefs.[5] Or (less plausibly) perhaps our affective responses to fiction can be adequately characterized in terms of states of feeling, such as moods, that do not depend on beliefs in the way that emotions do.[6] Or, again, perhaps they are to be understood as "imaginary" or "make-believe" emotions.[7]

However, leaving aside the difficulties involved in these strategies, it may be objected that their adoption would in any case be premature. As we have seen, our problem is generated by the claim that, given that we know that fictional characters *are* fictional, we cannot hold certain beliefs about them, such as a belief that they suffer misfortune. But this claim is, on the face of it, very odd. For surely we *do* believe, for example, that Emma Woodhouse was handsome, clever, and rich. Indeed, believing this would seem to be a criterion of having understood Jane Austen's novel. *Not* to believe it, or to disbelieve it, would suggest either that one has read *Emma* with so little attention that one could barely be described as having read it at all, or that one has simply got things very badly wrong.

One way of dispelling the mystery here, as a number of philosophers have noted, is by construing statements such as "Winnie Verloc had a pretty miserable time of things" as elliptical for statements of something like the form "it is *The Secret Agent*–fictional that Winnie Verloc had a miserable time of things." Thus while it is not true that Winnie had a miserable time, what *is* true is that it is *fictional* that she did; while we cannot (coherently) believe that Winnie had a miserable time, then, we *can* coherently believe that it is *fictional* that she did. And we can believe this without being committed to the belief that Winnie ever existed.[8]

Now if something like this is right, then a simple solution to the problem concerning our affective responses to what we know to be fictional

---

[5] Johnson advocates something like this in his *Preface to Shakespeare's Plays;* more recently versions of it have been advocated by Michael Weston, "How Can We Be Moved by the Fate of Anna Karenina? (II)," *Proceedings of the Aristotelian Society* Supplementary Volume 49 (1975); by Barrie Paskins, "On Being Moved by Anna Karenina and *Anna Karenina*," *Philosophy* 52 (1977); by Don Mannison, "On Being Moved by Fiction," *Philosophy* 60 (1985); and by William Charlton, "Feelings for the Fictitious," *British Journal of Aesthetics* 24 (1984).

[6] As perhaps is suggested by Charlton's remark in his *Aesthetics* (London: Hutchinson, 1970) that "in general, works of art seem to affect our feelings more by putting us into a *mood* than by exciting a directed *emotion*" (p. 97).

[7] Roger Scruton talks (very briefly) of "imaginary emotions" in "Fantasy, Imagination and the Screen," in his *The Aesthetic Understanding* (London: Methuen, 1983), p. 132. The role of make-believe in our responses to and understanding and appreciation of fiction is a subject that Kendall Walton has made his own; see especially his *Mimesis as Make-Believe*. (Cambridge, Mass.: Harvard University Press, 1990).

[8] Derek Matravers offers an account of belief about what is fictionally the case in his "Who's Afraid of Virginia Woolf?" *Ratio (New Series)* 4 (1991). I would emphasize that in what follows, I do not depend on any particular account of belief about fiction; I merely assume that a correct account is to be had.

suggests itself. For if those of our affective responses that seem to have fictional characters and events as objects *are* grounded on beliefs—beliefs about what is fictionally the case—then perhaps they *do* after all respect the constraints imposed by the cognitive theory of emotion, and hence *do* constitute emotions "proper." It is this possibility that I wish to consider in what follows.[9]

II

The question I shall be concerned with, then, is this: Can my belief that it is fictional that Winnie Verloc suffered (for example), together with certain other facts about me, make it true that I *pity* her?

But it may be objected at the start that this way of stating the question gets things wrong. After all, it may be said, in such cases we do not *actually* believe that anyone undergoes any suffering or misfortune at all. Some seeming support for this objection is offered by Bijoy Boruah, who characterizes attitudes of the kind we are concerned with here variously as "putative beliefs," as "insincere, hypothetical attitudes," as "no more than provisional assents to propositions about fictional phenomena."[10] But these characterizations are misleading. There is certainly nothing "putative," "insincere," "hypothetical," or "provisional" about my belief that Emma Woodhouse was handsome, clever, and rich. I *do, actually,* believe that (it is fictionally the case that) Emma had all of these attributes. There is nothing fictional about *beliefs* of this sort; it is their *content* that concerns the fictional. Beliefs about what is fictionally the case, that is, are just that: beliefs. They are not (as Flint Schier suggests)[11] "unasserted thoughts"; in believing that it is fictionally the case that *p* my attitude is one of judgment, the linguistic expression of which is assertion. In believing that it is fictional that *p*, I believe that it is *true* that it is fictional that *p*. Beliefs about what is fictional, like beliefs about the actual world, are open to assessment in terms of truth and rationality.

However, even if it is granted that beliefs about what is fictionally the case are genuine beliefs, it may be argued that this has little bearing on the real problem that we are faced with here. That problem, it will be said, arises not because in responding to *The Secret Agent* we do not *actually believe* that anything suffers—we do believe that (fictionally) Winnie suf-

---

[9] I am not the first to consider this possibility. That affective responses grounded on beliefs about what is fictional can be emotions proper has been suggested by Eva Schaper in "Fiction and the Suspension of Disbelief," *British Journal of Aesthetics* 18 (1978), by R. T. Allen in "The Reality of Responses to Fiction," *British Journal of Aesthetics* 26 (1986), and most recently by Derek Matravers in "Who's Afraid of Virginia Woolf?" As should become clear, I am broadly speaking in agreement with their conclusion, but take a rather different route in reaching it.

[10] Bijoy Boruah, *Fiction and Emotion* (Oxford University Press, 1988), pp. 60–63 and 68–70.

[11] Flint Schier, "The Claims of Tragedy: An Essay in Moral Psychology and Aesthetic Theory," *Philosophical Papers* 18 (1989), p. 13.

fers—but rather because in such cases we do not believe that *anything actual* suffers. The suggestion here is that in order to be correctly described as pitying someone or something, one must believe that the suffering or misfortune involved is actual, and thus that it is experienced by someone or something which actually exists. It is suggested that these beliefs are so central to pity that a person who does not hold them, a person who believes rather that it is fictional that the object involved suffers, and thus that it is fictional that the object exists, cannot properly be described as experiencing pity.

In support of this suggestion, it is sometimes held that beliefs about what is fictionally the case lack the *causal* power to move us. Thus Boruah suggests that such beliefs are no more than "mere recognitions on our part that, fictionally, something or other is the case," and that "mere recognition is not enough causally to explain why we feel any emotion towards fiction."[12] But this is unconvincing. For to the extent that my belief that fictionally Shylock is a victim of injustice can be construed as "a mere recognition that fictionally, something is the case," my belief that many Guatemalan refugees are victims of injustice can be construed similarly as "a mere recognition that, actually, something is the case." And there is no reason to suppose that "mere recognition" of what is fictional is any less casually efficacious with respect to emotion than "mere recognition" of what is actual.

In explaining the generation of many varieties of emotional response, a more helpful notion than those of "mere recognition" or bare belief is that of the adoption on the part of the subject of a certain sort of "perspective"; roughly speaking, one that involves *seeing things from another's point of view*. What makes my belief that many Guatemalan refugees are victims of injustice causally efficacious with respect to emotion, if it is, is the fact that in some way I can see what it must be like to be in their position; to some extent, at least, I can see things from their point of view. And there is no reason to suppose that we cannot adopt this kind of imaginative attitude with respect to fictional characters. Indeed, many works of fiction might plausibly be said to *demand* that we do so; the reader who doesn't see the world of *Tom Sawyer* through Tom's eyes will have understood the novel only in a very thin sense of "understand," if at all. And allowing the audience or reader to see and to understand his or her fictional world from a variety of perspectives and characters' points of view is a common criterion of an author's success.

The worry concerning the causal efficacy of our beliefs about what is fictionally the case thus looks misplaced. For on the one hand, if one takes belief to the crucial factor in the production of emotion, there is no reason to suppose that our beliefs about what is fictionally the case will be any

---

12 Boruah, *Fiction and Emotion*, p. 64. B. J. Rosebury makes a similar point in "Fiction, Emotion and 'Belief': A Reply to Eva Schaper," *British Journal of Aesthetics* 19 (1979), pp. 121–24.

more causally impotent with regard to emotion than our beliefs about
what is actually the case. On the other hand, if one takes the (I think more
plausible) view that the crucial factor in the generation of emotion is
something like the adoption of certain sorts of perspective, it seems clear
that this factor can be present in (and indeed is arguably often central to)
our dealings with fiction.

But we must not be too hasty here. Even if it is granted that many of
our affective responses to fiction are caused in much the same way as
many of our affective responses to what we take to be actual, the question
I raised at the beginning of this article, that of what *sort* of responses these
are, remains open. Furthermore, even if some emotions result from "seeing things from another's point of view," this is surely not true of all cases
of emotional experience. As my neighbor's rabid dog charges toward me,
slavering at the jaws, the only point of view with which I am likely to be
concerned is my own! And as the spectator at the horror movie shrieks
and sinks deeper into his seat, he is hardly interested in the perspective
that the monster on the screen has on things. Not all emotions, that is,
stem from adopting another's perspective. And this suggests that the various emotions to which we commonly appeal in attempting to describe
our affective responses to fiction may not be amenable to treatment as a
monolithic group, and hence that in discussing this issue we need to be
wary of generalizing, and alert to the differences between various sorts of
emotion and affective response.

III

Once again, then, the question I am concerned with is whether at least
some emotions may be based on beliefs about what is fictionally the case
as well as on beliefs about what is actually the case. In what follows, I
shall argue that there is at least one emotion which can be based on beliefs
about what is fictional. First, however, we should note that there is at least
one variety of emotional response that is *not* of this sort; namely, fear for
oneself. Central to fear for myself, as I noted earlier, is (roughly speaking)
a belief that I am threatened by or in danger from the object of my response. And just as I cannot coherently believe that it is actually the case
that I am threatened by something that I know to be fictional (for the only
monsters who can threaten *me* are actual monsters) so I cannot coherently
believe that it is fictionally the case that I am threatened by something that
I know to be fictional (for the only people that Nosferatu and the like can
threaten are fictional people).[13] Furthermore, because I do not believe that

---

[13] In *Mimesis and Make-Believe* Kendall Walton argues that it may be fictional that I *believe*
that I am threatened by a fictional character, if in responding to the work of which it is a part
I play a game of make-believe using the work as a "prop." In which case, Walton argues, it
may be fictionally rather than actually the case that I am afraid of the character. I have discussed Walton's account in my "Fear, Fiction and Make-Believe," *Journal of Aesthetics and
Art Criticism* 49 (1991), pp. 47–56.

(it is either actually or fictionally the case that) I am threatened by Nosferatu, I do not have the sorts of *desire* characteristic of fear for oneself; I do not have any desire to escape his clutches, or to warn my friends and family, and so on. Hence I am not afraid of Nosferatu, nor of any creature whom I know to be a creature of fiction. Nor, I suggest, can I be *jealous* of what I know to be a fictional character. For central to jealousy are (once again, roughly speaking) a belief that the person of whom I am jealous has, or has designs on, something that is rightfully mine, and a desire to regain or retain whatever that is. And this belief/desire combination is not one that I can coherently have where I know that the object of my response is fictional. The ontological gap between fictional characters and ourselves precludes rivalry with them as well as being threatened by and escaping from them.

Fear for oneself and jealousy are both sorts of response that do not typically result from adopting another's perspective, from seeing things from another's point of view. However, it is not the *causes* of these sorts of response that are problematic here; it is rather the kind of beliefs and judgments that they involve. Fear for oneself and jealousy (and I do not suppose that these are the only responses of this sort) have the following feature in common: They both depend on the subject seeing him- or herself as standing in a certain sort of relation to the object of the response, a relation that cannot obtain between the inhabitants of different ontological "worlds."

The fact that we cannot fear or be jealous of what we know to be fictional characters accords well with our experience; how often, after all, do we really want to describe ourselves as feeling jealous of a fictional character? Fear for oneself may be less obviously dispensable within this context; however, I would suggest that in most if not all cases where we might be prereflectively inclined to describe ourselves as afraid of something that we know to be fictional, our response will on reflection turn out to be better characterized in terms of fear of actual counterparts of what is represented in the fiction, or in terms of non-belief-dependent reactive states. Thus, for example, seeing Spielberg's *Poltergeist* may make me afraid of *real* ghosts that may, for all I know, be lurking in my bedroom closet; or it may make me afraid *that* there are real ghosts after all. Alternatively, or perhaps additionally, my response to the film may be better described in terms of states such as shock and alarm; states which a good director will induce through the expert use of camera angle and editing and sound, and which may *feel* very much like fear. Furthermore, we should remember that not all fear is fear for oneself; we may also experience fear sympathetically, or *for* others, and empathetically, or *with* others. And it may be that although we cannot be afraid *of* what we know to be fictional characters, we can be afraid for and with them.

Both fear for and fear with others, unlike fear for oneself, are sorts of response that (typically, at least) we experience as a result of imaginatively adopting another's perspective on things. And in the remainder of this article I shall argue that at least one other emotion of this sort can be based on our beliefs about what is fictionally the case. The emotion in question is pity. Along with fear, pity has received the lion's share of attention in the contemporary debate on the issues with which we are concerned, not least because it is one of the emotions to which we appear to be most inclined to refer in describing our affective responses to fiction. For my purposes, pity is also a good "test case" here because it can plausibly be argued that a paradigmatic instance of pity will have all the features or "ingredients" that any emotion of this kind could have. (In this respect, pity may be contrasted with envy, for example, which often does not involve bodily feelings and sensations; and with certain sorts of grief, which may not involve desires of any kind.) I shall proceed, therefore, by considering whether there are any necessary or characteristic features of pity which are such that if a response is founded on beliefs concerning what is fictionally the case, rather than on beliefs about what one takes to be actual states of affairs, then those features of the emotion will be missing from that response. If there are no such features, I suggest, then there will be no reason not to describe certain responses based on beliefs about what is fictionally the case as responses of pity.

IV

A characteristic if not necessary feature of many emotions, including pity, is a physiological/phenomenological one. And it is undeniable that we can be moved to bodily feeling and sensation by what we know to be fictionally the case. As Radford says, "We shed real tears for Mercutio. They are not crocodile tears, they are dragged from us and they are not the sort of tears that are produced by cigarette smoke in the theatre. There is a lump in our throats, and it's not the sort of lump that is produced by swallowing a fishbone." The occurrence of feelings and sensations of this sort clearly does not depend on a belief that the situation witnessed or described is actual.

However, it must be granted that in general the feelings and sensations that we experience in response to fiction tend to be rather different from those that may issue from our beliefs about what is actually the case. As Hume puts it, "The feelings of the passions are very different when excited by poetical fictions, from what they are when they arise from belief and reality." A passion experienced in response to poetry, he suggests, "lies not with that weight upon us: It feels less firm and solid."[14] I shall have more to say about this later, but two points should be noted here. First, whatever Hume may have meant by "weight" and "firmness" and "solidity," the difference between the feelings I experience in responding

[14] David Hume, *A Treatise of Human Nature*, ed. L. A. Selby-Bigge, 2d ed., rev. by P. H. Nidditch (Oxford University Press, 1978), p. 631.

to a fictional character or situation and those I experience in response to what I take to be actual cannot simply be understood in terms of *intensity*. What I feel for or about a fictional character may in fact be *more* intense than my feelings for or about the starving Ethiopians, or the Guatemalan refugees whose plight I hear about on radio or television. This may be morally worrying, but it appears nonetheless to be perfectly possible. Second, even if it could be established that beliefs about what is fictionally the case typically issue in "weaker" or less intense feelings than those that issue from beliefs about what is actually the case, it would not follow that responses founded on the former sort of belief cannot properly be construed as emotions. For the emotions cannot be defined in terms of the feelings and sensations that they may involve.[15] Whether or not it is a necessary part of pity, then, the "feeling" aspect of the emotion would appear to pose no difficulty for the position that I wish to defend here; namely, that a person may be correctly described as feeling pity for what he or she knows to be fictional.

However, Hume points to a further potential difficulty that we must address here. "A passion, which is disagreeable in real life," he suggests, "may afford the highest entertainment in a tragedy, or epic poem." Experienced as part of a response to what we know to be fictional, the emotion involved has "the agreeable effect of exciting the spirits, and rouzing the attention."[16] These remarks bring us up against a familiar problem in aesthetics, a problem which Hume addressed in more detail in his essay "Of Tragedy." His topic there is the "unaccountable pleasure which the spectators of a well-written tragedy receive from sorrow, terror, anxiety and other passions that are in themselves disagreeable and uneasy."[17] For our purposes, the problem that Hume is concerned with may be expressed with regard to pity as follows. A belief that the object of one's response is suffering is clearly not a sufficient condition of pity; in order to be correctly described as feeling pity, one must also be *distressed* by the suffering. If one reacts to the suffering of another with pleasure, one's response will be some form of *schadenfreude;* if one is simply indifferent to it, one will not be experiencing emotion at all. In responding to tragedy, however, we appear to take pleasure in experiencing emotions such as pity. And this raises the question (though it is not precisely Hume's question) of whether one's responses in such contexts really constitute *pity*.

In addressing this question, the first point to note is that our responses to the fictional depiction of suffering and distress do *not* always

---

[15] As is argued by George Pitcher, "Emotion," *Mind* 74 (1965); by Errol Bedford, "Emotions," *Proceedings of the Aristotelian Society* 57 (1956–57); and by William Alston, "Emotion and Feeling," *Encyclopedia of Philosophy* Vol. 2 (New York: Macmillan and The Free Press, 1967).

[16] Hume, *A Treatise of Human Nature*, p. 631.

[17] Hume, "Of Tragedy," reprinted in Section 7 of this book.

involve pleasure; what is depicted in a work of fiction may be so harrowing that we are forced to close the book or to leave the theater. And if we do not do so, it may be not because we take *pleasure* in what is depicted, but rather because we feel for one reason or another that we *ought* to endure it, as we may feel that we ought to suffer through Amnesty International's reports on torture and capital punishment. However, it seems clear that in many instances our experience of distressing fiction does involve pleasure; and it may be argued that in those instances, at least, our response is not correctly described in terms of intrinsically distressful emotions such as pity. For how can we be described as pitying something if we are taking pleasure in watching or reading about its suffering?

But this is unconvincing. For one thing, it is not clear that the pleasure that may be part of our response to a work of fiction even conflicts with, let alone rules out the possibility of, the distress that may *also* be a part of that response. In responding to a work of fiction as to anything else our attention may have more than one object; it may be, then, that our pleasure and our distress have different objects. (Thus we may be distressed by what is depicted in a work, yet be pleased by the manner of depiction.) If the object of the pleasure that we derive from a work of fiction really *is* the suffering depicted therein, then of course that will be a good reason for denying that our response is one of pity. But there is no reason to suppose that we are in general any more prone to take pleasure in fictional suffering than we are to take pleasure in actual suffering. Second, as Flint Schier remarked, the idea that we take *pleasure* in watching Oedipus or Gloucester with their eyes out (for example) is to say the least peculiar.[18] In discussions of this issue, that is, "pleasure" would appear to have a somewhat unusual sense, and one that needs to be spelled out. And the important point for our purposes here is that a major criterion of adequacy for any account of "tragic pleasure" is that it be able to show how this sort of pleasure is compatible with (and perhaps even involves) the distress that tragic fiction may also evoke in us.[19] The fact that we can take pleasure in tragic fiction, whatever "pleasure" may mean here, cannot plausibly be construed as ruling out the possibility that our responses to tragedy may also involve the distress that is an intrinsic part of emotions such as pity.

V

An examination of the feelings and sensations characteristic of pity thus supports, rather than casts doubt on, the suggestion that certain of our af-

---

[18] Flint Schier, "Tragedy and the Community of Sentiment," in Peter Lamarque, ed., *Philosophy and Fiction* (Aberdeen University Press, 1983), p. 76.

[19] The account that Schier began to develop in the two articles cited above is more successful in this respect than any other I have seen.

fective responses to fiction may in fact properly be described as responses of pity. The only element of pity that we have yet to consider is desire. If it can be demonstrated that a response founded on a belief that it is fictional that someone is suffering may involve the desires as well as the feelings and sensations that are characteristic of pity, then we shall have shown that there is every reason to describe such a response as one of pity.

It can plausibly be argued that a central and indeed necessary feature of pity is a want or desire that the misfortune suffered by the person or thing we pity should stop or could be avoided. It may then be argued further that we lack any such desire in responding to what we know to be fictional suffering, and that we do so precisely because we know that the suffering *is* fictional. Hence, it will be said, we cannot properly be described as pitying fictional characters. As it stands, however, this is unpersuasive. In responding to a work of fiction we may indeed desire that (fictionally) a character's suffering should come to an end, that (fictionally) his or her plight will be resolved happily. "How I hope that her father relents in time," we may think, or "How I wish that he didn't have to die." We sit tensed on the edges of our seats hoping that the heroine will get free of her bonds before the circular saw slices her up, wanting a character to realize his mistake before it is too late to rectify it, and so on.

However, with all but the most unsophisticated reader or spectator of fiction, the desires involves are likely to be more complex than this. Every time we see *Romeo and Juliet*, we may wish that Mercutio did not have to die; we may sit through many performances of *Lear*, wishing each time that Cordelia could survive. But suppose that one sees a performance of (what one initially took to be) *Romeo and Juliet* in which the director has obviously been so overwhelmed by the same desire that he arranges Mercutio's survival, letting him off with a minor flesh wound in the shoulder. Or suppose that one has not paid sufficient attention to the posters outside and realizes during a performance of *Lear* that one is watching Nahum Tate's version of the play, in which Cordelia survives. One's response in such situations is likely to be one of disappointment, if not outrage. It may be argued, then, that one does not *really* want Mercutio or Cordelia to survive; that at best one has conflicting desires with respect to the suffering of fictional characters: one both does and does not desire that their suffering should be prevented. Does this conflict of desire suggest that we are not properly described as pitying fictional characters?

Two points should be noted here. First, it is far from clear that we are in fact accurately described as having conflicting desires in cases such as those outlined above. We may genuinely and wholeheartedly wish that Mercutio *could* survive; our objection to the performance in which he does is not based on a conflicting desire that he should die, nor does it indicate that we do not really desire his survival. Rather, our objection is based on our knowledge that if Mercutio survives then we are no longer seeing *Romeo and Juliet* but another (and the chances are), inferior play. Our outrage at the "happy" ending, that is, need not conflict with our desire that the suffering involved could have been avoided, nor does it show that we do not really have any such desire. Second, even if we do have genuinely conflicting desires with respect to the suffering of a fictional character, this fact will not necessarily count against our being correctly described as pitying him or her. Our having mixed or conflicting desires with respect to another's suffering is not restricted to those cases in which the suffering involved is fictional; it is clear that we can also have conflicting desires with respect to suffering which we believe to be actual. Thus we may wish that the mental anguish and suffering undergone by a person recently bereaved could be ended, but also believe that this suffering has to be gone through if the person involved is to recover fully from his or her loss. Similarly, we might both wish that Lear's suffering could be avoided, and believe that for one reason or another he *should* undergo it. Indeed, there need be nothing altruistic about this conflict of desire; our pity may simply be mixed with a hint or more of *schadenfreude*. Whether or not we really *pity* Lear is to be decided in just the same way that we should decide whether or not we really pity the bereaved person; namely, by looking closely at the desires and beliefs that we have concerning them. The fact that we have conflicting desires concerning the suffering involved, if we do, no more rules out our being correctly described as feeling pity in one case than it does in the other.

A different aspect of the desires that are central to pity, and one that is more problematic, is pointed to by Charlton, who argues that "to be moved emotionally is to be moved to action. I am only moved by someone's plight if I want to help him."[20] (Here Charlton appears to construe "being moved" as synonymous with something like "feeling pity"; it is not true that all emotions conceptually involve some inclination to action—grief, for example, may well not.) Now the suggestion that a central component of pity is a desire to help the person whose suffering moves one does seem plausible. If it could be shown that it is in fact a *necessary* component of pity, then this would provide grounds for denying that any of our affective responses to fictional characters can properly be described as instances of pity. For typically we do *not* desire to come to the aid of what we know to be fictional characters. Indeed, it is arguable that we *cannot* have such a desire. For the "ontological gap" between fictional characters and ourselves is such that logically we *cannot* come to their aid, any more than we can escape from them or regain what is rightfully ours from them, and it can plausibly be argued that one cannot coherently desire what one knows to be logically impossible. However, even if desiring

[20] Charlton, "Feelings for the Fictitious," p. 206. Similarly, Robert Solomon suggests that central to pity is a desire "to soothe, heal, or at least comfort the other." Solomon, *The Passions* (Notre Dame: University of Notre Dame Press, 1983), p. 344.

to help what we know to be fictional characters is possible, there would clearly be something odd about having such a desire. For if we understand that the characters that we are faced with are fictional, then we know that nothing that we could possibly do would *count* as helping them. This explains why it is that most of us do not, as a matter of fact, experience any desire to leap onto the stage in order to wrench Desdemona from Othello's grasp, and why it is that we regard those who write in to soap-opera characters offering sympathy and advice as having got something fundamentally wrong.

In assessing Charlton's suggestion, then, we must ask first whether a desire to help the person whose suffering moves one is in fact a necessary component of pity. The fact that I can explain an action intended to aid or to comfort another by saying that I pitied him or her shows that pity *may* involve such a desire.[21] However, *need* I have a desire to help the person whose suffering moves me if I am to be correctly described as pitying him? Consider a case in which you can see that someone is suffering, and where you believe (i) that you have the power to help him, and (ii) that there are no other and overriding reasons not to do so. (This excludes such cases as those in which you may have reason to believe that in some way or other the person in question will ultimately benefit from being left to cope on his own, or in which you believe that your coming to his aid will cause you far more discomfort than you could possibly save him.) In such a case, if you simply have no inclination to help the person in question, then you are probably not accurately described as pitying him. For your lack of any such desire or inclination strongly suggests that you are indifferent to (or perhaps even pleased by) the fact that he is in the plight that he is. Your reaction, that is, suggests (though of course it does not establish) that you are not *distressed* by his plight, and is thus a good *prima facie* reason to deny that you are correctly described as pitying him.

However, this way of setting the matter up does not show that a desire to help the person whose suffering moves one is a necessary component of pity as such, but at most that such a desire is a necessary component of pity in certain cases. In some instances of pity, I suggest, there is no question of the subject having a desire to help the object of his or her pity. Pity for people from the past appears to be perfectly coherent—I may genuinely feel sorry for my late uncle or for Lady Jane Grey—and yet it seems clear that our emotional experience in such cases does not involve a desire to help the figure in question; the point being, of course, that we *cannot* (in any straightforward sense, at least) help such figures. And it is because we know this that a desire to help plays no part in our emotional response. To take a rather different kind of case, I may know

[21] Indeed, the fact that emotions may function as motives to behavior is explained partly by the fact that they often involve desires of this sort in addition to beliefs and feelings and sensations.

full well that I am utterly powerless to do anything to help a party of mountain-climbers caught in an avalanche, or a group of sailors trapped in a submerged submarine; and because I know this, my feelings with regard to them will typically not include any desire to help them. However, this does not in itself imply that I am indifferent to, let alone pleased by, their plight, and so that I do not pity them. As in the case of pitying historical figures, the distress I feel at their fate will be expressed in desires of a different form: broadly speaking, in a desire that their suffering should stop or could be ended (perhaps by someone who *can* do something to help); or, with respect to the suffering of an historical figure, a desire that it could have been avoided.[22] Although I know that I cannot do anything to help, that I am (in the case of historical figures, logically) powerless to influence the state of affairs that they find or found themselves in, and so do not desire to do so, I *can* desire that things should be or could have been otherwise for them. And if I do have such a desire, then this will constitute good grounds for describing my response as one of pity.

Pace Charlton, then, the desire to help another is not a *necessary* condition of pitying him. Thus the fact that we have no such desire in responding to the sufferings of a character whom we know to be fictional does not in itself rule out the possibility of describing that response as one of pity; the fact that our responses to fictional characters (typically, at least) involve no desires of this sort simply reflects our awareness that we cannot—logically cannot—help, heal, soothe or comfort them. The desire that is necessary to pity must be construed more broadly than Charlton suggests; roughly, as a desire that things should be otherwise and better for the object of one's pity. The question that we must address here, then, is whether a desire of *this* sort is dependent on a belief that the object of one's response and his or her plight are (or were) actual. Is this a desire that we can have with respect to what we know to be a fictional character?

As I have formulated it above, it is not. I cannot desire that things should have gone differently and more happily for Anna Karenina, simply because I do not believe that Anna ever existed. However, I *can* believe that it is fictionally the case that Anna existed, and that it is fictional that she had a pretty miserable time of things. And given that I hold these beliefs, I may also desire that fictionally things should have gone differently and better for her. (It should be noted that there is nothing fictional about such a desire itself; as with beliefs about what is fictionally the case, "fictionality" attachs only to the *content* of such desires.) If I do have such a desire, and if it is founded on a belief that fictionally Anna suffered, and if the depiction of her suffering causes me to experience the feelings of

[22] My distress may also be expressed in a wish that I *could* help them (which of course is not the same as a desire *to* help them), but it need not be. Nor, *pace* Charlton (in "Feelings for the Fictitious"), need my response involve a desire of the form, "Were anyone that I *could* help in Lady Jane Grey's situation, would that I might help them!"

distress characteristic of pity, then, I suggest, there are no good grounds for denying that my response to Anna Karenina is properly to be described as one of pity.

VI

At this point, however, it may appear that we are faced with a rather different problem.[23] For in wishing that fictionally things had gone differently for Anna, it would appear that I am in effect wishing that Tolstoy's novel had been written differently; that *Anna Karenina,* as well as Anna Karenina, were other than it is. Now I may, of course, wish just that. As a matter of fact, however, I do not; and it seems reasonable to assume that most of those who would describe themselves as pitying Mercutio or Winnie Verloc do not wish that *Romeo and Juliet* or *The Secret Agent* were other than they are. Indeed, it might plausibly be argued that to have such a desire would betoken a failing to engage with the work adequately and fully as a work of art, and hence that feeling pity for fictional characters, inasmuch as it involves having such a desire, is an inappropriate kind of response to them. Furthermore, we *value* certain works of fiction not least because they are capable of eliciting from us emotions such as pity for their characters. If responses of this sort involve our desiring that the work should be other than it is, however, we seem to be left with the very dubious conclusion that part of what we regard as valuable about certain works of fiction involves wishing that they were other than they are.

It would appear that we are faced here with two—equally unpalatable—alternatives. On the one hand, in pitying a fictional character, and hence wishing that fictionally things were otherwise with her, I also wish that the work of which she is a part were other than it is. And the fact that I have this desire suggests that my response to the work in question is in one way or another suspect. On the other hand, it may be that in pitying a fictional character I wish that fictionally things were different with her, and also want the work of which she is a part to be just as it is. And this latter scenario would appear to bring us very close to Radford's view that responses such as pity for fictional characters involve us in incoherence and irrationality. For it is logically impossible that (a) *Anna Karenina* (say) should be just as it is, *and* that (b) fictionally things should go differently for Anna Karenina. And if one cannot coherently desire what is logically impossible, our desiring both (a) and (b) above would involve us in incoherence.

However, this way of setting matters up neglects a third alternative

---

[23] I am very grateful to Aaron Ridley for pointing this out to me. A very illuminating discussion of this issue, to which I owe a great deal, can be found in his paper "Desire in the Experience of Fiction," *Philosophy and Literature* 16 (1992). This is a good place also to thank Curtis Brown and Marianne Melling for their help.

available to us here; namely, the possibility that in pitying a fictional character we desire that fictionally things were otherwise for her, without having any desires at all with respect to the work of which she is a part. It is true that were it to be fictional that Anna escaped her fate, then *Anna Karenina* would not be the novel that it is. However, it does not follow that in *wishing* that fictionally things had gone differently for Anna, I am in effect *wishing* that Tolstoy's novel had been written differently. Similarly, even though it may be a necessary condition of my losing weight that I stop eating iced buns, my desire to lose weight is not in effect a desire to stop eating iced buns; I may desire to lose weight without having any desires with regard to iced buns at all.

The important point to recognize here is that when I feel pity for Anna, and hence wish that things could have gone differently for her, I am focusing on a particular aspect of *Anna Karenina;* roughly speaking, on the *story* that Tolstoy tells. And in focusing on this aspect, I do not have desires with respect to other aspects of the novel, such as its plot structure or its language. When I adopt a different stance toward the novel—when I consider it *as* a novel, or as a work of art, or as a part of Tolstoy's *corpus*— then my desires and my feelings are likely to change. In particular, in looking at the work from these sorts of perspective I am unlikely to have any desires with regard to Anna herself. Recognizing that we can adopt different perspectives in responding to a work of fiction, that we may focus on one or another aspect of that work, allows us to see that wishing that things were otherwise for a fictional character does not involve us in the dilemma outlined above. We can wish that things had gone differently and more happily for Anna Karenina without thereby either being involved in incoherence or responding to the novel in a fashion that is in one way or another suspect.

Recognizing this feature of our responses to fiction also allows us to bring out the truth in Hume's remark that an emotional response to fiction "lies not with that weight upon us"; to explain, that is, why it is that our emotional responses to fictional characters and events are typically (though not invariably) of shorter duration, and are often (though again not invariably) less intense, than are our emotional responses to similar actual persons and events. In responding to a work of fiction, we tend to adopt a variety of attitudes or stances toward the work; the focus of our concern shifts between various aspects of that work. Thus in watching a performance of *Lear*, I may experience a variety of more or less intense emotional responses to one or more of the characters; as the lights go up, however, my attention is forced back to the fact that what I have been watching is a *play*, and in this case a supreme work of art. And my responses then change; the focus of my attention gradually moves from Lear to *Lear*. If I am moved now, it will probably be the performance, or the play, or Shakespeare's art, that I am moved by. Similarly, when I am "caught up" in a good thriller or spy novel, my attention and affective responses will be focused on the characters and events depicted. When I put the book down, this focus shifts; I think of the work as a novel, or as the new Le Carré, or in terms of its structure. And I may now realize that my attention and responses were entirely unmerited, that what has occupied me so intensely for the last hour or so is simply not worth it. Certain writers and directors—John Fowles, for one—are able to force us continually to shift the focus of our attention from one aspect of the work to another, and the ability to make this an integral part of our experience of the work rather than any annoying distraction is one criterion of mastery of the art of fiction.

The fact that our emotional responses to fictional characters tend to be shorter in duration and less intense than our responses to actual people does not mean that we do not or cannot really *care* about fictional characters, then, nor that our beliefs or feelings or desires with respect to such characters are in some way "substandard." It rather reflects the fact that those fictional characters that we do care about are typically part of something else that also demands, and gets, our attention.

VII

At the beginning of this article I raised the possibility that certain emotions may be based on beliefs about what is fictional as well as on beliefs about what is actually the case. By way of an examination of the structure of pity, I have argued that for that emotion, at least, this is in fact the case. All those features which can plausibly be argued to be necessary to pity— certain feelings and sensations, an attitude of distress, and desire—may be involved in an affective response that is founded on beliefs about what is fictionally the case. And what has been argued here with respect to pity will also hold true with respect to certain other emotions. Just as we may properly be said to feel pity for fictional characters, I suggest, a detailed examination of the structures of the emotions in question will show that certain of our responses to fictional characters may also be properly described in terms of *schadenfreude;* that without distorting either the responses themselves or the concepts in question we may describe ourselves as envying and admiring fictional characters, and as fearing *for* and *with* them. However, we do need to be wary of generalizing here; our affective responses to fiction cannot usefully be treated monolithically, or as though they formed a homogeneous class. What has been argued here certainly does not show that *any* emotion, other than fear for oneself and jealousy, can be experienced for or about fictions. However, the discussion above strongly suggests that at least some emotions, along with pity, can be so experienced, and has demonstrated the kind of examination that is necessary if we are to get clear about this issue.

SUGGESTIONS FOR FURTHER READING

General background on emotion:
Alston, William. "Emotion and Feeling," *Encyclopedia of Philosophy*, Vol. 2. New York: Macmillan and The Free Press, 1967.
Lyons, William. *Emotion*. Cambridge: Cambridge University Press, 1980.
Rorty, Amélie Oksenberg, ed. *Explaining Emotions*. Berkeley: University of California Press, 1980.
Solomon, Robert C. *The Passions*. New York: Doubleday, 1986.

On our emotional responses to fiction:
Boruah, Bijoy. *Fiction and Emotion*. Oxford: Clarendon Press, 1988.
Charlton, William. "Feelings for the Fictitious." *British Journal of Aesthetics* 24 (1984): 206–16.
Currie, Gregory. *The Nature of Fiction*. Cambridge: Cambridge University Press, 1990. Chapter 5.
Hanfling, Oswald. "Real Life, Art and the Grammar of Feeling." *Philosophy* 63 (1983): 237–43.
Lamarque, Peter. "How Can We Fear and Pity Fictions?" *British Journal of Aesthetics* 21 (1981): 291–304.
Levinson, Jerrold. "The Place of Real Emotion in Response to Fictions." *Journal of Aesthetics and Art Criticism* 48 (1990): 79–80.
Mannison, Don. "On Being Moved by Fiction." *Philosophy* 60 (1985): 71–87.
Mounce, H. O. "Art and Real Life." *Philosophy* 55 (1980): 183–90.
Mounce, H. O. "Hanfling and Radford on Art and Real Life." *Philosophy* 60 (1985): 127–28.
Neill, Alex. "Fear, Fiction and Make-Believe." *Journal of Aesthetics and Art Criticism* 49 (1991): 47–56.
Novitz, David. "Fiction, Imagination and Emotion." *Journal of Aesthetics and Art Criticism* 38 (1980): 279–88.
Paskins, Barrie. "On Being Moved by Anna Karenina and *Anna Karenina*." *Philosophy* 52 (1977): 344–47.
Radford, Colin. "The Essential Anna." *Philosophy* 54 (1979): 390–94. (Response to Paskins.)
Radford, Colin. "Philosophers and Their Monstrous Thoughts." *British Journal of Aesthetics* 22 (1982): 261–63. (Response to Lamarque.)
Radford, Colin. "Stuffed Tigers: A Reply to H. O. Mounce." *Philosophy* 57 (1982): 529–32.
Radford, Colin. "Tears and Fiction." *Philosophy* 52 (1977): 208–13. (Response to Weston.)
Ridley, Aaron. "Desire in the Experience of Fiction." *Philosophy and Literature* 16 (1992): 279–92.
Rosebury, B. J. "Fiction, Emotion and 'Belief': A Reply to Eva Schaper." *British Journal of Aesthetics* 19 (1979): 120–30.
Schaper, Eva. "Fiction and the Suspension of Disbelief." *British Journal of Aesthetics* 18 (1978): 31–44.
Walton, Kendall. "Fearing Fictions." *Journal of Philosophy* 75 (1978): 5–27.

Walton, Kendall. "How Remote Are Fictional Worlds from the Real World?" *Journal of Aesthetics and Art Criticism* 37 (1978): 11–23.

Walton, Kendall. *Mimesis as Make-Believe.* Cambridge: Harvard University Press, 1990. (Especially relevant are Chapters 5–7.)

Weston, Michael. "How Can We Be Moved by the Fate of Anna Karenina?" *Proceedings of the Aristotelian Society,* Supplementary Vol. 49 (1975): 81–93.

7

THE PLEASURES
OF TRAGEDY

Shakespeare, coming upon me unawares, struck me like a thunderbolt. The lightning flash of that discovery revealed to me at a stroke the whole heaven of art, illuminating it to its remotest corners. . . . But the shock was too great, and it was a long time before I recovered from it. A feeling of intense, overpowering sadness came over me, accompanied by a nervous condition like a sickness, of which only a great writer on physiology could give an adequate idea. . . .

Next day the playbills announced *Romeo and Juliet*. . . . After the madness and melancholy of *Hamlet*, after the pangs of despised love, the heartbreak and bitter irony, the continual brooding on death . . . to steep myself in the fiery sun and balmy nights of Italy, to witness the drama of that immense love, swift as thought, burning as lava, radiantly pure as an angel's glance, imperious, irresistible, the raging hatreds, the wild, ecstatic kisses, the desperate strife of love and death contending for mastery—it was too much. By the third act, hardly able to breathe—as though an iron hand had gripped me by the heart—I knew that I was lost. I may add that at that time I did not know a word of English.

—Hector Berlioz, *Memoirs*, pp. 109–12

INTRODUCTION

In the *Poetics*, Aristotle suggests that the function of tragedy is to give us a particular sort of pleasure. But the way in which he characterizes this pleasure is puzzling: "The tragic pleasure," he says, "is that of fear and pity." Part of what makes this puzzling is that in another work, the *Rhetoric*, Aristotle defines fear as "a *pain* or disturbance due to a mental picture of some destructive or painful event in the future." In the same work, he characterizes pity as *"a feeling of pain* caused by the sight of some evil, destructive or painful, which befalls one who does not deserve it and which we might expect to befall ourselves or some friends of ours." So Aristotle suggests that the emotions of pity and fear involve painful feelings. What can he mean, then, when he speaks of the *pleasure* of fear and pity? Assuming that the audiences of tragedies are typically not masochists, how is it that they can take pleasure in works that arouse in them painful or distressing responses?

The scope of the question here is not limited to tragedy. Many people claim that they get enormous pleasure from musical works such as Schubert's Piano Sonata in B flat (D.960), and from songs such as Patsy Cline's "Sweet Dreams"—and part of what makes these works so enjoyable, they say, is that they are so sad. Many more people seem to derive pleasure from horror movies and novels, works which seem designed to alarm, to shock, to terrify, to disgust, to horrify us. But, again, how is it that we can take *pleasure* in things which arouse in us what Hume calls "passions that are in themselves disagreeable and uneasy," from works that make us feel things which in everyday life we typically would go out of our ways to avoid?

This question lies at the heart of what is sometimes called the "paradox of tragedy." Given that tragedy typically arouses in us emotions which are distressing, how is it that we can take *pleasure* in tragedy? Indeed, the paradox can be formulated so as to give it more bite: Not only does tragedy seem to be the kind of thing that gives us pleasure as well as distress; it gives us pleasure at least partly *through*, or *by* causing us, distress. In Hume's words, "It seems an unaccountable pleasure which the spectators of a well-written tragedy *receive from* sorrow, terror, anxiety, and other passions that are in themselves disagreeable and uneasy." Or as Aristotle puts it, "The tragic pleasure is *that of* fear and pity." The pleasure of tragedy, in other words, is that of distress. This certainly looks paradoxical.

In attempting to dissolve this paradox, it might be suggested that we can take pleasure in tragedies just because we know that they are *stories*. We can take pleasure in watching *King Lear* when we would not take pleasure in watching a real man go mad, for example, simply because we know that *King Lear* is *fiction*. David Hume considers this suggestion in the first of the readings in this section, and suggests that it cannot be the whole answer. For one thing, he suggests, sometimes we enjoy distressing stories that we *don't* take to be fictional. Think here of all the made-for-TV movies which depict the misery suffered by actual people in actual situations, and which are enjoyed by millions of viewers. The success of such movies may even suggest that the fact that they are supposed to be *non*-fiction makes them *more* enjoyable than mere fiction to many viewers.

Hume begins his own answer to the question of how tragedy can be both distressing and pleasurable by suggesting that in responding to tragedy, the "disagreeable and uneasy" emotional responses that are aroused in us are directed at *what is depicted;* at the suffering of the characters, the awfulness of the circumstances they suffer through, and so on. In contrast, the pleasure that we experience is directed at *the manner of depiction;* at what he describes as "that very eloquence with which the melancholy scene is represented." This pleasure, he argues, "predominates" over the feelings of distress that we also experience, and "converts" them into pleasurable feelings. In watching *King Lear,* for example, we attend not only to the plight of Lear, but also to Shakespeare's eloquence, to the art of the actor, to the elegant costume and set design, and so on. And the pleasure that we take in the latter somehow overpowers and transforms the distress that we feel at the former.

Susan Feagin, in the second reading in this section, raises two questions about Hume's account which she suggests need to be answered if the account is to be persuasive. First, why is it that the pleasure which tragedy gives us typically "predominates" over the distress that it causes us? Why is it that our *overall* response to a well-written tragedy is typically pleasurable rather than distressing? Second, exactly how does the "conversion" of feeling that Hume speaks of work? How is it that our feelings of distress are "converted" into pleasurable feelings? In thinking about Hume's essay, it is important to consider how he might have answered these questions. For as Feagin suggests, unless we *can* answer them, in accepting Hume's account we should simply be exchanging one set of problems for another.

In proposing an alternative to Hume's account, Feagin suggests that if we look closely at our responses to tragedy, we find that they have two elements, which she labels the "direct response" and the "meta-response." The *direct response* is the distress we feel at the tragic events that are portrayed in the work, distress based on our sympathy with the characters involved. The *meta-response* is a response to the direct response, and it is one of pleasure: pleasure at the realization that we are sensitive human beings who care about what happens to others. So in the end, Feagin suggests, the fact that we can take pleasure in works which distress us is not paradoxical after all. It is not the distress itself that is pleasurable. What is pleasurable is rather the recognition that we are sensitive and sympathetic people who are *capable* of being distressed by what happens to others.

If Feagin is right, then, the pleasure that we get from tragedy is not in fact directed at tragedy at all; it is rather directed at ourselves. It may help to consider her proposal in the light of your own experience: When you take pleasure in tragedy, what exactly is the "focus" of your pleasure? It may also be helpful to consider Feagin's proposal in the light of Anthony Savile's suggestions about sentimentality in Section 8 of this book. Might it be argued that a consequence of Feagin's proposal is that many of our responses to tragedy are sentimental responses? If Hume is right, on the other hand, the focus of the pleasure that we take in tragedy is the tragedy itself. It is the work, rather than our own responses, Hume suggests, that we take pleasure in.

Despite their disagreements, however, Hume and Feagin do agree in their assumption that tragedy is typically a source of both pleasure and distress for us. In attempting to get clear about the nature of our experience of tragedy, it may pay to examine this assumption more closely. For one thing, is it so clear that tragedy does cause us real distress? Is witnessing the blinding of Gloucester in *King Lear* really anything like witnessing the blinding of an actual person? And if there is a difference between the two experiences, is it one of degree (so that one is *more* distressing than the other), or is it rather a difference in kind (so that they are different *sorts* of experience)?

On the other hand, is it clear that tragedy is typically a source of *pleasure?* Suppose you overhear someone coming out of a particularly harrowing performance of *King Lear* (or perhaps even an exhibition of Francis Bacon's paintings) exclaiming, "I really enjoyed that!" Does that response sound like an appropriate response to those works? If not, perhaps we ought not accept too quickly the assumption that tragedies are typically a source of pleasure. Feagin suggests that it would be hard to understand why we revere tragedies and seek them out if we did not get pleasure from them. But don't we often seek out things which do not typically give us pleasure (dentists, for example)?

Tragedies, and indeed all sorts of artworks that are, on the face of it, both distressing and pleasurable, have always played an important role in human life. So to attempt to understand just what the tragic experience involves—for example, to consider whether tragedy really is distressing/pleasurable, and if so *why* it is—is at the same time to attempt to arrive at a better understanding of ourselves.

Of Tragedy

David Hume

It seems an unaccountable pleasure, which the spectators of a well-written tragedy receive from sorrow, terror, anxiety, and other passions, that are in themselves disagreeable and uneasy.The more they are touched and affected, the more are they delighted with the spectacle; and as soon as the uneasy passions cease to operate, the piece is at an end. One scene of full joy and contentment and security is the utmost, that any composition of this kind can bear; and it is sure always to be the concluding one. If, in the texture of the piece, there be interwoven any scenes of satisfaction, they afford only faint gleams of pleasure, which are thrown in by way of variety, and in order to plunge the actors into deeper distress, by means of that contrast and disappointment. The whole art of the poet is employed, in rouzing and supporting the compassion and indignation, the anxiety and resentment of his audience. They are pleased in proportion as they are afflicted, and never are so happy as when they employ tears, sobs, and cries to give vent to their sorrow, and relieve their heart, swoln with the tenderest sympathy and compassion.

The few critics who have had some tincture of philosophy, have remarked this singular phænomenon, and have endeavoured to account for it.

L'Abbe Dubos, in his reflections on poetry and painting, asserts, that nothing is in general so disagreeable to the mind as the languid, listless state of indolence, into which it falls upon the removal of all passion and occupation. To get rid of this painful situation, it seeks every amusement and pursuit; business, gaming, shews, executions; whatever will rouze the passions, and take its attention from itself. No matter what the passion is: Let it be disagreeable, afflicting, melancholy, disordered; it is still better than that insipid languor, which arises from perfect tranquility and repose.[1]

It is impossible not to admit this account, as being, at least in part, satisfactory. You may observe, when there are several tables of gaming, that all the company run to those, where the deepest play is, even though they find not there the best players. The view, or, at least, imagination of high passions, arising from great loss or gain, affects the spectator by sympathy, gives him some touches of the same passions, and serves him for a momentary entertainment. It makes the time pass the easier with him, and is some relief to that oppression,

---

[1] [Jean-Baptiste Dubos (1670–1742), *Réflexions critiques sur la poésie et la peinture* (1719–33), translated as *Critical Reflections on Poetry, Painting and Music* (1748), pt. 1, chap. 1.]

under which men commonly labour, when left entirely to their own thoughts and meditations.

We find that common liars always magnify, in their narrations, all kinds of danger, pain, distress, sickness, deaths, murders, and cruelties; as well as joy, beauty, mirth, and magnificence. It is an absurd secret, which they have for pleasing their company, fixing their attention, and attaching them to such marvellous relations, by the passions and emotions, which they excite.

There is, however, a difficulty in applying to the present subject, in its full extent, this solution, however ingenious and satisfactory it may appear. It is certain, that the same object of distress, which pleases in a tragedy, were it really set before us, would give the most unfeigned uneasiness; though it be then the most effectual cure to languor and indolence. Monsieur FONTENELLE seems to have been sensible of this difficulty; and accordingly attempts another solution of the phænomenon; at least makes some addition to the theory above mentioned.[2]

"Pleasure and pain," says he, "which are two sentiments so different in themselves, differ not so much in their cause. From the instance of tickling, it appears, that the movement of pleasure, pushed a little too far, becomes pain; and that the movement of pain, a little moderated, becomes pleasure. Hence it proceeds, that there is such a thing as a sorrow, soft and agreeable: It is a pain weakened and diminished. The heart likes naturally to be moved and affected. Melancholy objects suit it, and even disastrous and sorrowful, provided they are softened by some circumstance. It is certain, that, on the theatre, the representation has almost the effect of reality; yet it has not altogether that effect. However we may be hurried away by the spectacle; whatever dominion the senses and imagination may usurp over the reason, there still lurks at the bottom a certain idea of falsehood in the whole of what we see. This idea, though weak and disguised, suffices to diminish the pain which we suffer from the misfortunes of those whom we love, and to reduce that affliction to such a pitch as converts it into a pleasure. We weep for the misfortune of a hero, to whom we are attached. In the same instant we comfort ourselves, by reflecting, that it is nothing but a fiction: And it is precisely that mixture of sentiments, which composes an agreeable sorrow, and tears that delight us. But as that affliction, which is caused by exterior and sensible objects, is stronger than the consolation which arises from an internal reflection, they are the effects and symptoms of sorrow, that ought to predominate in the composition."

This solution seems just and convincing; but perhaps it wants still some new addition, in order to make it answer fully the phænomenon,

---

[2] Reflexions sur la poetique, §36. [Fontenelle, "Reflections on the Poetic," sec. 36, which is contained in his *Oeuvres*, 3:34.]

which we here examine. All the passions, excited by eloquence, are agreeable in the highest degree, as well as those which are moved by painting and the theatre. The epilogues of CICERO are, on this account chiefly, the delight of every reader of taste; and it is difficult to read some of them without the deepest sympathy and sorrow. His merit as an orator, no doubt, depends much on his success in this particular. When he had raised tears in his judges and all his audience, they were then the most highly delighted, and expressed the greatest satisfaction with the pleader. The pathetic description of the butchery, made by VERRES of the SICILIAN captains,[3] is a masterpiece of this kind: But I believe none will affirm, that the being present at a melancholy scene of that nature would afford any entertainment. Neither is the sorrow here softened by fiction: For the audience were convinced of the reality of every circumstance. What is it then, which in this case raises a pleasure from the bosom of uneasiness, so to speak; and a pleasure, which still retains all the features and outward symptoms of distress and sorrow?

I answer: this extraordinary effect proceeds from that very eloquence, with which the melancholy scene is represented. The genius required to paint objects in a lively manner, the art employed in collecting all the pathetic circumstances, the judgment displayed in disposing them: the exercise, I say, of these noble talents, together with the force of expression, and beauty of oratorial numbers, diffuse the highest satisfaction on the audience, and excite the most delightful movements. By this means, the uneasiness of the melancholy passions is not only overpowered and effaced by something stronger of an opposite kind; but the whole impulse of those passions is converted into pleasure, and swells the delight which the eloquence raises in us. The same force of oratory, employed on an uninteresting subject, would not please half so much, or rather would appear altogether ridiculous; and the mind, being left in absolute calmness and indifference, would relish none of those beauties of imagination or expression, which, if joined to passion, give it such exquisite entertainment. The impulse or vehemence, arising from sorrow, compassion, indignation, receives a new direction from the sentiments of beauty. The latter, being the predominant emotion, seize the whole mind, and convert the former into themselves, at least tincture them so strongly as totally to alter their nature. And the soul, being, at the same time, rouzed by passion, and charmed by eloquence, feels on the whole a strong movement, which is altogether delightful.

The same principle takes place in tragedy; with this addition, that tragedy is an imitation; and imitation is always of itself agreeable. This circumstance serves still farther to smooth the motions of passion, and convert the whole feeling into one uniform and strong enjoyment. Objects of the greatest terror and distress please in painting, and please more than

---

[3] [Cicero, *Actionis Secundae in C. Verrem* (The second speech against Gaius Verres) 5.118–38.]

the most beautiful objects, that appear calm and indifferent.[4] The affection, rouzing the mind, excites a large stock of spirit and vehemence; which is all transformed into pleasure by the force of the prevailing movement. It is thus the fiction of tragedy softens the passion, by an infusion of a new feeling, not merely by weakening or diminishing the sorrow. You may by degrees weaken a real sorrow, till it totally disappears; yet in none of its gradations will it ever give pleasure; except, perhaps, by accident, to a man sunk under lethargic indolence, whom it rouzes from that languid state.

To confirm this theory, it will be sufficient to produce other instances, where the subordinate movement is converted into the predominant, and gives force to it, though of a different, and even sometimes though of a contrary nature.

Novelty naturally rouzes the mind, and attracts our attention; and the movements, which it causes, are always converted into any passion, belonging to the object, and join their force to it. Whether an event excite joy or sorrow, pride or shame, anger or good-will, it is sure to produce a stronger affection, when new or unusual. And though novelty of itself be agreeable, it fortifies the painful, as well as agreeable passions.

Had you any intention to move a person extremely by the narration of any event, the best method of encreasing its effect would be artfully to delay informing him of it, and first to excite his curiosity and impatience before you let him into the secret. This is the artifice practised by IAGO in the famous scene of SHAKESPEARE; and every spectator is sensible, that OTHELLO'S jealousy acquires additional force from his preceding impatience, and that the subordinate passion is here readily transformed into the predominant one.[5]

Difficulties encrease passions of every kind; and by rouzing our attention, and exciting our active powers, they produce an emotion, which nourishes the prevailing affection.

Parents commonly love that child most, whose sickly infirm frame of body has occasioned them the greatest pains, trouble, and anxiety in rearing him. The agreeable sentiment of affection here acquires force from sentiments of uneasiness.

Nothing endears so much a friend as sorrow for his death. The pleasure of his company has not so powerful an influence.

---

[4] Painters make no scruple of representing distress and sorrow as well as any other passion: But they seem not to dwell so much on these melancholy affections as the poets, who, though they copy every motion of the human breast, yet pass quickly over the agreeable sentiments. A painter represents only one instant; and if that be passionate enough, it is sure to affect and delight the spectator: But nothing can furnish to the poet a variety of scenes and incidents and sentiments, except distress, terror, or anxiety. Compleat joy and satisfaction is attended with security, and leaves no farther room for action.

[5] [Shakespeare, *Othello*, act 3, sc. 3.]

Jealousy is a painful passion; yet without some share of it, the agreeable affection of love has difficulty to subsist in its full force and violence. Absence is also a great source of complaint among lovers, and gives them the greatest uneasiness: Yet nothing is more favourable to their mutual passion than short intervals of that kind. And if long intervals often prove fatal, it is only because, through time, men are accustomed to them, and they cease to give uneasiness. Jealousy and absence in love compose the *dolce peccante* of the ITALIANS, which they suppose so essential to all pleasure.

There is a fine observation of the elder PLINY, which illustrates the principle here insisted on. *It is very remarkable,* says he, *that the last works of celebrated artists, which they left imperfect, are always the most prized, such as the* IRIS *of* ARISTIDES, *the* TYNDARIDES *of* NICOMACHUS, *the* MEDEA *of* TIMOMACHUS, *and the* VENUS *of* APELLES. *These are valued even above their finished productions: The broken lineaments of the piece, and the half-formed idea of the painter are carefully studied; and our very grief for that curious hand, which had been stopped by death, is an additional encrease to our pleasure.*[6]

These instances (and many more might be collected) are sufficient to afford us some insight into the analogy of nature, and to show us, that the pleasure, which poets, orators, and musicians give us, by exciting grief, sorrow, indignation, compassion, is not so extraordinary or paradoxical, as it may at first sight appear. The force of imagination, the energy of expression, the power of numbers, the charms of imitation; all these are naturally, of themselves, delightful to the mind: And when the object presented lays also hold of some affection, the pleasure still rises upon us, by the conversion of this subordinate movement into that which is predominant. The passion, though, perhaps, naturally, and when excited by the simple appearance of a real object, it may be painful; yet is so smoothed, and softened, and mollified, when raised by the finer arts, that it affords the highest entertainment.

To confirm this reasoning, we may observe, that if the movements of the imagination be not predominant above those of the passion, a contrary effect follows; and the former, being now subordinate, is converted into the latter, and still farther encreases the pain and affliction of the sufferer.

Who could ever think of it as a good expedient for comforting an afflicted parent, to exaggerate, with all the force of elocution, the irreparable

---

[6] Illud vero perquam rarum ac memoria dignum, etiam suprema opera artificum, imperfectasque tabulas, sicut, IRIN ARISTIDIS, TYNDARIDAS NICOMACHI, MEDEAM TIMOMACHI, & quam diximus VENEREM APELLIS, in majori admiratione esse quam perfecta. Quippe in iis lineamenta reliqua, ipsæque cogitationes artificum spectantur, atque in lenocinio commendationis dolor est manus, cum id ageret, extinctæ. Lib. xxxv. cap. 11. [*Natural History*, bk. 35, chap. 40, in the Loeb edition.]

loss, which he has met with by the death of a favourite child? The more power of imagination and expression you here employ, the more you encrease his despair and affliction.

The shame, confusion, and terror of VERRES, no doubt, rose in proportion to the noble eloquence and vehemence of CICERO: So also did his pain and uneasiness. These former passions were too strong for the pleasure arising from the beauties of elocution; and operated, though from the same principle, yet in a contrary manner, to the sympathy, compassion, and indignation of the audience.

Lord CLARENDON, when he approaches towards the catastrophe of the royal party, supposes, that his narration must then become infinitely disagreeable; and he hurries over the king's death, without giving us one circumstance of it.[7] He considers it as too horrid a scene to be contemplated with any satisfaction, or even without the utmost pain and aversion. He himself, as well as the readers of that age, were too deeply concerned in the events, and felt a pain from subjects, which an historian and a reader of another age would regard as the most pathetic and most interesting, and, by consequence, the most agreeable.

An action, represented in tragedy, may be too bloody and atrocious. It may excite such movements of horror as will not soften into pleasure; and the greatest energy of expression, bestowed on descriptions of that nature, serves only to augment our uneasiness. Such is that action represented in the *Ambitious Stepmother*,[8] where a venerable old man, raised to the height of fury and despair, rushes against a pillar, and striking his head upon it, besmears it all over with mingled brains and gore. The ENGLISH theatre abounds too much with such shocking images.

Even the common sentiments of compassion require to be softened by some agreeable affection, in order to give a thorough satisfaction to the audience. The mere suffering of plaintive virtue, under the triumphant tyranny and oppression of vice, forms a disagreeable spectacle, and is carefully avoided by all masters of the drama. In order to dismiss the audience with entire satisfaction and contentment, the virtue must either convert itself into a noble courageous despair, or the vice receive its proper punishment.

Most painters appear in this light to have been very unhappy in their subjects. As they wrought much for churches and convents, they have chiefly represented such horrible subjects as crucifixions and martyrdoms, where nothing appears but tortures, wounds, executions, and passive suffering, without any action or affection. When they turned their pencil from this ghastly mythology, they had commonly recourse to OVID,

---

[7] [Edward Hyde, First Earl of Clarendon (1609–74), *The True Historical Narrative of the Rebellion and Civil Wars in England* (1702–04). See Clarendon's description of the events of 1649.]

[8] [A tragedy by Nicholas Rowe (1674–1718), which was performed and printed in 1700.]

whose fictions, though passionate and agreeable, are scarcely natural or probable enough for painting.

The same inversion of that principle, which is here insisted on, displays itself in common life, as in the effects of oratory and poetry. Raise so the subordinate passion that it becomes the predominant, it swallows up that affection which it before nourished and encreased. Too much jealousy extinguishes love: Too much difficulty renders us indifferent: Too much sickness and infirmity disgusts a selfish and unkind parent.

What so disagreeable as the dismal, gloomy, disastrous stories, with which melancholy people entertain their companions? The uneasy passion being there raised alone, unaccompanied with any spirit, genius, or eloquence, conveys a pure uneasiness, and is attended with nothing that can soften it into pleasure or satisfaction.

The Pleasures of Tragedy

Susan L. Feagin

David Hume begins his little essay "Of Tragedy" with the observation: "It seems as unaccountable pleasure which the spectators of a well-written tragedy receive from sorrow, terror, anxiety, and other passions that are in themselves disagreeable and uneasy."[1] Here Hume addresses a paradox that has puzzled philosophers of art since Aristotle: tragedies produce, and are designed to produce, pleasure for the audience, without supposing any special callousness or insensitivity on its part (in fact, quite the opposite). I will introduce a distinction which enables us to understand how we can feel pleasure in response to tragedy, and which also sheds some light on the complexity of such responses. The virtues of this approach lie in its straightforward solution to the paradox of tragedy as well as the bridges the approach builds between this and some other traditional problems in aesthetics, and the promising ways in which we are helped to see their relationships. In particular, we are helped to understand the feeling many have had about the greatness of tragedy in comparison to comedy, and provided a new perspective from which to view the relationship between art and morality. The very close connection which is seen to hold here between pleasures from tragedy and moral feelings also gives rise to a potential problem, which is examined in the last three sections of the paper.

Hume himself alleged that imagination, imitation, and expression are all "naturally" pleasurable to the mind, and argued that when they "pre-

---

[1] David Hume, "Of Tragedy," reprinted in this book.

dominate" over the unpleasant feelings the latter are "converted" into the former. But it is not clear how the "dominance" of imagination and expression is to be achieved. It is not insured by the fact that what is depicted is fictional, or even by our knowledge that it is fictional, since Hume discusses a play where the events depicted (even though fictional) are so gory that no amount of expression can "soften" them into pleasure. More puzzling, however, is the process of "conversion" which imagination performs on the unpleasant feelings (and which those feelings, when dominant, perform on the natural pleasantness of the imagination). Pains are not merely mitigated by the pleasure, but converted or transformed into something different. The mechanics of this conversion are never explained, and as long as they remain obscure, even if we accept other features of Hume's view, many of which are quite insightful, we have merely substituted one puzzle for another.[2]

I. Preliminaries

The paradox of tragedy presupposes a position on the more general problem of how we can (not irrationally or absurdly) respond emotionally to a work of art at all, given that we do not really believe the events or characters depicted in it are real. I shall adopt the perspective of Ralph Clark who suggests a way of handling this more general problem which is ingenious for its simplicity.[3] Emotional responses to art are the result of entertaining various counterfactual conditionals: what would it be like if . . . (Iago were real, a 300-story building caught fire and all the elevators went out, someone had the characteristics and experiences of Anna Karenina).[4] Though this perspective is not essential to my view on the pleasures of tragedy, it does coincide nicely with some points I wish to make later. There are, moreover, some works of art for which Clark's approach will not do. But these tend to be parodies or other sorts of works within the comic genre, rather than tragedies. That is, such works make us laugh because there is no, or little temptation to entertain the supposition that that might really happen (*Godzilla Eats Toledo,* etc.). Even in those cases, however, we can imagine what it would be like to be a person about to suffer (and hence such works can excite fear) even as a result of something deliberately far-fetched. One could even argue that it is just the juxtaposition of such seemingly incompatible responses which often produces delight,

---

[2] *Op. cit.* The words in quotes are Hume's.

[3] Ralph W. Clark, "Fictional Entities: Talking About Them and Having Feelings About Them," *Philosophical Studies,* vol. 38 (1980), p. 347. For an elaboration of such a view see B. J. Rosebury, "Fiction, Emotion, and 'Belief': A Reply to Eva Schaper," *The British Journal of Aesthetics,* vol. 19 (1979), pp. 120–30.

[4] Cf. Barrie Paskins, "On Being Moved by Anna Karenina and *Anna Karenina,*" *Philosophy,* vol. 52 (1977), pp. 345–46.

or pleasure. But I am interested here in how to explain pleasure deriving from tragedy, rather than the problems of how we can respond emotionally to manifestly unrealistic works, or to any works of art at all. Clearly, my problem presupposes an answer to the more general problem, but in addition requires the resolution of a seeming incongruity between the pleasures produced and the feelings the tragic subject matter seems, morally, to call for.

It would not be surprising to find someone claiming that aesthetically developed persons do not feel pleasure or enjoyment from tragedy at all, and, that the appropriate response to such works of art is to be unnerved, disturbed, depressed, or even horrified. If this were true *and* this were all there was to say about the matter, then it would be very difficult indeed to understand why tragedies are so revered. People who pursue them would seem to be morbidly fixated on achieving their own unhappiness, which is more a sign of mental imbalance than aesthetic sophistication. The paradox of pleasure from tragedy would be replaced, then, by a different paradox: why we seek out things that displease us so.

Further, it would be difficult to accept that tragedy produces pleasure if pleasure were thought to be merely a kind of gaiety involving smiles or laughter, or purely sensuous, of short term interest and limited duration. But pleasures come in many shapes and sizes. Not all are highly spirited. Some are serene and calm, and may as well involve profound feelings of satisfaction. Pleasures from tragedy are of these latter sorts. Tragedy provides worthwhile experiences because it answers to important human interests, not superficial ones. These experiences include, as I shall argue, some of the most gratifying feelings human beings recognize themselves to possess. If this is so, and it is still claimed that these experiences are not pleasurable, then it seems we have embarked upon a merely terminological dispute.

Traditionally, the puzzle which is my topic has been posed as how we can derive pleasure from tragedy, and I shall follow suit. But I am using "tragedy" in a broad sense, including under this rubric the appropriate works in film, literature, dance, as well as theatre (operas and plays). My remarks here could even be extended, with appropriate modifications, to apply to paintings and sculpture—even though "tragedy" is not used to categorize works in those mediums. What this shows is that certain conclusions about the pleasurableness of tragedies are also seen to hold for other works as well, since the pleasures derive from comparable features of tragedies on the one hand and certain paintings and sculpture on the other. Naturally, then, my remarks do not apply merely to the narrow, Aristotelian sense of tragedy, in which sense there is question about whether such works as, e.g., Arthur Miller's *Death of a Salesman* or Eugene O'Neill's *A Long Day's Journey Into Night* are tragedies. I am concerned here with, to put it bluntly, the class of works of art with unhappy endings (even though the unhappiness of the endings is often punctuated with something we would judge to be felicitous—such as Othello's knowledge of Desdemona's faithfulness, or Alfredo's discovery of Violetta's love in *La Traviata*—in fact, one could argue that the "felicitous" discoveries are more poignant precisely because of the accompanying grief). To extend the concept to paintings and sculpture one would have to change this to "works with unpleasant subject matter." "Unhappy endings" and "unpleasant subject matter" are neither of them technically precise, but they do capture the feature of tragedy which leads to the puzzle. The unhappiness of endings and unpleasantness of subject matter are the aspects of works of art which give rise to the perplexity about how such works can give pleasure to anyone who is not an unfeeling brute, malicious, or unbalanced. It is unfortunate that Hume himself was not very clear on this, as he writes, "One scene full of joy and contentment and security is the utmost that any composition of this kind can bear; and it is sure always to be the concluding one."[5] Quite the contrary, scenes of joy are generally the opening ones, and tales with happy endings are not likely, in anyone's vocabulary, to be called tragedies.

Though my own discussion of the pleasures of tragedy does not utilize such notions as imagination and passion on which Hume depended, it does have its own special presuppositions. I shall speak of two kinds of responses to art: a direct response and a meta-response. A direct response is a response to the qualities and content of the work. A meta-response is a response to the direct response. The distinction is not one of epistemological or ontological status; I presuppose no view about sense data, epistemologically "primitive" experiences, or incorrigibility of mental status. A direct response is direct only in the sense that it is a response to the qualities and content of the work of art. Of course, there are complex questions about what is "in the work" and what constitutes the "work itself," but those need not be resolved for the purposes of this discussion. The important contrast is not between a direct response to the work as opposed to a direct response to what is not really in the work. The important contrast is between a direct response and a meta-response which is a response to the direct response: it is how one feels about and what one thinks about one's responding (directly) in the way one does to the qualities and content of the work. The meta-response is what Ryle called a "higher order" operation: it depends on (and is partly a function of) another mental phenomenon, i.e., a direct response. Ideally, my remarks will be independent of any specific view of the "logical category" of pleasure itself, and I fear perhaps the term "response" may cause some unwarranted discomfort in that sphere. Let me therefore make the following caveats: (1) by calling pleasure a response I do not imply that it is not essentially connected to its source (what one finds pleasurable), i.e., it is not

[5] Hume, *op. cit.*, p. 198.

distinguishable as a response independently of what the pleasure is a pleasure in; (2) a response is not necessarily a mental episode or occurrence (*a fortiori* it is not necessarily a private mental episode) but it may turn out to be a mood or even a disposition or a change of disposition, or some other type of thing.

Both direct and meta-responses exist in ordinary life as well as in artistic contexts. For example, the remains of a spectacular car crash may titillate our curiosity, and we may feel disgusted with ourselves for being so morbid. On the other hand, we may enjoy the enticement of hawkers outside seamy strip joints, and be pleased with ourselves for having overcome a puritanical upbringing. We can be depressed at our failure to meet a challenge, impressed with our ability to rise to an occasion, disgusted with our lack of sympathy for a friend's bereavement, or pleased with the commitment we are inclined to make to help a neighbor. It should be noted that in ordinary as well as aesthetic contexts the two kinds of responses cannot be distinguished merely by what words are used to describe them. "Pleasure," "shock," "melancholy," and "delight" may all describe direct or meta-responses, and the two are not always clearly distinguishable from each other. A blush of embarrassment may be intensified by embarrassment over the blush. That two things being distinguished cannot be infallibly distinguished, and that there are unclear cases of how and even whether the two are distinguishable, does not necessarily undermine the utility of the distinction.

II. A Solution

Direct responses to tragedy are responses to the unpleasantness of the work, and they are hence unpleasant experiences we would expect to have from works having unpleasant subject matter and/or unhappy endings. Direct responses draw on our feelings and sympathies: tear-jerkers jerk tears because of our sympathy with persons who are ill-treated or the victims of misfortune. Many people, in fact, dislike attending depressing plays and violent movies, or reading weighty books and poetry, precisely because these experiences are unpleasant and consequently depress and sadden them, making them too well aware of the evil of people and the perils of existence. These works of art, rather than being uplifting and inspiring, often instead produce feelings of torpor and futility as one is overwhelmed by the amount and variety of viciousness in the world. A dose of direct response unpleasantness is a good antidote to creeping misanthropy, as it feeds off of our concern for others. It is also, as John Stuart Mill discovered, a cure for ennui. Mill reported in his *Autobiography* (Sec. V) that it was his crying over the distressed condition of Marmontel as related in his memoirs that initially jogged Mill out of his "mental crisis" by showing him that he did have feelings, concerns, and cares, and that he was not just "a logic machine."

It is the nature of these direct responses to tragedy which we expect and in fact receive which gives rise to the question in the first place, how do we derive pleasure from tragedy? Certainly the typical person who appreciates and enjoys such works of art doesn't feel the direct response any less poignantly than those described above who don't enjoy these works. Lovers of Dostoyevsky, Verdi, and Shakespeare, let us hope, are no more callous than those who find them too hard to take. But whence the pleasure? It is, I suggest, a meta-response, arising from our awareness of, and in response to, the fact that we do have unpleasant direct responses to unpleasant events as they occur in the performing and literary arts. We find ourselves to be the kind of people who respond negatively to villainy, treachery, and injustice. This discovery, or reminder, is something which, quite justly, yields satisfaction. In a way it shows what we care for, and in showing us we care for the welfare of human beings and that we deplore the immoral forces that defeat them, it reminds us of our common humanity. It reduces one's sense of aloneness in the world, and soothes, psychologically, the pain of solipsism. Perhaps this is something like what Kant had in mind when he spoke in the *Critique of Judgment* of a "common sense." We derive pleasure from the communicability or "shareability" of a response to a work of art: it is something which unites us with other people through feeling something which could, in principle, be felt by anyone.

These meta-pleasures should not be confused with the pleasures from crying or other kinds of emotional release. The pleasure from giving vent or expression to one's pent-up feelings of anger, frustration, or sadness is different from the pleasure from being aware of the fact that you are the kind of person who feels those emotions in response to particular situations as represented in tragic works of art. The emotional release, stressed with a somewhat different emphasis by Aristotle, may in fact be pleasant, leaving one feeling refreshed and renewed. But these external expressions need not accompany one's feelings in any obvious way; many feel embarrassed about them and hence strive to avoid them (or, what is more unfortunate, to avoid the works of art which produce them). This may lead to a kind of frustration or it may not, I do not feel qualified to undertake any such "psychoanalysis." Nevertheless, one *need* not engage in overt expressions of feelings in order to *have* them, and hence one need not engage in the expression of the feelings (i.e., expressions of the direct responses) in order to feel the pleasures from tragedy. If so, we can conclude that the pleasures from tragedy are not derived merely from the *expression* of grief, sadness, etc. but must have some other source.

III. Tragedy and Comedy

The observation is often made that tragedies are much more important or significant artworks than comedies. The great works of Shakespeare are

Hamlet, King Lear, and *Macbeth,* notwithstanding the brilliance of *Twelfth Night* and *As You Like It.* The greatest plays of antiquity are the Oedipus Trilogy and the *Oresteia,* despite the cunning wit of Aristophanes. The greatness of Voltaire's *Candide* is due more to his portrayal of the fate of humankind than his avowedly clever humor. There are great comedies, but the significance of the greatest is not thought to reach the significance of even less great tragedies. Why?

It is not due, as one might suppose on first blush, to some essential morbidity in the outlook of those who defend this judgment. If it were, the greatness of tragedy would be due to the simple truth of the basic picture drawn by tragedy of the nature of man's lot: doomed to suffer injustice, wage war, suffer defeat, and be overcome by conniving women, conniving men, mistakes in judgment, accidents of birth, ignorance, and foolish advice. Tragedy then would be taken to confirm, or at least to echo, one's solemn conviction in the nastiness of human life. The pleasure from tragedy would then also be a morbid one, like the evil-doer who, in his every act, enjoys providing more evidence against the existence of a benevolent god. Whether or not one does believe in the existence of such a god, the pleasure taken in providing evidence against its existence by performing acts of evil is undoubtedly a morbid one.

But the greatness of tragedy is not due to any supposed truth of "profound" pictures such as these, and our pleasure in it is not therefore in recognizing this unpleasant truth. Tragedy is anything but morbid, for if people did not feel sympathy with their fellow human beings we would not have the initial negative responses we do to the tragic situation, the unpleasant direct responses. At the foundation of the aesthetic pleasure from tragedy is the same feeling which makes possible moral action: sympathy with, and a concern for, the welfare of human beings *qua* human beings, feelings which are increased if those human beings bear any special relationship to oneself such as friends or family, with an attendant increase in moral commitment to them. I do not wish to argue about the basis of morality, but I do wish to suggest that the basis for our judgments of the aesthetic *significance* of tragedy (as opposed to the lesser significance of comedy) can plausibly be its calling forth feeling which are also at the basis of morality. Judgments about tragedy's greatness derive from a recognition of the importance of morality to human life.

In comedy there must be a "butt" of the joke. The pleasure from comedy, then, is generally a direct response to the failures, defects, or absurdities of whomever (or whatever) is the object of ridicule or fun. Of course not all laughing is laughing *at* people—there is also laughing *with* people—and the two kinds of responses also provide a means for explaining what this means. One laughs *with* people when one is among those being laughed at. Depending on the joke, one's own emotional reactions to parts of the work may be the object of fun, or perhaps what one remembers having done or imagines one would have done under circumstances presented in the work. The response has then become more complex, requiring a kind of self-awareness, much like the meta-response that pleasure from tragedy requires.

Moreover, responses to comedy are to failures or defects judged to be insignificant. This judgment is important because if the imperfections were thought to be of great significance, the work would then take on the air of tragedy rather than comedy, it would be saddening rather than amusing that people were subject to such flaws. The arrogance and pomposity of Trissotin in Moliere's *The Learned Ladies* is comic because he is a parochial poet with little influence outside of an equally insignificant small circle of dotty old ladies. But the arrogance of Jason is of cosmic proportions: it ruins Medea, and she in turn destroys his children, his bride, his future father-in-law, and by that act unstabilizes the very order of society. Human foibles may be minor or major, and it is precisely the latter ones which tear at (rather than tickle) the hearts of an audience. Comedy, one might say, is skin deep: it generally goes no further than direct response, and requires that one's responses be to things which do not play major roles in maintaining the happiness and security of human life. Presuming an imperfection to be insignificant makes it possible to laugh at it, but believing it to be important makes one cry. The person who laughs at tragedy may justifiably be called "callous," and one might sensibly harbor serious doubts about that person's morality.

IV. Immoral Art

This excursion into the importance of tragedy as opposed to comedy has opened the back door to another issue concerning aesthetic value, one which has been infusing the discussion: the nature of the relationship between aesthetic and moral value. I have described the importance or significance of tragedy in comparison to comedy as due to an appreciation of the pleasure from tragedy being derived from feelings of sympathy with other human beings, which provide for the direct response, and the sympathy itself can plausibly be argued to be the basis also of moral feeling. The greatness of tragedy reflects the importance of morality in human life, and the aesthetic judgment of a particular work's greatness, therefore, would be an aesthetic judgment which reflects one's own particular moral commitments. Hume says at the end of his essay "Of the Standard of Taste" (in what seems to be a reluctant confession) that we cannot admit a work of art to have value unless we approve of its morality.[6] That is, a necessary condition of judging a work of art to be good is that it does not conflict with one's own ethical views. This is necessary in order to feel the direct response, and consequently to feel the pleasure

---

[6] David Hume, "Of the Standard of Taste" in *Of the Standard of Taste and Other Essays* (Indianapolis: Bobbs-Merrill, 1965), p. 22.

of the meta-response which is dependent on it. Hume illustrates this with some of his own moral judgments, but they of course involve cases where evaluators may differ.

I imagine that a work which conflicts with one's own ethical views would be called an immoral work, though both the conflict and the immorality of the work are hard to pin down. This is because a judgment that a work is immoral is a relational judgment, a judgment of the relationship between one's own ethical convictions and something about the work—what it expresses, says, shows, or approves. Judgments of immorality of a work will then vary according to different ethical convictions as well as different interpretations of the work. A work's supporting multiple interpretations even further complicates any judgment of its immorality.

Nevertheless, assuming good grounds can be given for a given interpretation of a work and, therefore, for the legitimacy of a given direct response, an immoral work would be one which manipulates our responses in a way which has us responding favorably towards something which we would in fact judge as evil, and unfavorably toward something we would in fact judge as good (to put the matter in black-and-white terms). Hypothetically, one might rewrite *Othello* so that one is led to feel pleasure at the victory of Iago, for example, though note there might be some doubt then about whether such a work should be called a tragedy (and *if* called a tragedy, it would be so called for quite a different reason—because of the eventual capture of Iago, not because of Desdemona's death). Some contemporary American horror films could also serve as examples. I am thinking specifically of a number of spin-offs of the well-reviewed film *Halloween* from a couple of years back. The morally horrifying thing about these films is that they are told through the eyes of the rapist/killer, as if to say, "you, too, can feel what it is like to be a homicidal maniac," as if there is something worthwhile in having that experience. We don't learn about their psychopathology, nor are we encouraged to identify with the victims since their characters are not developed enough to do so (but only enough to present them as victims). The thrill of the movie is, so to speak, the thrill of the chase. The point is that one finds a work morally disturbing when there is a conflict between the (immoral) feelings it produces (or attempts to produce?) in us and our (ordinary) judgments of morality. It is certainly a conflict which can occur, and which in general leads us to shun the work ourselves and, most likely, to arm our children against it.

The charge of a work's being immoral identifies the work's fault as influencing us immorally, or, if we have the strength of character to resist, attempting to do so. An immoral work, then, is one which encourages a direct response to which we have an unfavorable meta-response. The direct response, as manipulated by the author, if successful, would be pleasurable (exciting, enticing, etc.) but, given the state of one's ordinary moral feeling, one's meta-response would be *displeasure* at finding that one is capable of such callousness. (The work may be so successful as to prevent all of one's moral feelings, but notice that then the *problem* disappears, at least in one's own mind, for one no longer judges the work to be immoral). That is, in an immoral work one could not have the meta-pleasure characteristic of pleasure from tragedy, and hence one would certainly not judge it as good on the basis of that pleasure.

I have advanced this characterization of immoral art intending only to capture the possible immorality of tragedy. The meta-pleasure we feel in response to tragic situations is absent in immoral works, and this absence leads to a negative judgment of the work's aesthetic value. This characterization of immoral art could also be applied in obvious ways to comedy and even pornography. One may think it inhumane to laugh at people slipping on banana peels, or base to enjoy explicit depictions of sexual activity. In these one may also recognize the talent (if it takes talent) of the artist in producing the appropriate direct responses, but ultimately reach a negative verdict of its value because one disapproves of people having those sorts of responses to that sort of subject matter.

V. A Potential Problem

Given that, on this analysis, the same feelings are at the base of both morality and aesthetic pleasure from tragedy, it is necessary to explain how, consistently with this, one might respond aesthetically and be, for all intents and purposes, an immoral person, and also how one might be morally very upright but aesthetically insensitive. The first is what John Ruskin calls somewhere the "selfish sentimentalist." One can weep, groan, and cringe over a novel or in the theater, but remain blasé if the fictional events were to occur in reality. The pride one feels in one's theater tears is a selfish pride, and has actually very little to do with any concern for human welfare, or, consequently, one's virtue (though it may have a lot to do with one's supposed virtue). Wouldn't such an account as mine have to suppose that the moral feelings exist when one is in the theater, but that they dissolve when one walks outside?

In *The Concept of Mind*, Gilbert Ryle says, "Sentimentalists are people who indulge in induced feelings without acknowledging the fictitiousness of their agitations."[7] Their agitations are not real since their concern is not: without a genuine desire for people's welfare there is no opposition between that desire and the fate that eventually befalls them. They pre-

---

[7] Gilbert Ryle, *The Concept of Mind* (New York: Barnes & Noble, 1949), p. 107.

tend a concern for the poor devils, and then feel real distress when they suffer only because their pretense has been so effective. But then one wonders how people can feel real distress over pretended concerns.

There should be another way of explaining the situation which does not involve so much self-delusion. Indeed, there is. One might genuinely care for others but not nearly so much as for oneself. Hence, when there is no risk to oneself all the tears come pouring forth out of compassion: as a casual reader or theater-goer one is merely a witness to, and cannot be a participant in, the proceedings. That is one of the delights of fiction (even tragedy): one is free to feel as one wishes at no risk to oneself, incurring no obligation, requiring no money, time, or dirty fingernails. But once one gets outside, the situation changes, and one's concern for others may just not be strong enough to overcome self-interest. Concern for others does not miraculously disappear when one travels from the theater to the marketplace—it is overpowered by concern for self. And there is still another way to view the phenomenon, consistently with what I have said about sympathetic responses and meta-responses. Perhaps one identifies with the character in the novel, film, or play, and hence one's concern is self-interested in the sense that it exists *only* because of that identification. What one may never have learned to do is to be concerned about others even when one does *not* feel at one with them. In this case there is a genuine sympathetic response, but one's capacity for sympathy is limited. I, at least, would expect such individuals to show rather pronounced patterns of likes and dislikes with respect to fictional material: only characters with certain salient properties (divorced women, perhaps, or aristocrats, or characters plagued by self-doubt, etc.) would excite their compassion, while others (bachelors, immigrants, or the chronically self-assured, etc.) leave them cold. One of the things we generally expect from a good work of art is a capacity to evoke sympathetic feelings in us for some of its characters, and it is a measure of its goodness that it can melt the hearts even of those not disposed to any concern for others. Of course, there are "cheap" ways of doing this which we all recognize: there are tools for manipulating an audience that practically no one can resist. One such tool is to introduce someone who is young, intelligent, and good, but dies an untimely death (*Love Story, Death Be Not Proud*), and another is to capitalize on adorable youngsters who have been wronged in all their innocence and goodness (Cio-Cio-San's child, Trouble, in *Madame Butterfly*). Both are effective in disturbing even the weakest sense of injustice.

The other side of the potential problem is the unimaginative moralist, whose behavior is always exemplary but who cannot get worked up over a fictional creation. Isn't it even more difficult to explain how such a person will not respond sympathetically to fiction although he or she will do so in reality? We certainly do not have a case here of one's sympathy being overpowered by self-interest. The key to the solution is that this moralist is unimaginative, for it takes *more* effort of imagination to respond to a work of art than it does to respond to real life. In art one has to overcome the conventions of the medium, contemplate counterfactuals, and make the appropriate inferences and elaborations on the basis of them. Perhaps this is why some have thought that developing an appreciation of appropriate works of art is a good ingredient of moral education: if one can learn to respond morally in the imagined case, then it will be even easier to do so in reality. Too little, it seems to me, has been written on the role of imagination in art appreciation. The discussion has instead focused on the role of belief, and how we can respond emotionally without believing (or suspending disbelief) in the reality of the characters and events. If we pursue the suggestion mentioned earlier that our responses to art are from entertaining counterfactuals, which, *qua* counterfactuals are *imagined* characters and events (not believed ones), then the way is opened for examining traits of imagination which are involved in doing this. It seems we *are* at last, led back to Hume and imagination, in a way which has more potential for understanding our responses to art than his notion of imagination did. But this is a matter for separate study. For these purposes, we can explain the unimaginative moralist's failure to respond to art by virtue of that person's being unimaginative in a way which is required in the aesthetic context but not required in the actual moral one.

VI. Meta-Responses to Art and to Life

Given the nature of pleasure from tragedy as analyzed here, it is not surprising to find philosophers alleging the existence of special "aesthetic emotions," unlike those which exist in real life. Indeed, we don't generally feel pleasure from our sympathetic responses to real tragedies, and there needs to be some explanation of why the pleasurable response is appropriate to fiction and not to reality. The fact about fiction which makes this so is that in it no one *really* suffers; the suffering is fictional, but the fact that perceivers feel genuine sympathy for this imagined suffering enables perceivers to examine their own feelings without regard for other people. In real life, the importance of human compassion is easily overshadowed by the pain of human suffering. It is not possible in real life to respond to the importance of human sympathy as a distinct phenomenon, since that sympathy depends on, one might even say "feeds on," human misery. It is not, in life, an unequivocal good. In art, however, one experiences real sympathy without there having been real suffering, and this is why it is appropriate to feel pleasure at our sympathetic responses to a work of art, whereas it is not appropriate to feel pleasure at our sympathetic responses in reality. There the sympathy comes at too great a cost.

In real life, it is more appropriate to feel satisfaction, pride, or even pleasure with what one has done rather than with what one has felt. Though one should have some caution in how one feels about what one has done (because of unforeseen consequences), "caution" isn't the right word to describe the hesitation one should have in responding to how one felt. Actions can be completed so that one can respond to them in themselves in a way inappropriate with feelings. One can go to a funeral, and be glad, looking back on it, that one had the courage to do so, but sadness over the person's death has no determinate end. Feelings are not the sorts of things which can be completed; they are not tasks to be performed. Feelings reveal one's sensitivities, which can be revealed not only in first-hand experience but also when one simply thinks about or remembers a situation. In real life, to be pleased with the feelings one had reveals a smugness, self-satisfaction, and complacency with what one has already felt. To be pleased that one once was sensitive (though now insensitive), is to be (properly) pleased very little, because one is at best pleased that one *once* was a feeling person (and, as explained above, one is pleased—because one's sympathy exists—at the expense of other people's misfortune). One should be more displeased that one has lost the sensitivity one once had. Pleasurable meta-responses in real life are foreclosed by the continued call for direct (unpleasant) responses, even when one is confronted with just the idea or memory of the event.

But such is not the case with a work of art. The direct response is to the work of art as experienced in its totality, in the integration of all its sensuous elements. The direct response is possible only in the presence of the work; take away the work and one is left merely to memories and meta-responses. In this sense, a direct response to art has "closure" (unlike feelings in real life and somewhat like actions) so that those responses can, without smugness, self-satisfaction, and complacency, themselves be singled out and responded to.

Though a meta-response of pleasure to sympathy felt in real life would reveal smugness and self-satisfaction, a meta-response of displeasure to one's lack of sympathy is appropriate and even laudable. This shows that it is not the case that meta-responses are always inappropriate (or impossible) in real life, but that it depends on the nature of the situation. Discomfort, disgust, or dissatisfaction with oneself is desirable because it shows that we are aware of defects in our character, which is a first step to self-improvement. It is courting temptation to concentrate on how well one has done, for this makes us inattentive to the ways in which we might do better. It is also true that when one doesn't "reap the benefits" of, i.e., gain pleasure from, one's sympathy, we can be reasonably sure that it is genuine.

The differences between responses and meta-responses to real situations and to art have to do both with (1) the important role actions play in morality but not in our responses to art, and (2) the differing roles which emotions themselves play in the two cases. This latter, at least, turns out to be a very complicated matter, a complete examination of which would require an analysis of the importance of a first person, direct experience of a work of art for an appreciation of it (a phenomenon which I have suggested allows for "closure" of feelings in response to art which is not present in real life). But, most fundamentally, the meta-response of pleasure to the sympathy we feel for other people is appropriate to art but not in life because in the former there is no real suffering to continue to weigh on our feelings. In the latter case, real suffering easily commands our attention, so that any desirability of sympathy is of miniscule importance in comparison with the perniciousness of the conditions which gave rise to it.

In summary, pleasures from tragedy are meta-responses. They are responses to direct responses to works of art, which are themselves painful or unpleasant. But given the basis for the direct response, sympathy, it gives us pleasure to find ourselves responding in such a manner. That is, it is a recognition that there can be a unity of feeling among members of humanity, that we are not alone, and that these feelings are at the heart of morality itself. The judgment that tragedy is a great art form, much greater than comedy or farce, is based on the fact that our pleasures in it derive from feelings which are essential to the existence and maintenance of human society. Further, one's judgment of the goodness of a tragic work of art is dependent upon one's moral approval of it, since disapproval (or indifference) would not generate the pleasurable meta-responses on which judgments of a work's value are based. It is, of course, possible to respond appropriately to art, even when those responses require sympathy, and not with the appropriate sympathy in life, as it is also possible to be morally upstanding in life but insensitive to art. Explanations of these phenomena involve intricacies of their own, but they reinforce rather than resist the analysis given of pleasure from tragedy as a meta-response. The fact that pleasurable meta-responses to our sympathetic responses to tragedy are appropriate to art but not in life suggests one respect in which aesthetic emotions are different from emotions of life, and also has to do with the importance of direct experience of a work for an appreciation of it. The peculiarity of the responses hinges on the fact that what one initially responds to is *not* real, thus making continued sympathy idle, and allowing one to reflect on the sympathy one previously felt.

SUGGESTIONS FOR FURTHER READING

Aristotle. *Poetics.* Trans. by Ingram Bywater, in *The Basic Works of Aristotle,* ed. by Richard McKeon. New York: Random House, 1941.

Carroll, Noël. *The Philosophy of Horror.* New York: Routledge, 1990. (See especially Chapter 4.)

Eaton, Marcia. "A Strange Kind of Sadness." *Journal of Aesthetics and Art Criticism* 41 (1982): 51–63.

Heller, Terry. *The Delights of Terror: An Aesthetics of the Tale of Terror.* Urbana: University of Illinois Press, 1987.

Hill, Eric. "Hume and the Delightful Tragedy Problem." *Philosophy* 57 (1982): 319–26.

Hipple, Walter. "The Logic of Hume's Essay 'Of Tragedy.'" *Philosophical Quarterly* 6 (1956): 43–52.

Iseminger, Gary. "How Strange a Sadness?" *Journal of Aesthetics and Art Criticism* 42 (1983): 81–82.

Levinson, Jerrold. "Music and Negative Emotion." *Pacific Philosophical Quarterly* 63 (1982): 327–46.

Markowitz, Sally. "Guilty Pleasures: Aesthetic Meta-Response and Fiction." *Journal of Aesthetics and Art Criticism* 50 (1992): 307–16.

Morreall, John. "Enjoying Negative Emotions in Fiction." *Philosophy and Literature* 9 (1985): 95–102.

Neill, Alex. "Yanal and Others on Hume and Tragedy." *Journal of Aesthetics and Art Criticism* 50 (1992): 151–54.

Packer, Mark. "Dissolving the Paradox of Tragedy." *Journal of Aesthetics and Art Criticism* 47 (1989): 212–19.

Paton, Margaret. "Hume on Tragedy." *British Journal of Aesthetics* 13 (1973): 121–32.

Quinton, Anthony. "Tragedy." *Proceedings of the Aristotelian Society*, Supplementary Vol. 34 (1960): 245–64.

Ridley, Aaron. "Desire in the Experience of Fiction." *Philosophy and Literature* 16 (1992): 279–91.

Schier, Flint. "The Claims of Tragedy: An Essay in Moral Psychology and Aesthetic Theory." *Philosophical Papers* 18 (1989): 7–26.

Schier, Flint. "Tragedy and the Community of Sentiment." In *Philosophy and Fiction*, ed. by Peter Lamarque. Aberdeen: Aberdeen University Press, 1983.

Walton, Kendall. *Mimesis as Make-Believe.* Cambridge: Harvard University Press, 1990. Chapter 7, Section 3.

Yanal, Robert J. "Hume and Others on the Paradox of Tragedy." *Journal of Aesthetics and Art Criticism* 49 (1991): 75–76.

8

SENTIMENTALITY

For she was dead. There, upon her little bed, she lay at rest. The solemn stillness was no marvel now.

She was dead. No sleep so beautiful and calm, so free from trace of pain, so fair to look upon. She seemed a creature fresh from the hand of God, and waiting for the breath of life; not one who had lived and suffered death.

Her couch was dressed with here and there some winter berries and green leaves, gathered in a spot she had been used to favor. "When I die, put near me something that has loved the light, and had the sky above it always." Those were her words.

She was dead. Dear, gentle, patient, noble Nell was dead. Her little bird—a poor slight thing the pressure of a finger would have crushed—was stirring nimbly in its cage; and the strong heart of its child-mistress was mute and motionless for ever.

—Charles Dickens, *The Old Curiosity Shop*, Chapter 71

One must have a heart of stone to read the death of Little Nell without laughing.

—Oscar Wilde, quoted in *The Wit and Humor of Oscar Wilde*

Little Nell's death scene in *The Old Curiosity Shop*, which to many modern readers has seemed intolerably, soppily sentimental, may seem, to a reader who has lost a child of Little

219

Nell's age, quite consoling and even restrained and justified by the facts—as it must have seemed to those Victorians who lost so many more children than we do.

—Wayne C. Booth, *The Company We Keep*, p. 69

INTRODUCTION

What is it to be sentimental? "Sentimental" is a term that is often used in describing works of art and our responses to those works, and it is a term that appears to have undergone a great change in meaning over the last two centuries. Originally, the term meant something like "full of feeling." Flaubert used the term in this purely descriptive sense when he called his story about a young man's emotional development *A Sentimental Education*. Indeed, the term is often used in the same sense today: To describe someone's response as sentimental may be to say no more than that it is a response full of tender feelings. And to describe a work of art as sentimental may simply be to say that it tends to arouse responses full of feeling in us.

However, the term "sentimental," especially when it is used to describe art and responses to art, has increasingly come to have a negative connotation. For example, when the critic F. R. Leavis described the portrayal of Maggie Tulliver in George Eliot's novel *The Mill on the Floss* as "sentimental," he clearly meant to suggest that there is something wrong with that portrayal. Another critic, I. A. Richards, said that sentimental responses are responses that are "too great," or "crude," or in one way or another "inappropriate." And Oscar Wilde suggested that sentimentality somehow involves dishonesty when he characterized a sentimental person as someone "who desires to have the luxury of an emotion without paying for it." At least some of our everyday uses of the term "sentimental" echo these negative characterizations of sentimentality. For example, to describe people as sentimental about small children is to suggest that their responses to children are in some way inadequate: They (rightly) see toddlers as innocent, sweetly virtuous, and mischievously cute, but they consistently overlook such important features of toddlers as the dirty diapers they produce and their screaming fits and temper tantrums. Again, to describe a political advertisement as sentimental is to object to it on the grounds that it shamelessly tugs at our heartstrings while deliberately oversimplifying and glossing over difficult political realities.

So "sentimental" and "sentimentality" are not restricted to description and criticism of art and our responses to art. Sentimentality can be a feature of greeting cards, political conventions, ticker-tape parades, graduation ceremonies, news reporting, and indeed of more or less any aspect of public and private life. In attempting to understand how the term "sentimental" is typically used in art criticism, then, and in attempting to understand just what kind of flaw the term is intended to pick out, we will also be exploring a phenomenon which extends beyond art into many aspects of our lives.

In the first reading in this section, Anthony Savile suggests that "sentimentality is always open to criticism. There is always something wrong with it. . . . There are no situations the proper perception of which demands a sentimental response." This is a striking claim, and one that should give pause for thought to anyone who has ever wiped a tear from the eye while reading Dickens, or who has sobbed his or her way through *Love Story*. What exactly can Savile mean by "sentimental" in order to hold that sentimentality is so objectionable? It should be clear that Savile is not simply criticizing responses which are tender or full of feeling. For one thing, Savile suggests that it is not only "tender" feelings which can be sentimental: Anger, indignation, jealousy, and hatred, he says, may also be felt in sentimental ways.

What all sentimental responses have in common, according to Savile, is that they are based on partial or selective views of what they are responses to. (Think here of the sentimental view of small children described above—that view is certainly very selective.) A sentimental response, that is, is a response that is based on a false picture of the world. However, not every response based on a false picture of the world is sentimental. For example, if I mistakenly believe that you are hurt, I may be sad, but the fact that my sadness is based on a mistake about you does not mean that my sadness is *sentimental*. What makes a response sentimental, Savile suggests, is not *merely* that it is based on a false picture of the world, but that it is based on a false picture of the world which we adopt "under the guidance of a desire for gratification and reassurance." That is, Savile suggests, in responding sentimentally we are involved in a kind of self-deception. We *want* to feel in certain ways, so we selectively and deliberately (though not necessarily consciously) misrepresent the world to ourselves so that we *can* feel in those ways. For example, a man may be so determined to feel superior to a female colleague that he deliberately misrepresents her to himself, refusing to recognize her strengths and abilities and exaggerating her weaknesses, so that he can regard her as less competent than he is. In effect, he *makes* himself believe what he *needs* to believe if he is to feel the way he wants to feel. His comforting feelings of superiority depend upon his deceiving himself about his colleague's true qualities. The common name for his attitude toward his colleague, of course, is "sexism." But if Savile is right, it is also a kind of sentimentality.

In the second reading in this section, Ira Newman suggests that Savile's account, and others like it, may be too hard on sentimentality. Newman argues that the fact that a response involves "being false to the world," or is based on a deliberate misrepresentation of the way things really are, does not in itself mean that there is anything wrong with that response. Nor does the fact that a response involves "being false to oneself," or that it is based on some act of self-deception, mean that the response must necessarily be flawed or objectionable. Indeed, Newman suggests that the idealization and self-deception characteristic of sentimental responses may sometimes be "psychologically practical." Newman does not mean that such responses may be merely easier or more comfortable than unsentimental responses. His point is rather that without a certain measure of idealization and self-deception some aspects of our experience would not be tolerable at all. If Newman is right, then, sentimentality may simply be a way of coping with experiences of a world that can often be painful and disappointing. Not all of us—perhaps none of us—are strong enough all the time to face things as they really are. Life and the truth about the world can be awful. So perhaps it might be better sometimes to respond to the world sentimentally—to idealize it and deceive ourselves—than it would be to be broken by the world or to become incapable of responding to it at all. Sentimentality may always be objectionable, as Savile claims. But if Newman is right, it may nonetheless sometimes be the best mode of response available to us.

Sentimental art is art that is especially well suited to arouse sentimental responses in us. Works of art are not the only things that can evoke such responses. But some works of art are particularly effective at doing so. Indeed, some works of art seem designed for that very purpose. For example, in his novels, Charles Dickens often portrayed children in ways similar to those in which modern advertisers portray them—that is, as innocent, sweet, charming, wise, and, above all, good. The nineteenth-century French artist Bouguereau produced many paintings depicting children in much the same way—in essence, as idealized little angels. Part of the incredible popularity of both Dickens and Bouguereau in the last century (a popularity which continues today) is surely due to something that modern advertising agencies understand very well: that this sort of portrayal of children is one that people find heartwarming and comforting. Is the attempt to offer us comfort against the often difficult and unpleasant realities of everyday life a respectable goal for art? Or should art be concerned with showing us the truth about ourselves and our world? These questions raise others which we shall take up in Section 10 of this book. But in part, the answers we give to them will depend on which of the authors in this section we think comes closer to the truth.

Sentimentality

Anthony Savile

An initial clue to the nature of sentimentality is that there is no distinct feeling or content of thought that passes under that name. What qualify are our standard feelings of grief, anger, pity, and so on, and the thoughts internally associated with them. This is not to say that every occurrence of such feelings and thoughts is sentimental. That would be absurd. They are sentimental when they are felt or entertained in a particular way. Sentimentality is properly seen as a *mode* of feeling or thought, not as a feeling of a particular *kind*. The task of elucidation is to characterize that mode by describing the way in which we sentimentally think and feel what we do.

Another thing we know is that sentimentality is always open to criticism. There is always something wrong with it. Whereas for any standard affect there will be situations in which it is quite appropriately felt or in which not to feel it requires explanation, in the case of sentimentality there are no situations the proper perception of which demands a sentimental response or in which its absence needs to be accounted for. The thought in which sentimental grief or pity about something is grounded will always be defective in some way, and I surmise that in its essential defectiveness we find a pointer to its nature.

One property that lays thought open to criticism is falsity. Another, quite compatible with thought's truth, is lack of evidential justification. Now while it is certainly true that when I sentimentalize an object something in my thought about it will be false or evidentially unjustified, these faults, either singly or together, do not capture its essence. If, seeing you knocked down by a car and mistaking you for your brother, I feel sympathy for him, I need not do so sentimentally. Again, if my love for you is rooted in the true but in fact unjustified thought that you cherish me, my love is not on that account a sentimental one.

These two defects of thought are naturally enough envisaged as arising in the course of truth-seeking enquiry. I have supposed myself to form the belief that your brother is hurt and that you cherish me under the guidance of a quite general desire to believe what is true. But we have only to remind ourselves that this is not the only desire that contributes to the formation of belief[1] to see that the deficiency of thought that is characteristic of sentimentality does not arise under the aegis of this particular

---

[1] Cf. Freud, *Totem and Taboo*, Ch. III, 2: 'Our psychoanalytic work will begin at a different point. It must not be assumed that mankind came to create its first world system through a purely speculative thirst for knowledge. The practical need of mastering the world must have contributed to this effort.' And Freud was no stranger to the idea that one way of mastering the world was to make it up.

overarching desire. For given that a belief of mine is so formed, when it is pointed out to me that it is false or that I am not justified in holding it, I shall abandon it or at least suspend belief. If nothing else sustains such errors than my desire rationally to believe what is true, they die a reasonably swift death. By contrast, a man whose grief, anger, or love is sentimental will tend to resist the correction of the thought on which his emotion rests, and this very recalcitrance suggests that what holds the thought in place is not a desire for truth and knowledge but something else—a desire that can be satisfied by seeing the object in a false light. Hence the crucial belief about it is not so much mistaken as arrived at as a result of active false-colouring. And we can perhaps descry the element of purposeful activity in the formation of feeling in the way we speak of ourselves actively *sentimentalizing* something rather than simply passively finding ourselves with a sentimental view of it.

What then is the desire under whose guidance sentimental thought is conducted? Doubtless there are several answers to this question. The most straightforward seems to be that what the sentimentalist seeks is the occurrence of certain enjoyable emotions. And since no emotion can be felt except as supported by a certain thought about its object, an appropriate thought has to be entertained for the sake of the pleasure. Where the object itself does not properly support that thought I shall have to contrive it by projection. Thus for instance I may sentimentalize a duckling before eating it by falsely representing it to myself as eagerly waiting for the pot, and in doing so make possible a gratifying feeling of benevolence towards the bird and the natural order to which the bird belongs.

A more interesting case—and surely as common in its occurrence—is that in which what is desired is not so much a gratifying feeling as a gratifying image of the self that is sustained by a fabricated emotion. As before, what makes the emotion possible is a thought about its object (which may or may not be the self). Take for instance those very common objects of sentimentalization, children and domestic pets. Projecting onto them an exaggerated vulnerability and innocence, I encourage myself to feel a tender compassion for them, one I may make use of to support a view of myself as a man of gentleness and fine feeling. And the temptation to sentimentality here is obvious, for it is far harder to be a man of fine feeling by proper response to the objects around me than it is to fabricate such a characterization of myself by some factitious projection. Indeed, provided that the feeling I generate is one that does underpin the character I want, sentimentality may offer me the added advantage that I may not need to go on and actually do anything about it. My aim is achieved in the feeling.

It must not be thought that only those emotions which we experience with pleasure make for sentimental thought, for once the structure of the phenomenon is clear it is evident that this will not be so. Even when we do not find them pleasing, anger or indignation for instance can easily be fitted into the pattern just illustrated. Thus a man who idealizes a distant political cause may be sentimentally angry or indignant when one of its exponents is extradited from the country, even though he does not experience these feelings with pleasure.[2] What may happen is that in demonstrating against the extradition he may sustain a view of himself as righteous and just. His anger is fed by his sentimental view of the cause, and while it may bring him distress, it also works to enable him to take a gratifying view of his own character. In the same vein it is no more difficult to imagine self-gratifying jealousy or hatred even though these emotions are far more painful to experience than anger or indignation. So my jealousy could support a pleasing view of myself as a man of grand passion, and my hatred for some luckless neighbour serve to endow me with a gratifying heroism that otherwise I would not take myself to possess.

What we see in these various cases is how the sentimentalist achieves a certain kind of gratification by false-colouring an object in his thought. A fuller description would undoubtedly attempt more precision. It would in particular tell us more about typical ways in which the sentimentalist acts, and would show how very often his activity has a protective function, so that what is achieved through the false-colouring of the world that he goes in for is reassurance in a world that is found unsettling. He tends to protect himself against the resistance of other things by softening them down, filing down their uncomfortable edges, or makes what is in truth rather alien and off-putting quite docile to his wishes and tastes. Thus when the advertizers of David Hamilton's *Le Jardin secret* hold out that book of popular photographs as containing 'images d'un monde où le spectateur peut contempler la fragile beauté des jeunes filles aux premiers instants de leur éveil à la féminité; monde heureux qui ne connait ni violence, ni viellesse, monde d'élégance et de beauté, refuge contre les rigeurs de la realité,' they collude with the photographer in offering the reader a world in which he is comfortably and protectively cocooned. The appeal of these popular shots would scarcely be comprehensible if they did not encourage fantasy to deny the reality of a world in just the odious ways the publicity so glutinously describes.

However, it may seem that the description of sentimentality I have offered is too wide, for it suggests that almost any gratifying self-protective fantasy projected onto the world will be a sentimental one. And that is surely wrong. For example I may find myself unable to understand the work of some difficult philosopher, Kant, say, or Wittgenstein, and rather than admit that the fault lies with me, rather than abandon my pride, I may accuse the author himself of bad faith and of passing off as deep insight what is in fact little more than empty babble. Here I protect my pride by discovering in imagination the confidence trick that has taken every-

---

[2] The example comes from M. Tanner 'Sentimentality', *Proceedings of the Aristotelian Society* (1976/7), 127–47.

one else in. In consequence I represent the frustration arising from my own limitations as justified anger, and protect my self-esteem by detection of the intellectual fraud. Such a situation may appear to mirror those just set out, but it would scarcely be one in which I have sentimentalized the work of Kant or of Wittgenstein.

It is evident that this kind of case cannot be dealt with by pointing to some unacceptable harshness in the emotion that is involved. We have already noticed that *any* emotion can on occasion be sentimentally entertained—though it may well be that in some cases the object of the sentimentalization and the object of the emotion differ (as in the case of hatred that I mentioned). However, it may be right to suggest that what distinguishes the sentimental fantasy from the other one is its tendency to idealize its objects, to present them as pure, noble, heroic, vulnerable, innocent, etc., and that feature is quite absent in my mistreatment of Kant or Wittgenstein. There I went in for no idealization at all and have instead projected onto the obscure philosopher a kind of malevolent intent that permits me to divert frustration away from myself.

With this emendation made, my tentative suggestion is that a sentimental mode of thought is typically one that idealizes its object under the guidance of a desire for gratification and reassurance. Derivatively, emotion is sentimental which is supported by such as thought. And we can see that such an attitude is one that may be directed not only towards other people and abstract causes, as my illustrative examples have shown, but also towards the self and, at the other extreme, towards the inanimate natural world.

For an example of the former, consider Ruskin's remarks in 1865 to the cadets of the Royal Military Academy at Woolwich:

> You don't understand perhaps why I call you 'sentimental schoolboys' when you go into the Army? Because, on the whole, it is love of adventure, of excitement, of fine dress and of pride of fame, all of which are sentimental motives, which chiefly make a boy like going into the Guards better than into a counting-house . . . So far then, as for your own honour and the honour of your families, you choose brave death in a red coat before brave life in a black one, you are sentimental.[3]

To put it more fully than Ruskin did, the young man will be sentimental in his action if he goes into the Guards because by doing so he sustains a picture of himself as grand, glorious, honourable, and dashing in contrast with the mediocre and drab fellow he may dimly suspect himself to be. The idealization of Army life makes it possible for him to love and admire himself and incidentally at the same time does something to ward off the uncomfortable prospect of banality which is the lot of most. To accept that lot, to accept what Ruskin calls life in a black coat, is what would be truly

---

[3] Ruskin, *The Crown of Wild Olives*, §118.

brave, for as Ruskin sees it it is based on fact and does not enjoy the support of illusion that the sentimental young guardsman relies on.

Exactly the same structure can be discerned in the other case too, in that of the sentimentalization of the natural world. Typically we find this when we project onto an inert and separately existing world a warm concern for our human welfare and a tender amenability to our desires and needs. Instances of the strategy are to be found throughout the work of the Romantic poets, and one instructively complex example is supplied by Matthew Arnold's 'Dover Beach'. There the poet, put in mind of the ebb of Christian faith by the grating of the pebbles on the shore, apostrophizes his mistress in the lines:

> Ah, Love, let us be true
> To one another! for the world, which seems
> To lie before us like a land of dreams
> So various, so beautiful, so new,
> Hath really neither joy, nor love, nor light,
> Nor certitude, nor peace, nor help for pain;
> And we are here as on a darkling plain
> Swept with confused alarms of struggle and flight
> Where ignorant armies clash by night.

Now undoubtedly it is sentimentalization of the ego, and not of Nature, that we first detect here. Lover and mistress are presented as engagingly forlorn and bereft of all comfort but what they offer each other. What makes them forlorn is the departure from the world of faith, whose presence we are given to understand previously extended to Nature herself. With its departure the natural world cannot but be bleak, alien, and comfortless. *This* view of nature is not sentimental. What is sentimental though is the view on which it relies for contrast; the view that when the tide of faith was full Nature did minister to our needs and desires, and that we are now to be pitied because this is no longer so. Here we have a case of one piece of sentimentality facilitating another. For if it were clearly recognized that Nature is unchangingly inert, and therefore just as much capable of attaching the poet now as before his loss of faith, its distance could not be made a source of self-pity. The poet would not be able to think of it as having abandoned him. It is the suggested breakdown of the first idealization that makes way for the second. Both are gratifying, and both give the poet an easy picture of himself that is insulated from the more precise and better sustainable—the painful—view.

The Alleged Unwholesomeness of Sentimentality

Ira Newman

Nearly all philosophers and literary analysts who have commented on the subject agree with Anthony Savile that sentimentality—whether in art or in life—is a defective condition that deserves our censure, if not outright contempt.[1] I shall oppose this position by challenging two arguments these critics have frequently used: first, the argument that sentimental objects and attitudes, because they are based on pleasing idealizations of reality, are false to the world; and second, the argument that sentimental persons, because of the way they form pleasing fantasies about bits of their lives, are false to themselves. I shall conclude that, although there may be unwholesome instances of sentimentality, there may be laudable ones as well. Underlying my account is the linguistic observation that the term "sentimentality" has not only an evaluative sense (as a term assessing fault), but also a descriptive sense, which is free of evaluation.

1. The Meaning of "Sentimentality"

The central idea in sentimentality is the evocation, by some aspect of the sentimental subject matter, of a tender emotion (for example, compassion, sympathy, or affection). This emotion, furthermore, is a response to a pleasing idealization, resulting from some degree of exaggeration or misrepresentation in the sentimental subject matter.[2] Thus when war veterans grow sentimental at a commemorative reunion, they may feel fondness for the drama of the great campaign in which they fought as young soldiers.[3] Their fondness may be described as "sentimental" because that emotion may be possible for them only if they idealize a battle that, at the time of engagement, they experienced as a repulsive series of disconnected events. Their idealization suppresses, to a certain degree, some of the important stressful, psychologically unassimilable features of combat.

---

[1] Anthony Savile, *The Test of Time: An Essay in Philosophical Aesthetics* (Oxford: Oxford University Press, 1982), pp. 237–43, reprinted in this book.

[2] A variation of this idea is expressed by R. A. Sharpe ("Solid Joys or Fading Pleasures," in Eva Schaper, ed., *Pleasure, Preference and Value* [Cambridge: Cambridge University Press, 1983], pp. 86–98), who states that "sentimentality involves the taking of pleasure in an object without attending to the object in its comprehensive character" (p. 89). See also Mark Jefferson ("What Is Wrong with Sentimentality?" *Mind* 92 [1983]: 519–29) for another variation: "[The sentimentalist's] trick is to misrepresent the world in order to feel unconditionally warm-hearted about bits of it." Components of the central idea are also found in the formulations of several other writers.

[3] For other treatments of this example see I. A. Richards, *Practical Criticism* (1929; reprint ed., New York: Harcourt, Brace & Co., 1960), pp. 260–61, 267–68; and Robert C. Solomon, "In Defense of Sentimentality," *Philosophy and Literature* 14 (1990): 304–23 (see p. 321).

When applied to art, "sentimentality" surfaces prominently as the name of a particular literary genre, style, or form. Thus a chapter of literary history is devoted to the appearance in the eighteenth century of the "sentimental novel," where characters such as Richardson's Clarissa and Sterne's Yorick exhibit a certain idealized portrait of virtue (in particular, an unwillingness to compromise with the world) in distress (due to their defeat by the world), and it is this idealized portrait that elicits our pity.[4] Subsequently, in the nineteenth century the fiction of Dickens and the Victorian novelists developed sentimental literary paradigms of innocent children, death and family separation, the poor, and moral conversion (such as Scrooge's). What distinguished these cases was their eliciting, from audiences, tender emotions of sympathy and affection, aimed at fictional objects that were shorn of the genuinely repugnant and dissonant features that their unidealized counterparts might be expected to exhibit.[5]

Whether applied to artworks in this way or to subjects in life, as outlined previously, the term "sentimentality" can be understood in a purely descriptive sense, as simply ascribing certain properties to a subject, without expressing any evaluation of the worth of the subject. Clearly, this evaluation-free sense is not the only way the term is used. "Sentimentality" may also be used as a term of evaluative abuse, when, for instance, we call something "sentimental nonsense" or "sentimental slop." I am neither denying that the latter usage exists nor legislating that it ought not exist. I am merely saying that the abusive sense is not the only legitimate sense, because—for one thing—there is nothing in any of the term's instantiations I have thus far mentioned that is obviously or inevitably faulty.[6] Surely sentimental subjects (in art and in life) can be burdened by

---

[4] See R. F. Brissenden, *Virtue in Distress* (London: Macmillan, 1974), pp. 89–91; also pp. 159–86 (for an analysis of *Clarissa*) and pp. 218–42 (for an analysis of *A Sentimental Journey*).

[5] In the late eighteenth century sentimental fiction was thought to require suppression of the repulsive. J. M. S. Tompkins (The Popular Novel in England 1770–1800, 1932; reprint ed. [Lincoln: University of Nebraska Press, 1961], p. 104) quotes a critic of the day, when she writes: "There was a crying need for a 'new torture or nondescript calamity' in the world of fiction, and the need was the more difficult to supply because distress, in order to be pleasing, must avoid awakening disgust. Pity must always be associated with love and esteem; no idea must be admitted which destroys 'the grace and dignity of suffering,' and even scenes of poverty must be so chastened as to leave the imagination an amiable figure to dwell upon."

[6] Richards (op. cit., pp. 255–56) also wants us to know that there are different uses of "sentimentality"—in particular, an emotive use (lacking a descriptive core) and a descriptive use (which, contrary to Richards's label, is actually an evaluative use that merely presupposes, as any evaluation naturally must, a descriptive core). Thus, despite his linguistic interest, Richards fails to identify a purely descriptive and evaluation-free use of "sentimentality," as I am advocating. See also Solomon (op. cit., pp. 310–11) for ideas on how to define "sentimentality." One problem in Solomon's analysis is his having adopted a definition of "sentimentality" that is too weak ("an expression of and appeal to the tender emotions"). Without some further qualification, this definition articulates such a seemingly unobjectionable state of affairs that one may wonder where the fault in sentimentality is alleged to be found.

faults, but upon further analysis these faults turn out to be attributable to aesthetic, psychological, or moral qualities that can plague any subject, not just, or even primarily, sentimental ones. My suspicion is that when "sentimentality" *is* used as an evaluative term of abuse, it is actually these other factors—such as poor aesthetic design, psychological shallowness, or moral insensitivity—that are being called to our attention, not the central ideas of sentimentality I have outlined above.[7] And finally, I suspect that the insults heaped on sentimentality, by a virtually unanimous chorus of critics in this century, have been the result of an illicit merging of the evaluative and descriptive senses of the term.[8] These critics have simply failed to recognize that there are two distinct senses here, not merely one.

In order to prove my point I shall outline some of the prominent arguments that have claimed sentimentality amounts to a flaw in a subject, and I shall then show why these arguments are themselves flawed.

2. Being False to the World

If sentimentality is an idealization that suppresses many of the undesirable features in a subject matter, is this not a falsification of that subject matter? And if so, is this not a sufficient reason for condemning sentimentality, since being false to the world is either intrinsically or instrumentally bad? Such reasoning is one kind of attack perennially mounted against sentimentality. How valid is it?

A. Let us consider the claim, first, that there is something *intrinsically* bad about this kind of falsification. Underlying this view is a general presumption against falsification as a degenerate moral, aesthetic, or epistemological condition. When applied to art, this presumption leads to the view that although artworks may legitimately present fictional representations (for example, Scrooge is not a real person and the ghosts that visit him are incompatible with empirical views of reality), these fictional representations must be faithful, or true, to the psychology and morality of human beings and the events that befall them. Since the idealizing charac-

---

[7] M. H. Abrams (*A Glossary of Literary Terms*, 3d ed. [New York: Holt, Rinehart and Winston, 1971], pp. 156–57) expresses similar thoughts: "A useful distinction between sentimental and nonsentimental is one which does not depend on the intensity or type of the feeling expressed or evoked, but labels as sentimental a work or passage in which the feeling is rendered in commonplaces and *clichés,* instead of being freshly verbalized and sharply realized in the details of the situation as represented."

[8] Sentimentality's lone apologist, recently, is Solomon, who, in the article already cited and in "On Kitsch and Sentimentality" (*Journal of Aesthetics and Art Criticism* 49 [1991]: 1–14), argues that sentimentality is a virtue. While I sympathize with the attack on sentimentality's critics, Solomon's position, nevertheless, may tilt the balance too far in the direction of unqualified praise. That is one reason it is beneficial to carve out a descriptive, evaluation-free sense of "sentimentality."

teristics of sentimentality violate this requirement, sentimentality is intrinsically bad and deserves our censure.[9]

There are two reasons why this argument fails.

(i) Such falsification is not distinctive of sentimentality, but is found in many kinds of artworks and responses—even those of a clearly laudable nature. Thus Hector's tragic death in the *Iliad* is a blatant falsification, not simply because it is physiologically incredible that a man whose neck has just been speared could deliver a well-formed death speech, but because Homer purposely conceals from us the corporeal repulsiveness of blood and ripped flesh in order to cast a classical patina of grandeur on his warrior's death.[10] The butchery of death in war is purified by that remarkable Homeric light which converts the most vile act of violence into an epic tableau. In view of this sort of falsification, sentimental varieties, such as the antiseptic portraits of death by consumption in nineteenth-century romantic art, do not suffer for want of company.[11] There are plenty of targets around that are vulnerable to the same charge.

(ii) But is falsification of this sort—wherever it may be found—always a flaw? Perhaps not. There are times when we may regard competing values, such as kindness and concern for others, as more important than the value of telling the truth and, as a result, may come to view benevolent lies to a dying patient as morally appropriate in some cases. Examples like this suggest that truth telling and fidelity are only in *general* virtues; they are not virtues under *all* conditions.

We can extend such an analysis to the case of art, where the values of aesthetic excellence, audience pleasure, and cathartic release and escapism often override (and quite properly so) the commitment to present the whole truth. One wonders what the story of the *Iliad* would look like if Homer were denied the authority to suppress the details that he did. There would be no epic or tragic quality to his tale, and it would thus be a disappointingly diminished aesthetic achievement. For although the *Iliad* would still retain its abundantly faithful psychological and moral observations (it is the intricate story, after all, of an angry man and his mistakes), it would lack that special transcendent vision of war, death, and human choices, which, however much larger than—and hence untrue

---

[9] See Sharpe (op. cit., pp. 88–89), where the contempt for this sort of falsification, in sentimentality, is suggested: "*The Merry Widow* is sentimental because it presents intrigues amongst the privileged with no hint of the exploitation needed to preserve that society, or even of its darker side. *The Marriage of Figaro* is unsentimental because it does not duck that issue; we see the depth of corruption that power creates in the privileged" (p. 88).

[10] See Homer, *Iliad* (trans. W. H. D. Rouse), 22. Homer is careful to point out that Achilles' spear had not cut Hector's windpipe, and thus Hector "could still answer his foe." This may somewhat diminish our skepticism, but not by much.

[11] See Sharpe (op. cit., p. 88): "Puccini presents us with the cliché of the lovers reunited just in time for the heroine to die of that romantic disease, consumption. The soprano lead will manage a discreet little cough but producers never give us blood and phlegm."

to—life, nevertheless appeals to some deep and abiding need in our spiritual consciousness.

Therefore, basing a charge against sentimentality on its falsification of objects would once again be a confused accusation, because falsification is not always a flaw. In particular, it is not a flaw when aesthetic values deserve placement above truth in a ranking order.[12]

But, someone might object, falsification has its own dangers. It can lead to false or distorted beliefs and actions in those who encounter it. So while we might acknowledge the value of falsification to achieve some aesthetic ends, we would not be so generous toward it if we attended to many of the pathological beliefs and actions emerging in its wake. It is to these consequences that I shall now turn.

B. There are two kinds of consequentialist objections to falsification.

One kind claims that the falsifications in art generate false beliefs about reality and, consequently, unintelligent or ineffectual actions based on those false beliefs.[13] Dickens's novel *A Christmas Carol,* for instance, presents false views of the poor (their plight is attributed entirely to an immoral economic system, with surprisingly little responsibility given to their own character flaws); false views of moral improvement (Scrooge's miraculous conversion suggests nothing of the perseverance needed when the inevitable frustrations inherent in charitable giving surface); and false views of the solutions to social misery (a kind heart and distributed money, not basic changes in either the moral, educational, or social structures). Such false—and sentimental—views, the objection maintains, encourage audiences to acquire oversimplified beliefs and to act on these oversimplifications. Such actions, in all likelihood, will lack the sophistication to deal effectively with complex situations, such as social poverty. To compound matters, the defeated actors may become so resigned to their failure that they will be discouraged from attempting any further actions in the future.

While this first kind of objection addresses a person's inclinations to take action in the world, the second addresses a tendency found in many people to avoid action in the world altogether and to take refuge, instead,

---

[12] Solomon ("On Kitsch and Sentimentality," p. 12) asks a well-founded rhetorical question: "Should we insist that all paintings of young, adorable children be triptychs, an adorable centerpiece, perhaps, but two obligatory side panels displaying the child destroying a piece of furniture in one and throwing a temper tantrum in the other?" Solomon, however, attributes this all to a selective "focus" or "concern," rather than to "distortion" or falsification. I find Solomon's distinction unnecessarily coy here. The example *does* exhibit falsification, but there is nothing wrong with it in this sort of instance. See also Solomon, "In Defense of Sentimentality," pp. 318 and 321.

[13] See Mary Midgley, "Brutality and Sentimentality," *Philosophy* 54 (1979): 385–89; and Jefferson.

in a world of pleasing aesthetic fantasy. Sentimentality is conducive to such escapist inclinations because its falsifications involve projecting an appealing quality on its idealized subjects.[14] Thus if the Cratchits and Tiny Tim were presented as seething with resentment, or if Scrooge were not in the end presented as, in Chesterton's words, a "great furnace of real happiness"[15]—possibilities which would be, no doubt, psychologically and socially more true to life—we would probably not have the degree of fondness for them that we find ourselves so curiously possessing. This suggests the possibility that under some circumstances we might be tempted to remain within the aestheticized sanctuary of the sentimental "world" itself rather than deal with *real* poor people, whose intractable faults and problems may be the cause of deep discomfort to us.[16] For why bother with real poor people when we can deal exclusively with their more pleasing counterparts in art? But this spiral of thought clearly has a morally depraved character, which is forcefully illustrated by imagining a theatergoer who avoids encountering a homeless person, out of fear that this disturbing scene may ruin the delicious images of poor people he brings away with him from a dramatized performance of *A Christmas Carol*.[17]

What can we say in response to these consequentialist objections to sentimentality's falsification?

Based on my previous arguments, it is clear the response cannot be limited specifically to sentimentality, but must refer to the falsification found in art in general. This is because the falsifications of tragedy and epic poetry, for example, may be just as likely as those of sentimentality to lead to unwholesome consequences. Thus Hector's sanitized death may, in some way, lead to glamorized views of war, and, as a consequence, to an acceptance of or even eagerness for war. And reading the *Iliad* (as well as viewing its various reincarnations in contemporary war movies) may become a pleasing aestheticist alternative to the repellent, yet sometimes necessary, task of dealing with the psychological and moral horrors of real battlefield deaths.

Referring to the *Iliad* in this incidental manner, though, suggests an

---

[14] See note 5.

[15] G. K. Chesterton, *Charles Dickens, a Critical Study* (1906; excerpt reprinted in George H. Ford and Lauriat Lane, Jr., eds., *The Dickens Critics* [Ithaca, N.Y.: Cornell University Press, 1961], p. 124).

[16] For similar views, see Richard Shusterman, "Aesthetic Education or Aesthetic Ideology: T. S. Eliot on Art's Moral Critique," *Philosophy and Literature* 13 (1989), pp. 96–114; reprinted with some minor changes in his *Pragmatist Aesthetics: Living Beauty, Rethinking Art* (Oxford, England and Cambridge, Mass.: Blackwell, 1992), pp. 147–68.

[17] This illustration is a slight modification of Shusterman's basic example ("Aesthetic Education," p. 101 and *Pragmatist Aesthetics*, p. 155).

answer. Surely we do not condemn this work just because it may lead some audiences to develop undesirable beliefs or actions. While acknowledging that such effects do take place, we might also assert, quite legitimately, that blaming the *Iliad* would place far too much responsibility on the artwork itself. After all, audiences bring their own moral, intellectual, and psychological dispositions to artworks, and they should bear some of the responsibility for assessing the fidelity of various components of the artwork. An insensitivity to the realities of battlefield death, for example, reflects a shallow historical or intellectual background. The solution is to strengthen this background through an exposure to alternative reports of the sobering facts, such as photographs of war dead, or artworks expressing disillusionment with war (Wilfred Owen's poem "Dulce et Decorum Est," for instance). With this background, the *Iliad*'s narrative may be appreciated from a more balanced perspective, and those glorified views of dying on the battlefield can be taken for what they are: the transfigurations of art, not accounts of the truth. Much the same may be said about sentimentality's falsifications.

But isn't this reinstatement of falsification too sanguine in its expectations? Why should one assume that the audience can acquire the perspective needed to recognize the falsification for what it is? If the audience is fed a steady diet of such falsifications, or if a falsification is especially powerful (as it seems to be in Dickens), how is the audience to develop the resources to resist? The only answer to be given is that the match between artwork and audience is rarely an optimal one, and rarely a final one. Mistakes and misjudgments are bound to occur. The audience simply has to do its best to subject the artwork to various tests, and critics must continually prod the audience to persist in testing and to come up with the most balanced views. The fact that there is often failure is no justification for relieving the audience of its obligation.[18]

---

[18] An audience, therefore, must grow to understand that Dickens's *Christmas Carol* is operating on several, often clashing, levels. There is, first, a good deal of truth in the novel: The poor under capitalism are in desperate straits and their problems need our attention; people can, and ought to, change their moral outlook if they are too egoistic and lack compassion; repentant sinners should be forgiven and welcomed back to the community. On the other hand, there is a good deal of pleasing untruth, some instances of which I have already mentioned. Added to this list is one overriding untruth which a judicious audience must acknowledge. That is the view that it is easy to be a benefactor: just be jolly, shed a tear for Tiny Tim, keep Christmas, and throw some money around. But giving is not easy. We have to decide what projects to support and how to support them. We have to distribute goods and energies according to a rational scheme. And we have to decide on a psychologically and morally plausible balance between helping others and satisfying ourselves. The truth is that we struggle with our benevolence as much as with our greed. But Dickens's novel, in the interest of aesthetic pleasure and escapism—which we can admit as worthwhile values—chooses to conceal all that. As responsible audience members, who are experiencing these delights, we cannot afford to collaborate completely in the concealment.

3. Being False to Oneself

There is another sort of falsification argument that has been used to discredit sentimentality. This sort of argument maintains that sentimentality involves the expression of responses that are false to the genuine traits of the person exhibiting the response, and false, moreover, in some normatively objectionable way.

In I. A. Richards's eyes, for example, the sentimental response can often be viewed as a contrived way of dodging certain unpleasant memories that the person is afraid to face, yet should.[19] There are hints of personal insincerity here: The person senses where the sources of disturbance are and simply avoids thinking of them, replacing them instead with the rosy idealizations that sentimentality brings. And if one thinks there might be some redeeming reasons for these evasive maneuvers, Richards reminds us that our personal development and "mental health" require us, sometimes, to "envisage" the painful aspects of experience we are so deviously trying to avoid.[20]

In contrast to Richards's emphasis on mental flabbiness, Oscar Wilde draws attention to the moral shabbiness of sentimentality. In Wilde's view, sentimental people want to appear good, both to themselves and to others, through exhibiting emotional expressions they have not earned the right to exhibit, simply because they have not made the sacrifices required for a genuine expression of the emotion. Thus they weep in sorrow and compassion without feeling the full pain or meaning of the sorrow and compassion they appear to have. Or they choose thoughtless (and hence easy to exhibit) forms of expression, such as commercial condolence cards. Like many hypocrites in the moral sphere they want to cash in on the rewards that moral sacrifice brings (the sense of nobility, the pride, the good name) without having paid the full moral price for these rewards. In Wilde's words, sentimentalists desire "to have the luxury of an emotion" (or the air of refinement that an act of moral loftiness brings) "without having to pay for it." It is a desire to look moral, even to feel moral, without really being moral.[21]

---

[19] See Richards, op. cit., pp. 260–61, 267–70. "And those who contrive to look back to the War as 'a good time', are probably busy dodging certain other memories. . . . The sentimental response steps in to replace [a painful aspect of life] by some other aspect more pleasant to contemplate or by some factitious object which flatters the contemplator" (pp. 267–68).
[20] Ibid., p. 268.
[21] See Oscar Wilde, "De Profundis," The Letters of Oscar Wilde, ed. Rupert Hart-Davis (New York: Harcourt, Brace & World, 1962), pp. 500–07. In this cryptic, but intriguing, section of a letter Wilde wrote from Reading Prison, Wilde accuses his lover, Lord Alfred Douglas, of hypocrisy and moral tackiness. According to Wilde, Douglas adopted a noble stance of charity toward his mother (whom he thought financially too strapped to be burdened by a son's request for money) while, at the same time, sponging funds from Wilde, in order to support his expensive lifestyle (pp. 500–01). From this situation of financial and moral irresponsibility, Wilde develops a metaphor for sentimentality. "A sentimentalist is simply one

In a view reminiscent of both Richards's and Wilde's reflections, Anthony Savile calls attention to the desire, on the part of some sentimentalists, to maintain certain reassuring images of themselves even though such self-images are no more than pleasing fantasies, products of an often intricate set of fact-distorting manipulations. For example, a young man's sentimental attitude toward a military career may be traced to an initial, and distorting, idealization of army life, where he imagines adventure, fine dress, and bravery to rule the day, rather than the revulsion, humiliation, and terror that are often the soldier's true lot. When the young man, in a subsequent move, imagines *himself* to be a member of the military, his initial distortion of army life allows him to project a fantasy self he can love and admire, which in this case amounts to a "picture of himself as grand, glorious, honourable, and dashing in contrast with the mediocre and drab fellow he may dimly suspect himself to be." According to Savile, other sorts of sentimentalists may concoct still other kinds of pleasing fantasies: reassuring self-images, for instance, of compassion (on which Wilde seems to have focused), of righteousness, of forlornness, or of invulnerability to the assaults of a harsh reality.

To counter these stinging assessments, I shall contend that Richards, Wilde, and Savile are actually aiming their barbs at pathological or corrupt instances of sentimentality, and that not *all* instances of sentimentality are pathological or corrupt. My claim, then, is that there is more to sentimentality than the personal insincerity, hypocrisy, or fantasizing these writers attribute to it. Sentimentality can actually be displayed in circumstances where we might even heap praise on it for its exhibition of certain virtues—moral, aesthetic, and psychological.

For my support I shall return to Dickens, and this time to one of his acknowledged masterpieces, *Dombey and Son*. In that novel, Chapter 16 is

---

who desires to have the luxury of an emotion without having to pay for it. To propose to spare your mother's pocket was beautiful. To do so at my expense was ugly. You think that one can have one's emotions for nothing. One cannot. Even the finest and most self-sacrificing emotions have to be paid for. Strangely enough, that is what makes them fine" (p. 501). And immediately following this, Wilde lashes out at the willingness of "ordinary people" to settle for the convenience of adopting other people's stock emotional expressions, rather than working out thoughtful expressions of their own. Their "intellectual and emotional life," says Wilde, "is a very contemptible affair. Just as they borrow their ideas from a sort of circulating library of thought—the *Zeitgeist* of an age that has no soul—and send them back soiled at the end of each week, so they always try to get their emotions on credit, and refuse to pay the bill when it comes in" (p. 501). For remarks about Wilde's ideas, in particular the costs required in understanding one's feelings, see Michael Tanner, "Sentimentality," *Proceedings of the Aristotelian Society* 77 (1976–77), pp. 142–43. For eighteenth-century critical ideas about the "luxury" of noble emotions and the possibility of hypocrisy, see Tompkins, op. cit., pp. 100–03, and Brissenden, op. cit., pp. 81–84. For similar ideas from the nineteenth century, see Walter E. Houghton, *The Victorian Frame of Mind*, 1830–1870 (New Haven and London: Yale University Press, 1957), pp. 273–79.

devoted to the death of Dombey's young son, little Paul. It is a scene of overwhelming sentimentality, where the young boy virtually presides over his own deathbed, attempting to comfort the grief-stricken adults with kind and judiciously expressed words ("Don't be so sorry for me, dear Papa! Indeed I am quite happy!"). The self-possession of little Paul— the absence of any public display of fear on his part, as well as any need for psychological support from the adult world—lends an idealized quality to Dickens's representation of him. This appears so because one source of our horror at a young child's death is the sense that adults are forced to abandon a vulnerable creature, possessing only minimal command of the mental and moral tools of life, to the intractable grip of death. Dickens denies all that in his description, in the interest of presenting Paul as a character for whom we feel sympathy and affection, yet whose death is not a source of unrelieved disturbance. It is in this way that Dickens has sentimentalized the death of his young character.[22]

Almost immediately the challenges of Richards, Wilde, and Savile can be heard. Is Dickens's portrayal a way of dodging the anguish implicit in such an unhappy event, as Richards might maintain? Or, to invoke Wilde's analysis, is the response elicited from readers, narrator, or author a falsely noble one, where we are caused no real pain by Paul's death, and where our expressive gesture of compassion—like some commercial sympathy card—is not thought out and is, therefore, superficial? Or to allude to Savile, does the sweetness of Paul's death lead us to fantasize a reassuring self-image, in which we see ourselves "cocooned" in a world where normally painful and uncontrollable events appear "quite docile to our wishes and tastes"?

To follow these lines of attack would be a mistake, however. While they clearly provide plausible analyses, and may even be applicable in some cases, they are not applicable in the case of little Paul's death. Actually it is just the reverse that seems true, based particularly on a reading of some personal letters Dickens wrote in a period before his creation of *Dombey*. In those letters (which announced how he planned to deal with the death of his young sister-in-law, Mary Hogarth), Dickens promised

---

[22] For many readers, little Paul's death scene is a flawed literary performance, because of its sentimentality. See, for instance, H. M. Daleski, *Dickens and the Art of Analogy* (New York: Schocken Books, 1970), pp. 136–39. Other readers, however, argue persuasively for the death scene's considerable aesthetic merits, in terms of the overall structure of the novel and the subtlety of the psychological observations with which Dickens endows Paul. For some examples of critical praise, see Steven Marcus, *Dickens: from Pickwick to Dombey* (New York: Basic Books, 1965), pp. 322–29; Kathleen Tillotson, *Novels of the Eighteen-Forties* (Oxford: Oxford University Press, 1954), pp. 47–53; and Barbara Hardy, *Forms of Feeling in Victorian Fiction* (Athens, Ohio: Ohio University Press, 1985), pp. 63–77.

never to shrink from speaking of her, as if her memory were to be avoided, but rather to take a melancholy pleasure in recalling the times when we were all so happy.[23]

The suggestion here is that of encountering one's memories, not dodging them; of making oneself vulnerable to the pain of memory, rather than in-uring oneself to loss by refusing to dwell on any thought of the dead; of loyalty, forbearance, and respect in relation both to the memory and to the lost person, rather than egoistic desensitization.

There clearly is something odd about nineteenth-century expressions of this sort, which differ so markedly from the more stoic, or reserved, at-titudes toward death and sorrow that are the norm today. Such differ-ences must not lead us to any smug conclusions about the cultural superi-ority of our own historical period, however. For a person living at the present time may still recognize such virtues as loyalty and forbearance in Dickens's letter, and this suggests that the oddness we detect in Dickens's response may reflect only our own unfamiliarity with a perfectly legiti-mate way members of another culture choose to react to misfortune.

If we now turn to little Paul's death scene, we can see how the pattern of ideas and responses associated with Dickens's letters is realized.

In the first place, the cheery idealization of Paul's death does not sug-gest a way for readers, narrator, or author to suppress the painful re-sponse to misfortune (as Richards might have thought). Nor does it sug-gest a way for the same individuals to maintain a reassuring self-image of invulnerability to pain (as Savile might have speculated). On the contrary, we can view Dickens's portrayal as a way of *recovering* the pain in ques-tion. For what the idealization achieves is a suppression not of *all* aspects of the pain, but only of those features that might prove to be most repug-nant, and unbearably painful, to someone remembering them. It is these repugnant features—more precisely, the *anticipation* of having to remem-ber them—that may drive a person toward fantasizing, in an effort to avoid recalling them altogether. But while avoiding the most repugnant features might be a rather innocent thing, the tendency for such forms of avoidance to include the person, thing, or quality of life whose absence gives rise to the pain, might not be: for by avoiding recall of these things, one becomes vulnerable to inappropriate levels of forgetfulness, apathy, or disloyalty. So in the interest of faithfulness to the memory of the loss, idealization, by making recall more palatable, proves to be a psychologi-cal ally, not an obstacle.

---

[23] Charles Dickens, *The Letters of Charles Dickens,* ed. Madeline House and Graham Storey (Oxford: Clarendon Press, 1965), 1:323. (The omission of a comma following "her" in the original text may suggest an ambiguity in meaning that is clearly not the intent of Dickens's statement. To avoid such a suggestion I have inserted a comma in my transcription.) For an illuminating discussion of the relationship between Dickens's personal letters of this period and his sentimental literature, see Marcus, op. cit., pp. 132–35, 158–61.

Second, the compassion extended to little Paul does not fit either of the Wildean signs of hypocrisy. For one thing, as we have just seen, the pain of the loss is not denied, but is genuinely felt. For another, the expressive response Dickens elicits is one requiring a certain degree of reflection and novelty for its formation. That response can best be described, in the telling phrase Dickens uses in his letter, as a "melancholy pleasure." Whatever that phrase signifies, it clearly is not reducible to the thoughtless and stock responses associated with commercial condolence cards.[24] This is because, at the very least, the phrase suggests that the person responding is trying to hold together emotional elements—of happiness and meditative sadness—in an extraordinary union, which extends well beyond what we would usually expect of these conflicting feelings.[25] And since it requires an *expense* of mental and moral energy for the person responding to resolve to hold these two in conjunction, how could Wilde's contemptuous assessment—that the sentimentalist is unprepared to *"pay"* for his emotions—still stand up? Wilde undoubtedly has his sights correctly targeted on many sentimentalists, but that may say more about them than about sentimentality. Dickens's sentimentality seems to have manifested itself in a different, and—by contrast—quite laudable, direction.

To conclude: I have claimed, in this paper, that the jeers almost everyone hurls at sentimentality spring from a fallacious set of arguments. First, while we may admit that sentimental objects and attitudes are false to the facts, it does not follow from this that sentimentality is flawed, for in many situations falsification may enable values such as aesthetic excellence or audience pleasure to be realized. Second, while some sentimental persons are false to themselves (through initiating fantasies about aspects of their lives), the same cannot be said of other sentimentalists, who may display personal virtues, such as loyalty and forbearance, in dealing with painful memories or possibilities. In the end, then, we can say that instances of sentimentality are susceptible of either praise or blame. But

---

[24] Dickens's "melancholy pleasure" is not to be confused with the "pleasures of melancholy." The latter refers to the popular eighteenth-century view of melancholic states as sources of wisdom and spiritual rapture. Dickens saw no such exalted dimension in melancholy. Instead, he seemed to view melancholy as one component in a complex mental state (along with pleasure as the other component), much as we might view bitter and sweet as components of a complex (and puzzling) experience we call "bittersweet." For the "pleasures of melancholy" see Louis I. Bredvold, *The Natural History of Sensibility* (Detroit: Wayne State University Press, 1962), pp. 53–73.

[25] In commenting on another personal letter, Marcus (op. cit., p. 161) states: "With its distinctions that do not quite distinguish, with its qualifications that slide into blurred incertitude, this passage reveals Dickens' sentimentality as a condition of spirit in which doubt and pain and affirmation coexist, and in which affirmation is commanded forcefully, willfully, to prevail."

which assessment it is to be, is a matter to be decided by examining the particular contexts within which the sentimental instance emerges, not by complacently assuming a blanket evaluation of sentimentality itself.[26]

[26] An earlier version of this paper was presented at both national and Eastern Division meetings of the American Society for Aesthetics in 1992, and at the 1993 meeting of the American Philosophical Association, Central Division. I am grateful to the respective commentators—Robert Solomon, Cynthia Grund, and Paul D. Eisenberg—for their provocative criticisms. Thanks are also extended to Ellen Blais, Bernard Koloski, Alex Neill, Richard Shusterman, and Kathleen Thompson for helpful suggestions, and to Mansfield University for research support.

SUGGESTIONS FOR FURTHER READING

Budd, Malcolm. "Belief and Sincerity in Poetry." In *Pleasure, Preference and Value,* ed. by Eva Schaper. Cambridge: Cambridge University Pres, 1983.

Calinescu, Matei. "The Benevolent Monster: Reflections on Kitsch as an Aesthetic Concept." *Clio* 6 (1976).

Calinescu, Matei. *Five Faces of Modernity: Modernism, Avant-Garde, Decadence, Kitsch, Postmodernism.* Durham: Duke University Press, 1987.

Crick, Philip. "Kitsch." *British Journal of Aesthetics* 23 (1983): 48–52.

Dewey, John. "Quest for Certainty." In *John Dewey: The Later Works 1925–53,* Vol. 4, ed. by Jo Ann Boydston. Carbondale: Southern Illinois University Press, 1984.

Dorfles, Gillo, ed. *Kitsch: The World of Bad Taste.* New York: Universe Books, 1968.

Eaton, Marcia Muelder. "Laughing at the Death of Little Nell: Sentimental Art and Sentimental People." *American Philosophical Quarterly* 26 (1989): 269–82.

Greenberg, Clement. "Avant-Garde and Kitsch." In his *Art and Culture.* Boston: Beacon Press, 1965.

Henry, Lyell D., Jr. "Fetched by Beauty: Confessions of a Kitsch Addict." *Journal of Popular Culture* 13 (1989): 197–208.

Higgins, Kathleen. "Sweet Kitsch." In *The Philosophy of the Visual Arts,* ed. by Philip Alperson. New York: Oxford University Press, 1992.

Jefferson, Mark. "What Is Wrong with Sentimentality?" *Mind* 92 (1983): 519–29.

Kulka, Thomas. "Kitsch." British Journal of Aesthetics 28 (1988): 18–27.

Kundera, Milan. *The Unbearable Lightness of Being.* New York: Harper and Row, 1984.

Midgley, Mary. "Brutality and Sentimentality." *Philosophy* 54 (1979): 385–89.

Richards, I. A. *Practical Criticism.* New York: Harcourt, Brace and World, Inc., 1929, pp. 242–43.

Solomon, Robert. "In Defense of Sentimentality." *Philosophy and Literature* 14 (1990): 304–23.

Solomon, Robert. "On Kitsch and Sentimentality." *Journal of Aesthetics and Art Criticism* 49 (1991): 1–14.

Tanner, Michael. "Sentimentality." *Proceedings of the Aristotelian Society* 77 (1976–77): 127–47.

Wilde, Oscar. Letter to Lord Alfred Douglas, 1897. In *The Letters of Oscar Wilde,* ed. by Rupert Hart Davis. London: Hart-Davis Ltd., 1962, p. 501.

9

MUSICAL PROFUNDITY

The work of an architect, built in stone to withstand centuries, is something that originates in man's inner being and is then transformed into matter. The same is true of the works of sculptors and painters. These works are present externally and have taken on form.

Musical creations, however, must be generated anew again and again. They flow onward in the surge and swell of their harmonies and melodies, a reflection of the soul, which in its incarnations must always experience itself in the onward-flowing stream of time. Just as the human soul is an evolving entity, so its reflection here on earth is a flowing one. The deep effect of music is due to this kinship. Just as the human soul flows downward from its home in Devachan and flows back to it again, so do its shadows, the tones, the harmonies. Hence the intimate effect of music on the soul. Out of music the most primordial kinship speaks to the soul; in the most inwardly deep sense, sounds of home rebound from it. From the soul's primeval home, the spiritual world, the sounds of music are borne across to us and speak comfortingly and encouragingly to us in surging melodies and harmonies.

—Rudolf Steiner, *The Inner Nature of Music and the Experience of Tone*

INTRODUCTION

To describe a work of art as "profound" is to describe it with one of the most positive terms in the language of criticism. But how could *music* possibly be regarded as profound? A song might be thought profound at least partly in virtue of its text. An opera might be profound because of the characters and situations it contains. And perhaps an orchestral work based upon *Faust,* for instance, could inherit some of the profundity of Goethe's poetic masterpiece. But music all by itself? Purely instrumental music—music without the support of words, stage action, or program? How could a string quartet, or a symphony, or a fugue for organ be profound? How could mere sequences of sounds ever invite or justify such a description?

One answer, of course, is that they couldn't. You might think that pure instrumental music is simply too abstract, too free of content, possibly to qualify as profound. When one understands a piece of music, you might argue, there is nothing which one understands beyond the music itself, and thus, there is nothing which it can be profound about. But if this is the case, then why is it that so many people have in fact believed that certain pieces of purely instrumental music are indeed profound? Why is it that so many have described Beethoven's last string quartets, Bach's *The Art of Fugue,* or Brahms's Fourth Symphony as profound? Are they just mistaken? Or are they guilty of exaggeration, calling a piece of music profound when all they really mean is that they enjoy it or admire it very much?

Perhaps. But the existence of a *tradition* of describing music, or at least certain pieces of music, as profound might suggest that there is something more going on here than mere error or exaggeration. The tradition in question goes back a long time, but it finds one of its most memorable expressions in the philosophy of Schopenhauer. Schopenhauer thought that music was a "copy" of the "will"—and the "will," according to him, is the ultimate foundation of all reality. Thus Schopenhauer assigned to music a deeply metaphysical quality, and went on to talk about it in terms which have exerted a real influence over the ways in which musicians have conceived of, and have described, their art ever since:

> I recognize in the deepest tones of harmony, in the ground-bass, the lowest grades of the will's objectification, inorganic nature, the mass of the planet. . . . Those that are higher represent to me the plant and animal worlds. . . . Finally, in the *melody,* in the high, singing, principal voice, leading the whole and progressing with unrestrained freedom . . . I recognize the highest grade of the will's objectification, the intellectual life and endeavor of man. . . . [There is an] immediate knowledge of the inner nature of the world unknown to [the] faculty of reason. . . . [Music's] imitative reference to the world must be very profound, infinitely true, and really striking, since it is instantly understood by everyone. . . . Yet the

point of comparison between music and the world, the regard in which it stands to the world in the relation of a copy, or a repetition, is very obscure. (*The World as Will and Representation*, Vol. I: 256–63)

Schopenhauer's glorification of music is a good deal more evocative than it is clear, and altogether more baffling than it is illuminating. Few philosophers nowadays would accept his claims about music as they stand, nor would many accept the metaphysical views upon which those claims rest. But his claim that music is capable of being "very profound" has stuck. And implicit in what Schopenhauer says are a number of questions which are good questions to ask if we wish to determine whether and how music really can be profound.

These questions can be stated as follows: (1) What kind of property *is* profundity—what do we *mean* when we call something profound? (2) What do we understand when we understand a piece of music? (3) Is what we understand when we understand a piece of music capable of having the property of profundity? Schopenhauer's answers to these questions might have run as follows: (1) Profundity is a property of metaphysical knowledge. (2) In understanding music we understand the innermost nature of the world. Music, that is, may be a source of metaphysical knowledge. And, therefore, (3) Yes, music can be profound.

Peter Kivy would certainly disagree with the second of Schopenhauer's answers. The first reading in this section is taken from his book *Music Alone,* where Kivy argues for a version of musical "purism." By "purism" he means that music "is a quasi-syntactical structure of sound understandable solely in musical terms and having no semantic or representational content, no meaning, and making no reference to anything beyond itself" (*Music Alone,* p. 202). In this passage, we can already see an answer to question (2) above: What we understand when we understand a piece of music, according to Kivy, is something purely musical, which has no reference to anything outside the music itself. And he goes on to give an answer to question (1) as well. In order for a work of art to be profound, he says, "It must be able to be 'about' (that is, it must possess the possibility of subject matter); it must be about something profound (which is to say, something of abiding interest or importance to human beings); [and] it must treat its profound subject matter in some exemplary way or other adequate to that subject matter." This view of what profundity is makes the problem of profound *music* extremely puzzling for Kivy. For if music refers to nothing beyond itself, as he says in answering question (2), then there can be nothing profound for music to be *about*. But as Kivy says in answering question (1), a profound work of art *must* be *about* something profound. And this would seem to mean that no piece of music can be profound.

However, Kivy's intuitions suggest to him that this is the wrong answer. He wants to answer "Yes" to question (3)—to say that music *can* be profound. But on his view, this means that music must be *about* something. He goes on, then, to suggest that although music cannot have reference to anything *beyond* itself, it may yet have reference *to* itself—that is, music may be about music. And since music is a subject of abiding interest or importance, Kivy suggests that music itself might be the profound subject matter which certain musical works are about. Such musical works would then have a claim, on Kivy's model, to be regarded as profound. He subjects this account of what it is for music to be profound to close criticism, and admits that he is somewhat skeptical about it. In the end, he wonders whether the attribution of profundity to pieces of music is rationally justifiable after all.

In the second of the readings in this section, Jerrold Levinson takes a more optimistic line. He argues that Kivy's approach to the problem of musical profundity is misplaced, and that it overlooks three things we might mean when we describe a piece of instrumental music as profound. One of these is explored by Aaron Ridley in the final reading. Ridley agrees with Levinson that the sketch of profundity given by Kivy in answer to the question "What is profundity?" is mistaken. His own answer to this question is that profundity is a "structuring property which something has within a system of which it is a part." A thing will be profound, in Ridley's view, if it lies at the heart of, and gives structure to, a network of elements in which it is implicated. Ridley uses this model to suggest that certain *expressive* qualities can be seen to play a profound role within certain pieces of music. He also suggests that those expressive qualities reflect particular "ways of regarding the world," and that in recognizing an expressive quality as profound we somehow come to a deeper understanding of the way of regarding the world that that quality reflects. In answer to the question "What do we understand when we understand a piece of music?" Ridley argues that the roles played by these expressive qualities are part of what we understand in a piece of music when we understand it. And this leads Ridley to conclude that some pieces of music can indeed be profound.

The readings in this section suggest a number of ways, apart from Schopenhauer's, of answering the questions detailed earlier, and they should give us a sharper perspective on music's claim (or lack of it) to be considered profound. But the questions and answers outlined in this section should not be taken to apply to music only. For the issues raised are general issues about profundity. They ought, if followed through, to suggest ways in which we might think about what *literary* profundity is, for instance, or about what *scientific* profundity is, or about what *philosophical* profundity is. As so often happens, what looks at first glance like a fairly narrowly defined question about one of the arts turns out to be of broader significance, bearing on further questions both within and beyond the traditional concerns of aesthetics.

The Profundity of Music

Peter Kivy

Certain works of the instrumental repertoire are considered to be somehow "profound" musical works: Beethoven's late quartets, Bach's *Well-Tempered Clavier,* works like that. But does that belief in their profundity make sense?

The reason for the question is this. If I were to say that Goethe's *Faust* is a profound work of art where Oscar Wilde's *Importance of Being Earnest* is not, it is clear what I would mean. The former deals with deep philosophical and moral matters whereas the latter is a clever, frothy comedy of manners with no depth at all, meant to amuse and to be enjoyed. This is not to say that *The Importance of Being Earnest* is an imperfect work. Nor need I be saying, necessarily, that it is a lesser work of art. It *is*, of course. But it is possible for one work to be more profound than another yet less perfect and, perhaps, not as good. However, and this is the crucial point, we are clear that what makes one literary work more profound than another must be, at least, that it is about more profound matters.

Of course, being about something profound is not, by itself, sufficient for our ascribing profundity to a literary work. For profound subjects can be botched as well as beautiful, bungled as well as splendidly brought off. So we will surely have to add that for a literary work to be profound, it must not only have a profound subject but must treat it in a way adequate to that profundity. We may say, then, that for a work to be profound it must fulfill at least three conditions: it must be able to be "about" (that is, it must possess the possibility of a subject matter); it must be about something profound (which is to say, something of abiding interest or importance to human beings); it must treat its profound subject matter in some exemplary way or other adequate to that subject matter (function, in other words, at some acceptably high aesthetic level).

That being the case, the difficulty I am having with musical profundity is obvious. Music alone isn't about anything. Hence one musical composition cannot be more profound than another in virtue of being about a more profound subject. And indeed, if being a profound work of art requires being about a profound subject, it looks as if music cannot be profound at all, and when we call Bach's *Well-Tempered Clavier* "profound" we are just talking nonsense.

Now because the version of musical purism I espouse does countenance expressive properties, there appears to be an easy way out of this dilemma. It seems plausible for me to argue that music is profound in virtue of being expressive of the darker, which is to say "serious," emotions. Thus the somber seriousness of Brahms's first and fourth symphonies warrants their being considered more profound works than (say) his two serenades for orchestra, expressive as *they* are of the lighter end of the emotive spectrum.

Perhaps there is something to this suggestion in that it may correspond to the way many laypeople perceive and talk about instrumental music. I think such people do tend to perceive and to describe music expressive of the serious emotions as deeper, more profound, than music expressive of the cheerful or frivolous ones. And I think we can easily see why this is the case. There is obviously a connection between dark emotions and profound subjects. "Serious" literature, tragedy in particular, deals with death, crime and punishment, the problem of evil, human loss, sorrow and discontent, the human condition, freedom of will, human weakness—the whole litany of human complaints. These are the subjects we find profound and difficult, and the literature that deals with them we find profound (and difficult) on that account.

But although this may be an adequate account of what music the layperson tends to perceive and describe as profound, and perhaps even productive of a sound psychological explanation of why he or she does tend to perceive music expressive of the serious emotions as more profound than music expressive of the frivolous and cheerful ones, it hardly provides a *justification* for doing so. For if, as I argue, music alone is a quasi-syntactical structure of sounds, with no sense or reference, that happens to have as some of its properties expressive ones, there seems absolutely no reason for believing that a structure with serious expressive properties is any more profound than a structure with frivolous or happy ones. Perhaps profundity arises as a result of a work's concerning, being about, serious emotions. But as, on my view, music expressive of serious emotions is not about them, that it is expressive of them is no grounds at all for ascribing profundity to it.

I have suggested that laypeople tend to ascribe profundity to music expressive of the serious emotions and that there is no real justification for so doing. A logical next step would be to inquire what kind of music the musically learned tend to describe as profound and whether their ascriptions of profundity are any more justifiable than the layperson's. I begin this inquiry with an example.

In his book on J. S. Bach, Albert Schweitzer gives the following description of the now blind composer's last days and of his last musical composition.

> He appears to have passed his last days wholly in a darkened room. When he felt death drawing nigh, he dictated to Altnikol [his son-in-law] a chorale fantasia on the melody "Wenn wir in höchsten Nöten sind," but told him to head it with the beginning of the hymn "Vor deinen Thron tret ich allhier," that is sung to the same melody. . . .
>
> In the dark chamber, with the shades of death already falling round him, the master made this work, that is unique even among his creations. The contrapuntal art that it reveals is so perfect that no description can

give any idea of it. Each segment of the melody is treated in a fugue, in which the inversion of the subject figures each time as the counter-subject. Moreover the flow of the parts is so easy that after the second line we are no longer conscious of the art, but are wholly enthralled by the spirit that finds voice in these G major harmonies. The tumult of the world no longer penetrated through the curtained windows. The harmonies of the spheres were already echoing round the dying master. So there is no sorrow in the music; the tranquil quavers move along on the other side of human passion; over the whole thing gleams the word "Transfiguration."[1]

I think it requires no argument to convince the reader that Schweitzer thought Bach's last composition "profound," although the word does not occur in the passage. And it seems obvious too that the profundity has something to do, to his mind, with the "contrapuntal art . . . so perfect that no description can give any idea of it," manifested, in particular, in the fact that we have "a fugue, in which the inversion of the subject figures each time as the counter-subject." What can we make of this?

Counterpoint itself, since time out of mind, has been associated in the thinking of musicians with the profound and the serious. And in the modern musical era, composers of instrumental music have continually turned and returned to "learned" counterpoint, always in the interest of "deepening" their style. Is the association of counterpoint with profundity merely a psychological association, like the layperson's association of profundity with the serious emotions? Or is there a real connection, as there is between profundity in literature and profound subjects? That is to say, is there some rational justification for thinking that contrapuntal music is profound in virtue of being contrapuntal? I do not mean to suggest that contrapuntal music might be the only profound music. But if we can discover just what it is about counterpoint that so frequently elicits the judgment "profound," perhaps—if indeed that judgment is rationally justified—we may be able to generalize from that to all profound music properly so-called. Let us see, then, where this strategy may lead.

The *New Harvard Dictionary of Music* defines "counterpoint" as "[t]he combination of two or more melodic lines," and continues: "its nature is indissolubly linked to the nature of melody. A melody must have coherence; its tones follow one another in a musically sensible way, and this is true for melodies combined contrapuntally no less than for those that are not."[2] The challenge of counterpoint, therefore, is, most simply stated, to juggle successfully a complex function of two variables: the number of melodies combined together, and the intrinsic, melodic interest of each of those melodies. An additional parameter that has become inseparable

---

[1] Albert Schweitzer, *J. S. Bach*, trans. Ernest Newman (New York, 1950), I:223–224.
[2] Mark De Voto, "Counterpoint," *The New Harvard Dictionary of Music*, ed. Don Randel (Cambridge, Mass., 1986), p. 205.

from the art of counterpoint is what might be termed the principle of "melodic economy," which is to say, the use of as little melodic material as possible, commensurate with intrinsic melodic interest. This principle expresses itself in all of the familiar contrapuntal artifices that composers have indulged in throughout the centuries: combining a melody with itself (canon or imitation), combining it with itself in larger or smaller note values (augmentation and diminution), combining it with its mirror image (inversion), combining it with itself, back to front (crab). I call it the principle of melodic economy because, in all of the above-mentioned relationships, the trick is to combine a melody not with a different melody but with itself or some recognizable version thereof. This is particularly plain in the Bach chorale prelude that Schweitzer so admires for its use of the theme's inversion for the countersubject each time. And Bach's feat here is all the more remarkable, all the more difficult, because the theme he is using, that is, the chorale melody "Wenn wir in höchsten Nöten sind," preexists his use of it, thus putting an added constraint on the composer, since he is not free to invent any theme he likes that can go with its own inversion but has to do it with a theme already given. That theme he can, indeed, meddle with to a certain extent, but not beyond the point where it would become unrecognizable.

In the modern era, in which the institution of instrumental music as we know it came into being and flourished, this juggling act has come to represent perhaps the preeminent symbol of musical craftsmanship and learning, venerable with age and almost mystical in significance for the musician. Certainly it has come to be associated with the notion of profundity. But what makes that association more than psychological or sociological? Certainly, that contrapuntal music is difficult to write and venerable with age does not alone speak for its profundity.

Let me return to Bach's last composition: the chorale prelude on "Wenn wir in höchsten Nöten sind." In it each phrase of the melody is treated as a fugue theme, with the counter-subject always an inversion of the subject. Because the chorale melody preexisted the composition of his work, it seems entirely appropriate to describe what Bach did as *discovering* that the chorale melody could be treated in this way.[3] That is to say, Bach discovered that (with suitable tinkering) each phrase of the chorale could be accompanied with its mirror inversion. The chorale was there. Bach discovered and revealed to us through his chorale prelude that it contained this "potential" (if you will) within. Bach's contrapuntal art here is the "art of the possible": an art of discovery, of revelation.

Now this, of course, is a special case. But might we not generalize

---

[3] In suggesting the possibility of musical composition as discovery, I spin out a suggestion that I have made in a rather different context twice before: "Platonism in Music: A Kind of Defense," *Grazer Philosophische Studien* 19 (1983), and "Platonism in Music: Another Kind of Defense," *American Philosophical Quarterly* 24 (1987).

from it to counterpoint as a whole? What we find so mysteriously fascinating about contrapuntal music, I want to suggest, is that it seems to us to reveal in some deep sense the very possibilities of musical sound itself. Whether we start with preexistent material, as Bach did in his chorale prelude, or start from scratch, by devising our own fugue subject and then putting it through its paces, it is tempting to describe the process here, more perhaps than in any other kind of music, as the "discovery of possibilities." The contrapuntist seems to us as an explorer: he or she discovers what sound can do, reveals the possibilities of a theme: with what it can be combined and how. If melody appears to us as the most basic music—a melody, after all, is a complete musical composition—then counterpoint, whose "nature is indissolubly linked to the nature of melody," is the ultimate musical art, for it pursues to the outer limits the ultimate possibilities of melody, in terms of melody's possible combinations with itself. If melody is for us the simplest complete entity in the musical universe, then the contrapuntist, not the "tunesmith," is the ultimate "melodist" and, in so being, the Columbus and the Newton of our musical universe.

It appears now that we really do have a leg up on the problem of musical profundity. Recall that the first condition for a work's being "profound" is that it be able to have a subject matter, that it be able to be about something. And recall, further, that music alone, being without subject matter, being about nothing, posed a seemingly insuperable problem in that regard. But now we have found that one kind of music, contrapuntal music, seems, perhaps more frequently and consistently than any other, to be thought "profound" by the musically learned. We have found too that here we are more strongly tempted than anywhere else in music to think of composition as a discovery of possibilities and music hence to be about these possibilities, about the possibilities of musical sound or, in words we have previously used, about music itself. We have, then, a subject matter for just that kind of music which is most frequently associated in the mind of the musician with the musically profound. And the rest follows directly.

Our second condition for the profundity of a literary work was that it be about a profound subject: a subject of abiding interest or importance to human beings. That condition can immediately be seen to be fulfilled by contrapuntal music, for it is a matter of observable fact that instrumental music is of abiding interest and importance to a significant number of human beings. And as the subject matter of counterpoint is the possibilities of musical sound—that is, music—it is a subject matter *eo ipso* of abiding interest and importance to the same significant number of human beings.

It is clear, of course, that we would not call all contrapuntal music "profound." But that coincides completely with our third condition for profundity, namely, that the profound subject matter be treated in an exemplary way, a way appropriate to the subject matter's profundity. We find Bach's counterpoint matchlessly worked out, that of his lesser contemporaries clumsily or pedantically or inadequately worked out. That is why we find Bach's works profound, his contemporaries' trivial. The subject matter of his contemporaries' fugues and canons is as profound as the subject matter of Bach's, for it is the same subject matter. But Bach was a match for it, and they were not.

To sum up, then, we find that contrapuntal music tends to be called "profound" by the musically learned and that there seems to be some rational justification for their doing so. The justification is that such music seems to fulfill the three requirements for the profundity of (for example) literary works. We are tempted to say that this music is about something, namely, the possibilities of musical sound itself; what it is about is of abiding interest and importance to many of us; and at least some of this music is matchlessly executed—executed with aesthetic distinction. The problem is that contrapuntal music is not the only kind of music the musically learned tend to call profound. And if it is the only kind of music that there *seems* to be any rational justification for calling profound, I think that would cast grave doubt on whether there is in fact any real justification for it. I myself would rather give up the notion that any music is profound than accept the notion that only contrapuntal music is. Surely I find the fugues of Bach profound, but so also Brahms's symphonies. And it would seem to me naked prejudice or dogmatism to give up the latter judgment while holding on to the former. Here I think we need to insist on all or nothing. Perhaps we can have it all.

I suggested, when I began this discussion of counterpoint, that we might find in it that which elicits the judgment of profundity; that something, moreover, might be the very thing we find profound in other kinds of music as well. I think we are now in a position to determine what that something is and to generalize it for all music within the tradition with which we are concerned.

I said that in the modern era counterpoint became the preeminent symbol of musical *craftsmanship*. That, I think, is the key. Supreme musical craftsmanship is, I believe, the common denominator between counterpoint and other instances of musical profundity. Where music is great, and where its greatness is seen as the result, *significantly*, of its consummate craftsmanship, it elicits the judgment "profound" from the musically learned.

But the crucial point is that although counterpoint may be the ultimate musical craftsmanship, perhaps the one most admired by the learned, it is not the only one. Craftsmanship is a relative notion. Every major style or idiom will have a concept of craftsmanship defined relative to it. The classical style, for example—and an important example it is— provides another preeminent symbol of musical craftsmanship. The style that came of age, many would say, in Haydn's String Quartets, Op. 33, and reached various climaxes of perfection in the mature works of Haydn, Mozart, and Beethoven, provides us with another concept of craftsmanship in music, one devolving on its notably "syntactic" character.

What justification, though, is there for attributing profundity to musical craftsmanship? Well, it is the same justification, generalized, that we have in the special case of counterpoint. Craftsmanship in music is the exploration of musical possibilities within some given set of stylistic parameters. What I am suggesting here is that if anything tempts us to refer to music as being about itself, it is musical craftsmanship in general and, in particular, counterpoint, its most prestigious special case.

But how, it is fair to ask, do we know when musical craftsmanship is to be singled out as an element in a composition important enough to warrant our calling the music profound? The most obvious answer is that when the craftsmanship obtrudes, when it presses itself forcefully enough upon our musical attention, we then are motivated and (perhaps) licensed to judge the music importantly craftsmanlike and hence profound, at least to a degree. But this obvious answer must be resisted, for the obvious reason that, at least in one sense, the obtrusion of musical craftsmanship is not only not a sign of musical profundity but, quite to the contrary, a form of musical ineptitude (at least when measured against the highest standards of musical achievement). The musical craftsmanship and learning of Mendelssohn's youthful string symphonies is truly prodigious. Their counterpoint and classical techniques of symphonic exposition and development stick out all over the place. But, to appropriate Alfred Einstein's fine phrase, these youthful works still "smell of the lamp."[4] Their craftsmanship and learning have not yet been integrated into the composer's distinctive style. The same might be said of Haydn's String Quartets, Op. 20; marvelous and satisfying as the fugal finales are, they are not yet part of the classical style as are, for example, the fugal finales of Mozart's G-Major Quartet, K. 387, and "Jupiter" Symphony. Haydn had not yet achieved the integration and perfection of craftsmanship that Einstein called "that 'second naïveté' for which only a few masters in all the arts were pre-destined."[5] It is this same mastery of the craft, making the difficult seem transparent, which Schweitzer recognized in Bach's last composition, when he wrote that "the flow of the parts is so easy that after the second line we are no longer conscious of the art."

Thus to a certain extent, it is just when the craftsmanship does not obtrude that we want to call the musical work profound. The craftsmanship must be there, and it must demand our attention as a primary factor in our musical experience of the work. But craftsmanship must be supremely well brought off for us to call a work possessing it profound on

---

[4] Alfred Einstein, *Mozart: His Character, His Work* (New York, 1951), p. 155.
[5] Ibid., p. 156.

that account, and supremely well brought off craftsmanship is just the kind that is so well integrated into the musical work—and into the composer's personal style—that "we are no longer conscious of the art. . . ."

Nor is this inconsistent with our intuitions about the profound in the literary arts. A novelist may deal with a profound subject matter and may, indeed, have original and important things to say about it. But if the subject matter, regardless of how profound and informative it might be, fails to be treated in a novelistically successful way, fails to become "literature," we will not see the work as a profound novel, although we may see it, perhaps, as a profound contribution to its subject. The dialogues of Plato are profound literary as well as philosophical works; those of Bishop Berkeley, for all of their philosophical profundity, fail to achieve literary profundity for just the reason cited above. The characters are wooden, and the philosophy sticks out, when the works are viewed as literature.

We are now in a position to ask whether this proffered analysis of profundity in music fulfills the conditions laid down previously for success. And on first reflection it does seem to do so. The first condition, it will be recalled, is that a work be about something. In the case of profound musical works, that condition is fulfilled, in the present analysis, in that such works are profound in virtue of their consummate craftsmanship, which, we are tempted to say, makes them "about" music itself: "about" the possibilities of musical sound.

The second enabling condition for profundity is that the work be about something profound, have a profound subject matter. And as musical sound appears to be, for many people, of abiding interest and supreme importance, that condition too seems to be satisfied by at least some musical works.

Finally, we said that the subject matter of a profound work must not only be profound but be treated in a way adequate to that profundity: must be treated in some artistically supreme and exemplary way. And that condition seems, indeed, to be embodied in Einstein's requirement that supreme musical craftsmanship not "smell of the lamp" but achieve the transparency of what he calls the "second naïveté" and in Schweitzer's observation that in such supreme musical craftsmanship as Bach's "we are no longer conscious of the art."

It would *seem*, then, that we do now have adequate rational justification for the ascription of profundity to some musical works, and that justification does seem to apply just where we want it to: to just those works which, in fact, musical experts and connoisseurs tend to call "profound" or its equivalent. But I underscore "seem" because the reader is likely to detect some sleight of hand here; and I think there are at least two reasons to be somewhat uncomfortable with this rather facile exercise.

One problem rests with the second condition for profundity: that the subject matter of a profound work be a profound subject matter. For we slipped rather easily—too easily, as it turns out—from "of abiding interest and importance" to "profound." The second condition is too weak if it takes as a sufficient condition for something's being a profound subject merely that it is of very great interest, even of great concern, to a large number of people. It omits a vital normative component. For profundity to obtain, we seem to require that something be not just of great concern but *worthy* of great concern, in some suitably strong sense of "worthy" (to be discussed in a moment). I dare say far more people are vitally concerned with and interested in the subject of baseball than are in the subject of determinism and freedom of the will or the problem of evil. Yet with all due respect to the national pastime, it is a *pastime;* we would hardly take it to be a more profound subject than human freedom—or a subject with pretensions to profundity at all—just because it commands great and intense interest among us, indeed greater and more intense interest, overall, than the alternative subject.

Now I say a suitably strong sense of "worthy" because there are, it would seem, subjects of abiding interest and concern to human beings, and justifiably so, that do not merit or receive the judgment "profound." Certainly, to take an example, proper nutrition is a subject of abiding interest and concern to human beings, and surely it is worthy of such abiding interest and concern. Yet we would hardly want to say that nutrition is a profound subject matter or works about nutrition, no matter how well brought off, profound works.[6]

Why is the nature of the universe (say) a profound subject and nutrition not? Not because nutrition is of no importance to us: it *is* of importance and worthy of our concern. And not, I think, because it is of "practical" rather than "theoretical" significance. For I dare say there are environmental issues, obviously "practical," that we would surely want to call "profound." I would think those practical issues which we call profound are just those which go to the moral heart of the human condition. A life without "Nature" in something like the form we now know it in does not measure up to our moral ideal of the good life for human beings; and environmental issues addressing that concern are, therefore, "profound." A life without proper vitamin supplements is not on that account morally bankrupt, desirable as proper nutrition might be; and if the study of nutrition goes no further—in particular, does not touch the vital center of our moral and metaphysical concerns—it surely is worthy of interest and concern but not profoundly so.

We have a pretty good idea about why such questions as freedom of the will and the problem of evil are of great concern to us. Knowing why makes clear to us why we feel justified in thinking of these as profound subjects of interest, whereas the collection and contemplation of baseball cards, no matter how intense and widespread the interest, would fail to be

---

[6] I owe this objection, as well as the accompanying example, to Christopher Peacocke.

seen as anything but trivial pursuits. The problem is that we—at least *I*—have no clear idea at all about why serious, well-educated, adult human beings should find pure musical sound of *such* abiding interest that we are moved to call the subject "profound." And without such understanding, I cannot see that we have any real rational justification for doing so. That is to say, I cannot see that we have, to paraphrase Bentham, any reason for thinking that music is better than pushpin or more worthy of our vital and enduring interest. I believe that it is, and my belief is intense, but the strength of my belief hardly counts as an argument.

Furthermore, it is not altogether clear whether the general strategy of construing musical sound as the subject of profound musical works is free of a vicious circularity?[7] For, it might be argued, the question whether musical sound is a profound subject matter cannot be answered without first answering the question whether there are any profound musical works. If musical sound just is the class of musical works, then for it to be a profound subject matter it must, one might insist, contain at least some profound musical works. Thus there being some profound musical works would be a necessary condition for musical sounds being a profound subject matter, and the circle would be closed. There are profound musical works only if musical sound is a profound subject matter; musical sound is a profound subject matter only if there are profound musical works.

The question of circularity, then, turns on the question whether it makes sense to think of musical sound as a profound subject matter independently of its containing profound musical works. And an answer, one way or the other, seems to me to be difficult to make out. If one can prise apart the question whether musical sound is a profound subject matter from the question whether there are profound musical works, then the project of understanding profound musical works as being profound (in part) in virtue of having a profound subject matter (namely, musical sound itself), although in an unsatisfactory state, may be so merely because it is temporarily incomplete, awaiting assurance that it fulfills the strengthened normative requirement of profundity. If one cannot so prise them apart, then the project is hopelessly compromised by the fatal logical flaw of circularity.

Which of these alternatives is correct I do not presently know. But even if it is the more favorable one, I must end here on a note of mystery and puzzlement. Those of us who cultivate a taste for the instrumental music of the West seem to find certain examples of it so enormously compelling and of such enduring interest that "profound" forces itself upon us as the only (and fully) appropriate term to describe them. Yet there seems to be no rational justification for our doing so. For even if the works we describe as profound have a subject matter, and that is debatable, the

[7] I am grateful to Christopher Peacocke and Kendall Walton for pressing me on this point.

only subject matter they can plausibly be thought to have, namely, musical sound itself, does not bear, at least on the face of it, any obvious mark of profundity, as do such subject matters as freedom of the will or the problem of evil, love and marriage or crime and punishment, and so forth: the subjects of "profound" literary works.

Now in saying that I have so far failed to find any rational justification for calling musical works profound, I do not want to be misunderstood as denying that I have rational grounds for thinking certain musical works great works of art. I am not using the word "profound" as synonymous with the word "great" or any other word like it. I think all but not only profound musical works are great musical works. And I think we do have rational grounds for thinking some musical works great and some greater than others. These are just the usual grounds for evaluations that abound in the music-critical literature. But I take the word "profound" as not simply a portmanteau evaluative epithet. I have taken it, when applied to music, as having the same implications as it would have when applied to literature or philosophy. In other words, I have taken it seriously. And in spite of the fact that there seems to me to be substantial agreement among enthusiasts about which musical works deserve the description "profound," I fail to see any rational justification for their deserving it. Yet, for certain works, I can find no other word as appropriate. Yes: the *Well-Tempered Clavier* and the late Beethoven quartets are great works of art. So also are Mozart's divertimenti for winds. But the former are something else, they are profound, and there's an end on it.

I find myself at present, then, unable to refrain from thinking that some musical works are profound yet unable, as well, to provide any rational grounds for my thinking it. So if you ask me, now, what my justification is for thinking the *Well-Tempered Clavier* profound, the only response that comes readily to mind is that notorious misquotation: "Play it again, Sam."

Musical Profundity Misplaced

Jerrold Levinson

Peter Kivy has addressed the issue of profundity in music in his usual careful and common-sense way, and has come up with a result that will not ruffle the feathers of those given to thinking of music as primarily structural and syntactical, nor alarm those—often the same folk—who are unsettled by any hint of mysticism in discussions of musical significance. He claims that music is profound when it is about the possibilities of musical sound, and displays or explores those possibilities with the utmost craftsmanship. This counts as profundity, according to him, first, because there is a subject of the music to which we can point (namely, music itself), second, because music is of abiding interest (and as he later adds, rightly so), and thirdly, because in such cases the subject—music and its possibilities—is so well treated. I do not think this view is at all adequate. We can see pretty clearly how Kivy was driven to it, however, since he has done us the favor of not covering his tracks. Let us go back and try to discover the wrong turning.

The profundity of music, it is often said, has something to do with its emotional or, perhaps more broadly, human content. Kivy briefly considers the suggestion that music's being expressive of dark emotions, in particular, might have something to do with its profundity. But he rejects this, and in principle anything along similar lines, on the grounds that music which is expressive of emotions is not thereby *about* emotions, and if not about them, then not possibly profound in virtue of that connection.

Kivy's reasons for eschewing any claim of "aboutness" are given in the penultimate chapter of his book *Music Alone*.[1] A work's expressive properties, he claims, are as deservedly considered musical as either its technical ones or its other aesthetic but non-expressive ones, and that where prominent in a successful piece of music, they contribute to structure just as other properties do; thus, they needn't be thought to be necessarily adverting to the human world outside the music.[2] Furthermore, if we were justified in taking notably sad music to be about sadness, we would be equally justified—which is absurd—in taking notably tranquil music to be about tranquility, or notably turbulent music to be about turbulence.

Taking the last point first, I would rather accept the supposedly absurd conclusion than give up any idea that much music is, in some sense, about emotional life. But frankly, it doesn't strike me as absurd. Notably tranquil music is a very paradigm of tranquility; we might very well use it to indicate to someone the essence of tranquility, or to deepen someone's

---

[1] Peter Kivy, *Music Alone* (Cornell University Press, 1990).

[2] Kivy goes further than this at one point in what I regard as a mistaken effort to assimilate expressive properties to structural or formal ones, strictly speaking: "Other expressive properties serve as structural properties in their own right." (p. 196). This seems an attempt to soothe and win over by newspeak the music analyst skeptical of the expressive dimension of music. To be sure, expressive properties are aesthetically and structurally relevant ones—unlike the location of the work's original manuscript, or the total number of quarter-notes it contains—but that alone doesn't make them structural in the sense Kivy is after. Expressive properties might themselves form a structure, and that structure might be formally related to the other structures of the work, but they are not themselves structural or formal in the way being a rondo, being monothematic, being cyclic, exhibiting throughout the proportions of the Golden Section, or involving the succession of keys G, F, A, etc. are. By analogy with this last one might say that involving a certain expressive sequence was a structural or formal property, but it still wouldn't follow that the individual expressions were structural properties.

appreciation of what tranquility was like. Is it wholly implausible that serving in such a capacity was part of a composer's motivation or intention in writing such music, which would seem to license our regarding the music as about the state it aims to be a paragon of? Anyway, I don't see that it is incumbent on the defender of certain music's aboutness in regard to certain extra-musical conditions to rely on or accept the principle generally that *any* piece of music is about *all* the extra-musical properties it may express. Rather, musical aboutness might be best defended on a case-by-case basis.

The first, more extensive observation that expressive qualities function musically and structurally, seems perfectly consistent with their also functioning, in some cases, to draw attention to emotional states themselves. Surely we can defend a loose notion of music's "aboutness" in regard to the emotions (if not one of strict exemplification, à la Goodman) despite Kivy's qualms. If musical works have expressive properties, if composers generally intend them to have such, if listeners generally expect them to have such, and if it is widely acknowledged that a considerable (though not the greatest) part of the interest in much music resides there, I don't see why we should be barred from saying that one of the things music as a whole is *about*, i.e. is concerned with, is emotional expression, and so by extension the realm of emotions expressed, nor from saying that some particular piece of music is partly *about*, i.e. concerned with, the emotions it reaches out to through its structure, when properly construed in context. In addition, if we consider that when music is expressive of emotional states, listeners who grasp that are often led to reflect, if obscurely, on such states—possibly through inhabiting them temporarily in imagination—and that this result must often be envisaged by the creators and transmitters of music, then it is hard to see what can be so wrong in allowing that some music is about emotional states and their musical expression—when it is often an express point of the music to bring such to the consciousness of listeners. There is no reason we should restrict our useful informal notion of *aboutness* to systematic or conventional relations of reference or denotation.

But I have a second reason for urging that there is no reason for Kivy to deprive himself of any help that music's aboutness in relation to the emotions might provide. Kivy is willing, when it comes to counterpoint and its implicit examination of melodic possibilities, to help himself to musical aboutness on no stronger, and possibly weaker, grounds than I have just appealed to above. If contrapuntal music can be about melodic possibilities which few are privy to, then surely much music—including contrapuntal music—can be about the emotional states it explores, with whose potential for doing so everyone is familiar. So I think Kivy has given us insufficient ground to exclude from among the possible bases of profundity in music the particular kind of expressive or psychological content a piece of music may carry.

I turn now to Kivy's second condition for profundity, that a work be about something of abiding interest or importance. Kivy thinks this satisfied by (some) contrapuntal music, since it is about music's possibilities of self-combination. To my mind this is not an adequate resting-place for the explanation. If music's possibilities of self-combination did no more than ground (virtually) unlimited diversion for the ears, then those possibilities would not have an *importance* sufficient to fill the bill, though the *interest* they provide might indeed be an abiding one. It is true that Kivy, at least at most junctures, requires only that such possibilities sustain one or the other—abiding interest or abiding importance—in order to anchor profundity. But here I just disagree. Lasting importance, not just perennial interest, is needed for something to make music profound in virtue of music's being about it. This difficulty is only partially ameliorated toward the end of Kivy's chapter, when he suggests that being *worthy* of abiding interest, and not just being abidingly interesting, is the property required. For consider chess: the possibilities of the game are of abiding interest, and are worthy of such, but they are not yet *important* in the way I think required to underpin profundity.[3]

But let us continue with contrapuntal music. Kivy says that what makes it a *candidate* for profundity is that it seems to reveal the "very possibilities of musical sound itself." To my mind, that by itself could not ground profundity, but rather only, as Kivy puts it, "fascination." I would hold, by contrast, that what makes intricate and yet apparently effortless counterpoint a potential basis on which musical profundity can rest is its ability to present an aural image of the transfiguration of conflict and complexity into something higher—an image of a state in which the imperfections of partial perspectives are transcended, where all differences are ultimately ironed out or, as we might aptly say, resolved. Kivy says Bach's counterpoint, in particular, is *in fact* often profound because it is technically able to explore the possibilities of its materials, whereas Kuhnau's, say, is not. But again, this stops too short, and confuses the scaffolding for the building. Bach's counterpoint is profound where Kuhnau's is not because of the kind of experience it provides, and the kind of vision into human and even metaphysical possibilities that it enables, not just the possibilities of structural or grammatical combination that it so masterfully, to be sure, exemplifies.

Broadening his formula at the end, Kivy says that supreme musical *craftsmanship*—whether contrapuntal or other in nature—is the common factor in all profound music. I will just note a danger of analyticity here: if a piece manages to be profound—understood in some independent way,

---

[3] If the example of chess is controversial here—for those who regard it as being profound in subject matter or implication—then I think the point could be made as well with reference to *weather patterns:* these too are of abiding interest and worthy of same, but hardly capable of profundity.

or just preanalytically—then, naturally, we must say that the craftsman-ship in it—the musical means marshalled to create it—is supreme. To put this worry a bit differently, how do we determine, when push comes to shove, whether a piece displays supreme musical craftsmanship, if we are not going to restrict that in advance to the successful employment of such and such enumerated musical techniques? I suspect we will not be able to do this in at least some cases without making an *independent* assessment of the profundity—or other achievement—of a piece of music, and then re-flecting back on, and belatedly admiring, the means that somehow brought that about. If this is right, then the essence of musical profundity is, of course, still to seek.

On Kivy's reductive view of musical profundity, the semantic con-nection between "profound" and "deep" seems to have been, so to speak, buried. I believe that is some indication of what is missing in his account.

So, finally, what might it plausibly mean to say that a piece of instru-mental music was profound, beyond the rather self-regarding sense that Kivy has offered us? The following, it seems, are still worth considering: 1) it explores the emotional or psychic realm in a more insightful or eye-opening way than most music;[4] 2) it epitomizes or alludes to more inter-esting or complex extra-musical modes of growth and development than most music, and it gives us a vicarious experience of such modes;[5] 3) it strikes us as touching, in some fashion or other, on the most fundamental and pressing aspects of human existence—e.g. death, fate, the inexorabil-ity of time, the space between aspiration and attainment.[6] Of course these are just suggestions, brief promissory notes which only a more extensive analysis could redeem. But at least they do not prematurely sell the prob-lem short.

On the other hand, and not necessarily incompatible with the tenta-tive program above, profundity in music is perhaps best formulated in terms of the kind of experience that a sensitive and adequately back-grounded listener has of a piece termed profound. Perhaps the experi-encer of a profound piece of music centrally has the impression of having been *shown or revealed* something particular about how life is, or goes, or might be, something previously undisclosed to him. Of course it might turn out to be "particular" in the intransitive sense described by Wittgenstein, so that to the query "*what* has been revealed to you?," the listener can only appeal back to the experience. But even if that be the

---

[4] See, for example, Susanne Langer, *Philosophy In A New Key* (Harvard University Press, 1942), and J.W.N. Sullivan, *Beethoven: His Spiritual Development* (Vintage, 1924).

[5] See Monroe Beardsley, "Understanding Music" in *On Criticizing Music*, ed. K. Price (Johns Hopkins University Press, 1981).

[6] See, for example, Arthur Schopenhauer, *The World As Will And Representation*, Vol. II, ed. and trans. E.F.J. Payne (Dover Publications, 1969) or Leonard Bernstein, *The Unanswered Question* (Cambridge: Harvard University Press, 1984).

case, there is more for such a listener in certain music than the kinetic pleasure of following the music's unfolding structure—perhaps the core reward of music listening; more than the pleasure of cognizing the music's representational and expressive dimension, or even partaking in the latter imaginatively; and more, even, than being profoundly—that is to say, strongly—moved by the music and its various excellences. There is, in addition, an impression of knowledge—of having *seen*. Known or seen *what*? Again one hesitates to pass beyond reiterating that it is something about how life is, or goes, or might be. But it would be equally foolish to deny outright that one is vouchsafed some sort of vision by certain music: Mahler's, Scriabin's, late Beethoven's, late Brahms'—and of course, much of Bach's. The sense of such a vision, whether or not its content can be elucidated propositionally or its objective validity sustained, is the *sine qua non* of music that I, at least, am willing to call profound.

Profundity in Music

Aaron Ridley

Peter Kivy has recently attempted to explain how a piece of music can be profound, although with results which he himself appears to think unsatisfactory.[1] And so they are. But in raising the question he has done us a service, and in trying to answer it, he has drawn our attention to an area which cries out for exploration. In what follows, I will attempt to elucidate two senses in which a piece of music can be described as profound (there are other ways, to be sure—but I believe that the ways explored here are central ones). I won't consider objections to what I am saying as I go along—I'll save all of those for the final section: so bear with me. First, though, to Kivy.

I

In my view, Kivy goes wrong at the very beginning. He opens with a sketch of profundity which is at once partial and monolithic, and which contributes directly to the air of unreality surrounding his eventual conclusion: namely, that music might be profound in virtue of being profound about *itself*. To be profound, he says, a thing must be *about* something profound, and must be about it in a manner *adequate* to its profundity. Which of course is going to make music, which isn't much

---

[1] "The Profundity of Music," in Kivy's *Music Alone* (Ithaca: Cornell University Press, 1990), reprinted in this book.

good at being about things, an outsider from the start. But far too much has been conflated in this sketch, and even more left out.

Take an example. Suppose that Natasha believes profoundly in a religion. It is clearly her belief which is being described as profound. Her belief is *about* something (more naturally, we would say "in" something); that something is a religion, so we would assume it to have the kind of moral and metaphysical content which religions standardly have, and which Kivy suggests are the hallmarks of properly profound subject matter.[2] But what can we say about the "adequacy" of her belief to the profundity of its subject? The answer is, nothing. For the appeal to "adequacy" is unhelpful in at least two ways. First, it invites a regress: The profundity of one thing (e.g., of a belief) is made conditional upon its adequacy to something else (the profundity of its subject matter), in which case the profundity of the subject matter ought itself to be conditional upon the subject matter's adequacy to the profundity of some third thing, and so on. And second, the demand for "adequacy" presumably requires that a thing, for instance a belief, have some property (apart from profundity) *relevant* to the profundity of what it's about. But its possession of that property will establish only that the belief is a belief of a certain kind, and not that it is a profound belief. So the appeal to adequacy leads us nowhere, and we should conclude accordingly that it is a mistake to make the profundity of one thing dependent on the profundity of something else, or on the first thing's measuring up in some way to the profundity of the second. For neither condition is necessary.

Let us return to Natasha. Her profound belief is a religious belief. But suppose now that the religion she adheres to is devoid of any but the most trivial metaphysical and moral commitments; indeed suppose it an utterly trivial religion. Would this mean that her belief could not, after all, be profound? Of course it wouldn't. It might make it hard to understand why she holds the belief as she does. But because profundity is a quality of the *belief*—and not, as Kivy would have it, a quality of the subject matter which the belief somehow inherits by being adequate *to* it—the apparent triviality of what the belief is about is irrelevant to the ascription of profundity to the belief itself. One can believe profoundly in all kinds of shallow nonsense, just as one can believe casually in the deepest of truths.

So what is it for a belief to be profound? What, if not its subject matter, would justify us in describing Natasha's belief as profound? In one sense, I think this question is rather easy to answer (another sense will be detailed in Section IV, together with objections to what I am just about to say). We can answer the question by looking at what would lead us to say that a belief was *not* profound. We would be likely, for instance, to doubt that Natasha's belief was profound if we suspected that she might drop it at any minute for something different; or if we saw that she did not take at

[2] Ibid, p. 245.

all seriously whatever rituals or devotions her religion might enjoin; or if she never acted on such moral recommendations as her religion might make; or if she held other beliefs which she believed to be incompatible with her religious belief, without seeming much bothered by the fact; or, in short, if her religious belief appeared to have no real *significance* for her life. A profound belief, then, must be one which gives structure to a person's other beliefs, which informs her actions and enters into how she leads her life. It is a belief held in a certain *way*.

The profound nature of a belief can in fact be understood in much the same fashion as Quine claims that the analytic nature of a judgment can be understood.[3] Quine pictures judgments as forming a kind of net or web of interrelated propositions, in which some judgments are more centrally placed than others—more deeply enmeshed in the interrelations constituting the web. An analytic judgment is one which occupies a position close to the center of the web, and is deeply implicated in the web of judgments as a whole. As such, an analytic judgment is one which it would be very difficult (although not impossible) to give up. Abandoning such a judgment would require a restructuring of the entire web.

Whatever its merits for describing analytic judgments, Quine's model works well for the kind of profound belief which we have been talking about. A profound belief, on this account, will be a belief which ties in to a large number of other beliefs, such that were the belief to be given up it would necessitate the abandonment or modification of all those other beliefs to which it is connected. A casual or shallow belief, by contrast, will occupy a position on the periphery of a person's mental life, and will be subject to abandonment without causing much, if any, disruption to the web as a whole. This is why it would be not merely surprising to find one had to give up a profound belief, but also shocking, disorienting, and even painful. One has an *investment* in beliefs of this kind, and the degree of one's investment is registered by the quantity of havoc that abandoning them would cause among the rest of one's mental life (some of which will itself be profound), and by the sheer cognitive inconvenience which one would suffer in attempting to reconstitute the web along other lines, incorporating beliefs different from, and incompatible with, those to which one had grown accustomed. A profound belief, then, isn't necessarily a belief about a certain sort of thing (for example, a profound thing); it is a belief which stands in a certain sort of relation—a *structuring* relation—to other aspects of one's mental life.

II

So where does this get us? Certainly we seem to have made little enough progress with the question of profound *music.* Indeed, we might even

---

[3] "Two Dogmas of Empiricism," in Quine, *From a Logical Point of View* (Cambridge: Harvard University Press, 1956).

seem to have gone backward. For it would surely be a fearsome task, and probably a thankless one too, to try to show that music could somehow have, or *be,* a belief, profound or otherwise. I, for one, would go to considerable lengths to avoid the job. But happily it doesn't have to be done.

For we are actually in quite a good position. Not only can we now see that a thing doesn't need to be about something profound in order to be profound itself; we ought also to be able to see that a thing needn't be about *anything at all* in order to be profound. Beliefs, to be sure, are always about something. But beliefs are not the only kind of psychological trait capable of standing in the right sort of (structuring) relation to our *other* psychological traits. Suppose, for instance, that Natasha is astonishingly *gullible.* Gullibility is a disposition. It means that one hàs a propensity to fall for nonsense about all kinds of things. But the disposition is not itself about anything; there is no particular piece of nonsense which one must be gullible *about* if one is to count as gullible. Now imagine that Natasha is capable of being persuaded of just about anything; that most of her actions are determined by beliefs far less critically acquired than they might have been; that she is continually surprised to learn that what she has just taken for gospel is really baloney; that her whole life is structured, at every level, by her tendency too willingly to believe whatever she is told. Clearly, and (I take it) uncontroversially, Natasha is profoundly gullible. If so, then there is nothing necessarily referential or intentional about profundity; something can be profound, but about nothing. This opens the door to any mental item, trait of character, habitual attitude, or propensity, which is capable of structuring significant aspects, or simply significant quantities, of a person's life. Thus one might be profoundly cheerful, profoundly mean, profoundly suspicious, profoundly courageous, and so on. And in each case it can be true of one's cheerfulness, meanness, courage, etc., that it is *profound.* This accords well with common usage, and is also quite unmysterious.

In the next section such thoughts will prove useful in addressing one kind of *musical* profundity. But we should notice first that the present account is not limited to the profundity of psychological or behavioral things. For in claiming that a defining feature of the profound lies in the structuring role which it plays in the context of some wider system, the account is limited only to such systems as are capable of being so structured, and it is clear that a good number of those are neither psychological nor behavioral. Thus, a profound economic indicator will be one which sits at or near the center of a web of economic variables; a profound alteration in an ecosystem will be one which determines the subsequent nature and development of the ecosystem in all its aspects; and so on. This, I think, allows one to appreciate rather directly why Kivy's musical conclusions have that air of unreality about them which I mentioned earlier. He suggests that certain contrapuntal music might be called profound because it is in some sense about (and adequately about) the possibilities inherent in music, which are themselves profound. Now this might very well be true. But how much simpler to say that the music is *profoundly contrapuntal*—that every aspect of the music is informed, controlled, and given shape by the counterpoint which lies at its heart! It seems to me that this is a vastly more natural way of speaking. And it has the added advantage of making attributions of profundity open to rational disagreement. I can't imagine what you'd have to show in order to establish that a piece *wasn't* profound in Kivy's sense (i.e., that it wasn't *actually* about the profound possibilities inherent in music, or if it was that it wasn't adequately so), whereas it is clear what you'd have to show on the present account—namely, that the music was not in fact informed in all its aspects by counterpoint. This might not always be easy to do in practice, but it is certainly possible in principle.

III

So Kivy's kind of profound music—essentially, music which is informed by profound *musicianship*—can be captured tolerably well by the account advanced so far. But I am primarily interested in another kind of profound music: music which is profound in virtue of its *expressive* properties.[4]

Now here, if we are to get the emphasis right, we shall have to tread carefully. It might, for example, appear tempting to claim that a piece of music will be, say, profoundly cheerful if it is frequently or exclusively expressive of cheerfulness.[5] But there is a difference between being profoundly cheerful and being merely regularly or relentlessly cheerful. Consider Natasha again (after another of her metamorphoses). Suppose now that—unencumbered by too much religion or gullibility—she leads an immensely agreeable life, surrounded on all sides by engaging companions and diversions, with never a cloud in her sky. She is almost always cheerful. Now this would be quite insufficient to establish that her cheerfulness was profound. We would want to see how she responded to misfortune, for example, or how she would be if she were surrounded by drudges, pedants, and bores. If her responses seemed *still* to be unchanged, or to be suffused by a kind of underlying cheerfulness, which gave form to each of her passing feelings, then—and only then—would we be warranted in concluding that her cheerfulness was profound. For cheerfulness would now be a *key* to Natasha's character, rather than merely an accidental product of her circumstances. We could attempt to

---

[4] This kind of profundity is one of those suggested by Jerrold Levinson in his response to Kivy. See Levinson, "Musical Profundity Misplaced," *Journal of Aesthetics and Art Criticism,* 1992, reprinted in this book.

[5] A temptation succumbed to, I think, by David White, in "Toward a Theory of Profundity in Music," *Journal of Aesthetics and Art Criticism,* 1992. See especially his discussion of the sadness of Beethoven's Quartet op. 131 (pp. 31–32).

understand and to interpret Natasha as a personality *structured* by her profoundly cheerful nature, rather than as merely happening to be having a reasonably agreeable time of things. What this means for the musical case is that we shall have to be careful not to confound the mere preponderance of some expressive quality with the kind of quality which underlies, and breathes life into, the various expressive episodes which the music contains. It is only the second kind of quality which will have any claim to be described as profound. Consider two examples.

Beethoven's Fifth Symphony is rather famously associated with defiance. But on the surface (as we might say) it is only intermittently expressive of defiance in a direct way: The expressive character of its surface is—variously—turbulent, rumbustious, jolly, laconic, triumphant, anguished, benign, and, from time to time, defiant. Yet the defiance of the piece seems to permeate its other expressive qualities, so that underlying the various episodes of laconic good humor, for instance, is always a sense that the latter quality is maintained either against the odds, or only as a respite from the chief business of outfacing the world. The quality of defiance, in other words, appears to structure the expressive content of the symphony as a whole—to be the interpretative key to understanding the affective terrain which the work, in all its various aspects, inhabits. Which of course means that, in my view, Beethoven's Fifth Symphony is profoundly defiant—that the expressive quality of defiance is a profound quality of the work. But compare this with the prevailing expressive quality of, for instance, Scarlatti's B-flat Major Sonata K.529 (a delightful piece). Its principal thematic idea, which is lighthearted and cheerful, alternates with a section of very slightly darker music, whose modest shadow looms briefly, before being deftly dispelled. Its musicianship aside, nothing in this sonata invites description as profound. Its cheeriness lies on the surface only, for although that quality is almost constantly in evidence, it does not relate to any other qualities which—taken collectively—could, without strain, be regarded as a *system* of any kind. Scarlatti's sonata simply *has* no underlying expressive quality, for there is nothing which such a quality might be heard to underlie or to structure. Thus it cannot be expressively profound. These examples ought to indicate somewhat more clearly the kind of distinction I mean to draw between music which is expressive in a profound way, and music which is—merely—frequently or exclusively expressive of some particular feeling.

Now suppose it is *Natasha* who is profoundly defiant, in a way analogous to that in which Beethoven's Fifth is defiant. We could simply describe her as profoundly defiant, and leave it at that. Or we could, if we wished, say more. For although her defiance is not *about* anything in particular, it certainly does presuppose an attitude *toward* things in general. One would not be likely, in any specific case, to respond defiantly to an event which one regarded as amenable or devoid of threat, or to an event which one thought threatening but altogether impossible to outface. There is, in other words, a description—perhaps "the threatening but out-faceable"—which one has to perceive an event as fitting if one is to re-spond to it defiantly. This is so for particular episodes of defiance. But Natasha's defiance is of a profound kind. There is nothing in particular which she perceives as threatening but outfaceable—rather, she has a dis-position to regard things in general as fitting that description. She has, one might say, a distinctive attitude toward the world which is intimated through the profoundly defiant quality of her character. Thus, in describ-ing Natasha as profoundly defiant, we at the same time impute to her a distinctive outlook on the world, or, more grandly, a *Weltanschauung* (which she herself may be only imperfectly aware of having). And I think that this would be true, *mutatis mutandis,* were *any* profound characteristic of a psychological kind to be attributed to her.

Something similar is also true when such a characteristic is attributed to a piece of music. I am not suggesting, of course, that the music literally *has* an outlook of some kind, or that it has some particular way of viewing the world. That would be as futile as trying to show that pieces of music can hold, or be, beliefs. But I am suggesting that, in experiencing certain pieces of music intently, and responsively, and so coming to grasp their profoundly expressive qualities, we at the same time gain an intimation of the outlook on the world implicit *in* those qualities: so that, for example, in grasping the profoundly defiant character of Beethoven's Fifth Symphony we gain an intimation of what it would be to have a defiant outlook on the world, of what it would be to view the world as threaten-ing but outfaceable. Indeed, if our experience of the music is especially in-volved, we may even come for a time to share that outlook, to enter imag-inatively into the attitude implicit in the music's profoundest qualities. This, I think, is why one writer on music can say:

> There are some works, of which I take *Tristan* to be, probably, the supreme example, though the *St. Matthew Passion* runs it a close second, if it doesn't equal it, of which it is a prerequisite that one suspends disbe-lief, not in this or that aspect of the work, nor in the verisimilitude of events in the work, but in the ethos which the work embodies and pro-mulgates. This means that subsequent reflection, in so far as it involves rejection or critique of the work's ethical or metaphysical dimensions, also involves critique of one's reactions to them; but nonetheless it is im-portant that one should have had those dubious feelings and near-be-liefs.[6]

The responses described in this passage reflect rather fully, I believe, the kind of engagement with music which I have suggested is central to un-

---

[6] Michael Tanner, "The Total Work of Art," in Burbidge and Sutton, eds., *The Wagner Companion* (London: Faber, 1979), p. 182.

derstanding the expressive qualities of certain musical works as *profound*. Those qualities underlie and give structure to the music's surface expressive features, and *in* those qualities are implicit certain attitudes, or ways of regarding the world, which we grasp as we come to grasp the qualities themselves as profound.

IV

Those, then, are the bones of the account that I want to give of music which is profound in virtue of its expressive properties. In this last section I will try to put a little flesh on those bones by considering an objection to what I have said—an objection which has no doubt suggested itself to everyone, and which cannot be put off any longer.

Surely, it will be objected, the account given here simply *ignores* what is most interesting about profundity, musical or otherwise. It simply ignores the kind of metaphysical or moral content characteristic of the profound—the kind of content which Peter Kivy attempts to capture when he insists that profound things must be *about* "something of abiding interest or importance to human beings."[7] Indeed, the present essay gives only an adverbial account of profundity; to be profound, it claims, is merely to be implicated in a system of some kind in a certain way. Thus the essential link with *evaluation* has been severed. When we call something profound, after all, we are surely—among other things—meaning to commend it, meaning to indicate that we think it worthy of more than ordinary regard. But the adverbial account carries with it no such connotation. Natasha's gullibility is described as "profound," but no one would think of commending her gullibility. And the fact that some factor might play a pivotal, structuring role in a system of the uttermost triviality would hardly qualify it for the kind of regard which we expect profundity to warrant. No. When we say that someone expresses a profound view, we mean not that he or she holds the view in a particular way, nor that the view stands in a "structuring" relation to that person's other views and beliefs, but that the view itself—regardless of who holds it, or how—is peculiarly deep, or especially worthy of contemplation and reflection. *That* is what an account of profundity ought to be explaining—and that is what the present account fails so much as to address. It will also be objected that the present account fails to make the right kind of sense of *musical* profundity. For certain music which might be regarded as flawed would, on the present account, qualify as profound, and qualify for precisely the reasons which might be given for *objecting* to the music. Ernst Bloch, for instance, comments as follows on Strauss's *Elektra:* "A soul is lacking, however lyrical-erotic the prevalent mood. . . . In its deepest passages Strauss'

---

[7] Kivy, op. cit., p. 245.

music wears at the best the melancholy expression of a brilliant hollow-ness."[8] Clearly Bloch is not intending to praise Strauss's music. But on the account given here, the "brilliant hollowness" which disturbs Bloch would almost certainly count as a profound quality of *Elektra*. But to at-tribute profundity of this kind to a piece of music—neither commending it, nor even suggesting that it is worth hearing—is surely to miss some-thing rather important about what is profound about profound pieces of music.

This objection raises some valid concerns. Yet I think that what is valid about them tends to strengthen rather than to undermine the posi-tion I've been arguing for. To begin with, let me bite a couple of bullets. It still seems to me appropriate to call Natasha's gullibility profound, and—assuming that Bloch's characterization of Strauss's music is right—I would indeed claim that the "brilliant hollowness" of *Elektra* was a pro-found quality of it. But—and this is the important point—biting *those* bul-lets doesn't oblige me to chew my way through an entire ammo-dump; in particular, it doesn't commit me to denying the connection between pro-fundity and value, or between profundity and worthiness of regard.

Quite the reverse, in fact. If you're *interested* in Natasha, then her pro-foundly gullible quality will strike you, without doubt, as worthy of re-gard (of reflection, of contemplation), because it will strike you as *valuable* in your efforts to *understand* her. If you're wholly indifferent to Natasha, on the other hand, and have not the least desire to understand her, then, to be sure, you won't find much in her gullibility to get excited about: but nor, in that case, will you be in a position to *appreciate* it *as* profound. The appreciation of a thing's profundity both depends upon, and pays divi-dends for, one's interest in, and one's desire to understand, the system in which the thing is profoundly implicated—the "system" in this case being Natasha's personality. And similarly with the Strauss example: If I'm gen-uinely interested in *Elektra,* and really do want to understand it, or what's off-putting about it, then I may well be glad to recognize (with Bloch's help) just how profoundly hollow it is. Appreciating its "brilliant hollow-ness" might unlock for me the (soulless!) heart of the music's expressive world. But my recognition of *Elektra*'s hollowness as profound is condi-tional upon my desire to understand *Elektra,* and the value which that recognition has for me lies in the understanding of *Elektra* which it yields. I suggest, then, that the link between profundity and value, or between profundity and worthiness of regard, is not only not severed in my ac-count, but is in fact central to it.

The objection also charges that my explication of someone's holding a profound view only relates that view to the other views and beliefs which the person holds; it says nothing about the profundity of the view itself,

---

[8] *Essays on the Philosophy of Music* (Cambridge: Cambridge University Press, 1985), p. 38.

however held or by whom. But that is a charge which derives from the kind of conflation which I suggested that Kivy's account was guilty of at the beginning. For there is indeed a difference between the profundity of the *content,* or subject matter, of a view, and the profundity of the role played by the view in the life of the person who holds it, and it is no criticism to claim that an account of the latter fails at the same time to account for the former. These are separate issues and should be treated separately. But of course the account defended here is *eminently* capable of addressing the (allegedly neglected and more important) issue of the profundity of a view's content, in its turn. For what do we mean when we say that someone's view, however held, is a profound one? We mean, surely, that the view occupies a central, structuring position in a web of concerns which is, to us, of great interest and importance; and that our attempts to make sense of those concerns, and of their interrelations, will be facilitated by our appreciation of the profundity of the view. If we think that someone has a profound view about the meaning of life, for instance, or about the nature of the world, then we presumably think that his or her view is, or could be, pivotal to explaining or to grasping the essential nature of life or of the world. The present account makes sense of this kind of profundity in exactly the way it makes sense of the profundity of the role played by a view in someone's life. In both cases profundity is explained as the structuring property which something has within a system of which it is a part.

Now this conclusion—or clarification—has an interesting consequence for musical profundity. The defiance which I argued earlier to be a profound quality of Beethoven's Fifth Symphony, for example, is a quality possessing the musical equivalent or the first kind of profundity—defiance plays a structuring role within the work, and is interesting and valuable for that, at least to anyone with a desire to understand Beethoven's Fifth Symphony. Call this kind of profundity "work-profundity." But the attitude toward the world which I claimed was implicit in that quality—an attitude for which the world falls under the description "threatening but outfaceable"—is of course a candidate for having the second kind of profundity attributed to it (call this second kind "world-profundity"). For such an attitude, or rather, the unique shade of such an attitude, as intimated through the unique shade of defiance with which the symphony is suffused, might plausibly be regarded by someone as a principle about which to organize, or with which to give *structure* to, certain of his or her moral and metaphysical perplexities. The attitude contains one possible answer to the metaphysical question, What is the world really like? (Answer: threatening.) And one possible answer to the moral question, How ought one to regard such a world? (Answer: as something to be outfaced.) Probably the attitude implicit in Beethoven's Fifth (whose *precise* shade is of course only to be found there) could only be taken thus by a listener whose perplexities and character were of a particular kind.

But the point is that music which has a quality which is work-profound—and, of course, *only* such music—may also have a quality which is world-profound, in virtue of the role which the attitude implicit in the music may play in giving sense to someone's experience of the world; and when it does have world-profundity, it is exactly the same quality which is responsible for this as is responsible for its possession of work-profundity. The defiance which profoundly structures the expressive world of Beethoven's Fifth Symphony is also, when grasped as an attitude, that to which a structuring role is assigned amongst the moral and metaphysical perplexities of someone who regards the attitude as profound. Of course, the temptation to regard such an attitude as profound will *only* arise for someone who has the appropriate perplexities. But that is just to underline the connection between profundity (as I have explicated it), interest, and worthiness of regard, or value.

I believe that these reflections allow us to go a good way toward accounting for the attribution of profundity to the pieces of music which Kivy and others take as paradigmatically profound—Beethoven's late quartets. That they exhibit profound musicianship (a variety of profundity treated in Section II) I think no one will deny. But this by itself is inadequate to account for their paradigmatic status. What they owe *that* to, I surmise, is something like the following: In listening intently, with complete absorption, to the C sharp Minor Quartet one gains the impression (as perhaps from no other music, except the quartets in B flat and A minor) of a profoundly expressive quality which is forever eluding one's grasp, by a whisker, like a magical word on the tip of one's tongue. And to the *Weltanschauung* implicit in it, of which one can catch only glimpses, elusive hints, one attributes a profundity commensurate with its refusal finally to yield itself up. There is a sense that if one could but *grasp* that attitude, *that* view of the world (as for fleeting instants one believes, almost, that one has), then the question of how one should *be* in the world would be, if not resolved, at least rendered less unanswerable. It is the tantalizing, all-but, nature of the quartets' profundity which instates them as paradigms, and the sense of forever coming close which dramatizes the searching essential to an engagement with them. That search (and the hope it presupposes) is at the heart of the experience of the profound: It is the search for understanding, for some principle of organization, for some structure which will give sense to even the most inchoate of our concerns. And the account offered here, I suggest, of profundity in music (and in general) provides the beginnings of an explanation of why and how that might be.[9]

---

[9] I would like to thank Jerrold Levinson and Alex Neill for their comments on an earlier version of this paper.

SUGGESTIONS FOR FURTHER READING

Budd, Malcolm. *Music and the Emotions*. London: Routledge and Kegan Paul, 1985. (See especially Chapter 5 for a discussion of Schopenhauer's views about music.)

Godwin, Joscelyn, ed. *Music, Mysticism and Magic*. New York: Routledge and Kegan Paul, 1986.

Goldman, Alan. "The Value of Music." *Journal of Aesthetics and Art Criticism* 50 (1992): 35–44.

Kerman, Joseph. "Analysis, Theory and New Music." In his *Contemplating Music: Challenges and Musicology*. Cambridge: Harvard University Press, 1985.

Meynell, Hugo. *The Nature of Aesthetic Value*. London: Macmillan, 1986. Chapter 5.

Schopenhauer, Arthur. *The World as Will and Representation*. Trans. by E. F. J. Payne. New York: Dover, 1969. Vol. I. See especially pp. 255–67.

Walton, Kendall L. "What Is Abstract about the Art of Music?" *Journal of Aesthetics and Art Criticism* 46 (1988): 351–64.

White, David A. "Toward a Theory of Profundity in Music." *Journal of Aesthetics and Art Criticism* 50 (1992): 23–33. (This essay includes a discussion of the piece by Kivy reprinted in this section.)

On understanding music:

Budd, Malcolm. "Understanding Music." *Proceedings of the Aristotelian Society*, Supplementary Vol. 59 (1985): 233–48.

Kivy, Peter. *Music Alone: Philosophical Reflections on the Purely Musical Experience*. Ithaca: Cornell University Press, 1990. (Chapters 4–7 are especially useful.)

Kraut, Robert. "Perceiving the Music Correctly." In *The Interpretation of Music*, ed. by Michael Krausz. Oxford: Oxford University Press, 1993.

Levinson, Jerrold. "Musical Literacy." *Journal of Aesthetic Eduction* 24 (1990): 17–30.

Meyer, Leonard. *Emotion and Meaning in Music*. Chicago: Chicago University Press, 1956.

Ridley, Aaron. "Bleeding Chunks: Some Remarks about Musical Understanding." *Journal of Aesthetics and Art Criticism* 51 (1993): 589–96.

Scruton, Roger. *The Aesthetic Understanding*. London: Methuen, 1983. (Chapter 8 is especially useful; Chapters 2–7 are also about music.)

Scruton, Roger. "Notes on the Meaning of Music." In *The Interpretation of Music*, ed. by Michael Krausz. Oxford: Oxford University Press, 1993.

Tanner, Michael. "Understanding Music." *Proceedings of the Aristotelian Society*, Supplementary Vol. 59 (1985): 215–32.

10

FEMINISM AND AESTHETICS

Not that [the fifth century B.C. Greek sculpture] the Esquiline Venus represents an evolved notion of feminine beauty. She is short and square, with high pelvis and small breasts, far apart, a stocky little peasant such as might be found still in any Mediterranean village. . . . But she is solidly desirable, compact, proportionate; and in fact her proportions have been calculated on a simple mathematical scale. The unit of measurement is her head. She is seven heads tall; there is the length of one head between her breasts, one from breast to navel, and one from the navel to the division of the legs. . . . [T]he sculptor has discovered what we may call the plastic essentials of the feminine body.

—Kenneth Clark, *The Nude*, pp. 67–68

Yesterday we went to a show of the classical nude in marble form. It was nice to see some women looking so cool and neutral in the heat. They weren't quite in the altogether, though, these nudes, having been figleafed by a recent hand. It's ridiculous, said Martina, the tiny wraps and sprigs they've added on. Oh I don't know, I said: don't be too hasty—it's good to leave a little something to the imagination. She didn't agree. In my view, of course, the chicks would have looked even better if they'd added stockings and garter belts, G-strings and ankle-strapped shoes: but that's aesthetics for you. Tomorrow we go to the big new show by Monet or Manet or Money or some such guy.

—Martin Amis, *Money*, p. 327

In the average European oil painting of the nude the principal protagonist is never painted. He is the spectator in front of the picture and he is presumed to be a man. Everything is addressed to him. Everything must appear to be the result of his being there. It is for him that the figures have assumed their nudity. But he, by definition, is a stranger—with his clothes still on. . . .

In the art-form of the European nude the painters and spectator-owners were usually men and the persons treated as objects, usually women. This unequal relationship is so deeply embedded in our culture that it still structures the consciousness of many women. They do to themselves what men do to them. They survey, like men, their own femininity. . . .

[T]he essential way of seeing women, the essential use to which their images are put, has not changed. Women are depicted in a quite different way from men—not because the feminine is different from the masculine—but because the "ideal" spectator is always assumed to be male and the image of the woman is designed to flatter him. If you have any doubt that this is so, make the following experiment. Choose . . . an image of a traditional nude. Transform the woman into a man. Either in your mind's eye or by drawing on the reproduction. Then notice the violence which that transformation does. Not to the image, but to the assumptions of a likely viewer.

—John Berger, *Ways of Seeing*, pp. 54, 63, 64

INTRODUCTION

Throughout the history of aesthetics, and particularly of Anglo-American aesthetics, there has been a strong tendency to ignore, marginalize, deny, or condemn any connection between works of art and politics. It has often been felt that to acknowledge such connections would be to undermine the essential purity of art. It would be to surrender art to political interests, to a realm of experience in which concern for qualities such as beauty or craftsmanship would inevitably be lost. Above all, it would be to weaken drastically the assumption, central to much traditional aesthetics, that *genuine* works of art stand apart from the currents of ideology—that genuine works of art speak to and for humankind as a whole, to persons of every condition, in every time and place. The capacity of art to be universal, then, its capacity to speak to and for all of us, has been thought to depend upon the segregation of art from politics. And aestheticians have tended to assume, or to enforce, that segregation accordingly. For example, to classify a piece of would-be art as "propaganda" has traditionally been to condemn it, to suggest that in getting its hands dirty in the alien world of politics the work has forfeited its claim to be taken seriously as *art*. Where aesthetic intentions have been subordinated to political ones, aestheticians have been swift to object. The presuppositions, the theories, the very methods of aesthetics combine to emphasize the transcendence of art over the worldly and mundane. Aesthetics, as it has traditionally been conceived, is the apolitical science *par excellence*.

But inevitably, in a century which has seen the expansion of political analysis into almost every aspect of life, this traditional conception of aesthetics has increasingly been interpreted as ideologically motivated. The self-image of aesthetics as the apolitical study of a body of works which stand above and beyond politics has been challenged. The very denial of political content has been construed as a political, and a very conservative, stance. It is no longer possible simply to *assume* that aesthetics can or should be apolitical, any more than it is still possible to assume that the works of art which it studies are without political implications. Aesthetics has been politicized, and a variety of ideological perspectives now claim the right to pose *openly* political questions about the arts—questions of a kind which, it is argued, were previously excluded by the *covertly* political program embodied in aesthetics as it has traditionally been understood. Aesthetics now finds itself facing serious and unfamiliar challenges to its assumptions, its methods, and even its legitimacy.

Some of the most interesting of these challenges have come from feminist thinkers, and one of their central charges—briefly—is this. Most of the art considered "great" has been created by men, or has been created within a culture dominated by men. Most of that "great" art reflects, not a *human* view of the world, or a universal view, but an identifiably masculine view, which embodies and promotes a particular set of attitudes toward women. Feminist critics have argued that it does this at a number of levels. For example, in its manner of portraying women (for instance, as mother or as whore) art reinforces the cultural assumption that women derive their roles from men, or that the role of the "second sex" requires masculine validation. And at a deeper, more insidious level, art employs conventions (for instance, narrative conventions) whose apparent innocence masks an attempt to claim a monopoly on objectivity, on the power to "tell it like it is." As a result, the male-dominated view of the world, including its view of women, unjustifiably acquires the air of natural truth. All the time, of course, while this has been going on, aestheticians (usually male) have stood on the sidelines and cheered. They have insisted on the separation of art from ideology, and in doing so they have endorsed the pretensions to universality of the masculine view of women and the world which is embodied in the "great" works of art. Aesthetics, feminist critics argue, stands in need of a radical overhaul.

These charges are among those discussed by Mary Devereaux in the first reading of this section, as she expounds and explores the feminist challenge to aesthetics. She does not conclude that "all traditional aesthetics is useless." But she does suggest that feminism points up a "cognitive dissonance which marks the current situation in aesthetics," and which deserves our attention. She goes on to describe various aspects of that dissonance, and to outline some of the changes which might be made in order to resolve it, both in the practice of philosophical aesthetics and in the production of new works of art.

Devereaux suggests that we need to ask "how far the old model of aesthetics and the new are commensurable. Is traditional aesthetics contingently or necessarily associated with patriarchy? Can the 'gender-neutral' aesthetics of the traditional model be reformed or must it be rejected?" Suppose we accept that the art of the past has indeed tended to portray women in dubious ways. Does this commit aesthetics to doing any more in future than paying close attention to the way women are treated in art? Suppose we also accept that the effect of certain artistic conventions is to lend a false air of completeness to what is in fact a partial view of the world. Would this recognition mean that we must in some sense reject or disparage those conventions? Or would it mean merely that we must maintain an alert and critical attitude toward them and look harder at the ways in which they perform their various political functions? Suppose that, having answered these questions, we conclude that the world of art and the world of male ideology cannot after all be kept distinct from each other. Would this mean that aesthetics itself ought to become overtly ideological? Or would it mean merely that, as aestheticians, we ought to be wary of sinking thoughtlessly into a kind of covert conservatism? Finally, we might ask whether our answers to any of these questions commit us to rejecting the notion that certain "great" artworks of the past speak with a universal voice, equally valid for men and women. Perhaps many of them don't (and it will be important to develop techniques for deciding which ones don't, and why). But perhaps other works of art, when interpreted with an eye to the snares of ideology, will be able to justify their claim to represent a peculiarly and deeply *human* response to the world. In which case, we might conclude that aesthetics needs not so much to radicalize itself, as merely to proceed with rather more care—both in its selection of analytical tools and in its selection of exemplary artworks upon which to put those tools to work.

Curtis Brown takes up Devereaux's suggestion that we need to address these questions in the second reading of this section. Brown explores in detail two "Principles of Autonomy," each of which holds that art and aesthetics are to some extent, at least, "insulated" from facts about the oppression of women. The first principle holds that facts about the history of production of a work can have no bearing on its aesthetic value. The second holds that a large body of works of art, namely fictions, say nothing about the real world. Both principles may *seem* to show that some feminist criticisms of art are misguided. If the history of a work of art is irrelevant to its value, then the fact that women were oppressed in its production is also aesthetically irrelevant. And if fictions say nothing about the real world, then the way women are portrayed in works of fiction cannot be oppressive. Brown uses pornography as a "test-case" against which to assess these principles. He argues that, on the one hand, both principles, when properly understood, are correct, but that, on the other hand, the principles do not in fact protect art from feminist criticism.

Does the legitimacy of aesthetics as a responsible mode of inquiry depend upon a radical, feminizing overhaul of its basic methods and assumptions? Or should we conclude that, while it would benefit from including a number of questions and techniques which it has hitherto thought marginal, traditional aesthetics is essentially sound, and needs only to consider minor revisions to its presuppositions and procedures? Whatever conclusions we reach, one thing is certain: that aesthetics—whether it emerges feminized from its encounter with feminism, or merely somewhat altered—can hardly fail to benefit. It can hardly fail to derive from the challenge it faces an increase in that critical alertness which, whatever else aesthetics requires for its legitimacy, is surely essential to it.

Oppressive Texts, Resisting Readers and the Gendered Spectator: The "New" Aesthetics

Mary Devereaux

I

At the heart of recent feminist theorizing about art is the claim that various forms of representation—painting, photography, film—assume a "male gaze." The notion of the gaze has both a literal and a figurative component. Narrowly construed, it refers to actual looking. Broadly, or more metaphorically, it refers to a way of thinking about, and acting in, the world.

In literal terms, the gaze is male when men do the looking. Men look both as spectators and as characters within works. In figurative terms, to say that the gaze is male refers to a way of seeing which takes women as its object. In this broad sense, the gaze male whenever it directs itself at, and takes pleasure in, women, where women function as erotic objects. Many feminists claim that most art, most of the time, places women in this position. In Laura Mulvey's words, man is the bearer of the gaze, woman its object.[1]

Feminist theorists, like many other theorists, take as basic the tenet that no vision, not even artistic vision, is neutral vision. All vision is colored by the "spectacles" through which we see the world. The notion that all seeing is "a way of seeing" contrasts sharply with the traditional realist assumption that observation can be cleanly separated from interpretation, at least under certain ideally specified conditions. In part, feminist theorists can be understood as reiterating a familiar, but still important, objection to the naive notion of the innocent eye. As E.H. Gombrich convincingly argues, observation is never innocent. In his words, "Whenever we receive a visual impression, we react by docketing it, filing it, grouping it in one way or another, even if the impression is only that of an inkblot or a fingerprint. . . . [T]he postulate of an unbiased eye demands the impossible."[2] Observation is always conditioned by perspective and expectation.

Yet, feminist claims that our representations inscribe a male gaze involve more than a denial of the eye's innocence. They involve asserting the central role that gender plays in formulating those expectations.

[1] Laura Mulvey, "Visual Pleasure and Narrative Cinema," in *Film Theory and Criticism*, 3rd ed., eds., Gerald Mast and Marshall Cohen (Oxford University Press, 1985), pp. 803–816.
[2] E. H. Gombrich, *Art and Illusion: A Study in the Psychology of Pictorial Representation* (Princeton University Press, 1960), pp. 297–298.

Feminist theorists insist, moreover, that these expectations are dispropor-
tionately affected by male needs, beliefs and desires. Both men and
women have learned to see the world through male eyes. So, for example,
women throughout their lives expend enormous amounts of time and energy and money making themselves "beautiful." In undertaking this
costly process, women judge themselves according to internalized standards of what is pleasing to men. As Sandra Bartky observes, adolescent
girls "learn to appraise themselves as they are shortly to be appraised."[3]
In this sense, the eyes are female, but the gaze is male.

Feminist theorists object to seeing the world "through male eyes."
They equate the male gaze with patriarchy. The notion of patriarchy is
key here. Defined as a social system structured upon the supremacy of
the father and the legal dependence of wives and children, patriarchy
makes women depend upon men not only for status and privilege, but
for their very identity. The assumption is that this arrangement oppresses women. It also, as both feminists and non-feminists have argued, oppresses men, although not necessarily in the same way as it
oppresses women.

This oppression occurs at the symbolic as well as the material
level. Women, as the first editorial of the film journal, *Camera
Obscura,* announced, "are oppressed not only economically and politically, but also in the very forms of reasoning, signifying and symbolical exchange of our culture."[4] Thus, to take a familiar but powerful example, in English "he" functions as the unmarked term, "she" as the
marked term. "His" attributes define all humanity (i.e., "mankind");
"hers" define only women. The higher priority assigned to male attributes
passes unnoticed because our language, like our thinking, equates "male"
gender with "gender neutral."

Art, as another form of symbolical exchange, also participates in this
oppression. In both its high and low forms, feminist theorists argue, art
inscribes "a masculinist discourse" which we learn to reproduce in our
everyday lives. Feminist theorists here draw on the insight that art both
reflects the conditions of life and helps to establish and maintain them.
The male gaze inscribed in art triggers what Elizabeth Flynn and
Patrocinio Schweickart describe as a deep-seated impulse for women to
adapt themselves to the male viewpoint.[5] Griselda Pollock goes further,
arguing that the history of art itself is a series of representational practices which actively encourage definitions of sexual difference that

---

[3] Sandra Bartky, "Women, Bodies and Power: A Research Agenda for Philosophy," *APA
Newsletter on Philosophy and Feminism* 89 (1989), p. 79.
[4] Robert Lapsley and Michael Westlake, *Film Theory: An Introduction* (Manchester University
Press, 1988), p. 23.
[5] Elizabeth A. Flynn and Patrocinio P. Schweickart, eds., *Gender and Reading: Essays on
Readers, Texts, and Contexts* (Johns Hopkins University Press, 1986), xix.

contribute to the present configuration of sexual politics and power relations.[6]

For this reason, much of feminist theorizing about art is critical in tone. From its perspective, the artistic canon is androcentric, and hence, politically repressive. In Schweickart's words, "For a woman, then, books do not necessarily spell salvation."[7] Briefly summarized, the feminist critique of representation rests on the equation: the medium = male = patriarchal = oppressive.

Some will greet this equation as exaggerated, even absurd. The idea that art is political or ideologically charged contradicts the deeply held belief that art speaks to and for all human beings. Socrates' charges against the poets notwithstanding, the Western European tradition characterizes art as liberating, enlightening, uplifting. Art's effects are positive; the experiences it offers intrinsically valuable. In categorizing art with other forms of patriarchal oppression, feminist theorists reject the division of art and politics basic to Anglo-American aesthetics.

The implications of this rejection are important and far-reaching. In dividing the artworld into male and female, feminist theorists irrevocably link the production and consumption of art with issues of power and control. Outside the Anglo-American paradigm, this linkage is not new. The Marxist tradition in aesthetics has long placed the concept of power at the center of the discussion of art. Marxism's emphasis on how class and other social forces and practices enter into the reading of any text lays the groundwork for feminist investigations of how gender enters the exchange with the text.

What is original to feminism is the linkage of art with sexual politics. Issues of sexual politics lie at the center of current academic debate in English Departments, Film Studies programs and feminist theory groups. Aesthetics, at least in America, has been slower to notice or respond to this debate. Although an occasional feminist paper has appeared on the program at the annual American Society for Aesthetics meetings, *The Journal of Aesthetics and Art Criticism* has prior to this writing never published a work of feminist theory. This omission is even more surprising given that philosophers from Plato to Nelson Goodman have been preoccupied with issues of representation—an issue that feminism, from another direction, centrally addresses.

This lack of attention to issues transforming the discussion of art in other disciplines is frequently attributed to a difference in vocabulary. Feminist theory has its roots in Foucault and Lacan, not in Plato, Aristotle and Kant. Confronted with talk of "mirror stages," "voyeurism," and "difference," practitioners of traditional aesthetics may feel trapped by

---

[6] Griselda Pollock, *Vision and Difference* (New York: Routledge, 1988), p. 11.
[7] Patrocinio Schweickart, "Toward a Feminist Theory of Reading" in *Gender and Reading*, p. 41.

the jargon of a foreign discourse, one not bound by rules their own train-
ing insists upon. Stanley Cavell describes the experience of reading these
works as involving a different set of satisfactions.[8] Whatever the promise
of these satisfactions, some will maintain, it is difficult not to lose patience with contemporary writers whose texts demand the exegetical
labors normally reserved for the dead and the "truly great."

On this account, feminist theories remain marginalized due both to
their difficulty and unfamiliarity. But this explanation does not, I think,
tell the whole story. Regular readers of the *Journal* have no doubt noticed
the growing number of articles dealing with the latest developments in
literary theory (the work of Stanley Fish, Jacques Derrida, Mikhail
Bakhtin), hermeneutics (Hans-Georg Gadamer) and the philosophy of
language (Donald Davidson). In each of these cases, vocabulary and
methodology pose formidable challenges. Not every reader will find such
challenges worth the time or effort. But clearly, in aesthetics, as in philosophy generally, difficulty alone never warrants exclusion.

The reason feminist theories of art and aesthetics have so long remained unmentioned lies deeper, I think. At stake in the debate over feminism are deeply entrenched assumptions about the universal value of art
and aesthetic experience. The overthrow of these assumptions—linchpins
of aesthetic theory since Kant—constitutes what art historian, Linda
Nochlin, describes as a Kuhnian paradigm shift.[9] The new paradigm is a
feminist paradigm and what we face is a conceptual revolution. If I am
right, then the deeper explanation for the lack of attention to feminist theories lies in the natural resistance of those suddenly faced with the overthrow of an entrenched way of thinking.

As recent developments in the philosophy of science and ethics high-
light, aesthetics cannot simply "add on" feminist theories as it might add
new works by Goodman, Arthur Danto or George Dickie. To take feminism seriously involves rethinking our basic concepts and recasting the
history of the discipline. And that requires more than adding women's
names to the canonical list of great philosophers.

The requirement that we engage in such radical rethinking may seem
burdensome and unnecessary. It is helpful to the self-esteem of women or
to women who are feminists. But what of those who do not fit into either
of these two categories? What, they may wonder, do they have to gain
from feminist aesthetics?

In part to answer such questions, I want in the next section to return
to the notion of the male gaze. In examining this key feminist notion more
carefully, I hope to make clear the intrinsic interest of this approach to
aesthetics and to suggest why its concerns merit serious consideration.

---

[8] Stanley Cavell, *In Quest of the Ordinary: Lines of Skepticism and Romanticism* (University of
Chicago Press, 1988), p. 131.
[9] Linda Nochlin, *Women, Art and Power and Other Essays* (New York: Harper and Row, 1988),
p. 146.

To this end, I want to investigate how gendered vision works in one specific representational practice, namely film. Film is a natural choice for such a study because it is a medium so fundamentally built around the activity of looking. It is also, not surprisingly, the medium where the male gaze has been most extensively discussed.

The relationship of gender and cinematic vision is extremely complicated. A complete analysis of this topic would require several hundred pages. In what follows, I focus on two key claims, namely, that in cinema the gaze is male and that the cinematic text is a male text. I seek to make clear how these claims should be understood and then to situate them philosophically. In confining myself to what I take to be the core claims of this debate, I will of necessity leave aside many important, but internal, issues in film theory.

II

Despite the extensive literature which refers to and relies upon it, the concept of the male gaze remains difficult to understand. It is so in part because, as noted above, the male gaze refers both to literal and metaphorical vision. A further difficulty in understanding the male gaze arises from the failure to distinguish three different gazes: that of film-maker, the characters within the film and the spectator. With each of these gazes, literal and figurative seeing interact in a variety of ways.

In the first case, that of the film-maker, someone looks through the viewfinder of a camera, someone (often the same person) looks at the rushes after the day's shooting and someone looks at the film's final cut. This person may be male, but need not be. Women, too, make movies and have done so since the early days of the medium (e.g., Maya Deren, Dorothy Artner, Leni Riefenstahl).

What does it mean then to say that at this level the gaze is male? It means that despite the presence of women directors and screenwriters, the institutions of film-making remain largely populated by men. Not all films have male authors, but whoever makes movies must work nonetheless within a system owned and operated by men. At the level of the film-maker, then, men do not always do the looking, but they generally control who does. The male gaze is not always male, but *it is always male-dominated.*

By male-dominated, feminist theorists mean male-gendered, not simply possessed of male anatomy. A key move distinguishes sex from gender. A child is born sexed; through education and experience, it acquires gender. On this account, education and experience create the particular way of seeing which the term, "the male gaze," describes. Male institutional control thus refers not to the anatomy of film world personnel, which includes both men and women, but to the way film, however authored, contributes to the hegemony of men over women.

From a feminist point of view, this control matters because it "builds in" a preference for a particular type of film, i.e., one which positions women in ways consistent with patriarchal assumptions. Movies promote a way of seeing which takes man as subject, women as object. Simone de Beauvoir's *The Second Sex* puts the point succinctly. "Representation of the world, like the world itself, is the work of men; they describe it from their own point of view, which they confuse with absolute truth."[10]

As de Beauvoir explains, women, unlike men, do not learn to describe the world from their own point of view. As the "other," woman learns to submerge or renounce her subjectivity. She finds her identity in the subjectivity of the men to whom she is attached (father, husband, lover). In the eyes of men, she finds her identity as the object of men's desire.

In arguing that cinema, too, assigns woman this position, feminist theorists link male control of film institutions with a patriarchal way of seeing. At this point it should be clear that in attempting to describe the literal gaze of the film-maker, the question of whether men or women do the looking is not at root the issue. The real issue centers on whether, whoever stands behind the camera, a patriarchal way of seeing the world prevails. The discussion of the literal gaze thus very quickly becomes a discussion of the figurative gaze.

I do not want to deny the heuristic usefulness of talking about "literal" looking in film. Someone does look through the lens of the camera, and film-going is irrefutably a visual experience. Moreover, the medium itself offers a range of devices for representing what characters on screen themselves see, e.g., the long sequences in Alfred Hitchcock's *Vertigo* in which we see what the protagonist, Scottie, sees as he follows Madeleine.

A deeper and more damaging objection to the literal/figurative distinction emerges from the claim that literal seeing is always already figurative. Men—like women—do not simply look. Their looking—where and when they do it and at what—mimics a particular way of thinking about and acting in the world. So understood, seeing never escapes *a way* of seeing.

How then does the figurative way of seeing deemed "male" translate to the screen? How *are* women represented from the male point of view? And, with what effect on the spectator? To answer these questions requires shifting our attention from the film-maker's gaze to the manipulation of the gaze within film. At the textual level, feminist theorists have focused most directly on the story films of Hollywood as opposed to the international art cinema, experimental film or documentary film. Attention to the Hollywood film arose naturally from the broad popularity and profound influence which this tradition exercised on American cultural life.

Feminist theorists initially attacked the Hollywood film for its patriar-

---

[10] Simone de Beauvoir, *The Second Sex,* trans. and ed. H. M. Parshley (New York: Vintage Books, 1974), p. 134.

chal content. Early feminist works such as Molly Haskell's *From Reverence to Rape*[11] examined how the portraits of the Good Girl, the Vamp and the Dutiful Wife presented so forcefully in westerns, detective films and melodramas reinforced a cultural mythology. In film after film, that mythology defined the value of women as their value to men. The good girl was a dutiful daughter who preserved herself (i.e., her virginity) for the right man "to take" from her. The bad girl, in contrast, flaunts her sexuality indiscriminately, "losing" her virginity or "giving it away."

Haskell's broadly sociological approach understood movies to tell the same stories we heard outside the theatre. In the movies, as in life, good girls were rewarded, bad girls punished. Any alternative point of view, one which might tell a different tale or the same tale differently, was effectively excluded. Put in the strongest terms, the charge was that the Hollywood film "belonged to patriarchy."[12] This commitment need not be intentional. Nor need it be confined to the works of male directors. Yet, as an institution, cinema, like television, was held to participate in and help to perpetuate a system of social organization which assigns power and privilege by gender.

Admittedly, not all films perpetuate patriarchy. Individual films may resist this arrangement. The strong-headed heroines typically played by Katharine Hepburn, Lauren Bacall and Bette Davis do not conform to this stereotype, nor do films such as Howard Hawks' *His Girl Friday*. As feminist critics themselves have demonstrated, the films of Hollywood evidence more variation and internal tension than a charge of monolithic patriarchy allows.

In speaking of Hollywood film as "belonging to patriarchy," something more subtle is at work than overt stereotyping. At the simplest level, Haskell and others had maintained, film reinforced women's dependence on men. As noted above, women on screen regularly won their happiness in the service of others (Griffith's Dear One, Marion as the amiable spouse in *Shane)*. When they depart from societal norms, as Hepburn's high-level diplomat does in *Woman of the Year*, they are revealed to be cold-hearted and in need of "re-education." Tess learns from her husband Sam to place work second to companionate time with spouse and the duties of parenting. Those who refuse this role, find themselves alone and lonely (e.g., Tess' Aunt Ellen). Those who opt for illicit instead of married love, end up dead (e.g., Marion in *Psycho*, Alex in *Fatal Attraction*).

Thus, as Mary Ann Doane convincingly argues, at a more complex level, the Hollywood film functions as "a recuperative strategy" designed

---

[11] Molly Haskell, *From Reverence to Rape: The Treatment of Women in the Movies* (Harmondsworth: Penguin Books, 1974).
[12] E. Deidre Pribram, ed., *Female Spectators: Looking at Film and Television* (New York: Verso, 1988), p. 1.

to return the wayward woman to the fold.[13] This return operates both within the narrative and externally, in the narrative's effect on its female audience. Internally, the Hollywood narrative typically charts the course by which a woman in a non-normative role cedes her control to a man.[14] The happy ending in which Tess returns to Sam serves externally to "recuperate" wayward members of the female audience as well. The message is that for a woman, unlike for a man, the satisfactions of solitude, work, or adventure cannot compare to those of caring for husband and children.

The classic Hollywood film reinforces this message stylistically by confining the spectator to the point of view of the narrative hero. In Tania Modleski's words, "the film spectator apparently has no choice but to identify with the male protagonist, who exerts an active, controlling gaze over a passive female object." By consistently stressing the man's point of view, the Hollywood film thus negates the female character's view.[15]

Stressing the male protagonist's point of view need not involve confining us consistently to his visual field. The one well-known experiment which confined us consistently to the first-person visual field of a character, Robert Montgomery's *The Lady in the Lake,* failed miserably to convey that character's figurative point of view. We saw what he saw, but we didn't feel what he felt. More typical narrative films, such as *The Big Sleep,* alternate between what the protagonist sees and what other characters see. Hawks gives us not only Marlowe looking at Vivian but Vivian looking at Marlowe. The gaze is thus not directly that of the protagonist.

Nevertheless, within the Hollywood film there is a long tradition of women performing for the camera. Women sing, dance, dress and undress, all before the steady, often adoring, gaze of an implied spectator. Frequently, female performance plays a role in the plot, as when Vivian sings for Marlowe and the audience at Eddie Mars' nightclub. But whether playing fictional characters who sing and dance before an audience or not, Marlene Dietrich, Marilyn Monroe, Ingrid Bergman and other female "stars," perform *for* the camera. As Stanley Cavell has pointed out, in photographing beautiful women, the cinema has found one of the subjects most congenial to it. But "congenial" here means the congeniality of men making films for men.

The male controlled institutions of film-making thus place women on screen in a particular position. As eroticized objects, women are doubly victimized. As Ann Kaplan argues, the male gaze involves more than simply looking; it carries with it the threat of action and possession. This

[13] See Mary Ann Doane, *The Desire to Desire: The Woman's Film of the 1940s* (Indiana University Press, 1987), ch. 2.

[14] Mary Beth Haralovich, cited in Annette Kuhn, *Women's Pictures: Feminism and the Cinema* (London: Routledge and Kegan Paul, 1982), p. 34.

[15] Tania Modleski, *The Women Who Knew Too Much: Hitchcock and Feminist Theory* (New York: Methuen, 1988), p. 73.

power to act and possess is not reciprocal. Women can receive and return a gaze, but they cannot act upon it.[16]

To be fully operative as a mechanism of oppression, the male gaze depends upon a second condition. Not only must looking come with some "back-up"—physical, economic, social—but "being looked at" must also activate some level of female narcissism. Women themselves must not be indifferent to the gaze turned upon them; they must have internalized a certain assignment of positions.[17]

It is this disequilibrium in power both inside and outside the arena of looking which makes the male gaze different from what some have called a female or gender-neutral gaze. Consider the oft-cited cases where men serve as the object of the gaze, as in the recent spate of Richard Gere movies (*Breathless, American Gigolo*). Despite the "role reversal," the degradation which women suffer in occupying the role of "looked at" is not matched by their male counterparts.

It would be useful at this point to make a distinction, one between objectification, aestheticization and degradation.[18] 'Objectification,' as I am using the term, means no more than to make someone or something the object of my gaze. There is nothing inherently oppressive about objectification understood in this way. Nor is the filmic male gaze any more objectifying than any other gaze. Aestheticization, defined here, means simply treating people or things as objects of aesthetic contemplation. There is nothing inherently oppressive about aestheticization. Both objectification and aestheticization may be degrading, but they need not be. 'Degradation' is a complex notion, associated with such concepts as respect, human dignity and worth. To degrade is to demean or debase someone, where this involves not only failing to respect, but also, in some sense, actively diminishing the value or dignity of the person. Rape, slavery and torture provide three obvious examples of degradation.[19]

---

[16] E. Ann Kaplan, "Is the Gaze Male?" in *Women and Values: Readings in Recent Feminist Philosophy*, ed., Marilyn Pearsall (Belmont, California: Wadsworth Publishing Co., 1986), p. 231.

[17] The idea that women's oppression depends upon the fulfillment of both of these conditions I owe to a conversation with Tim Gould.

[18] I base these distinctions on Lydia Goehr's helpful commentary on an earlier version of this paper. Her comments were presented at The American Society for Aesthetics, Eastern Division Meeting, State College, Pa., March 16, 1990.

[19] In saying that acts such as rape degrade their victims, I do not mean to endorse the conventional view of women according to which rape is degrading because it destroys or damages a woman's 'purity.' I do, however, want to maintain that there is a sense in which rape (along with slavery and torture) is truly degrading. The notion of degradation is complicated and we are likely to have conflicting intuitions. Many of us would like to uphold the Kantian idea that human dignity is inviolable. In this view, human dignity is such that no act can diminish it. On the other hand, there is the also compelling view that certain acts are such that they do degrade and diminish persons. In this latter view, it is the potential for real degradation that makes the rapist's acts so horrible.

Given these distinctions, it is easy to see that male characters, like their female counterparts, may be objectified or even, as in the case of Richard Gere, aestheticized (or eroticized). And they, like women, may also be portrayed in degraded or less than fully human ways. It is with respect to actual degradation that the asymmetry between men and women reappears. For in the case of women, unlike that of men, real life degradation often runs parallel to portrayals of degradation. Because women frequently lack power off screen, they are more likely to be degraded by their portrayals on screen. Even if men are portrayed in degrading ways, their real life power shields them from actual degradation.

As I've said above, objectification and aestheticization are not in themselves degrading. Nevertheless, feminist theorists are correct that Hollywood films reflect and encourage a cultural proclivity to treat the female body and the female self *only* as objects of aesthetic contemplation. And they are also correct in suggesting that this way of treating women *is* degrading. While, as I have argued, movie-making and movie-watching cannot be held solely responsible for the oppression of women, feminist theorists rightly emphasize the connection between how we represent our lives and lived experience itself.

In turning, finally, to the effect of the film text on its spectators, I want first to consider the means by which the gender bias of many Hollywood films remains hidden. The Hollywood film conventionally presents its telling as, to quote Beauvoir again, "absolute truth." It depends for its effect upon creating a narrative illusion. The film story must unfold transparently, as though happening before our very eyes. It is crucial to such film-making that it proceed without calling attention to itself as a story. In this, the stylistic conventions of Hollywood follow those of the 19th century realist novel. For a film to acknowledge its status as a story or fiction admits a point of view, a place from which its story gets told. Devices such as Godard's use of stop-action and words written across the screen aim to resist narrative illusionism. They announce the film as a film, as a fiction, a construct.[20]

For many feminists, as for many Marxists, the narrative illusion central to the classic Hollywood film is politically compromised. Hollywood films are said to foster strong character identification and full absorption in the action. This absorption in turn is believed to encourage viewer passivity. At its worst, warned Max Horkheimer and Theodor Adorno, such film-making undermines individual autonomy. It renders its audience a "mass" easily manipulated in the interests of the status quo.

In an effort to encourage active, critically engaged spectatorship, feminist theorists often exaggerate the connection between conventional Hollywood techniques of storytelling and passive spectatorship. Passive

---

[20] Interestingly, what is termed the "new" Hollywood cinema has adopted some of the techniques and self-conscious strategies of the international art cinema.

spectatorship is not, however, restricted to Hollywood narratives, nor do all such films aim for, or achieve, such an effect, e.g., Spike Lee's *Do the Right Thing*. To the extent that the average Hollywood product *does* encourage passivity, it renders *both* male and female spectators passive. Unfortunately, feminist critics often lose sight of this point.

In calling for active reading to replace this passivity, feminist critiques of the Hollywood film here parallel Brecht's critique of Aristotelian drama. Both denounce what they see as efforts to elicit the passive empathy of the spectator; both ask for art to break the narrative illusion. However, feminist theorists go beyond Brecht's analysis to examine how identification differs in male and female spectators. Gender, they rightly assert, plays a key role in eliciting the empathy and identification typical of narrative film.

The analysis of film's effects on the spectator brings us to the third and, I would argue, most important site at which the male gaze operates. In developing a theory of spectatorship, feminist theorists move beyond an initial concern with film content and style to explore the mechanisms of viewing. To the question "how does film represent women?" is added the question "what sources of satisfaction do these representations of women offer the spectator"? At what many now call its second stage, feminist film theory shifts attention from the literary critical and sociological reading of individual films to the more broadly theoretical project of describing the unconscious mechanisms involved in watching movies.[21]

Primary among these mechanisms is voyeuristic pleasure. In this view, enormously influential among film theorists, spectators derive erotic pleasure through the opportunities for looking which the cinema affords. As Christian Metz argues in *The Imaginary Signifier* (1975), the darkened theatre, the absence of the object viewed, and its inability to return the gaze all contribute to the idea that film viewing constitutes unauthorized looking.[22] From its early association with the Nickelodeon, the motion picture has come to function as a metaphor for the illicit activity of the voyeur, as Alfred Hitchcock's 1954 film, *Rear Window*, illustrates. Lest one miss the point, Hitchcock makes L.B. Jeffries—an inveterate voyeur—a photographer.[23]

The question of how film plays to our already existing desires, fantasies, and fears received one of its most influential treatments in Laura

---

[21] This division of feminist film theory into first and second stages can be found, for example, in Lapsley and Westlake, *Film Theory*, p. 25. The same division emerges less explicitly in Claire Johnson, "Women's Cinema as Counter-Cinema," in *Movies and Methods*, ed. Bill Nichols (University of California Press, 1976), pp. 209–215.

[22] Christian Metz, from *The Imaginary Signifier*, *Film Theory and Criticism*, 3rd ed., eds. Gerald Mast and Marshall Cohen (Oxford University Press, 1985), pp. 799–801.

[23] See Modleski's chapter on *Rear Window* for a discussion of the film's critical reception.

Mulvey's now classic, "Visual Pleasure and Narrative Film." Mulvey begins from the premise that film reflects the psychical obsessions of the society which produces it. In making this assumption, Mulvey, like most other second wave theorists, draws heavily on psychoanalysis, particularly Freud and Lacan. She sets out to analyze the characteristic sources of pleasure and unpleasure offered by the cinema.

Narrative cinema, by which she means narrative in the unself-conscious mode described above, provides the spectator with two sources of pleasure. First, it provides what Freud calls "scopophilic" pleasure, the pleasure of viewing another as an erotic object. As we saw above, this pleasure characteristically takes the form of looking at women. In film after film, women function both as erotic objects for characters within the movie, as Vivian does for Marlowe, and as erotic objects for the spectator in the movie-house, as Lauren Bacall does for us. Thus, women's presence on screen presupposes the appreciative glance of a male spectator.

Men, in contrast, only rarely function as eroticized objects for female (or male) spectators. Men, Mulvey points out, feel uncomfortable in such a role. Neither the ruling assumptions of patriarchy "nor the psychical structures that back it up" encourage the male "to gaze at his exhibitionist like."[24] Instead, man's role is to function as the locus of narrative action. His role, on screen as off, involves shooting the bad guys and blazing the trails. The male movie star attracts our admiration and respect by his deeds. We are encouraged to *identify with* him, to imagine ourselves doing what he does.

In Freudian terms, the male functions as an "ego-ideal," not as an object of erotic desire. The possibility of identifying with this ego-ideal offers the spectator a second, contrasting source of pleasure, i.e., the pleasure of identifying with the characters projected on screen. Since, on Mulvey's analysis, it is the male hero who makes things happen and controls them, we typically identify with him. Thus, the spectator's gaze is male in two senses, both in its direction at women as objects of erotic fascination and in its identification with the male protagonist. The division of male and female roles on screen mimics traditional gender roles: women functioning as the passive objects of the viewer's gaze; men functioning as the active subjects of the viewer's imagination.

In playing to our existing desires, fantasies and fears, film also offers what Mulvey calls unpleasure. In the patriarchal unconscious, woman represents the threat of castration. This threat the Hollywood film typically meets in one of two ways. It may contain the threat posed by the mystery and fearsomeness of women by domesticating them, typically through marriage (e.g., *Notorious*), or, more drastically, by killing them off, as in *Fatal Attraction*. Alternatively, the threat may be denied alto-

---

[24] Mulvey, "Visual Pleasure and Narrative Cinema," p. 810.

gether by elevating the woman to the status of a fetish. In the latter case, the woman becomes reassuring instead of dangerous.[25]

To summarize, then, the male gaze refers to three interlocking forms of control. With respect to the film-maker, it refers to male control of the practices of film-making. This control leads, at the level of the film text, to a product whose content and style inscribe the patriarchal unconscious of the culture at large. Lastly, these devices position the male or female audience member to find in film a way of seeing which calms our fears and satisfies our desires.

This is a provocative account of film spectatorship. To ask who is doing the looking assumes all spectators are not similarly positioned, i.e., that factors such as gender have a role to play in structuring—maybe even in constituting—what we see. Mulvey's original analysis, however, leaves the *female* spectator with no active viewing position except to identify with the male protagonist. In identifying with the women on screen, the female spectator is assumed to align herself with the female-as-object.[26] More recent feminist theory rightly inquires how Mulvey's account explains the pleasure which women derive from going to the movies. As Ann Kaplan has asked, is the female spectator's pleasure, like the man's, the pleasure of looking at women, the masochistic pleasure of enjoying objectification, or the sadistic pleasure of identifying with the men who oppress her?[27]

In "Afterthoughts on Visual Pleasure and Narrative Cinema," Mulvey herself proposes, more positively, that identification with the male allows the female spectator to revert, at least imaginatively, to the active independence of what Freud termed the female child's "early masculine period." In this "tomboy" phase, she takes pleasure in a freedom that correct femininity will later repress.[28]

In moving beyond the static model of active male/passive female, current theories of spectatorship acknowledge women's resistance to the position assigned to them in patriarchal culture. There remains, however, a tendency to speak of *the* female spectator as if all women shared the same aims and aspirations and came to film texts similarly equipped. To make these assumptions overlooks important differences between women of color and white women, rich and poor, women and feminists and different varieties of feminists.

Similarly, feminist theories of spectatorship tend to speak of *the* male spectator as though all men's gazes are male. This assertion assumes, unjustifiably, that all men are equally powerful and that they stand equally

---

[25] Ibid, p. 811.
[26] Pribram, *Female Spectators*, pp. 1–2.
[27] Kaplan, "Is the Gaze Male?" p. 252.
[28] Laura Mulvey, *Visual and Other Pleasures* (Indiana University Press, 1989), p. 37.

to gain from the arrangements of patriarchy. Such assumptions contradict feminism's own insistence on the relationship between power and variables such as economic standing, education, ethnic identity, sexual orientation and so on. Thus, for example, in feminist terms, the male gaze is not only sexist but also heterosexist. Should not then an adequate theory of spectatorship also include an account of how the male gaze operates when the spectator is not heterosexual?

As these objections suggest, a more fine-grained analysis of spectatorship undermines the easy identification of male viewer with "the male gaze." The characterization of the male gaze as "totally active" is, I suggest, difficult to sustain once we move beyond the assumption that all men occupy the same position in a patriarchal social system. Moreover, the assumed activity and control of the male spectator is at odds with the widespread notion that the Hollywood film monolithically encourages a form of passive spectatorship. Equating the male gaze with the active gaze ignores the passive element involved in looking at movies. The male spectator, whatever his real political and social power, cannot interact with the on-screen woman. She appears, but is physically absent.

As I hope to have made clear, the notion of the male gaze cannot simply be identified with the way men see the world. The gaze, properly understood, has undergone certain refinements. It describes a way of seeing the world which is typically male. But it is not a way of seeing confined to men nor is it the province of all men.

Part of what makes feminist theories interesting and powerful is their attention to factors which affect how we see and respond to texts. Gender is one of these factors. As they evolve, feminist film theories, like feminist theories more generally have, however, increasingly recognized the necessity to move beyond a simple binary analysis of gender. In articulating the inter-connections between gender and other variables, such as sexual orientation, race, and class, a feminist orientation serves to fine-tune our understanding of art and its effects upon us.

III

What general conclusions can we draw from this analysis of the male gaze? That film works to reinforce societal norms? That it is male? That film, like art generally, may be harmful to women? Such conclusions are now common in film studies. As noted earlier, we find similar arguments in older, more entrenched, fields such as literature and art history. As a body of theory, feminism has succeeded in placing the question of gender at the center of contemporary literary and artistic theory. As I suggested earlier, this new agenda has unsettling consequences for traditional aesthetics. The new agenda seeks not only to have us surrender certain long-standing assumptions, but to replace them with whole new ways of thinking about art and our relationship to it. I want to conclude therefore by sketching briefly some of these changes and raising several questions for us to consider.

First, feminist theorists ask us to replace the conception of the artwork as an autonomous object—a thing of beauty and a joy forever—with a messier conception of art. Seen in these terms, the artwork moves from an autonomous realm of value to the everyday realm of social and political praxis. It gains a history which overflows the former bounds of "art history." Who makes art and what type of art gets made depend, we learn, on the interaction of the artworld with other worlds.

In drawing our attention to culture in the broadest sense, feminist theorists rely on an alternative, European view of art. In this, feminist aesthetics constitutes part of a larger movement away from "autonomous" aesthetics. Even within Anglo-American aesthetics, the old paradigm no longer holds the place it once did. Our understanding of representation, of the pleasures and powers of art, and of spectatorship have been immeasurably enriched by the expanded context in which we now look at art. Yet, in this enlarged context, how does a concept of the "aesthetic," if by that we mean the *purely* aesthetic, function? Is the discipline of aesthetics possible apart from sociology, cultural studies, identity politics?

Second, feminist theorists propose that we re-examine art's claim to speak for all of us. Does art speak in a gender-neutral voice or does it privilege some experiences and ways of seeing over others? Traditional aesthetics inherits from Aristotle belief in a universal human condition of which art, at least great art, speaks.

Feminist theorists challenge the adequacy of the classic, Aristotelian model not only with respect to the Hollywood film (which some might argue is not great enough to qualify as "great" art), but with respect to all art. The films of Sergei Eisenstein and Jean Renoir, like the plays of Shakespeare, all speak in "particular" voices. On the new view, the artwork, like the generic pronoun, speaks for "mankind," but mankind includes only some of us.[29]

To question art's autonomy and universality, need not imply that these artworks are without value—quite the contrary—although their value may differ from what we once supposed. Nothing in feminist theory precludes ranking Henry James a more important novelist than Jane Austen or Alice Walker a greater writer than John Steinbeck.

In making these evaluative rankings, feminist theorists do insist, however, that we acknowledge the criteria used in defining "important" and "great." Does "great" mean the forcefully written or the spare, the heartfelt or the coolly reasoned, the typical or the innovative? When is a

---

[29] For a more detailed analysis of the concepts of art's autonomy and universality, see my "The Philosophical and Political Implications of the Feminist Critique of Aesthetic Autonomy" in *Turning the Century: Feminist Criticism in the 1990s,* Glynis Carr, ed., *The Bucknell Review,* Vol. XXXVI, No. 2 (Cranbury, NJ: Associated University Presses, 1992).

text forcefully written and who decides? Feminist theorists offer a framework from within which we may—indeed, should—raise such questions. Only when we explicitly acknowledge the criteria used in making these judgements do we create space for competing criteria.

In denying that artworks or the criteria we use to judge them are value-neutral, feminist theorists also urge a third proposal. We are asked to reconsider our relationship to established artistic traditions. The canon, still heralded by some as a reservoir for the best of human thinking, is accused of excluding and silencing women (among other groups). At the very least, a feminist perspective requires that we rethink our relationship to the artistic tradition in terms which do not assume a monolithic "we." Describing existing artistic traditions as uniformly enlightening and liberating ignores those for whom the authority of those traditions is unquestionably problematic. Thus, we must ask whether the coming of age stories of Holden Caulfield and David Copperfield affect adolescent girls in the same way as adolescent boys, and what significance this difference, if any, makes. Being willing to ask *who* is doing the reading forces us to question whether the pleasures of art are invariant and impervious to factors such as class, race and gender.

Fourthly, feminist theorists alter the characterization of reading or viewing as neutral activities. Like hermeneutics and reader-response theories, they seek to explain how the social and historical placement of the spectator affects the meaning derived from the text. Meaning is no longer determined exclusively by the text. Aside from emphasizing the social and historical context in which interpretation occurs, feminist theorists break new ground in demonstrating how texts themselves "assume" a particular reader through narrative and stylistic devices. The best of feminist theorizing executes this demonstration through a careful analysis of texts.

In advancing new theories of readership, however, what justifies feminist theorists in assigning "the woman reader" a central place in the analysis of texts? If it is meaningful to think in terms of "the woman reader," then why not in terms of "the lesbian reader,"[30] "the adolescent reader," "the ideal reader," "the over-educated reader"? Are all of these categories equally important, and according to what theoretical or political criteria?

Lastly, feminist theorists, like other post-structuralist theorists, endeavor to make the unnoticed noticed. They adopt from the Frankfurt School the belief that the informed spectator is a more critical spectator, and the critical spectator is one less likely to be victimized by the text.

Calls for critical reading are unlikely to meet resistance among aestheticians. But what of claims that art may not be good for us?—At the

[30] Jean E. Kennard, "Ourself Behind Ourself: A Theory for Lesbian Readers" in *Gender and Reading*, p. 63.

very least, not all art and not for all of us. In adopting a *politics of art,* feminist theorists confront Anglo-American aesthetics head-on. They replace reverence for art with skepticism. They ask that we be willing to rethink what we value and the reasons we value it.

In suggesting that this challenge deserves serious consideration, I might be understood to claim that all traditional aesthetics is useless, that the accomplishments of the last century are a chimera. This is not my intent. My intent is instead to describe the cognitive dissonance which marks the current situation in aesthetics. If feminism constitutes a new paradigm, then we may wish to ponder how far the old model of aesthetics and the new are commensurable. Is traditional aesthetics contingently or necessarily associated with patriarchy? Can the "gender-neutral" aesthetics of the traditional model be reformed or must it be rejected?

Aside from these theoretical issues, feminist theory raises several practical issues which demand attention. If art contributes to the disequilibrium in power between the sexes, then what should we do? Should we simply quit going to the movies?

Raising such questions returns us to the Socratic tradition which urges caution in the face of art's power. Socrates followed that warning with a call for censorship. With this suggestion, however, many feminists would not agree. Feminist theory confronts the ancient problem of art's potential for harm with two other, far more promising, strategies. Neither appears to have occurred to Socrates. I want therefore to conclude by looking very briefly at these solutions.

IV

The first proposed solution consists in a call for a new type of art. Some feminists, Claire Johnson for example, have proposed the creation of a counter-cinema to compete with the mainstream Hollywood cinema.[31] This strategy, like establishing public radio and television stations aims to offer an alternative to the usual fare.

The suggestion to create an alternative art might please Socrates. It would allow him to replace Homer's epics with his own, more philosophically informed, tales. This so-called revision of the canon would meet the Socratic objections to art whose content and form encouraged a weakening of the requisite moral virtues.

Creating new artistic traditions provides an alternative to the passive reception of dominant traditions. This strategy is most often described as creating a female voice or female gaze. It allows women to write their own texts, their own history. Achieving such a "female gaze" requires more than simply providing women with access to the means of filmmaking. As Diane Waldman correctly argues, women don't make better,

---

[31] Johnson, "Women's Cinema as Counter-Cinema" [Work referred to in note 21].

less "patriarchal" films simply because they are women, as if women automatically had access to resources not available to the male psyche. The required transformation of film depends not upon some female essence, but upon a consciously adopted political perspective.[32]

Adopting such a perspective has resulted in interesting films by Mulvey, Sally Potter, Lizzie Borden, Barbara Hammer and others. These films strive in a variety of ways to disrupt or rework the narrative conventions of the dominant cinema. Sally Potter's *Thriller*, for example, retells the story of *La Bohème*. In Potter's *film noir* version of the doomed love affair, Mimi investigates her own death. Her voice-over and the fragmented narrative through which her story unfolds resist the character identification and narrative closure typical of traditional narrative. Films such as *Thriller* strive to critique the dominant moods of cinematic representation by privileging heterogeneity and multiplicity of meaning. In this, these films aim to free the spectator to engage more actively with the text. Other films, such as those of Barbara Hammer, seek alternatives to the forms of cinematic pleasure provided by the glossy image of the professional photographer. The range and variety of feminist film-making far exceeds what I can survey here. However, these films are shown primarily in film courses and private film societies. Thus, despite their importance in providing an alternative tradition, their influence on mainstream audiences and film-practices is limited.

The second feminist strategy consists in developing methods of dealing with existing texts. This strategy is variously described as re-reading, as reading against the grain, or as "re-vision." It involves active readership, where I mean reading in the broad sense to include both visual and written texts. These strategies have in common the aim of critique and reappropriation. Thus, they do what good criticism always does. But more than this, they involve learning to see through what Kuhn calls a "new pair of spectacles."[33] This new pair of spectacles provides an education not in *what* to think but *how*. Reading against the grain is a strategy designed by out of power groups to counterbalance the dominant textual traditions by offering alternative interpretations of works within those traditions.

Thought of in these terms, feminist theories offer a different critical perspective. They provide a means of resistance, and an alternative to, the male gaze. Admittedly, just as the male gaze involves a distinct political position, so too a feminist perspective is not, nor should it be regarded as, politically neutral.[34] Yet, as a way of seeing, it importantly differs from its male counterpart in acknowledging itself *as* a way of seeing.

---

[32] Diane Waldman, "Film Theory and the Gendered Spectator: The Female or the Feminist Reader?" *Camera Obscura* 18 (1988), p. 81.
[33] Kuhn, *Women's Pictures*, p. 70.
[34] Ibid.

The possibility of such textual strategies is politically important not only for feminists but for others concerned with "neutralizing" the effects of certain artworks or forms of art within a cultural setting committed to the protection of free speech. Reading "against the grain" offers an alternative to the passive readership which censorship assumes, and in its paternalism, encourages.

As an interpretative strategy, it opens to all of us—male and female—the possibility of finding our own way through the text. For various historical and cultural reasons, feminist theorists look more optimistically than did Socrates on the capacity of each of us to find that way. Yet, producing new forms of art and reading against the grain of the old will not by themselves topple the existing gender hierarchy. For that, women must also have power off-screen.

Art, Oppression, and the Autonomy of Aesthetics

Curtis Brown

I. Introduction

Mary Devereaux has suggested, in an overview of feminist aesthetics,[1] that feminist aesthetics constitutes a revolutionary approach to the field: "Aesthetics cannot simply 'add on' feminist theories as it might add new works by [Nelson] Goodman, Arthur Danto or George Dickie. To take feminism seriously involves rethinking our basic concepts and recasting the history of the discipline." In particular, feminist theory involves a rejection of "deeply entrenched assumptions about the universal value of art and aesthetic experience." Overthrowing these assumptions "constitutes what art historian, Linda Nochlin, describes as a Kuhnian paradigm shift."[2] Near the end of her essay, Devereaux returns to this theme: "If feminism constitutes a new paradigm, then we

---

[1] Mary Devereaux, "Oppressive Texts, Resisting Readers and the Gendered Spectator: The 'New' Aesthetics," reprinted in this volume.

[2] This attribution could be a little misleading, since Nochlin (a) is not talking about the overthrow of quite these assumptions; (b) does not mention Kuhn; and in fact (c) doesn't even explicitly mention paradigm *shifts*. But she does say that "the so-called woman question . . . can become a catalyst, an intellectual instrument, probing basic and 'natural' assumptions, providing a paradigm for other kinds of internal questioning, and in turn providing links with paradigms established by radical approaches in other fields" (Linda Nochlin, "Why Have There Been No Great Women Artists?" in Nochlin, *Women, Art, and Power and Other Essays* [New York: Harper & Row, 1988], p. 147).

may wish to ponder how far the old model of aesthetics and the new are commensurable. Is traditional aesthetics contingently or necessarily associated with patriarchy? Can the 'gender-neutral' aesthetics of the traditional model be reformed or must it be rejected?"

At first glance, we may be uncertain why feminist aesthetics should *either* replace traditional aesthetics *or* be added to it. Concerns about the relation between art and women's oppression seem to be broadly speaking *moral* concerns rather than aesthetic ones, and we may wonder why aesthetics cannot acknowledge that the concerns are important and interesting, but deny that they ought to form part of the subject matter of aesthetics itself. This is precisely the attitude we take toward many other concerns that are germane to issues about art: the economics of the art market, however interesting to aestheticians, is thought of as part of economics, not as part of aesthetics; the interpretation and evaluation of particular works of art are a matter for art criticism rather than for aesthetics; the chemistry of pigments is part of natural science rather than of aesthetics; and so on. From the point of view of traditional aesthetics, one might well wonder what makes feminist aesthetics *aesthetics* at all, rather than ethics, social and political theory, or art criticism.

In order to regard feminist aesthetics as aesthetics, it may seem, we need to show that aesthetics is not, or should not be, as isolated from other subject matters as much modern aesthetics has taken itself to be. A good deal of modern aesthetics has taken itself to be *autonomous*. The term "autonomy" here is broad and not terribly clear. I shall use it to describe the general view that artworks may and should be studied and appreciated as objects in their own right, without regard to the causes of their production, their historical context, their effects on an audience, or even their relation to the (rest of the) real world, and, moreover, that the contemplation or study of artworks should appeal only to some of the properties of the artwork, namely its aesthetic properties—as opposed especially to its moral properties, but also to its economic or physical or practical properties.[3] Harold Osborne describes the view as involving:

> the concentration of attention on the work of art as a thing in its own right, an artifact with standards and functions of its own, and not an instrument made to further purposes which could equally be promoted otherwise than by art objects. . . . A work of art, it is now held, is in concept an artifact made for the purpose of being appreciated in the special mode of aesthetic contemplation; and although particular works of art

---

[3] The doctrine of aesthetic autonomy seems to have its origins in the eighteenth century, especially in the work of Kant; it is closely related to the nineteenth-century notion of "art for art's sake," and versions of it have played a role in the twentieth century in the "New Criticism" and, more recently, in poststructuralist criticism. For the early history of the notion, see the interesting Chapter 22, "Art for Art's Sake," of William K. Wimsatt and Cleanth Brooks, *Literary Criticism: A Short History* (New York: Random House, 1957).

may be intended to do other things and may in fact serve other purposes as well as this, the excellence of any work of art *as art* is assessed in terms of its suitability for such contemplation. This is what is meant by claiming that art is autonomous: it is not assessed by external standards applicable elsewhere, but by standards of its own.[4]

As this quotation suggests, the doctrine in question is often described as the doctrine that *art* is autonomous, but this is misleading. The artwork *itself* is not held to be independent of its context, its causes and effects, and so on. Rather, the point is that the appropriate *examination* of art *as art* is an examination which abstracts from or ignores these factors. That is, what is held to be independent of external factors is not the artwork itself, but rather its appropriate study or contemplation. In short, it is *aesthetics* rather than art which is held to be autonomous.

It is no accident that feminists have attacked the view that aesthetics is an autonomous discipline.[5] For the autonomy of aesthetics seems to show that any relation art might bear to the oppression of women is irrelevant to its aesthetic value. Were women oppressed in the production of the work, or by the actions of people influenced by the work? No matter; the concern of aesthetics is the work itself, not its causes or effects. Are women represented by an artwork in false and degrading ways? Again, no matter, for, first, the work says nothing about the real world but merely sets up a fictional world; or, second, if the work can be construed as saying something about the world, nevertheless its representational content is irrelevant to its aesthetic value; or, third, even if representational content is relevant to aesthetic value, *moral* evaluations of this content are irrelevant to the artwork's value *as art*. To make the case that the oppressive character of some artworks is aesthetically relevant, it seems, feminist aesthetics will have to challenge the doctrine of aesthetic autonomy.

I will be arguing in this essay in favor of two specific kinds of insulation of the aesthetic, two ways in which aesthetics is autonomous. I will suggest, first, that the history of production of a work of art is relevant to its artistic value only by way of its effects on the work's sensory properties or its content, and second, that the content of a fictional work of art says nothing about the real world, but only describes a fictional world. Both of these doctrines threaten to render at least some facts about women's oppression irrelevant to the philosophy of art. But I will also argue

---

[4] Harold Osborne, *Aesthetics and Art Theory: An Historical Introduction* (New York: Dutton, 1970), pp. 262–63.

[5] Devereaux's brief discussion of this topic in "Oppressive Texts" is much amplified and developed in her helpful article "The Philosophical and Political Implications of the Feminist Critique of Aesthetic Autonomy," in Glynis Carr, ed., *"Turning the Century": Feminist Theory in the 1990s* (Lewisburg, Pa.: Bucknell University Press, 1992). The specific doctrines I will describe as "autonomy principles," however, are different from any Devereaux discusses.

that the insulation provided by these principles is not as thick as might at first appear: Feminist criticisms of art are sometimes legitimate aesthetic criticisms despite the fact that in the respects I have mentioned aesthetics is autonomous.

This conclusion opens up the possibility of a kind of reconciliation between feminist aesthetics and traditional aesthetics. Feminist aesthetics need not overthrow the two autonomy doctrines I will defend in order to legitimize itself, and at the same time traditional aesthetics cannot employ the doctrines in question to dismiss feminist aesthetics as an impostor. Of course, the two doctrines I will discuss express only two of the many ways in which aesthetics has been held to be autonomous, and the doctrine of autonomy is only one of many traditional doctrines of aesthetics called into question by feminists. But my admittedly limited conclusion may give some reason to hope that feminist aesthetics and traditional aesthetics will in the end turn out to be more compatible than many have thought.

II. Oppression and the Production of Art

Can oppressive treatment of women in the production of a work of art affect the artistic value of the work of art itself? The view that aesthetic value is autonomous, that we can and should determine an artwork's aesthetic value without considering such external facts as how the work came to be, seems to provide a powerful reason for insisting on a negative answer to this question. In this section I will defend a restricted version of the independence of aesthetic value from history, while arguing that this principle is compatible with the view that in some important cases, oppression of women in the production of art is aesthetically relevant.

A. The Nymph of Fontainebleau   Let us begin with an example from the realm of sculpture. The following memorable account may be found in the autobiography of the sixteenth-century Italian goldsmith and sculptor Benvenuto Cellini. Cellini describes asking one Pagolo Micceri to keep watch both over Cellini's property and over "that poor young girl Caterina; I keep her principally for my art's sake, since I cannot do without a model; but being a man also, I have used her for my pleasures, and it is possible that she may bear me a child."[6] Pagolo later sleeps with Caterina. Enraged, Cellini at first threatens to kill him, then forces him to marry Caterina. There follows the incident in which I am principally interested. Cellini writes:

> If I did not confess that in some of these episodes I acted wrongly, the world might think I was not telling the truth about those in which I say I acted rightly. Therefore I admit that it was a mistake to inflict so singular

[6] Benvenuto Cellini, *Autobiography of Benvenuto Cellini*, trans. John Addington Symonds (New York: Modern Library, n.d.), p. 334.

a vengeance upon Pagolo Micceri. . . . Not satisfied with having made him take a vicious drab to wife, I completed my revenge by inviting her to sit to me as a model, and dealing with her thus. I gave her thirty sous a day, paid in advance, and a good meal, and obliged her to pose for me naked. Then I made her serve my pleasure, out of spite against her husband, jeering at them both the while. Furthermore, I kept her for hours together in position, greatly to her discomfort. This gave her as much annoyance as it gave me pleasure; for she was beautifully made, and brought me much credit as a model. At last, noticing that I did not treat her with the same consideration as before her marriage, she began to grumble and talk big in her French way about her husband. . . . [T]he wretch redoubled her insulting speeches, always prating big about her husband, till she goaded me beyond the bounds of reason. Yielding myself up to blind rage, I seized her by the hair, and dragged her up and down my room, beating and kicking her till I was tired. . . . When I had well pounded her she swore that she would never visit me again. Then for the first time I perceived that I had acted very wrongly; for I was losing a grand model, who brought me honour through my art. Moreover, when I saw her body all torn and bruised and swollen, I reflected that, even if I persuaded her to return, I should have to put her under medical treatment for at last a fortnight before I could make use of her. [The next morning Caterina returns.] Afterwards I began to model from her, during which occurred some amorous diversions; and at last, just at the same hour as on the previous day, she irritated me to such a pitch that I gave her the same drubbing. So we went on several days, repeating the old round like clockwork. There was little or no variation in the incidents. (pp. 344–47)

Let us ignore questions about Cellini's reliability as a source.[7] And let us pass over a number of disturbing features of this story—the way in which Cellini regards his torment of Caterina as an injury to her husband rather than to her; the fact that he apparently believes he acted wrongly only because he placed himself at risk of "losing a grand model"; the fact that his sexual relationship with Caterina consists, as he cheerfully writes, in his having "used her for my pleasures"; his apparent failure to see anything out of the ordinary in his becoming furious because Caterina brags about her husband, or in his acting on this fury by beating her.

B. First Autonomy Principle: The Independence of Value from History
The incident is useful for my purposes because during the modeling sessions in question, Cellini was sculpting what has come to be a famous work, the *Nymph of Fontainebleau,* designed to appear over a doorway but now on display in the Louvre. The question I want to ask is whether Cellini's mistreatment of Caterina while producing the *Nymph* has any

---

[7] Much of Cellini's autobiography seems incredible to the contemporary reader. But John Pope-Hennessy, observing that the book's credibility is often questioned, indicates his own belief that "almost every direct statement in the *Life* (direct as distinct from reported statement) is correct." John Pope-Hennessy, *Cellini* (New York: Abbeville Press, 1985), p. 13.

aesthetic significance. Does it affect the way we ought to see the work? My own view is that it does not. Granted, it has had an effect on the way I *do*, in fact, see the work: I cannot now look at photographs of the *Nymph* without thinking about Caterina, and without trying to glean from the *Nymph*'s features some sense of what Caterina herself might have been like. But isn't this strictly irrelevant to the properties the object has *as an artwork*? Examining the *Nymph* to discover what Caterina looked like seems exactly on a par with, say, studying ancient Greek statues of athletes to glean information about the sports popular at the time[8]—both endeavors may be intrinsically interesting, but they are at best indirectly relevant to the way in which we view the object as a work of art. The artistic value of the *Nymph*, I would suggest, is unaffected by Cellini's mistreatment of Caterina in producing the work.

This conclusion is underwritten by a version of the autonomy doctrine which holds that the history of production of a work can affect its value only indirectly, by virtue of affecting properties of the work itself. If this is correct, then oppressive treatment of women in the production of a work will affect the artistic value[9] of the work only to the extent that it leads the artist to produce a work which is, say, uglier or tawdrier or more vacuous or inane than it would otherwise have been.

This formulation of the doctrine will not do, however. It is completely empty to say merely that the history of production of a work is relevant to its value only to the extent that it affects properties of the work itself. *Which* properties of the work itself? After all, *having a certain history* is a property of the *Nymph*, and Caterina's beatings certainly affect *that*! We could say that a work's history affects its value only to the extent that the history affects the work's *artistically relevant* properties. If "artistically relevant" merely means something like "relevant to artistic value," however, the doctrine has an unpleasantly circular character. If the principle is to have any content, we need an independent way of specifying which properties are artistically relevant. I suggest that there are really two such properties. First, there is the work's *appearance*, including under this heading the way the object appears to any of the senses, not just its appearance

---

[8] Of course, the knowledge thereby gleaned might be *indirectly* relevant to the aesthetic properties of artworks; for instance, once we learned from whatever source about sports and the way they were practiced, such knowledge might enable us to characterize particular sculptures as realistic or idealized.

[9] I use the terms "artistic value" and "aesthetic value," and the terms "artistic property" and "aesthetic property," interchangeably. The term "aesthetic" in these contexts has the virtue of greater familiarity, but runs the risk of misleading, since historically and etymologically "aesthetic" properties have been understood to be restricted to properties of a work's appearance. The terms "artistic value" and "artistic property," though they sound a bit unnatural, have the virtue of suggesting precisely the notions I have in mind: "Artistic value" is the value of a work as art; an "artistic property" is a property relevant to a work's status as a work of art.

to the sense of sight. In the case of a sculpture, for example, such properties as shape and texture are directly relevant to the appearance of the
sculpture. Second, in addition to the work's appearance, its meaning or
content is artistically relevant.[10] This second artistically relevant property,
content, does not reduce to the first, appearance, since content may be affected by features of the work's history or context that do not directly affect the work's appearance. We know for example that the *Nymph* illustrates a legend about the origin of Fountainebleau.[11] But this fact is not
completely determined by the shape, size, texture, and so on of the
work. It depends as well on facts about the legends of the region and
their influence on Cellini's creation of the work.

We are left, then, with the following version of the principle that
value is independent of history: Facts about a work's history are irrelevant to its artistic value *unless* they affect *either* its appearance *or* its
content. I think that, provided we construe the notion of "content"
broadly, this principle is correct—though it must be admitted that the
notion of content, so construed, is not as clear as one might wish.[12] I
intend the notion to include *at least* linguistic representation, pictorial
depiction, and the expression of emotion.

The autonomy principle I have just formulated has affinities with
more radical principles which have been widely accepted. The New
Critical doctrine that the artist's intention is irrelevant to the interpretation of a work of art,[13] and the poststructuralist doctrine of the "death of
the author,"[14] may both be seen as effecting a similar, though more extreme, separation of the work from its genesis. These affinities may or

[10] This has of course been denied, notably by Clive Bell: "If a representative form has
value, it is as form, not as representation. The representative element in a work of art
may or may not be harmful; always it is irrelevant" (Bell, *Art* [New York: Capricorn
Books, 1958], p. 27). On Bell's view, aesthetic value is independent not only of history,
but also of representational content. But for rhetorical purposes, I need not defend my
view that content is relevant, since I am defending a less extreme autonomy principle
against those who would reject the autonomy of aesthetics altogether.

[11] Pope-Hennessy, op. cit., p. 137.

[12] It is also not clear to me precisely what sort of effect on the content of a work its history must have in order to be relevant to its artistic worth. For instance, suppose that
Cellini had mistreated Caterina deliberately in order to produce a certain kind of expression which he could then sculpt, as the photographer Karsh is reported to have
stolen Churchill's cigar just before photographing him to produce the precise look of
outrage he wanted for the portrait. Would this affect the artistic value of the *Nymph*? If
so, how?

[13] The classic source is of course William K. Wimsatt and Monroe C. Beardsley, "The
Intentional Fallacy," in Wimsatt, *The Verbal Icon: Studies in the Meaning of Poetry* (Lexington,
Ky.: University of Kentucky Press, 1954).

[14] See Roland Barthes, "The Death of the Author," in Barthes, *Image-Music-Text*, trans.
Stephen Heath (London: Fontana, 1977), pp. 142–48. In the context of film criticism, see the
discussion in Chapter 4, "Authorship," of Robert Lapsley and Michael Westlake, *Film
Theory: An Introduction* (Manchester: Manchester University Press, 1988).

may not be seen as support for the principle. Affinities aside, why should we accept the principle? The main attraction of the view, I think, is simply the thought that, if the notion of a discipline devoted to the study of art as art is to make any sense at all, there must be some way of discriminating between features of artworks which are the proper concern of that discipline and features which are not. Indeed, if the notion of an artwork itself is to have any content, there must be a distinction between features of an object which are relevant to its status as an artwork, and features of the object which have nothing to do with that status. If so, then there must be some autonomy principle which states that certain features of artworks are not related to their status as artworks. Any particular proposal about how to distinguish relevant from irrelevant features will be more controversial than the simple claim that some such principle is true. But I offer my principle as a reasonable first approximation, since appearance and content are the features which figure most prominently in discussions of art in criticism and in aesthetics. In particular cases, the clearly relevant facts I can think of all seem to pertain either to a work's appearance or to its content.[15]

C. Pornography   I think that our first autonomy principle is correct: The artistic value of a work *is* independent of its history of production. I am quite content to accept the consequence that the artistic value of the *Nymph* is unaffected by Caterina's mistreatment during its production. I turn now, however, to a second example in which women are oppressed in the production of works of art—an example which I find more troubling and more puzzling than that of Cellini and Caterina. The example I have in mind is that of certain sorts of pornography—namely pornographic films depicting abusive treatment of women, produced by recording on film acts which are genuinely abusive of women.[16] Of course

[15] I don't mean to be dogmatic about this. There *may* be further kinds of facts which are relevant. For example, the *originality* of a work may be germane to its value; originality clearly isn't a matter of appearance, and perhaps is also not a feature of the work's content. Similarly, in the performing arts, difficulty of execution may be an aesthetically relevant quality which does not affect the appearance or content of a work. The crucial thing is that there must be a distinction between relevant and irrelevant facts. My suspicion is that, whatever the right account of the distinction turns out to be, it will classify Caterina's oppression on the "irrelevant" side.

[16] One might insist that pornography is not art. Perhaps some of it is not. But I don't see how one could describe, say, a typical Hollywood movie as art and still insist that the better productions of the pornographers are not. At any rate, precisely the same points I will be making about pornographic films could be made about nonpornograhic films. For example, it may be that the fictional mistreatment of the Peruvian Indians who pushed a steamboat over a mountain in Werner Herzog's movie *Fitzcarraldo* was produced in part by filming real mistreatment. (See "Art of Darkness," *The Progressive* 46 [August 1982]: 20–21; George Dolis and Ingrid Weiland, "The Floating Opera," *Film Comment* 18 [September–October 1982]: 56–59.)

the abusive acts performed in the course of making such a film are objectionable. But what effect does their existence have on the artistic value of the resulting pornographic film?

Feminist critics of pornography often stress that pornographic films at least sometimes are produced in ways that abuse women.[17] Here is Catherine MacKinnon: "Pornography is . . . routinely defended as 'fantasy,' meaning not real. It is real: the sex that makes it is real and is often abuse, and the sex that it makes is sex and is often abuse."[18] And compare this vivid passage from Andrea Dworkin's book *Pornography: Men Possessing Women:*

> This book is distinguished from most other books on pornography by its bedrock conviction that the power is real, the cruelty is real, the sadism is real, the subordination is real: the political crime against women is real. . . . In this book, I wanted to dissect male dominance; do an autopsy on it, but it wasn't dead. Instead, there were artifacts—films, photographs, books—an archive of evidence and documentation of crimes against women. This was a living archive, commercially alive, carnivorous in its use of women, saturating the environment of daily life, explosive and expanding, vital because it was synonymous with sex for the men who made it and the men who used it—men so arrogant in their power over us that they published the pictures of what they did to us, how they used us, expecting submission from us, compliance; we were supposed to follow the orders implicit in the pictures.[19]

This passage raises more issues than I will be able to discuss. But at this point, notice that Dworkin, like MacKinnon, stresses that the acts which pornographic films record are real acts between real people. The films are typically, of course, fictions; the characters in the films are imaginary, the plots invented. Nevertheless, these fictional characters and events are portrayed on film by recording real events involving real people. So, for example, Linda Marchiano, who appeared in the infamous pornographic movie *Deep Throat* under the name Linda Lovelace, has claimed that her treatment in the production of the film was deeply abusive—indeed, that "every time someone watches that film, they are watching me being raped."[20]

The principle of the independence of value from history would seem to suggest that the reality of the abuse involved in producing a film is irrelevant to the artistic value of the film. Given two similar films of fic-

---

[17] It may be that radical feminist critics overestimate the proportion of pornography of which this is true. For some relevant data, see Ronald J. Berger, Patricia Searles, and Charles E. Cottle, *Feminism and Pornography* (New York: Praeger, 1991), pp. 95–96.

[18] Catherine MacKinnon, "Sexuality, Pornography, and Method," *Ethics* 99 (1989): 314–46, at 342.

[19] Andrea Dworkin, *Pornography: Men Possessing Women* (New York: E.P. Dutton, 1989), pp. xxxvii–xxxviii.

[20] Quoted in Dworkin, *Pornography*, p. xvi.

tional abusive scenes, one of them produced by filming real abuse and one of them produced by filming feigned abuse, the autonomy principle suggests that, so long as their content is the same, this difference between the two has no bearing on their relative artistic merit, though of course it has a great deal to do with the relative *moral* status of the two filming episodes. What matters to the artistic merit of the film is only the features of the fictional scene it depicts, not the features of the real scene the cameras recorded. (One might argue—perhaps Dworkin and MacKinnon would—that the filming of pornography is *always* abusive of women. I am skeptical about this, but my point does not depend on denying it. The same point could be made with respect to nonpornographic fictions which portray abusive treatment, and it surely is not the case that *any* depiction of abuse must itself be abusive. Moreover, even in the pornographic case, there are presumably *more* and *less* abusive ways of depicting abuse; the disturbing point about the autonomy principle is that it seems to imply that this difference is irrelevant aesthetically.)

This view leads to consequences I find it difficult to accept. Suppose that a filmmaker wants to make a fictional film about a male character, "Bill," who beats a female character, "Jane." He has in his studio two actors named, coincidentally, "Bill" and "Jane." (Or maybe it isn't a coincidence; these are not experienced actors, and it may be easier for them to remember their characters' names if they coincide with their own.) He makes his movie by having Bill actually beat Jane, and recording the beating on film. Suppose that the same filmmaker also wants to make a documentary film recording the beating. He can set up a second camera (call it "camera B," and call the first one "camera A") and record the very same scene through it. Now, although cameras A and B are recording the same scene, the film produced by camera A is a fiction, while the film produced by camera B is a documentary. Isn't there something odd about this? Odder still, suppose it occurs to our filmmaker that it is a needless waste of resources to have two cameras recording the same scene. Why not make do with one? Then two copies of the same film can be made, one a documentary and one a fiction. In a final burst of economy, the filmmaker may even make do with a single copy of the film, simply changing the way he labels it depending on where it is to be shown.

It seems a cruel joke to suggest that a film of a beating can, by a simple relabeling, be turned into a harmless fiction. And it is precisely this cruel joke that feminists like Dworkin and MacKinnon argue is being told by many pornographic filmmakers. What the pornographers claim are harmless fictions are precisely what Dworkin insists are in fact "an archive of evidence and documentation of crimes against women."

D. A Way Out: Films as Recorded Performances   What shall we say about this? We have three choices. First, we might bite the bullet and concede that, odd as it may seem, there is a world of difference between the films recorded by camera A and camera B—one is a fiction, the other not—while at the same insisting that there is no artistic difference between the fictional beating produced by recording a real beating, and the fictional beating produced by recording a feigned beating. Second, we might give up the principle of autonomy. Perhaps the two fictions are different in some artistically relevant way, despite being the same in appearance and content. Or, third, we might give up the idea that the content of a film is separable from the facts about the actual scene the camera records. Perhaps you cannot prevent a film from representing or being about a real beating simply by relabeling it as about a fiction. In that case we can preserve the principle of autonomy while still insisting that the two fictional films are as different as can be, and that the products of cameras A and B are alike in that each represents a real beating (though one of them *also* represents a fictional beating).

I think that the third option is the correct one. The autonomy principle is correct: The only things relevant to an artwork's aesthetic value are its appearance and its content. But the content of the film cannot be insulated from the difference between a real and a feigned beating. A film is not *just* a presentation of fictional characters engaged in fictional actions. It is also a recording of a performance. The artistically relevant features of the film include features of the performance. In criticizing the film, we quite legitimately talk not only of the characters, but also of the actors who play them, and we distinguish between the traits of the two: It's one thing to say that a particular character was inexpressive and unemotional; it is another to say that an actor's performance was wooden.

In this respect, films are like stage productions, and unlike novels (and unlike some painting, sculpture, and poetry). When we watch a stage play, the aesthetic object to which we attend is not simply the fiction presented, but also the presentation, the way that flesh-and-blood actors portray the fictional characters they represent. I want to suggest that in some ways, a fictional film is like a documentary film which records a stage production. (The thinness of the line between the two may perhaps be suggested by a film like Bergman's *The Magic Flute,* which is a kind of borderline case.) There is more to a film than this, of course. Many of the aesthetic features of the film will not have been present in the performance: The cinematography, the editing, the special effects are all aesthetically relevant features of the film which have little or nothing to do with the recorded performance. But the addition of these features does not erase the film's documentary character, does not negate the fact that among the functions of the film is to record performances, which are real actions of real people.

Now, let us return to the difference between real and feigned abuse in the production of what is claimed to be a work of art. But let us shift the scene for a moment: Consider now a stage production. We are sitting in the audience watching a play in which a woman is beaten. In version one of this example, the actors perform the fictional beating by feigning a beating. In version two, the beating is not feigned but genuine: The woman is genuinely being beaten before our eyes. Now, in this second case, we are liable to refuse to take the real beating as just part of the play. We will want to call the police, or to jump up on stage and stop the beating. But suppose we are somehow convinced to take the real beating as just a particularly vivid way of performing a fictional beating. Perhaps all the actors, including the victim, have agreed beforehand that the performance will be conducted in this way. (If Chris Burden can have himself shot as part of a work of "body art," surely a beating can also be part of a work of art. And if actors can portray fictional walking and talking by means of real walking and talking, surely it is possible in principle to portray a fictional beating by means of a real beating.) Despite our acceptance of the beating as part of the performance, however, we will legitimately feel not only moral indignation at the beating, but also that the resulting artwork is aesthetically inferior.

In saying this, I am explicitly rejecting one doctrine which has sometimes been described as the autonomy of art, namely the doctrine that aesthetic value is independent of moral value. This is the idea that art "might draw off by itself and be content with an emphatic assertion of autonomy—its own kind of intrinsic worth . . . apart from, and perhaps in defiance of, the rival norms of ethics and politics."[21] To show that real abusive treatment is explicitly represented in a film is not enough to show that the film is *aesthetically* inferior; one must also show that our negative moral evaluation should carry over to our aesthetic evaluation. I wish I had more to say in defense of this view; all I can offer at present is that some moral views are not just false but ugly, and some actions are not just immoral but repulsive. Of course, under some circumstances even ugliness and repulsiveness can be turned to worthwhile artistic purposes. But in the absence of a rather special redeeming context, they are likely to be aesthetically debilitating. As much as I would like to have more to offer on this point, perhaps in the present dialectical context I need no more, since my main purpose is to defend and discuss the consequences of two principles of aesthetic autonomy; my dialectical opponents, the critics of autonomy, may reasonably be presumed to grant the relevance of moral to aesthetic concerns.

The point I have been making about the difference between two staged portrayals of a fictional beating applies as well to films. Recall Linda Marchiano's claim that she was raped in the production of *Deep Throat*. When we reach the scene in the movie in which this occurs, we

---

[21] Wimsatt and Brooks, op. cit., p. 476.

cannot leap onto the stage and stop the rape. We might take the view that the movie stops being an artwork at that point, just as we might regard the play as effectively over when the real beating commences. But suppose that we are persuaded to take the film as an art object. It remains the case that it records a real rape, and this fact is not only morally relevant but also aesthetically relevant.[22]

Let us return to our original question: Can oppressive treatment of women in the production of a work of art affect the artistic value of the work of art itself? It now appears that we can answer this question in the affirmative *even if*, as our first autonomy principle maintains, the artistic value of a work is independent of its history of production except insofar as that history affects the work's appearance or content.

III. Oppression and the Content of Art

Let us turn now to a second question: Can fictional artworks be oppressive by virtue of their content? I will defend a second principle of autonomy which may seem to show that they cannot. I will then argue that in fact, the truth of the principle is compatible with the view that artworks may constitute assertions of oppressive claims.

A. Second Autonomy Principle: The Independence of Fiction from Reality As in our previous section, a fairly plausible autonomy principle would seem to insulate fictions from the real world in such a way that they could not possibly be oppressive. The principle is this: Fictions represent fictional worlds; they do not represent the actual world. Fictions may of course *resemble* the actual world in various ways, and our efforts to discover their similarities to and differences from the actual world may lead us to surprising discoveries. But fictions do not *say* anything about the real world, so they cannot be oppressive or libelous or slanderous or defamatory or degrading—nor can there be "orders implicit in the pictures," as Dworkin puts it.

In defense of the independence of fiction from reality, I would offer the following argument. No one will maintain that *every* representation in a fiction is to be taken to be an accurate portrayal of the world. At most, the defender of the view that fictions should be taken to represent the world accurately may hold that some represented features are to be taken

---

[22] I suspect that this fact is not of much interest to Dworkin—nor is there any reason it should be. For Dworkin does not take herself to be doing aesthetics; she is interested in moral and political issues rather than artistic ones. Regardless of one's view about whether the artistic content of a film includes facts about the real people and events filmed, a film which records real abuse will constitute evidence of that abuse in the way that footprints or tire tracks constitute evidence of the presence of people or automobiles.

to be accurate and some are not. This raises the problem of how we can determine which features are which. I take the following to be a useful way to think about this problem. Works of history or science carry a kind of implicit "It is true that . . ." operator. We are to take the representations they contain to be at least attempts at an accurate portrayal of the world. Similarly, works of fiction carry an implicit "It is fictional that . . ." or "It is true in this fiction that . . ." operator. Now, there *can* be mixed cases— cases in which some sentences of a work[23] are to be taken to be fictional and others to be truthful. For example, it is common for philosophical essays to include brief fictional examples designed to illustrate a point. (For concreteness, consider Judith Jarvis Thomson's famous essay on abortion, in which the following interjection occurs: "It sounds plausible. But now let me ask you to imagine this. You wake up in the morning and find yourself back to back in bed with an unconscious violinist . . . [whose] circulatory system [has been] plugged into yours."[24] The phrase "imagine this" notifies the reader that what follows will be a fictional interlude in a largely nonfiction piece.) But it is *very* difficult to imagine a mixed case which is predominantly fiction rather than predominantly nonfiction. In the philosophical case, we have a work we take to be implicitly prefaced with "It is true that. . . ." Within this work, we hit a paragraph or two implicitly prefaced with "It is fictional that. . . ." Now we have one operator embedded inside the scope of another, yielding "It is true that it is fictional that. . . ." If it is true that it is fictional that a violinist is plugged into you, then it is fictional that a violinist is plugged into you. So far so good: A little fiction within a nonfiction work seems entirely possible.

But now consider a predominantly fictional case. The entire fiction is implicitly prefaced with "It is fictional that. . . ." Now the author attempts to insert some material we are to take to be factual. How can the text indicate that this material is to be taken to be factual? It must include something tantamount to the "It is true that . . ." operator. The result is again that one operator is embedded within the scope of another, yielding "It is fictional that it is true that. . . ." But to say that it is fictional that something is true is precisely *not* to say that it is true! Any claim to truth *within* a fiction is just one more part of the fiction. And of course creators of fictions take advantage of this fact all the time, producing fictionally true prefaces, fictionally true footnotes, fictionally true dictionary or encyclopedia entries, and so on. These fictionally true items may happen also to be actu-

---

[23] I take a literary work as my example here because it is difficult to formulate the point in a general enough way to be neutral as between literary fiction, cinematic fiction, painted fiction, and so on.
[24] Judith Jarvis Thomson, "A Defense of Abortion," *Philosophy and Public Affairs* 1 (1971), reprinted in Marshall Cohen, Thomas Nagel, and Thomas Scanlon, eds., *The Rights and Wrongs of Abortion* (Princeton: Princeton University Press, 1974), pp. 3–22, at pp. 4–5.

ally true, but it cannot be part of the content of the fiction that they are (really) true.[25]

B. Devereaux on Movies   If this second autonomy principle is correct, then some of Devereaux's criticisms of Hollywood movies must be questioned. Devereaux distinguishes between different levels of feminist criticism of the content of movies. At the simplest level, feminists "attacked the Hollywood film for its patriarchal content." These films perpetuated a "mythology [which] defined the value of women as their value to men." In particular, these films portrayed women as falling into one of several stereotypical categories, such as "the Good Girl, the Vamp, and the Dutiful Wife."

This indictment is problematic even apart from considerations of autonomy. In the first place, a particular film cannot be said to imply that all women fall into one of these categories simply because it portrays women who do. No doubt there are real women who fit these stereotypes reasonably well, women who value themselves largely in terms of their value to men. So a particular film, in portraying women who fit the stereotypes, may simply be presenting fictional characters who in fact are significantly like (some) real women. Presumably, then, the indictment must be an indictment, not of any particular film taken in isolation, but of "the Hollywood film" taken as a whole: The objection must be that since all (most? many?) movies present women only in terms of their value to men, the body of Hollywood films taken as a whole implies that this is women's only value. But this would be a difficult claim to defend, as Devereaux herself recognizes. Although she writes at one point that "any alternative point of view, one which might tell a different tale or tell the same tale differently, was effectively excluded," by the next paragraph she is acknowledging that "not all films perpetuate patriarchy. . . . The strong-headed heroines typically played by Katharine Hepburn, Lauren

---

[25] There may be special cases in which we have conventions dictating that certain portions of a predominantly fictional work are to be taken to be factual. Easy cases are prefaces and postscripts to literary works; consider Henry James's long introductions to the New York edition of his novels. This is an easy case because the introductions are outside the fiction proper; the initial "It is fictional that . . ." operator does not take effect until *after* the introduction. A little more difficult is a case like Eliot's footnotes to "The Waste Land," but again we may take the notes as simply external to the work itself. A very puzzling case is Henry Fielding's essays in *Tom Jones*. Perhaps we are to take them as nonfiction intermingled with the fiction. But it is very hard to be certain; for all we can glean from the work itself, they may be intended to be taken as the product of a fictional narrator, and so to be just more fiction. The only case I can think of in which clearly nonfictional bits occur within a predominantly fictional work is the case of fables in which a little story ends with an explicitly stated "moral." But this is surely a very special case.

Bacall and Bette Davis do not conform to this stereotype, nor do films such as Howard Hawks' *His Girl Friday."*

What we are left with is the claim that many or most Hollywood films, though not all, present their female characters from a masculine perspective according to which their chief, perhaps only, value is their value to men. This will permit us to say neither that any particular film endorses the view that all (real) women are valuable only insofar as they are valuable to men, nor that "the Hollywood film" as a whole endorses this view. This is not to say that frequent stereotyping is innocent or innocuous. (A very plausible account of what precisely is wrong with it has been offered by Noël Carroll.)[26] But the problems with stereotyping do not have to do with what films say, or film in general says, about women.

If the content of a fictional artwork says nothing about the real world, as the autonomy principle claims, however, then an even stronger conclusion is possible: Not only is it unlikely on empirical grounds that "the Hollywood film" asserts or implies that women's only value is their value to men, but no (fictional) film or set of films *could* assert or imply this. Characters in the film may assert, or reveal by their actions that they believe, that women are valuable only insofar as they are valuable to men, but that is not the same thing as the film itself endorsing this view. And, according to the defender of autonomy, this is what the film cannot do. All it can do is to present an imaginary world, and let viewers connect this imaginary world to the real one in any way they like.

The insulation of fictional content from claims about the real world also bears on other criticisms Devereaux offers. Citing the work of Mary Ann Doane, Devereaux writes that "at a more complex level, the Hollywood film functions as a 'recuperative strategy' designed to return the wayward woman to the fold." She goes on to say that in such films, "The message is that for a woman, unlike for a man, the satisfactions of solitude, work, or adventures cannot compare to those of caring for husband and children." But if films are insulated from the real world in the way the autonomy principle suggests, then they cannot carry "messages" about the real world. Again, Devereaux suggests that Hollywood films degrade women by portraying them *"only* as objects of aesthetic contemplation." This complaint too seems to presuppose that such films make general assertions about actual women. Portraying fictional characters as only objects of aesthetic contemplation may be degrading to the fictional characters, but cannot be degrading to actual women unless portraying fictional charac-

---

[26] Noël Carroll, "The Image of Women in Film: A Defense of a Paradigm," *The Journal of Aesthetics and Art Criticism* 48 (1990): 349–60.

ters in this way expresses something about actual women rather than about fictional women—and this is precisely what the second autonomy principle says cannot happen.

C. Pornography Again Some feminist discussions of pornography also take the view that fictional material may nevertheless make assertions about real people. Helen Longino, in fact, *defines* pornography in a way which presumes this:

> Pornography . . . is verbal or pictorial material which represents or describes sexual behavior that is degrading or abusive to one or more of the participants *in such a way as to endorse the degradation*. . . . Pornography communicates its endorsement of the behavior it represents by various features of the pornographic context: the degradation of the female characters is represented as providing pleasure to the participant males and, even worse, to the participant females, and there is no suggestion that this sort of treatment of others is inappropriate to their status as human beings.[27]

Many other writers make similar claims, usually without doing as much as Longino to explain on what basis pornography is said to communicate an endorsement. Susan Brownmiller: "Pornography is the undiluted essence of anti-female propaganda."[28] Ann Garry: "Some pornographic films convey the message that all women really want to be raped, that their resisting struggle is not to be believed."[29] And we remember Dworkin's reference, quoted earlier, to "the orders implicit in the pictures."

All these claims are, I think, deeply problematic. Let us distinguish between two slightly different kinds of things pornography is supposed to assert. First, it is claimed to assert falsehoods about women, for example that all women want to be raped, or that women exist only for the satisfaction of men. Second, it is claimed to assert pernicious value judgments: that rape is a good thing, that women ought to be bound and

---

[27] Helen E. Longino, "Pornography, Oppression, and Freedom: A Closer Look," in Laura Lederer, ed., *Take Back the Night* (New York: Morrow, 1980), reprinted in Marilyn Pearsall, ed., *Women and Values: Readings in Recent Feminist Philosophy* (Belmont, Calif.: Wadsworth, 1986), pp. 167–76, at p. 169.

[28] Susan Brownmiller, *Against Our Will: Men, Women and Rape* (New York: Simon and Schuster, 1975), p. 374, quoted in Ann Garry, "Pornography and Respect for Women," *Social Theory and Practice* 4 (1978): 395–421, reprinted in Jeffrey Olen and Vincent Barry, ed., *Applying Ethics*, 4th ed. (Belmont, Calif.: Wadsworth, 1992), pp. 127–35, at p. 128.

[29] Garry, "Pornography and Respect for Women," op. cit., p. 128. Garry also writes that included among the most objectionable pornography are "movies which recommend that men rape women, molest children and puppies, and treat nonmasochists very sadistically" (p. 131).

tortured, and so on.[30] I claim that pornography does, and can do, neither of these things. Consider as an analogy the case of action films—the sort of films that star Arnold Schwarzenegger or Jean-Claude Van Damme or Sylvester Stallone. In these films, people often move their limbs through the air so fast they make a whistling sound, and blows to the face or body typically make a loud thwacking noise. Do the movies therefore represent the real world as working this way? Hardly! At most, they depict a world in which hitting someone in the face makes a thwacking noise, but they cannot assert that the world they depict is the actual world, or is like the actual world in this particular way.[31] The same point applies to moral features of the fictional world as well as to factual ones. In the world of action heroes, it may be an appropriate response to a perceived insult to punch the offending person in the face. I for one am quite prepared to cheer when a Schwarzenegger character punches an offensive boor for making an inappropriate remark. But although I accept this as appropriate behavior in the fictional world of certain films, I would be horrified if someone acted that way in the real world.[32] As I experience and interpret action films, the moral values presupposed in the fictional world are just further elements of the fiction; they may correspond to real values, but they need not. I believe this to be a common experience. And unless this common experience is missing something rather important, a film's acceptance of a particular set of values does not represent an implicit claim to the *truth* of the values it accepts. I would argue that, similarly, a pornographic film's depiction of a world in which it is a good thing to rape women does not constitute an assertion that in the actual world it is a good thing to rape women. Indeed, if the autonomy principle is correct, as I believe it to be, a film *could* not make this assertion, or any other.

Even films which may appear to be commentaries on the relation be-

[30] This is virtually the same distinction drawn by Alan Soble between the criticism of pornography that it defames women and the criticism that it endorses the degradation of women. Soble offers some valuable arguments against both of these criticisms—without, however, going quite as far as I would: Soble stresses that "I have not claimed that depictions . . . never implicitly or explicitly endorse." Alan Soble, "Pornography: Defamation and the Endorsement of Degradation," *Social Theory and Practice* 11 (1985): 61–87, at p. 79.

[31] Alex Neill has suggested to me that the thwacking noises are not even part of the fictional world, but function rather like the lines trailing behind an object in a cartoon which indicate that the object is moving quickly. The suggestion is that the thwacking noises, like the cartoon lines, are part of the representation, but not part of the fictional world represented. I would be surprised to discover, however, that this is a common way of "reading" action films.

[32] In fact, I *was* horrified when I read that Texas congressman Henry B. Gonzalez had in fact responded to a perceived insult in a restaurant near my university by punching the offender off his seat at the counter. I might add that I am puzzled by Thomas Nagel's remark that there's something peculiarly appropriate about a punch to the nose as a response to insult—footnote 6 of "War and Massacre," in Nagel's book *Mortal Questions* (Cambridge: Cambridge University Press, 1976), p. 66.

tween fiction and reality cannot really be said to represent the real world. Consider *The Last Action Hero*, a Schwarzenegger movie in which an action hero is transported from his fictional world into the "real" world, and is surprised by the differences between the two. In such a film, what we really have is a commentary on the relation between two fictional worlds, one of them a fiction "inside" the other. The relation between the fictional fiction and the fictional reality is, to be sure, analogous to the relation between fictional reality and real reality. But there is no way for a fiction to specify the respects in which it is like the real world and the respects in which it is not, so there is no way for a fiction to assert anything about reality.

The second autonomy doctrine, although I believe it to be correct, is bound to sound rather hollow in some contexts. Let me offer one example among many. In the movie *I Posed for* Playboy, several women decide to pose for *Playboy* magazine.[33] One of these women is the editor of the Yale student newspaper, a woman who has recently written an editorial protesting the presence of *Playboy* photographers on campus and urging students not to be photographed. She comes to realize that posing for the magazine can be a valuable affirmation of her independence and her femininity; in a monologue addressed directly to the audience, with the camera in a tight close-up on her face, she explains the reasons for her choice to pose and her satisfaction with that decision. It seems clear that the audience is supposed to find her reasons convincing. Moreover, it also seems clear that, in finding her reasons convincing, the audience is also supposed to recognize the potential value to real women of really posing for the real magazine. The movie, in short, seems to be more than a mere portrayal of a fictional world: It seems to make value judgments about the real world, and in fact to be a bit of propaganda for *Playboy* magazine.

Wayne C. Booth expresses a similar sense of the hollowness of appealing to the autonomy principle in his discussion of John Donne's "Song," which includes these lines: "Ride ten thousand daies and nights,/Till age snow white haires on thee,/Thou, when thou retorn'st, wilt tell mee/All strange wonders that befell thee,/And sweare/No where/Lives a woman true, and faire." Booth describes discussing the poem with "a large group of English teachers" and finding some of the women present defending something very like the autonomy principle we have been discussing:

> Some of those who thought of themselves as professional critics scoffed at the very idea of worrying about "message." Why should we let annoyance at the male poet's direct assertion that women are inherently false and fickle interfere with our aesthetic responses? One said, "I can

[33] I saw parts of this movie on network television. In what I would be surprised to learn was a coincidence, the movie played at the same time that another channel was showing a Miss Texas pageant.

enter imaginatively into the world of the poem just as well as any man. Besides, Donne is not speaking in his own person—he is creating a persona." Uh huh. Perhaps. Nobody could ever disprove the claim. But meanwhile we do know one thing for sure: many male readers, including at least one young male English teacher (myself years ago), have found in the poem a delightful reinforcement, from "high culture," of our "natural" sense of male superiority. Can we really claim that such a fact is irrelevant to critical talk about the poem's true worth *"as poetry"*?[34]

D. A Way Out: Semantics and Pragmatics   It can seem obvious that fictions do not say anything about the real world. Indeed, a number of accounts of the nature of fiction define fiction in terms of this sort of independence from reality.[35] On the other hand, it can seem equally obvious that the author of a fiction may, in creating the fiction, be asserting all sorts of things about the real world. As Kendall Walton notes:

> There is no reason why, in appropriate circumstances, one should not be able to make an assertion by writing fiction. Indeed there is a long tradition of doing just that. There is what we call didactic fiction—fiction used for instruction, advertising, propaganda, and so on. There is the not uncommon practice, even in ordinary conversation, of making a point by telling a story, of speaking in parables.[36]

Is there any way to reconcile these obvious, but apparently conflicting, views? Is there any way to account for our feeling that fictions can reinforce disagreeable values, or false beliefs, without abandoning the autonomy principle? I think that there is. What I would like to appeal to is a distinction analogous to the linguistic distinction between *semantics* and *pragmatics*.[37] We need to distinguish between the content of a film or other fiction, on the one hand, and the information it may be used pragmatically to express, on the other. To borrow Nathan Salmon's terminology,[38] we need to employ a distinction analogous to that between *semantically encoded* information and *pragmatically imparted* information.

---

[34] Wayne C. Booth, *The Company We Keep: An Ethics of Fiction* (Berkeley: University of California Press, 1988), p. 393.
[35] See especially Monroe C. Beardsley's account in *Aesthetics: Problems in the Philosophy of Criticism* (Indianapolis: Hackett, [1958] 1981), pp. 419–23. See also Beardsley's updating of his view in his 1980 Postscript to this book, at pp. xliv–xlviii.
[36] Kendall Walton, *Mimesis as Make-Believe: On the Foundations of the Representational Arts* (Cambridge: Harvard University Press, 1990), p. 78.
[37] The distinction we need is only analogous to the semantics/pragmatics distinction, since many fictions are presented largely in media which lack precise semantic rules. Paintings and movies may be fictional, but there isn't literally a semantics of painting or cinema. Nevertheless, there are general conventions which enable us to extract from a painting or a movie a description of a fictional scene or world, and there is a genuine distinction between these general conventions and the context-dependent ways in which such a painting or movie may be used to impart propositions which are not a part of its content.
[38] Nathan Salmon, *Frege's Puzzle* (Cambridge: MIT Press, 1986).

Consider some straightforward examples to get a sense for this distinction. If I say, to someone who has telephoned me, "Well, I don't want to run your phone bill up," my words do not have the semantic content "I would like to stop talking now," but they may pragmaticaly impart that information. If I say "Good question!" to a student in class, I have not said that I don't know the answer, but I may have pragmatically imparted the information that I do not. If, in response to the question, "Don't you think he's smart?" I respond, "He works very hard," my words do not mean that he isn't all that smart, but in all likelihood I do, by uttering them, impart the information that I don't believe he is smart.

Many literary devices rely on the distinction between pragmatics and semantics for their success. Consider, for example, Jonathan Swift's essay "A Modest Proposal." This essay is a textbook example of irony. But irony is a pragmatic, not a semantic, phenomenon.[39] Semantically, the piece expresses the view that eating children is an appropriate response to famine. But the view pragmatically imparted by the piece is quite the opposite. Again, metaphor is best understood pragmatically rather than semantically.[40] "Richard is a lion" semantically expresses only the proposition that Richard is a lion—an obvious falsehood. But this sentence may be used to pragmatically impart the proposition that, for example, Richard is brave.

The crucial distinction between semantic and pragmatic phenomena is that the semantic content of an expression is determined by general linguistic conventions about the meaning of expressions, while what is pragmatically imparted by a given utterance depends upon features of the context of the utterance. The semantic content of the same expression will remain the same from one use to the next, but its pragmatic content will vary with the context of the particular use. Thus the movie *Reefer Madness* presents a fictional world in which a few puffs of marijuana suffice to induce instant addiction and all sorts of bizarre behavior. It was originally used to pragmatically impart the idea that marijuana is a deeply dangerous drug which should be scrupulously avoided. By the time I was a college student, screenings of the movie were often used instead to pragmatically impart the idea that antidrug propaganda is often factually

---

[39] See H. P. Grice's brief discussion of irony in "Logic and Conversation," reprinted in Steven Davis, ed., *Pragmatics: A Reader* (New York: Oxford University Press, 1991), pp. 305–15, at p. 312; and Dan Sperber and Deirdre Wilson, "Irony and the Use-Mention Distinction," in Davis, ed., *Pragmatics*, pp. 550–63.

[40] There are by now a number of detailed accounts of metaphor which take it to be a pragmatic phenomenon. Two early and very influential pieces in this vein are Donald Davidson, "What Metaphors Mean," in Sheldon Sacks, ed., *On Metaphor* (Chicago: University of Chicago Press, 1979), pp. 29–46, and John R. Searle, "Metaphor," in Andrew Ortony, ed., *Metaphor and Thought* (Cambridge: Cambridge University Press, 1979), pp. 92–123. Both essays are reprinted in Davis, ed., *Pragmatics*, op. cit., along with relevant essays by Merrie Bergman and A. P. Martinich.

inaccurate and absurdly overstated.[41] The fictional world of the movie remains the same from screening to screening, but the relations between that fictional world and the real world which are pragmatically suggested may vary widely from one context to another.

The implication of this view for our evaluation of pornography is this. We cannot indict a *work* for its degrading or defamatory treatment of women. But we can indict an artist, or a producer or curator or anyone else for *using* a work to pragmatically impart a message which is defamatory or endorses degradation. This is, I think, a result feminists ought to applaud; it has the consequence that one may criticize a pornographer for using pornography to propagate falsehoods about women, while not criticizing a feminist who shows all or part of the pornographer's work in a critical context. Fictional works are not intrinsically truthful or untruthful any more than technological innovations are intrinsically good or bad: Everything hinges on how they are used.

IV. Conclusion

Devereaux suggests in her penultimate section that feminist aesthetics radically challenges a number of features of traditional aesthetics, and thus constitutes "a new paradigm" in aesthetics. My own suspicion is that Devereaux overstates the incompatibility of traditional and feminist aesthetics.

One of the challenges Devereaux notes is that "feminist theorists ask us to replace the conception of the artwork as an autonomous object . . . with a messier conception of art." My essay has largely been an attempt to take Devereaux's advice to "ponder how far the old model of aesthetics and the new are commensurable." I have tried to explore the extent to which two versions of the doctrine that aesthetics is autonomous protect art from feminist criticism. A diehard traditionalist might argue that these autonomy doctrines show that feminist aesthetics is simply not aesthetics at all; rather, it is "merely" social and political philosophy, or sociology, or art criticism. On the other hand, some feminists will insist that the autonomy doctrines are simply false; traditional aesthetics, which is committed to these doctrines, is moribund and needs to be replaced with feminist aesthetics. I hope to have shown one way to avoid both extremes, at

---

[41] Soble, in "Pornography: Defamation and the Endorsement of Degradation," cited above, also discusses *Reefer Madness* (p. 79). He uses the example to support the claim that "whether an item of pornography implicitly endorses degradation is partially a function of the nature of the audience" (p. 80). I would want to suggest instead that pornography itself never endorses anything, but that it can be *used* to pragmatically impart an endorsement. This view avoids the awkwardness of Soble's apparent view that content depends on features of the audience.

least with respect to these two specific doctrines. The autonomy principles are correct, I have suggested, so at least two of the challenged doctrines of traditional aesthetics survive criticism. But the autonomy principles do not do as much as one might have thought to protect art from
feminist criticism. The survival of traditional aesthetics may yet leave
room for feminist aesthetics.[42]

[42] I am indebted to Alex Neill for detailed and very helpful comments.

SUGGESTIONS FOR FURTHER READING

Battersby, Christine. *Gender and Genius: Towards a Feminist Aesthetics.* Bloomington:
Indiana University Press, 1989.

Beauvoir, Simone de. "Women and Creativity." In *French Feminist Thought,* ed. by
Toril Moi, Oxford: Blackwell, 1987.

Berger, John. *Ways of Seeing.* New York: Viking Press, 1973.

Brand, M., and Korsmeyer, C. *Feminism and Traditional Aesthetics.* Special Issue of
the *Journal of Aesthetics and Art Criticism* 48 (1990).

Broude, Norma, and Garrard, Mary D., eds. *The Expanding Discourse: Feminism and
Art History.* New York: Harper Collins, 1992.

Case, Sue-Ellen. "Toward a Butch-Femme Aesthetic." In *Making a Spectacle,* edited
by L. Hart. Ann Arbor: University of Michigan Press, 1989.

Devereaux, Mary. "The Philosophical and Political Implications of the Feminist
Critique of Aesthetic Autonomy." In *Turning the Century: Feminist Criticism in
the 1990s,* ed. by Glynis Carr. *Bucknell Review* 36 (1992): 164–86.

Devereaux, Mary. "Protected Space: Politics, Censorship, and the Arts." *Journal of
Aesthetics and Art Criticism* 51 (1993): 207–15.

Ecker, Gisela, ed. *Feminist Aesthetics.* Boston: Beacon Press, 1986.

Felski, Rita. *Beyond Feminist Aesthetics: Feminist Literature and Social Change.*
Cambridge: Harvard University Press, 1989.

Haskell, Molly. *From Reverence to Rape: The Treatment of Women in the Movies.*
Harmondsworth: Penguin Books, 1974.

Hess, Thomas, and Baker, Elizabeth, eds. *Art and Sexual Politics.* New York:
Macmillan, 1973.

Kaplan, E. Ann. "Is the Gaze Male?" In *Powers of Desire,* edited by Snitow, Stansell,
and Thompson. New York: Monthly Review Press, 1983.

Korsmeyer, C. "Pleasure: Reflections on Aesthetics and Feminism." *Journal of
Aesthetics and Art Criticism* 51 (1993): 199–206.

Korsmeyer, C., and Hein, H., eds. *Aesthetics in Feminist Perspective.* Bloomington:
Indiana University Press, 1993.

Kuhn, Annette. *Women's Pictures: Feminism and the Cinema.* London: Routledge
and Kegan Paul, 1982.

Lauretis, Teresa de. *Technologies of Gender: Essays on Theory, Film, and Fiction.*
Bloomington: University of Indiana Press, 1987.

Lippard, Lucy. *Mixed Blessings: New Art in a Multicultural America.* New York:
Pantheon, 1990.

McClary, Susan. *Feminine Endings: Music, Gender, and Sexuality.* Minneapolis: University of Minnesota Press, 1991.

Mulvey, Laura. *Visual and Other Pleasures.* Bloomington: Indiana University Press, 1989. (Includes her article "Visual Pleasure and Narrative Cinema," discussed in Devereaux's article in this section.)

Nochlin, Linda. *Women, Art and Power, and Other Essays.* New York: Harper and Row, 1988.

Owens, Craig. "The Discourse of Others: Feminists and Postmodernism." In *The Anti-Aesthetic: Essays on Postmodern Culture,* ed. by Hal Foster. Port Townsend, Wash.: Bay Press, 1982.

Shrage, Laurie, and Tuana, Nancy, eds. *American Philosophical Association Newsletter on Feminism and Philosophy* 89, Nos. 2 and 3 (1990).

11
THE IDEA OF
THE MUSEUM

Over the last half-century, the Museum has supplanted the Church as the main focus of civic pride in American cities. . . . The basic form of virtuous social display, for early nineteenth-century Americans, was the giving of tithes to the Church and the support of religious philanthropies. But the later nineteenth century, in America as elsewhere, saw the rise of that intense belief in the reformative and refining powers of art which was, in itself, one of the taproots of the *avant-garde*. Paintings (especially landscape paintings) were conceived as vehicles of moral instruction, and the museum, in assembling them, performed some of the functions associated with a religious gathering place. . . .

By the mid-sixties the museum was the natural habitat of "vanguard" art, which accordingly took some traits from its new surroundings. The museum was so eager to help propagate the new that it became the artist's accomplice, a nearly equal partner, providing a set of permissions that earlier art had never had—or, indeed, bothered to ask for. So it was with, among other *oeuvres*, that of Carl André, the Minimalist sculptor. The essential difference between a sculpture like André's *Equivalent VIII* (1978) and any that had existed in the past is that André's array of bricks depends not just partly, but entirely, on the museum for its context. A Rodin in a parking lot is still a misplaced Rodin; André's bricks in the same place can only be a pile of bricks. The museum alone supplies the etiquette that identifies it as art, slotting the bricks into the formal debate about contexts which enables a visually inert heap of material to be seen as part of an art movement called "Minimalism.". . .

[W]ith the colossal enlargement of the museum audience, to the point where the successful museum must now be regarded as a low-rating mass medium (as preoccupied, in its own way, with audience levels as network television), the old distance between the coterie and the mass audience was swiftly being abolished. The work of art no longer had a silence in which its resources could develop. It had to bear the stress of immediate consumption. When people are engaged in the ritual of making "authoritative" judgments on something that happened two minutes ago, when there is no room for settling, the discourse is apt to degenerate into fetishised, exaggerated pronouncements about quality, into the making and promoting of cliques and the assembly of unreal movements.

—Robert Hughes, *The Shock of the New*, pp. 391–94

INTRODUCTION

Imagine yourself in an art museum. The building itself is very grand, with an impressive exterior, and indoors there are vast, high-ceilinged rooms. The atmosphere inside is serious and reverential—a little like the atmosphere in a cathedral—and no one shouts or runs around. Ropes and warning signs keep you from getting too close to the pictures. Uniformed guards prowl between rooms and fix you with bored but vigilant eyes. You're not allowed to take photographs. You're not allowed to eat. You mustn't expect your favorite picture to be always on show.

We're all accustomed to museums being like this. But when we stop to think about it, perhaps there is something a little strange about these temples of culture, with their watchdogs and their powerful but invisible priesthoods. Look at the walls. Why exactly are *these* pictures hung there? Who bought them? Who has decided which pictures will be on show, and which will be consigned to the storerooms? Why are they hung in this order, and on these particular walls? Who thought it wise to display a plank with nails sticking out of it next to a Matisse? Indeed, who thought it wise to display the plank at all? Somewhere or other there are curators—you know that—and museum directors. But they're nowhere to be seen. What exactly are they up to? And somewhere even further in the background you know that there must be boards of trustees, composed of the great and the good, or at any rate of the rich. How much control do the trustees have? Do they care about art? Do they want to shape or to influence the nature of your aesthetic experiences? There's no easy way of knowing. Indeed, the more you think about it, the more arbitrary—and even sinister—the whole institution of the art museum can come to seem, and the more perplexing it can become to ask just what sort of experience the art museum is supposed to provide.

Perplexities of this kind raise difficult questions about the role of cultural institutions within a society, and about the relations between institutions such as art museums and the specific artworks which they exist to house and to preserve. According to one influential theory, the relationship between artworks and the cultural institutions which surround them is so intimate that neither can be understood without the other. What makes something art, according to this account, is that it receives a certain kind of recognition from a representative of the so-called "art-world." An example of a representative of the "art-world" would be a museum curator; and an example of the kind of recognition which he or she might bestow upon something would be to hang it on the wall of an art museum.

This account, which makes the very nature of art dependent upon its relation to certain cultural institutions or agencies, is called the Institutional theory of art. On one reading, the Institutional theory can be seen as an attempt to describe what does in fact go on in art museums, and in the cultural institutions of a society. But on another reading, it might be seen as an attempt to *justify* the appropriation of works of art which may not really be related to the cultural institutions of a society— such as its art museums—in any more than the most indirect or inessential ways. On this second reading, the Institutional theory represents the "art-world's" effort to justify itself, its practices, and its agencies—for example, its art museums—to the sceptical art lover. To the questions posed at the beginning of this introduction, then, the "art-world," adopting the Institutional theory, might answer: "Things are as they are because the art-world makes them so. And things *must* be as they are: for without the art-world there would be no art."

Perhaps this is to paint a somewhat paranoid and Big Brotherly picture of art museums and of the forces which stand behind them. But such a picture would have been recognized at once by the great American philosopher John Dewey, whose essay "The Live Creature" appears as the first of this section's readings. ("The Live Creature" was originally Chapter 1 of Dewey's book *Art as Experience*.) Dewey is extremely suspicious of the art museum as an institution. Art, in his view, is—or should be—continuous with ordinary, everyday experience. The task, he says, "is to restore continuity between the refined and intensified forms of experience that are works of art and the everyday events, doings, and sufferings that are universally recognized to constitute experience." Art has its roots in common, and often communitarian, life. The aesthetic is encountered in all kinds of experiences, not only in experiences of art. And so, Dewey argues, when we put art on a pedestal—when we incarcerate artworks in museums—we cut off the aesthetic from our common experience, and we cut off artworks from the contexts within which they have their meaning. "When artistic objects are separated from both conditions of origin and operation in experience, a wall is built around them that renders almost opaque their general significance."

The "art-world," with its self-conferred role in the life of our culture, would have struck Dewey as the enemy of art and of aesthetic experience. Rather than making art and aesthetic experience possible, as the Institutional theory claims that the "art-world" does, Dewey would have said that the "art-world" impoverishes both. The art museum, as an agency of the "art-world," serves to obscure the significance of artworks. And by setting up the art museum as *the* proper place for aesthetic experience, the "art-world" distracts us from recognizing the aesthetic qualities of our common or everyday experience. Or so, at least, Dewey would claim.

Albert William Levi, in the second of the readings in this section, disagrees. He defends art museums (and, by implication, the "art-world") against Dewey's charges. Indeed, he suggests that since many of the most revered masterpieces of art were created in social contexts that no longer exist—for instance, Renaissance Italy—the art museum is now the *only* place where such works can be experienced at all. Under these circumstances, he says, it is futile to moan about art being cut off from the soil in which it has its true significance. For the mere passage of time has seen to that. To experience artworks in a museum, then, is at least better than not experiencing them at all. And Levi goes further. He doubts whether Dewey's vision of the experience of art is actually compatible with any experience which is truly *aesthetic*. Dewey thinks that the experience of art should occur in an appropriate social context. But Levi points out how distracting such contexts might be. When "we glimpse a Gainsborough in an eighteenth-century town house in London or a Holbein in a great Elizabethan country estate, we see them not as freestanding works of art, but as mere additional elements of luxury and nobility in the overall decorative scheme." To place such works in art museums "may, in fact, be the major salvation of the genuinely *aesthetic* experience!"

Levi examines a range of the productive roles which art museums can play as "agencies of culture" and details some of the practical measures which might be taken to make museums as valuable, and as aesthetically rewarding, as possible. A point which Levi does not make, however, is that art museums have themselves become the social context within which many works of art are now created. As Robert Hughes points out in the passage reprinted at the start of this section, much contemporary art—for example, some interactive art and certain kinds of "installation"—has been conceived entirely with the art museum in mind. Indeed this was true even in the 1930s, when Dewey was writing, for many Dada and surrealist works depended for their impact upon being displayed in museums alongside more traditional artworks. Thus the experience of art was already partly defined by museums, by the institutions of the "art-world," and the same is even more true today.

Does this mean that Dewey was simply crying in the wind when he suggested that art was not best experienced or best understood in the context of a museum? Or does his warning against the power of the "art-world" survive in spirit, if not always in letter? These questions ought to disturb us whenever we next mount the grand sweep of steps before one of our imposing temples of culture. We should ask ourselves: What role does this art museum *really* play? Does it alienate us from the possibility of true aesthetic experience, as Dewey claims? Does it represent a regrettable necessity? Or does it, as Levi suggests, offer us rich possibilities of experience, without which we would be greatly—and aesthetically—impoverished? What, we should ask ourselves, are art museums really *for*? And how might they best perform whatever their true function is?

The Live Creature

John Dewey

By one of the ironic perversities that often attend the course of affairs, the existence of the works of art upon which formation of an esthetic theory depends has become an obstruction to theory about them. For one reason, these works are products that exist externally and physically. In common conception, the work of art is often identified with the building, book, painting, or statue in its existence apart from human experience. Since the actual work of art is what the product does with and in experience, the result is not favorable to understanding. In addition, the very perfection of some of these products, the prestige they possess because of a long history of unquestioned admiration, creates conventions that get in the way of fresh insight. When an art product once attains classic status, it somehow becomes isolated from the human conditions under which it was brought into being and from the human consequences it engenders in actual life-experience.

When artistic objects are separated from both conditions of origin and operation in experience, a wall is built around them that renders almost opaque their general significance, with which esthetic theory deals. Art is remitted to a separate realm, where it is cut off from that association with the materials and aims of every other form of human effort, undergoing, and achievement. A primary task is thus imposed upon one who undertakes to write upon the philosophy of the fine arts. This task is to restore continuity between the refined and intensified forms of experience that are works of art and the everyday events, doings, and sufferings that are universally recognized to constitute experience. Mountain peaks do not float unsupported; they do not even just rest upon the earth. They *are* the earth in one of its manifest operations. It is the business of those who are concerned with the theory of the earth, geographers and geologists, to make this fact evident in its various implications. The theorist who would deal philosophically with fine art has a like task to accomplish.

If one is willing to grant this position, even if only by way of temporary experiment, he will see that there follows a conclusion at first sight surprising. In order to understand the meaning of artistic products, we have to forget them for a time, to turn aside from them and have recourse to the ordinary forces and conditions of experience that we do not usually regard as esthetic. We must arrive at the theory of art by means of a detour. For theory is concerned with understanding, insight, not without exclamations of admiration, and stimulation of that emotional outburst often called appreciation. It is quite possible to enjoy flowers in their colored form and delicate fragrance without knowing anything about plants theoretically. But if one sets out to *understand* the flowering of plants, he is committed to finding out something about the interactions of soil, air, water and sunlight that condition the growth of plants.

By common consent, the Parthenon is a great work of art. Yet it has esthetic standing only as the work becomes an experience for a human being. And, if one is to go beyond personal enjoyment into the formation of a theory about that large republic of art of which the building is one member, one has to be willing at some point in his reflections to turn from it to the bustling, arguing, acutely sensitive Athenian citizens, with civic sense identified with a civic religion, of whose experience the temple was an expression, and who built it not as a work of art but as a civic commemoration. The turning to them is as human beings who had needs that were a demand for the building and that were carried to fulfillment in it; it is not an examination such as might be carried on by a sociologist in search for material relevant to his purpose. The one who sets out to theorize about the esthetic experience embodied in the Parthenon must realize in thought what the people into whose lives it entered had in common, as creators and as those who were satisfied with it, with people in our own homes and on our own streets.

In order to *understand* the esthetic in its ultimate and approved forms, one must begin with it in the raw; in the events and scenes that hold the attentive eye and ear of man, arousing his interest and affording him enjoyment as he looks and listens: the sights that hold the crowd—the fire-engine rushing by; the machines excavating enormous holes in the earth; the human-fly climbing the steeple-side; the men perched high in air on girders, throwing and catching red-hot bolts. The sources of art in human experience will be learned by him who sees how the tense grace of the ball-player infects the onlooking crowd; who notes the delight of the housewife in tending her plants, and the intent interest of her goodman in tending the patch of green in front of the house; the zest of the spectator in poking the wood burning on the hearth and in watching the darting flames and crumbling coals. These people, if questioned as to the reason for their actions, would doubtless return reasonable answers. The man who poked the sticks of burning wood would say he did it to make the fire burn better; but he is none the less fascinated by the colorful drama of change enacted before his eyes and imaginatively partakes in it. He does not remain a cold spectator. What Coleridge said of the reader of poetry is true in its way of all who are happily absorbed in their activities of mind and body: "The reader should be carried forward, not merely or chiefly by the mechanical impulse of curiosity, not by a restless desire to arrive at the final solution, but by the pleasurable activity of the journey itself."

The intelligent mechanic engaged in his job, interested in doing well and finding satisfaction in his handiwork, caring for his materials and tools with genuine affection, is artistically engaged. The difference between such a worker and the inept and careless bungler is as great in the shop as it is in the studio. Oftentimes the product may not appeal to the esthetic sense of those who use the product. The fault, however, is oftentimes not so much with the worker as with the conditions of the market for which his product is designed. Were conditions and opportunities different, things as significant to the eye as those produced by earlier craftsmen would be made.

So extensive and subtly pervasive are the ideas that set Art upon a remote pedestal, that many a person would be repelled rather than pleased if told that he enjoyed his casual recreations, in part at least, because of their esthetic quality. The arts which today have most vitality for the average person are things he does not take to be arts: for instance, the movie, jazzed music, the comic strip, and, too frequently, newspaper accounts of love-nests, murders, and exploits of bandits. For, when what he knows as art is relegated to the museum and gallery, the unconquerable impulse towards experiences enjoyable in themselves finds such outlet as the daily environment provides. Many a person who protests against the museum conception of art, still shares the fallacy from which that conception springs. For the popular notion comes from a separation of art from the objects and scenes of ordinary experience that many theorists and critics pride themselves upon holding and even elaborating. The times when select and distinguished objects are closely connected with the products of usual vocations are the times when appreciation of the former is most rife and most keen. When, because of their remoteness, the objects acknowledged by the cultivated to be works of fine art seem anemic to the mass of people, esthetic hunger is likely to seek the cheap and the vulgar.

The factors that have glorified fine art by setting it upon a far-off pedestal did not arise within the realm of art nor is their influence confined to the arts. For many persons an aura of mingled awe and unreality encompasses the "spiritual" and the "ideal" while "matter" has become by contrast a term of depreciation, something to be explained away or apologized for. The forces at work are those that have removed religion as well as fine art from the scope of the common or community life. The forces have historically produced so many of the dislocations and divisions of modern life and thought that art could not escape their influence. We do not have to travel to the ends of the earth nor return many millennia in time to find peoples for whom everything that intensifies the sense of immediate living is an object of intense admiration. Bodily scarification, waving feathers, gaudy robes, shining ornaments of gold and silver, of emerald and jade, formed the contents of esthetic arts, and, presumably, without the vulgarity of class exhibitionism that attends their analogues today. Domestic utensils, furnishings of tent and house, rugs, mats, jars, pots, bows, spears, were wrought with such delighted care that today we hunt them out and give them places of honor in our art museums. Yet in their own time and place, such things were enhancements of the processes of everyday life. Instead of being elevated to a niche apart, they belonged to display of prowess, the manifestation of group and clan membership, worship of gods, feasting and fasting, fighting, hunting, and all the rhythmic crises that punctuate the stream of living.

Dancing and pantomime, the sources of the art of the theater, flourished as part of religious rites and celebrations. Musical art abounded in the fingering of the stretched string, the beating of the taut skin, the blowing with reeds. Even in the caves, human habitations were adorned with colored pictures that kept alive to the senses experiences with the animals that were so closely bound with the lives of humans. Structures that housed their gods and the instrumentalities that facilitated commerce with the higher powers were wrought with especial fineness. But the arts of the drama, music, painting, and architecture thus exemplified had no peculiar connection with theaters, galleries, museums. They were part of the significant life of an organized community.

The collective life that was manifested in war, worship, the forum, knew no division between what was characteristic of these places and operations, and the arts that brought color, grace, and dignity, into them. Painting and sculpture were organically one with architecture, as that was one with the social purpose that buildings served. Music and song were intimate parts of the rites and ceremonies in which the meaning of group life was consummated. Drama was a vital reënactment of the legends and history of group life. Not even in Athens can such arts be torn loose from this setting in direct experience and yet retain their significant character. Athletic sports, as well as drama, celebrated and enforced traditions of race and group, instructing the people, commemorating glories, and strengthening their civic pride.

Under such conditions, it is not surprising that the Athenian Greeks, when they came to reflect upon art, formed the idea that it is an act of reproduction, or imitation. There are many objections to this conception. But the vogue of the theory is testimony to the close connection of the fine arts with daily life; the idea would not have occurred to any one had art been remote from the interests of life. For the doctrine did not signify that art was a literal copying of objects, but that it reflected the emotions and ideas that are associated with the chief institutions of social life. Plato felt this connection so strongly that it led him to his idea of the necessity of censorship of poets, dramatists, and musicians. Perhaps he exaggerated when he said that a change from the Doric to the Lydian mode in music would be the sure precursor of civic degeneration. But no contemporary would have doubted that music was an integral part of the ethos and the institutions of the community. The idea of "art for art's sake" would not have been even understood.

There must then be historic reasons for the rise of the compartmental conception of fine art. Our present museums and galleries to which works of fine art are removed and stored illustrate some of the causes that have operated to segregate art instead of finding it an attendant of temple, forum, and other forms of associated life. An instructive history of modern art could be written in terms of the formation of the distinctively modern institutions of museum and exhibition gallery. I may point to a few outstanding facts. Most European museums are, among other things, memorials of the rise of nationalism and imperialism. Every capital must have its own museum of painting, sculpture, etc., devoted in part to exhibiting the greatness of its artistic past, and, in other part, to exhibiting the loot gathered by its monarchs in conquest of other nations; for instance, the accumulations of the spoils of Napoleon that are in the Louvre. They testify to the connection between the modern segregation of art and nationalism and militarism. Doubtless this connection has served at times a useful purpose, as in the case of Japan, who, when she was in the process of westernization, saved much of her art treasures by nationalizing the temples that contained them.

The growth of capitalism has been a powerful influence in the development of the museum as the proper home for works of art, and in the promotion of the idea that they are apart from the common life. The *nouveaux riches,* who are an important by-product of the capitalist system, have felt especially bound to surround themselves with works of fine art which, being rare, are also costly. Generally speaking, the typical collector is the typical capitalist. For evidence of good standing in the realm of higher culture, he amasses paintings, statuary, and artistic *bijoux,* as his stocks and bonds certify to his standing in the economic world.

Not merely individuals, but communities and nations, put their cultural good taste in evidence by building opera houses, galleries, and museums. These show that a community is not wholly absorbed in material wealth, because it is willing to spend its gains in patronage of art. It erects these buildings and collects their contents as it now builds a cathedral. These things reflect and establish superior cultural status, while their segregation from the common life reflects the fact that they are not part of a native and spontaneous culture. They are a kind of counterpart of a holier-than-thou attitude, exhibited not toward persons as such but toward the interests and occupations that absorb most of the community's time and energy.

Modern industry and commerce have an international scope. The contents of galleries and museums testify to the growth of economic cosmopolitanism. The mobility of trade and of populations, due to the economic system, has weakened or destroyed the connection between works of art and the *genius loci* of which they were once the natural expression. As works of art have lost their indigenous status, they have acquired a new one—that of being specimens of fine art and nothing else. Moreover, works of art are now produced, like other articles, for sale in the market. Economic patronage by wealthy and powerful individuals has at many times played a part in the encouragement of artistic production. Probably many a savage tribe had its Maecenas. But now even that much of intimate social connection is lost in the impersonality of a world market. Objects that were in the past valid and significant because of their place in the life of a community now function in isolation from the conditions of their origin. By that fact they are also set apart from common experience, and serve as insignia of taste and certificates of special culture.

Because of changes in industrial conditions the artist has been pushed to one side from the main streams of active interest. Industry has been mechanized and an artist cannot work mechanically for mass production. He is less integrated than formerly in the normal flow of social services. A peculiar esthetic "individualism" results. Artists find it incumbent upon them to betake themselves to their work as an isolated means of "self-expression." In order not to cater to the trend of economic forces, they often feel obliged to exaggerate their separateness to the point of eccentricity. Consequently artistic products take on to a still greater degree the air of something independent and esoteric.

Put the action of all such forces together, and the conditions that create the gulf which exists generally between producer and consumer in modern society operate to create also a chasm between ordinary and esthetic experience. Finally we have, as the record of this chasm, accepted as if it were normal, the philosophies of art that locate it in a region inhabited by no other creature, and that emphasize beyond all reason the merely contemplative character of the esthetic. Confusion of values enters in to accentuate the separation. Adventitious matters, like the pleasure of collecting, of exhibiting, of ownership and display, simulate esthetic values. Criticism is affected. There is much applause for the wonders of appreciation and the glories of the transcendent beauty of art indulged in without much regard to capacity for esthetic perception in the concrete.

My purpose, however, is not to engage in an economic interpretation of the history of the arts, much less to argue that economic conditions are either invariably or directly relevant to perception and enjoyment, or even to interpretation of individual works of art. It is to indicate that *theories* which isolate art and its appreciation by placing them in a realm of their own, disconnected from other modes of experiencing, are not inherent in the subject-matter but arise because of specifiable extraneous conditions. Embedded as they are in institutions and in habits of life, these conditions operate effectively because they work so unconsciously. Then the theorist assumes they are embedded in the nature of things. Nevertheless, the influence of these conditions is not confined to theory. As I have already indicated, it deeply affects the practice of living, driving away esthetic perceptions that are necessary ingredients of happiness, or reducing them to the level of compensating transient pleasurable excitations.

Even to readers who are adversely inclined to what has been said, the implications of the statements that have been made may be useful in defining the nature of the problem: that of recovering the continuity of esthetic experience with normal processes of living. The understanding of art and of its rôle in civilization is not furthered by setting out with eulogies of it nor by occupying ourselves exclusively at the outset with great works of art recognized as such. The comprehension which theory essays will be arrived at by a detour; by going back to experience of the common or mill run of things to discover the esthetic quality such experience possesses. Theory can start with and from acknowledged works of art only when the esthetic is already compartmentalized, or only when works of art are set in a niche apart instead of being celebrations, recognized as such, of the things of ordinary experience. Even a crude experience, if authentically an experience, is more fit to give a clue to the intrinsic nature of esthetic experience than is an object already set apart from any other mode of experience. Following this clue we can discover how the work of art develops and accentuates what is characteristically valuable in things of everyday enjoyment. The art product will then be seen to issue from the latter, when the full meaning of ordinary experience is expressed, as dyes come out of coal tar products when they receive special treatment.

Many theories about art already exist. If there is justification for proposing yet another philosophy of the esthetic, it must be found in a new mode of approach. Combinations and permutations among existing theories can easily be brought forth by those so inclined. But, to my mind, the trouble with existing theories is that they start from a ready-made compartmentalization, or from a conception of art that "spiritualizes" it out of connection with the objects of concrete experience. The alternative, however, to such spiritualization is not a degrading and Philistinish materialization of works of fine art, but a conception that discloses the way in which these works idealize qualities found in common experience. Were works of art placed in a directly human context in popular esteem, they would have a much wider appeal than they can have when pigeon-hole theories of art win general acceptance.

A conception of fine art that sets out from its connection with discovered qualities of ordinary experience will be able to indicate the factors and forces that favor the normal development of common human activities into matters of artistic value. It will also be able to point out those conditions that arrest its normal growth. Writers on esthetic theory often raise the question of whether esthetic philosophy can aid in cultivation of esthetic appreciation. The question is a branch of the general theory of criticism, which, it seems to me, fails to accomplish its full office if it does not indicate what to look for and what to find in concrete esthetic objects. But, in any case, it is safe to say that a philosophy of art is sterilized unless it makes us aware of the function of art in relation to other modes of experience, and unless it indicates why this function is so inadequately realized, and unless it suggests the conditions under which the office would be successfully performed.

The comparison of the emergence of works of art out of ordinary experiences to the refining of raw materials into valuable products may seem to some unworthy, if not an actual attempt to reduce works of art to the status of articles manufactured for commercial purposes. The point, however, is that no amount of ecstatic eulogy of finished works can of itself assist the understanding or the generation of such works. Flowers can be enjoyed without knowing about the interactions of soil, air, moisture and seeds of which they are the result. But they cannot be *understood* without taking just these interactions into account—and theory is a matter of understanding. Theory is concerned with discovering the nature of the production of works of art and of their enjoyment in perception. How is it that the everyday making of things grows into that form of making which is genuinely artistic? How is it that our everyday enjoyment of scenes and situations develops into the peculiar satisfaction that attends the experience which is emphatically esthetic? These are the questions theory must answer. The answers cannot be found, unless we are willing to find the germs and roots in matters of experience that we do not currently regard as esthetic. Having discovered these active seeds, we may follow the course of their growth into the highest forms of finished and refined art.

It is a commonplace that we cannot direct, save accidentally, the growth and flowering of plants, however lovely and enjoyed, without understanding their causal conditions. It should be just a commonplace that esthetic understanding—as distinct from sheer personal enjoyment—must start with the soil, air, and light out of which things esthetically admirable arise. And these conditions are the conditions and factors that make an ordinary experience complete. The more we recognize this fact, the more we shall find ourselves faced with a problem rather than with a final solution. *If* artistic and esthetic quality is implicit in every normal experience, how shall we explain how and why it so generally fails to become explicit? Why is it that to multitudes art seems to be an importation into experience from a foreign country and the esthetic to be a synonym for something artificial?

The Art Museum as an Agency of Culture

Albert William Levi

I

John Dewey is probably the greatest philosopher that America has produced, and his book *Art as Experience* perhaps the most significant treatise on aesthetics to come out of the American twentieth century. Yet in the first few pages of this book Dewey has seen fit to begin his argument with a sharp, direct, and sustained attack upon the institution of the modern art museum and exhibition gallery.

Dewey, of course, wants to restore continuity between those refined and recondite objects that are "works of art" and the everyday experiences with which they were originally associated. He deplores the acts of collection and segregation by which they are removed from their original place in the ongoing life of society. He is alarmed at the remoteness which they enjoy by being taken from their original habitat and placed in a special repository. He rejects the rationale by which they are separated from their original role as agents of general cultivation and civic enhancement.

It is clear that Dewey is upset by those forces that have glorified fine art by setting it upon a far-off pedestal and that his argument is against aesthetic abstraction, estrangement, *artificiality.* But as the argument proceeds, it becomes clear that a social critique is also under way and that, without explicit acknowledgement, Dewey's strictures have been profoundly influenced by Thorstein Veblen and his great classic, *The Theory of the Leisure Class.* And this causes him to search out some of the historic reasons for the rise of "the compartmental conception of fine art" and to accuse the modern art museum, to which works of fine art are removed and where they are stored, as a chief agency in this segregation.

"An instructive history of modern art," he said,

> could be written in terms of the formation of the distinctively modern institutions of museum and exhibition gallery. . . . Most European museums are . . . memorials of the rise of nationalism and imperialism. Every capital must have its own museum . . . devoted in part to exhibiting the greatness of its artistic past, and, in other part to exhibiting the loot gathered by its monarchs in conquest of other nations; for instance the accumulations of the spoils of Napoleon that are in the Louvre. They testify to the connection between the modern segregation of art and nationalism and militarism. The growth of capitalism also has been a powerful influence in the development of the museum. . . . The *nouveau riches,* who are an important by-product of the capitalist system, have felt especially bound to surround themselves with works of fine art which, being rare, are also costly. Generally speaking, the typical collector is the typical capitalist. For evidence of good standing in the realm of higher culture, he amasses paintings and statuary as his stocks and bonds certify to his standing in the economic world.

Dewey's point is not simply the moral critique that historically the art museum has been associated with the less than admirable qualities of nationalism, imperialism, militarism, and capitalism, but that the very *motive* of acquisition has been a kind of elitism or snobbery or holier-than-thou attitude, itself far removed from the aesthetic. And he thereby makes the vulgarity of class exhibitionism which is responsible for the modern art museum also a basic source of that artistic isolationism he deplores.

One would think the critique devastating unless one had managed to remember the front materials of Dewey's book. It is dedicated "To Albert C. Barnes, in gratitude," and Dewey's preface continues: "My greatest indebtedness is to Dr. A. C. Barnes. . . . I have had the benefit of conversations with him through a period of years, many of which occurred in the presence of the unrivaled collection of pictures he has assembled. . . . Whatever is sound in this volume is due more than I can say to the great educational work carried on in the Barnes Foundation." And to cap it off, five of the nine illustrations for Dewey's book (a Renoir, a Cézanne, a Matisse, as well as some African sculpture and Pueblo Indian pottery) are of the treasury of the art museum which is the Barnes Foundation.

The contradiction is mind-boggling! A treatise which begins with a virulent attack upon art museums and capitalist art collectors admits to the inspiration of an art museum and a capitalist art collector for its own insights and existence. And if we take this irony more deeply to heart and ponder its inner meaning, we shall come closer, I think, to the real significance of the contemporary art museum: its place in the spectrum of culture, its role within a context of civic humanism, as well as some of the crucial philosophical problems involved in the strategies of its educational presentations.

How does one answer Dewey's charges that the art museums remove works of fine art from their original place in the ongoing life of their society? Surely the answer lies in the necessities imposed by the inexorable passage of time. In this connection the case of Venice and her great fifteenth- and sixteenth-century painters is instructive. For, where the original building sites are still extant, every effort has been made to preserve them whole, along with the massive painterly treasures they contain. The mighty guild hall of San Rocco (Scuola di San Rocco) has managed to continue without interruption since the sixteenth century, and the forty Tintorettos which hang upon its walls make it the temple of that fertile artist. The smaller guild hall of the Dalmatian sea captains (the Scuola di San Giorgio degli Schiavoni) has been less fortunate, but the wonderful St. George and St. Jerome series (its patron saints) which Carpaccio painted for it between 1490 and 1515 still hang upon its walls, and for this reason the whole smaller edifice has been turned into a Carpaccio museum. Titian's great altarpiece *The Assumption of the Virgin* still graces the cathedral of Santa Maria dei Frari, and the smaller parish church of San Sebastiano, containing the frescoes, the marvelous ceiling painting, and even the tomb of Paolo Veronese, remains both an active religious institution and the living monument to that great painter. But what of the Scuola di Sant'Orsola (which once stood close to the church of San Giovanni e Paolo), founded in 1306, suppressed in 1810, and since demolished? And what was the inevitable fate of the marvelous series of monumental *teleri*, *The Legend of St. Ursula* painted by Carpaccio and "homeless" since that time? Had they not been taken in, wonderfully reassembled, and exhibited in the gigantic "Room XXI" of the Academy Gallery—the city art museum of Venice—they might have tragically been lost forever. For this deprivation even Dewey might have been expected to shed a tear! This is the obvious counterargument to the blanket attack which Dewey mounts in the first few pages of *Art as Experience*. It is in just such cases as this that the modern art museum asserts its right to exist. For it has become the surrogate home for precisely those aesthetic masterpieces which through the unavoidable ravages of time have been deprived of their own original residence.

Of course not all museum acquisitions have the overwhelming significance of the Academia's Carpaccios. Many donations and acquisitions are of doubtful or secondary merit or, at best, ambiguous in this respect, and this leads to the most primitive concept of *the art museum as warehouse,* as agency of mere storage and preservation, as simple repository of catalogued specimens of the genus "art object." Few museums are without their "basement" or their "attic" where labels are attached, the dust settles, and the public is never permitted to set foot.

Fortunately this primitive concept of the art museum as warehouse, as mere vehicle of preservation and storage, is supplanted by one more worthy and more just, one in which the concept of "aesthetic merit" becomes central. The great palace of the Habsburgs in Vienna—the Hofburg—contains a room which is called the *Schatzkammer*—the treasure room—where are stored the fabulous relics of the Habsburg dynasty: the jewelry, brocades, and costly artefacts, including the solid-gold, jewel-encrusted crown of the Holy Roman Empire. But hardly a stone's throw away, down on the Ringstrasse, stands another "Schatzkammer"—the great neo-Renaissance palace created between 1872 and 1889 by Gottfried Semper and Carl von Hasenauer on orders of Franz Josef to house the great collection of Brueghels and Velázquezes, the Holbeins and the Rubenses, as well as individual masterpieces by Raphael, Vermeer, and Giorgione. And the relation between the two "Schatzkammers" is even more symbolically intimate, for the art museum on the Ring also houses the famous solid-gold salt-cellar that Benvenuto Cellini made for Francis I and the equally solid-gold breakfast set from which the Empress Maria Theresa drank her chocolate every morning.

Here, I think, we have a second and even more decisive answer to Dewey's strictures against the art museum. For if conquest and ostentation were the original motives for its formation, civilized evaluation is the later. Now with measured judgment of aesthetic merit, art museums are no longer mere warehouses for storage and preservation, but *Schatzkammers*—repositories of aesthetic treasure, custodians of the "aesthetic valuables" of the community. And with this transformation it can no longer be said that art museums are the vehicle for the *removal* of aesthetic objects from the ongoing life of society, but rather that *the art museum as a whole, as an institution of civic consequence has itself been taken into, incorporated in the ongoing life of society.* At this point the art museum, like the cathedral, the town hall, and the university, has become an adjunct of that civic humanism which the evolution of every great *Kulturstadt* illustrates.

It is a commonplace that what we have come to call "culture" is primarily an urban phenomenon, and that all the great "culture cities" possess visible institutions which represent all their major cultural concerns. Thus, different as they are in ground plan and in profile, Venice, Paris, and Vienna are alike as centers of power, piety, and learning. Palazzo Ducale is balanced by Rathaus and Hôtel de Ville; Nôtre Dame by St. Stephens and St. Marks, the university in the fifteenth century Ca'Foscari in Venice by the Baroque Sorbonne and the late-nineteenth-century "Renaissance" palace of the University of Vienna. Universally, the city hall is the art-embellished seat of civic humanism. The cathedral, decorated with all the resources of painting, sculpture, and the minor arts, is a monument to sacred beliefs about human destiny. The university consecrates the sciences and the liberal arts, a visible embodiment of the powers of mind within the city environment. These institutions all go back as far as the middle ages.

But sometime during or after the European eighteenth century a new set of institutions begins to appear: L'Opéra and Musée de Louvre in Paris, La Fenice and Gallerie dell'Accademia in Venice, Staatsoper and Kunsthistorisches Hofmuseum in Vienna. Thus to cathedral, city hall, and university as agencies of culture have been added art museum and opera house or concert hall and even in some intances academies of music and fine art. How and why has this augmentation come about?

Perhaps just here a brief incursion into history is justified. The practice of serious art collecting began with the Italian Renaissance, partly out of a new-found sense of history, partly out of a passionate enthusiasm for the art of classical antiquity. Early collectors include artists like Raphael and Ghiberti, humanists like Poggio and Niccoli, princes like Alfonso of Aragon and Cosimo di Medici. The term 'museum' begins to appear in the late sixteenth century, and for good reason: great collections remained private, but by special dispensation they could be visited. Albrecht of Bavaria opened his collection in Munich in 1569, the Gonzaga Palace in Mantua became a center of display in 1570, and the east wing of the Uffizi was set aside as an art gallery from 1574 onward. Later, in the eighteenth century, enlightened princes began to feel that their collections should belong to their subjects as well, and they began to build separate edifices to house them that would be open to the public. This was true of the Belvedere in Vienna for Prince Eugene from 1721 onward and of Frederick the Great's Sanssouci at Potsdam from 1756. And in Florence in 1739 the last of the Medici presented her great collections to the city.

But if the time between the Renaissance and the late eighteenth century served as the incubation period for the modern civic art museum, the late nineteenth century is the moment of its flowering. New York's

Metropolitan and the Boston Museum of Fine Art both opened their doors in 1870. The Philadelphia dates from 1875, the Art Institute of Chicago from 1879, the great Kunsthistorisches Hofmuseum on the Ringstrasse in Vienna from 1889. But, once again, where is the inspiration, what is the ideological foundation which made this flowering possible?

It might appear that this development from the Italian Renaissance to the late nineteenth century in America formed a single continuum—one seamless web in which each century contributed equally its own insights into the meaning of aesthetic culture. In fact this is not so, for the European eighteenth century—the "enlightenment," so to speak—marks the great divide and, in reality, provides the ideology, the philosophical presupposition, so to say, by which the modern public art museum becomes possible. For the concept of culture and the idea of civilization as we now know them first made their appearance in the French and German eighteenth century.

With Turgot's discovery of the unity of human history, the Encyclopedist's insistence that all the arts and sciences form one unified structure of human creativity, and Voltaire's emphasis not upon economics or politics, but upon literature and art as the chief elements constituting a "historical epoch" in France, and with Herder's emphasis upon our common humanity, Kant's attention to what the human individual has it in him to become, and Winckelmann's passion for painting and sculpture and particularly the arts of classical antiquity in Germany, the conviction slowly grows that we are all part of one man-made civilization, one *Menschliche Kultur*, one *civilisation humaine*. And as a corollary of this conviction comes the additional insistence that *Bildung* or *La Culture*—culture of cultivation—education in the humanities and the arts, has become the inescapable obligation of the human individual. This whole movement culminates in Schiller's great series of letters of 1793—*The Aesthetic Education of Man*—the theme of which is the education of humanity through the instrument of art, a mode of viewing aesthetic cultivation as the highest conceivable level of human attainment, with the clear implication that a major strategy in this education is that the fine arts be opened up to the general public through access to their immortal examples. And it is only in the light of this new insight and enthusiasm that we can understand Hirt's famous memorandum to Friedrich Wilhelm III of Prussia in 1798: "The rare remains which we possess are a heritage for the whole of mankind. . . . Only by making them public and uniting them in display can they become the object of true study, and every result obtained from this is a new gain for the common good of mankind." With this recognition we reach the third and final definition of the independent public art museum of today: not as mere warehouse, or even as Schatzkammer and aesthetic treasury, but as showcase, purposive display area, as basic agency for the dissemination of culture, as *indispensable instrument in the great task of aesthetic education*.

In light of this whole historical excursus we have one more counterargument to the stern original attack of John Dewey. For the art museum with its insularity and its isolation may in fact be the only environment in which a true aesthetic experience is possible. It is important to remember that there is one whole school of aesthetic theory which defines the aesthetic experience as "the attitude of disinterested and sympathetic attention to, and contemplation of, the work of art *for its own sake alone.*" This, of course, tends to neglect subject matter, representation, and cognitive content in favor of exclusively formal values, and it suggests (in opposition to Dewey) that a religious, civic, or domestic context might detract from or destroy just that "distanciation" which makes true aesthetic appreciation possible. Thus, when we observe Giovanni Bellini's great *Virgin with Child* with its infinitely enigmatic four saints which hangs on the side wall of San Zaccaria in Venice, or his Triptych in the Sacristy of the Frari, or the infinitely moving *Coronation of the Virgin* by Cima da Conegliano which hangs on the wall of San Giovanni e Paolo, the ever-present religious atmosphere is a distraction from a purely aesthetic contemplation. By the same token, when we view Lorenzetti's frescoes *Good Government* in the town hall of Siena, or Tintoretto's *Bacchus and Ariadne Crowned by Venus* in the antechamber of the Hall of the Signoria in the Ducal Palace in Venice, or even such second-rate work as the monumental decorative canvases *The Life of St. Geneviève,* which Puvis de Chavannes painted for the Panthéon in Paris, we are so overcome by the sense of civic grandeur that the exclusive attention to aesthetic merit becomes secondary. And finally, in the case of the private dwelling, if we glimpse a Gainsborough in an eighteenth-century town house in London or a Holbein in a great Elizabethan country estate, we see them not as freestanding works of art, but as mere additional elements of luxury and nobility in the overall decorative scheme. Thus, paradoxically enough, those "acts of collection and segregation by which works of fine art are removed from their original place in the on-going life of their society" and placed in art museums may, in fact, be the major salvation of the genuinely *aesthetic* experience!

II

In what has gone before I have tried to explore the historical process by which the modern art museum has come into being and the various transformations by which it has finally established itself as an instrument of culture and a primary agency in the task of aesthetic education. And to this end I have used the paradoxical attack which Dewey makes upon the entire museum idea in the first few pages of *Art as Experience.* But anyone with some degree of philosophic sophistication will recognize that something infinitely more is taking place here than a mere institutional critique and that underneath this attack lies an unexpressed philosophical premise. It is the virulent opposition between the atomistic independence, the stark isolationism, the unregenerate individualism of John Stuart Mill and the pervasive organicism, contextualism, and institutionalism of Hegel. Dewey's attack merely gives this opposition a local habitation and a name. It espouses the Hegelian alternative and applies it aesthetically by demanding for the aesthetic object a living institutional embodiment which should resist the isolating, bracketing, insulating influence of museum residence. And indeed the occasional strategy of individualistic, timeless presentation in the museum, as opposed to the much more usual historical contextualizing practice through the use of such classifications as "Renaissance," "Baroque," "Rococo," "Impressionist," and the like, does show that even the philosophical quarrel between Mill and Hegel has implications for museum policy and practice. Earlier we dealt with the art museum in terms of institutional role. Here we will be more concerned with philosophic approach, inner significance, and ideological commitment.

It is certainly true that the presentation of the individual work of art by itself alone is a relatively rare practice by the contemporary art museum and generally used only to call attention to perhaps the latest notable acquisition which the museum has made, as in the case of the New York Metropolitan which some few years ago displayed Rembrandt's *Aristotle before the Bust of Homer* in a room by itself. But the public that flocked to see it was probably drawn more by rumor of the fabulous price that had been paid for its acquisition than by thirst for any genuine aesthetic experience. On the other hand, another Rembrandt—the great *Company of Captain Frans Banning Cocq,* better known as *The Night Watch,* completely cleaned, revarnished, and repaired, has been placed freestanding and alone in an enormous room of the Ryksmuseum in Amsterdam, huge in its dimensions, breathtakingly beautiful in its coloration, volcanic in its sheer dramatic impact; a permanent invitation to aesthetic contemplation, one of the great aesthetic adventures of the Western world.

Strangely enough, it may even be that what on the surface appears as Hegelian contextualism is in reality invitation to purely individual contemplation. This I think is the case for one of the most genial, exquisite, and deeply satisfying museums that I know, the sumptuous palace at 70th Street and Fifth Avenue in New York, which Henry Clay Frick had constructed in 1913–14 and planned primarily as a setting for his paintings.

The entire case of Frick is instructive. A fabulously wealthy industrialist, he retired at fifty and began to collect pictures. His early taste was "popular" and of questionable merit: he bought Bouguereau, Rosa Bonheur, Daubigny, and Mauve, which, as his taste matured, he subsequently disposed of. He began to study painting assiduously, slowly acquiring the capacity of real taste and discrimination, finally becoming a true "connoisseur" in the Berenson sense. In 1899 he purchased his first Rembrandt; in 1919 his last painting was Vermeer's *Lady Reading a Letter.* In between come the superb Bellini, the Holbeins, the Ruisdaels, El Grecos, Velázquezes, Dürers, and at least fifteen Rembrandts more. To the end he continued to improve his collection by exchanging earlier purchases for works of higher quality.

The results are breathtaking. When one first walks through the Frick museum and notes the fabulous collection of paintings spread out within their sumptuous background of early Italian furniture, French eighteenth-century pieces, and enormous and infinitely beautiful Isfahan rugs, one has the sense of Hegelian contextualism at its most sensitive; but further reflection convinces one that this is far from being the case. There is embodied here no *unified* sense of time, space, or culture. Instead one walks from a Rembrandt *Self Portrait* to Vermeer's *Lady Reading a Letter* to Holbein's *Sir Thomas More* to Giovanni Bellini's *St. Francis in the Desert.* And from there to Velázquez's *Philip the Fourth,* a second Holbein, *Sir Thomas Cromwell,* and from there to a wonderful but *limited* quantity of works by Ruisdael, Vermeer, Titian, Van Dyck, and Veronese, each individually inviting the spectator to stop, attend, regard; each soliciting its own measure of rapt contemplation, formal appreciation, and sustained admiration. And one begins to sense here not a synthesized organic whole, but a loose and almost random aggregate of Millian singulars, each making its individualistic aesthetic claim.

Then, finally, when one begins to be aware of the small-scale bronzes on the Renaissance tables, the names here are those of Benvenuto Cellini, Giovanni da Bologna, Verrocchio, and Michelangelo. And when one begins to notice the Black Hawthorn vases of the K'ang and Hsi period placed almost at random, it is apparent that they are among the choicest in existence! Only then it begins to dawn on one what the Frick museum really is: a presentation of works of art in their naked individuality, a temple of pure aesthetic experience, a virtual embodiment of the idea of *the art museum as an exclusive assembly of nothing but masterpieces.* (Reflection on the essence of the Frick museum suggests that this too is not without its suggestiveness for what the Getty museum has in it to become: the consequence of a private trust, with infinite financial resources of acquisition, and guided by the most enlightened artistic knowledge, and with directive powers with both creative imagination and the appetite for perfection.)

The concept of the art museum as an exclusive assemblage of nothing but masterpieces invites an interpretation of pure aesthetic contemplation, of a consideration of the work of art for its own sake alone. And this reinforcement of the "purity" of the aesthetic experience, like the purity of the apprehension of logical and mathematical universals, places the entire transaction outside of space and time. There is no effort within the Frick collection to call specific attention to date, original function, or place of

origin of any of the masterpieces it contains. In this sense the entire enterprise is profoundly antihistorical.

But there is another conception of what an art museum ought to be
which is directly antithetical to this—one, in fact, which views it as a lesson in, and an illumination of, cultural history. Here the Hegelian notion
of "context" is central, and the entire enterprise is guided by what I
should like to call "the doctrine of essential temporality." The shift here is
drastic, and it has profound epistemological consequences as well. A contemplative act in the pure present is very different from an act of historical comprehension whose goal is somehow "to recapture" the past, an act
of "recovery" or "restoration" of materials only incompletely and inferen-
tially known. To use the art museum as a demonstration of how the various arts and crafts are *associated as a way of life* constituting a particular historical period like "the Middle Ages" or "the Italian Renaissance" or "the
Dutch seventeenth century" or "Georgian England" means the use of
techniques of assemblage and presentation which stimulate a particular
and very elusive attitude—one which a very important philosopher of
historical method of the last century, Wilhelm Dilthey (1833–1911), used
two words to describe: *Verstehen* (or sympathetic intuitive *understanding*)
and *Nacherleben* (or profoundly imaginative *re-experiencing*). Here contextualizing, the placement in space and time of art objects in their intercon-
nectedness, is what makes *Verstehen* and *Nacherleben* possible, and the
aesthetic and the historical sense may even unite cooperatively in two
very different but mutually supportive acts.

One further thing must be presupposed in conceiving the art museum
as primarily an institution for instruction in cultural history: some prior
agreement upon the conventions of historical classification; one must
know in advance what it means to be a historical epoch. Once again, our
origins here go back to the eighteenth-century Enlightenment and chiefly
to Voltaire's short but revolutionary treatise, the *Siècle de Louis XIV*, published in 1751. Here, probably for the first time, the concept of a *Zeitgeist* is
taken seriously, and a historical epoch is defined less in terms of politics,
power, and dynastic conquest than in terms of the advance of literature
and the arts. Only from this time onward is it possible to write books with
titles like Karl Vossler's *Mediaeval Culture* or the Oxford *Legacy of the
Middle Ages* or Walter Pater's *The Renaissance* or Burckhardt's *The
Civilization of the Renaissance in Italy* or the two notable Oxford collections,
The Age of Shakespeare and *The Age of Johnson*, respectively. Any one of
these titles might also be the title of an exhibit arranged by any art museum devoting itself to the illumination of cultural history.

In fact, there are at least three ways in which this illumination can be
carried out. The first is by total dedication. The Musée de Cluny, situated
in the heart of Paris, a stone's throw away from the Sorbonne and the
Collège de France, houses perhaps the finest collection of mediaeval arts
and crafts in the world, all superbly exhibited in a mansion of the Middle

Ages—one of only two surviving examples of mediaeval domestic architecture in the city of Paris. Its riches are incalculable. It contains sumptuous tapestries like *La Dame à la Licorne, La Vie Seigneuriale,* and *Saint Etienne,* chalices and reliquaries of chased gold and silver, illuminated manuscripts with brilliantly painted miniatures, limoges enamels on religious subjects of the twelfth century, fragments of stained glass and cathedral sculpture, psalter covers in carved ivory, carved wooden chests and cupboards of the twelfth, thirteenth, and fourteenth centuries, embroidered taffeta robes, richly carved choir stalls, limoges caskets and plaques of cloisonné, massive stone fireplaces of the period with their cooking utensils, chairs, tables, and other pieces of domestic furniture, and, in fact, innumerable exemplars of the decorative and industrial arts, both for ecclesiastical and domestic purposes, all arranged to promote maximum intelligibility, all calculated to stimulate just that *Verstehen* and *Nacherleben* of which Dilthey spoke. The French philosopher Henri Bergson begins one of his most famous essays as follows: "Les philosophes s'accordent, en dépit de leurs divergences apparentes, à distinguer deux manières profondément différentes de connaître une chose. La première implique qu'on tourne autour de cette chose: la seconde qu'on entre en elle." After one has carefully and attentively worked one's way through the Musée de Cluny, one does not feel that one has "walked around" the Middle Ages, but that one has "entered into" them!

A lesser way is the single room or series of "period" rooms. Almost any art museum of size or distinction has to some degree the interest to exhibit its aesthetic treasures in historical context, as icons of the aristocratic way of life in a notable period of Western culture. If it is lucky enough to have transported the fireplace and wood panelling from some stately townhouse of Georgian England, it hangs a Joshua Reynolds portrait over the mantel, a Gainsborough landscape over the mahogany Sheraton sideboard, which already holds a massive Georgian coffee-and-tea service, and its finest Spode or Wedgewood or Chelsea china on the polished Hepplewhite dining room table surrounded by its Hepplewhite chairs which already occupies the center of the stage. And in the same spirit it can equip other "period" rooms as well: its "Louis XV Boudoir," its Austrian "Biedermeier," and its American "Federal" parlors. The possibilities are endless, and their variety and quality are dependent only upon the state and quality of the collections the art museum possesses. (Occasionally, such assemblages are actually authentic. In the "Museum der Stadt Wien" [Museum of the City of Vienna], for example, I have seen both the Biedermeier drawing room of the great Austrian dramatist Franz Grillparzer [1791–1872] and the interesting and bizarre self-designed study of Adolf Loos [1870–1933], the real European founder of architectural modernism, both taken bodily from their respective original apartments and reassembled whole.)

A third and least way is simply to promote suggestiveness by the loose association of such cognate works of fine art or craft as the museum possesses and sees as historically related. A few years ago I saw just such a display at the rather modest art museum of the city of Detroit. In at least one of its very long and rather narrow galleries, at intervals of perhaps fifty feet, it had hung pictures done by the better-known of American Colonial portrait painters—Copley, Stuart, Hoppner, and a few others—and standing against the walls between these pictures were splendid examples of the furniture made by the finest American Colonial cabinetmakers of Boston, Baltimore, and Philadelphia: exquisite and imposing Chippendale highboys in mahogany made in Philadelphia, lowboys and tables of Virginia walnut made in Baltimore, block-front desks from Newport, Rhode Island, and a multitude of Hepplewhite and Sheraton chairs made in all four cities. And on some of the flat surfaces of the lowboys and tables were placed elegant silver tea services and pitchers and porringers of the period and style of Paul Revere. The overall impression was both casual and stately and led the mind inevitably to a sense of the elegance, dignity, and culture of patrician Colonial America—a total civilization, if you will, but constructed out of an array of disparate particulars.

Hitherto I have taken up the ideologies of the art museum: (1) as the temple of pure aesthetic experience, as ideally a collection of masterpieces, and (2) as an agency for the presentation of cultural history, as illumination of the major cultural "epochs" in the history of the West. Now I want to turn to (3) the art museum as the special protegé of the academic field of art history and (4) the use of the art museum to present the fine arts as "liberal arts," that is to say, the exploration of "art" as a "humanity." In the case of (3) there is less original material to explore, since in some sense that is the way that most art museums currently function. Most of those responsible for the direction of art museum aesthetic policy have been trained as art historians, and it is therefore natural that they should be subconsciously aware of the doctrines they have absorbed by the influential theorists of their field: Berenson's emphasis upon "tactile values," Fry's emphasis on "significant form," Wölfflin's distinction between the "painterly" and the "linear" styles, Panofsky's obsession with "iconographic meanings," Gombrich's investigations of "the a priori of the spectator's anticipations." These distinctions have probably often subconsciously influenced the placement of the individual artwork in the museum space.

But there are other art-historical conventions which are even more powerful: classificatory designations like "Mannerist," "Baroque," "Rococo," "Impressionist," and the like, and these may even guide the sophisticated visitor to the museum as to where to go and what to look for. It is therefore much more traditional to present the painterly materials by historical placement than, say, by genres. So one might have a Dutch seventeenth-century room combining landscapists like Hobbema, Ruisdael, and Van Goyen with the interior wizards like De Hoogh, Ter Borch, and Vermeer, or a French nineteenth-century room in which Renoir's portraits, Monet's country landscapes, and Pissarro's and Sisley's paintings of the Grand Boulevards of Paris are all projected into one giant "Impressionist" space. But imagine the educational potential if a revolution occurred (and, if one can appeal to a musical analogy, the "serial" was supplanted by the "variation" form) and *genre* took priority over the principle of mere temporal succession. Then Titian and Joshua Reynolds, Copley and Franz Hals, Ingres and Modigliani, Rembrandt and Holbein, Goya and Van Dyck, Raphael and Memling, Manet and Dürer, El Greco and Velázquez might hang together in fascinating opposition, leaving the spectator in bemused but active consideration of valences of attitude, style, characterization, technique, and ultimate value. Then portraiture might take its rightful place in the spectrum of human concern, and painting might be transformed before our very eyes from a "fine art" into a "humanity."

This, of course, leads directly into our final topic: (4) the art museum devoted exclusively to *the presentation of art as a humanity.* Here again I wish to concentrate my attention primarily upon painting. The humanities, I have long maintained, are identical with the liberal arts, and the liberal arts consist primarily of the languages and literatures, history, and philosophy. Thus the humanities may alternatively be defined as the arts of *communication*, the arts of *continuity*, and the arts of *criticism*. Any move, therefore, to turn the fine art of painting into a humanity involves its being interpreted simultaneously as an act of communication, of historical significance, and of moral, social, or political criticism.

First the matter of communication. Painting is, of course, nonlinguistic; its magic is created neither with speech nor with words, but with paint and canvas in the form of shapes and images. Yet it is highly suggestive to consider paintings metaphorically as acts of writing or of speech, with each individual painter having his own unique "vocabulary" of line, color, calligraphy, and overall mood. Consider the obvious matter of chromatic preference. Van Gogh loved yellow, Rembrandt brown, El Greco alizerin crimson. Chardin paints in the darker "shades," Bonnard in the lighter "tints," Fra Angelico in "tones" of purest blue, red, and purple. Monet, like Bonnard, works in tints, especially lavender, turquois, and powder blue, whereas Mondrian with his black lines will have only the unmixed primaries red, yellow, blue, and green.

Or, consider the vocabulary of line: the clarity of Raphael, Holbein, and Ingres compared with the cloudiness of Rembrandt and the Impressionists. Or, in our own time, the hard edges of Albers and Noland compared with the smudginess of DeKooning or the careless drips and blots of Jackson Pollock. Or the actual calligraphy of the brush strokes: the rough ones of Franz Hals or Van Gogh compared with the smooth ones of Manet and Van Dyck, or the obsessive fussy dots of the Impressionists and Seurat. How can Cézanne get from the gutteral speech of his early thick impastos to the whispers of those thin washes (almost like watercolors) of the very last paintings? Isn't some brushwork bold or nervous, careless or deliberate, slashing or exact? Or consider the matter of characteristic mood: the violent gesturing of Michelangelo and Van Gogh, the good humor of Franz Hals; the angry and violent Soutine, the gloomy Munch, the sullen Vlaminck; the serenity and sweetness of Raphael and Cima da Conigliano, the quiet peacefulness of Vermeer and De Hoogh.

Finally as to content. What does the painter talk about? What are the subjects of his conversation? Mostly religion and God as with Giotto, Fra Angelico, and Giovanni Bellini. Or important people as with Clouet, Holbein, and Van Dyck. Or fine clothes and interior decoration and beautiful domestic objects as with Ter Borch, Vermeer, and De Hoogh. Or the East Anglian countryside by Constable, or the countryside around Aix-en-Provence by Cézanne, around Arles by Van Gogh, or around Delft, Leyden, and The Hague by Ruisdael, Hobbema, and Van Goyen. Or perhaps they speak about beautiful nude women, as with Boucher, Ingres, and Titian as he grew old. Or about old men, rabbis, solid citizens, and himself, as did Rembrandt throughout his life.

The last two categories need hardly detain us further: they are almost too obvious to require elaboration. For painting as ingredient in history, as an "art of continuity," it is only necessary that the museum display and discuss it as finding its place in a determinate *tradition:* say, that of portraiture from Titian to Modigliani, or that of still life from Claez to Braque, or that of landscape from Bellini to Cézanne. And for painting as philosophy, as social criticism, for example, it might be highly instructive to display examples of painters like Gentile Bellini and Carpaccio, whose pageants and processions glorify and revere the city of whose life they are a part, close to, but in opposition with, the spirit of that other persuasion—of those like Goya and Hogarth and Daumier, or like Ben Shahn or Jacob Lawrence in our own century, whose works are living critiques of courtly corruption or of civic poverty, squalor, and vice.

To conclude. In the first half of my consideration of the art museum as an agency of culture, I have tried to examine its institutional role (1) as warehouse, (2) as showcase and custodian of the aesthetic valuables of the community, and finally (3) as indispensable instrument in the great task of aesthetic education. Analogously, in the second half I have tried to present four conceptually different strategies through which the art museum's efforts of aesthetic education might be directed: (1) by the idea of the art museum as a collection of supreme masterpieces presented for pure aesthetic contemplation, or (2) by the idea of the art museum as an agency of cultural history, or (3) by the idea of the art museum as primarily an adjunct of the discipline of art history, or finally (4) by the idea of the art museum as the presentation of fine art as a humanity.

I have not meant that these last four alternatives should of necessity be mutually exclusive. It is only necessary, I think, that they should be un-ambiguously clear in the minds of those who are currently responsible for the direction of art museum policy.

SUGGESTIONS FOR FURTHER READING

Aagaard-Mogensen, Lars, ed. *The Idea of the Museum: Philosophical, Artistic and Political Questions.* Lewiston, N.Y.: E. Mellen Press, 1988.

Alexander, Edward P. *Museums in Motion: An Introduction to the History and Functions of Museums.* Nashville: American Association for State and Local History, 1979.

Bazin, Germain. *The Museum Age.* New York: Universe Books, 1967.

Bloom, Joel N., et al. *Museums for a New Century: A Report of the Commission on Museums for a New Century.* Washington, D.C.: American Association of Museums, 1984.

Burt, Nathaniel. *Palaces for the People.* Boston: Little, Brown, 1977.

Danto, Arthur. "The Artworld." *Journal of Philosophy* 61 (1964): 571–84.

Dickie, George. *Art and the Aesthetic: An Institutional Analysis.* Ithaca: Cornell University Press, 1974.

Draper, Linda, ed. *The Visitor and the Museum.* Washington, D.C.: American Association of Museums, 1974.

Gombrich, Ernst. "The Museum: Past, Present, and Future." *Critical Inquiry* 3 (1977): 449–70.

Hein, Hilde. "Exhibits and Artworks: From Art Museum to Science Center." In *The Philosophy of the Visual Arts,* ed. by Philip Alperson. New York: Oxford University Press, 1992.

Hein, Hilde. *The Exploratium: The Museum as Laboratory.* Washington, D.C.: Smithsonian Institution Press, 1990.

Hooper-Greenhill, Eilean. *Museums and the Shaping of Knowledge.* London: Routledge, 1992.

Hudson, Kenneth. *Museums of Influence.* New York: Cambridge University Press, 1987.

Hughes, Robert. *The Shock of the New.* New York: Alfred A. Knopf, 1981. (Chapter 8.)

Karp, Ivan, Kreamer, Christine M., and Lavine, Steven D. *Museums and Communities: The Politics of Public Culture.* Washington, D.C.: Smithsonian Institution Press, 1992.

Karp, Ivan, and Lavine, Steven D. *Exhibiting Cultures: The Poetics and Politics of Museum Display.* Washington, D.C.: Smithsonian Institution Press, 1991.

Larrabee, Eric, ed., *Museums and Education.* Washington, D.C.: Smithsonian Institution Press, 1968.

Lee, Sherman E. *Present, Past, East and West.* New York: George Braziller, 1983.

Lee, Sherman E., ed. *On Understanding Art Museums.* Englewood Cliffs, N.J.: Prentice-Hall, 1975.

Meyer, Karl E. *The Art Museum.* New York: William Morrow, 1979.

O'Doherty, Brian. *Inside the White Cube: The Ideology of the Gallery Space.* San Francisco: The Lapis Press, 1976.

Ripley, Sidney Dillon. *The Sacred Grove: Essays on Museums.* New York: Simon and Schuster, 1969.

Smith, Ralph, ed. *The Art Museum as Educator.* Special Issue of the *Journal of Aesthetic Education* 19 (1985).

Weil, Stephen E. *Beauty and the Beasts: On Museums, Art, The Law, and the Market.* Washington, D.C.: Smithsonian Institution Press, 1983.

Weil, Stephen E. *Rethinking the Museum and Other Meditations.* Washington, D.C.: Smithsonian Institution Press, 1990.